Collins

Maths EXPERT 6

Series Editor | Mona Jhunjhunwala

Components of DigiSuite

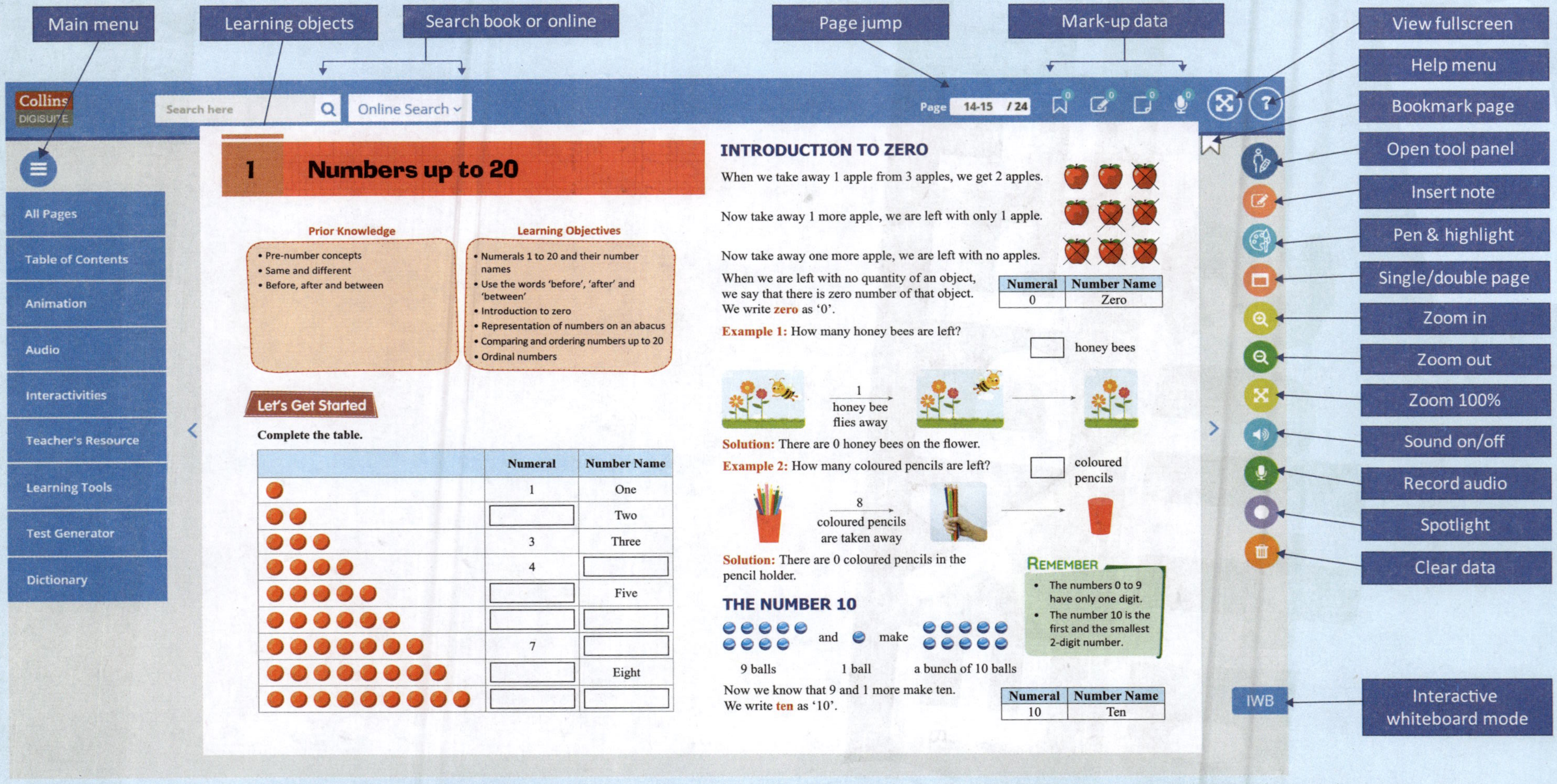

Student + Teacher			Teacher-only	
animations	activities	games	lesson plans	teacher's notes
ilt instructor-led tutorials	ia activities	g games	lp lesson plans	tn teacher's notes
ilt instructor-led tutorials	w worksheets	v videos	w worksheets	ak answer keys
	audio			

Preface

Collins Maths Expert is a series of eight books for Classes 1 to 8. The series is based on the **syllabus** prescribed by the **Council for the Indian School Certificate Examinations** for mathematics education. The series adheres to the guidelines of the **National Education Policy (NEP) 2020** and aligns with the vision of the ***National Initiative for Proficiency in Reading with Understanding and Numeracy* (NIPUN Bharat)**.

In this series, the approach is **"Less Is More"** and **"Drill and Practice"**. It provides all the basic information considered essential in attaining the objectives of mathematics education. All concept explanations are *simple* and *concise* with more *focus on Solved Examples*. The content has also been organized in a horizontal and vertical progression. The language used is child friendly and age appropriate.

This series aims to provide adequate opportunities to help students develop problem solving and critical thinking skills through solved examples, practice questions, formulas, tables, images and illustrations. Most of the solved examples are constructed from daily life situations requiring the student to apply mathematical principles and formula for their solution. Varieties of questions have been included to cater to all level of students. Sufficient provision for practice, revision and review have been provided through adequate number of questions. While citing examples from real life, an effort has been made to make the content inclusive with respect to race, gender, regions, religion, food, flora, fauna, festivals, etc.

We would like to take this opportunity to thank all the teachers who reviewed the books and provided their invaluable feedback, which helped in improving the quality of the content. Any suggestions or constructive criticism from the users are welcome. We shall try to incorporate those in the future editions.

Authors

About the Features

The key features of ***Collins Maths Expert*** series are completely aligned with National Education Policy (NEP) 2020.

Let's Recap!

A variety of questions based on the previous grade for quick recapitulation

Prior Knowledge:

List of topics to help construct connections between old and new knowledge

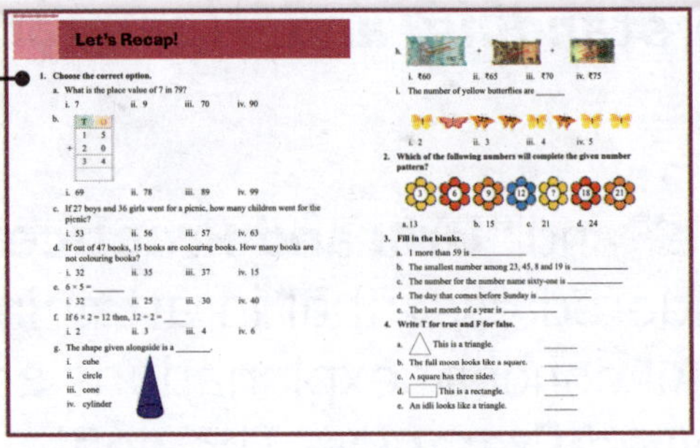

Let's Recap!

1. Choose the correct option.
   a. What is the place value of 7 in 79?
   i. 7 ii. 9 iii. 70 iv. 90
   b. T O / 1 5 / + 2 0 / 3 4
   i. 69 ii. 78 iii. 89 iv. 99
   c. If 27 boys and 36 girls went for a picnic, how many children went for the picnic?
   i. 53 ii. 56 iii. 57 iv. 63
   d. If out of 47 books, 15 books are colouring books. How many books are not colouring books?
   i. 32 ii. 35 iii. 37 iv. 15
   e. 6 × 5 = ______
   i. 32 ii. 25 iii. 30 iv. 40
   f. If 6 × 2 = 12 then, 12 ÷ 2 = ______
   i. 2 ii. 3 iii. 4 iv. 6
   g. The shape given alongside is a ______.
   i. cube ii. circle iii. cone iv. cylinder
   h. i. ₹60 ii. ₹65 iii. ₹70 iv. ₹75
   i. The number of yellow butterflies are ______
   i. 2 ii. 3 iii. 4 iv. 5
2. Which of the following numbers will complete the given number pattern?
   3 6 9 12 ? 18 21
   a. 13 b. 15 c. 21 d. 24
3. Fill in the blanks.
   a. 1 more than 59 is ______
   b. The smallest number among 23, 45, 8 and 19 is ______
   c. The number for the number name sixty-one is ______
   d. The day that comes before Sunday is ______
   e. The last month of a year is ______
4. Write T for true and F for false.
   a. This is a triangle. ______
   b. The full moon looks like a square. ______
   c. A square has three sides. ______
   d. This is a rectangle. ______
   e. An idli looks like a triangle. ______

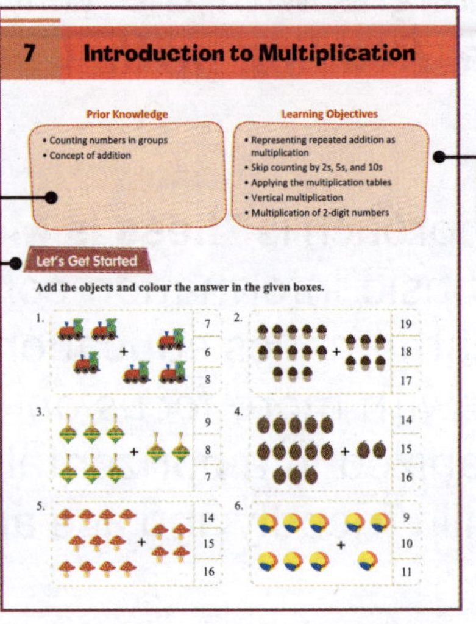

7 Introduction to Multiplication

Prior Knowledge
- Counting numbers in groups
- Concept of addition

Learning Objectives
- Representing repeated addition as multiplication
- Skip counting by 2s, 5s, and 10s
- Applying the multiplication tables
- Vertical multiplication
- Multiplication of 2-digit numbers

Let's Get Started

Add the objects and colour the answer in the given boxes.

1. 7 6 8
2. 19 18 17
3. 9 8 7
4. 14 15 16
5. 14 15 16
6. 9 10 11

Learning Objectives:

List of main topics that will be covered in a chapter

Let's Get Started:

Interactive exercise to begin a chapter with real-life connect and addressing 21st Century Skills

Solved Examples:

A variety of worked out examples based on each topic

Alert:

Snippets to clear common misconceptions and mistakes

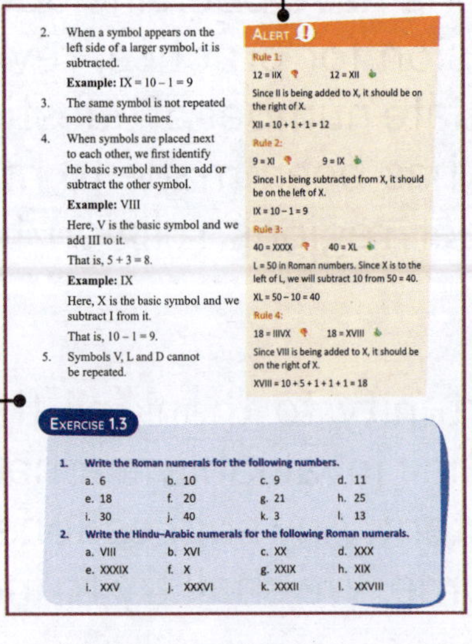

2. When a symbol appears on the left side of a larger symbol, it is subtracted.
   Example: IX = 10 – 1 = 9
3. The same symbol is not repeated more than three times.
4. When symbols are placed next to each other, we first identify the basic symbol and then add or subtract the other symbol.
   Example: VIII
   Here, V is the basic symbol and we add III to it.
   That is, 5 + 3 = 8.
   Example: IX
   Here, X is the basic symbol and we subtract I from it.
   That is, 10 – 1 = 9.
5. Symbols V, L and D cannot be repeated.

ALERT

Rule 1:
12 = IIX 12 = XII
Since II is being added to X, it should be on the right of X.
XII = 10 + 1 + 1 = 12

Rule 2:
9 = XI 9 = IX
Since I is being subtracted from X, it should be on the left of X.
IX = 10 – 1 = 9

Rule 3:
40 = XXXX 40 = XL
L = 50 in Roman numbers. Since X is to the left of L, we will subtract 10 from 50 = 40.
XL = 50 – 10 = 40

Rule 4:
18 = IIIVX 18 = XVIII
Since VIII is being added to X, it should be on the right of X.
XVIII = 10 + 5 + 1 + 1 + 1 = 18

EXERCISE 1.3

1. Write the Roman numerals for the following numbers.
   a. 6 b. 10 c. 9 d. 11
   e. 18 f. 20 g. 21 h. 25
   i. 30 j. 40 k. 3 l. 13
2. Write the Hindu–Arabic numerals for the following Roman numerals.
   a. VIII b. XVI c. XX d. XXX
   e. XXXIX f. X g. XXIX h. XIX
   i. XXV j. XXXVI k. XXXII l. XXVIII

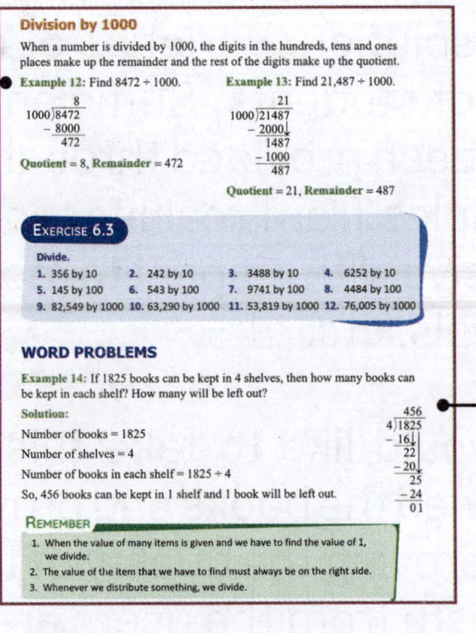

Division by 1000

When a number is divided by 1000, the digits in the hundreds, tens and ones places make up the remainder and the rest of the digits make up the quotient.

Example 12: Find 8472 ÷ 1000.

1000) 8472 (8; – 8000; 472

Quotient = 8, Remainder = 472

Example 13: Find 21,487 ÷ 1000.

1000) 21487 (21; – 2000; 1487; – 1000; 487

Quotient = 21, Remainder = 487

EXERCISE 6.3

Divide.
1. 356 by 10 2. 242 by 10 3. 3488 by 10 4. 6252 by 10
5. 145 by 100 6. 543 by 100 7. 9741 by 100 8. 4484 by 100
9. 82,549 by 1000 10. 63,290 by 1000 11. 53,819 by 1000 12. 76,005 by 1000

WORD PROBLEMS

Example 14: If 1825 books can be kept in 4 shelves, then how many books can be kept in each shelf? How many will be left out?

Solution:
Number of books = 1825
Number of shelves = 4
Number of books in each shelf = 1825 ÷ 4
So, 456 books can be kept in 1 shelf and 1 book will be left out.

4) 1825 (456; – 16; 22; – 20; 25; – 24; 01

REMEMBER
1. When the value of many items is given and we have to find the value of 1, we divide.
2. The value of the item that we have to find must always be on the right side.
3. Whenever we distribute something, we divide.

Exercise:

Purposefully designed in-text exercises

Remember:

Important points for quick reference

Word Problems:

Textual questions based on real-life situations

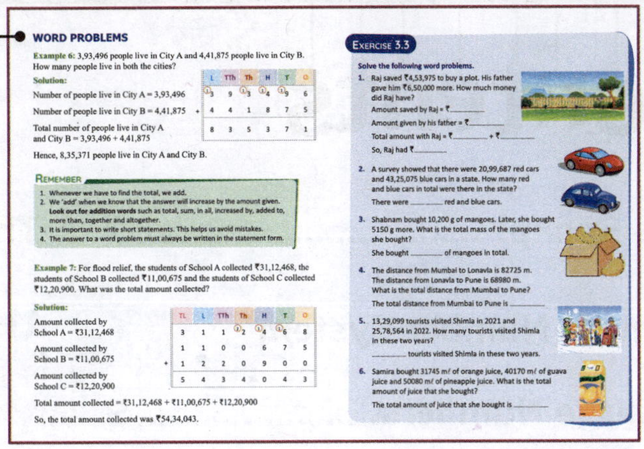

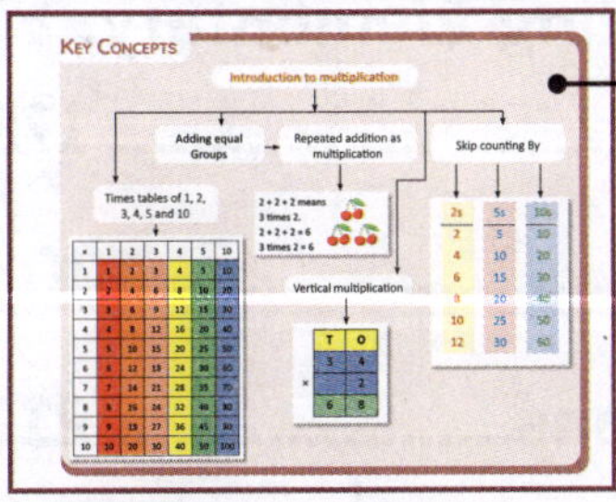

Key Concepts:

A graphic organizer to recap the chapter

Revision Exercise:

Variety of questions based on the topics covered in the chapter

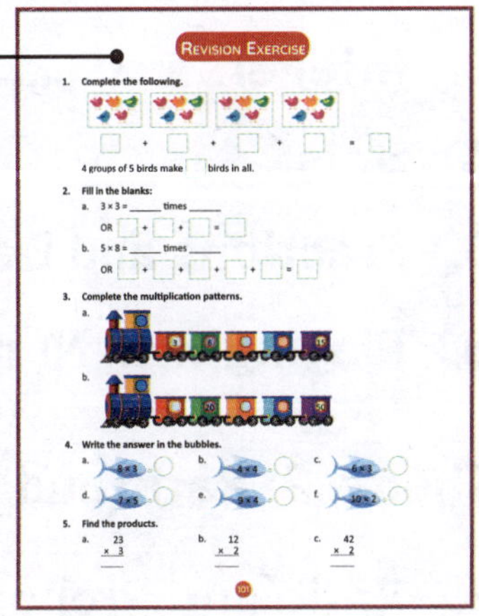

Test Paper:

Variety of questions based on the entire book

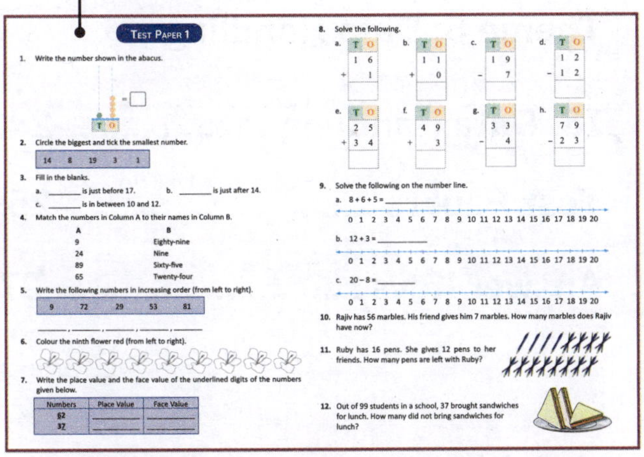

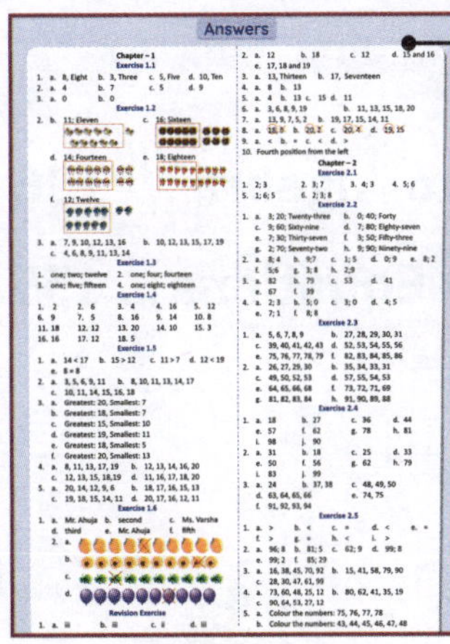

Answer Keys:

Solution to Exercises and Revision Exercise

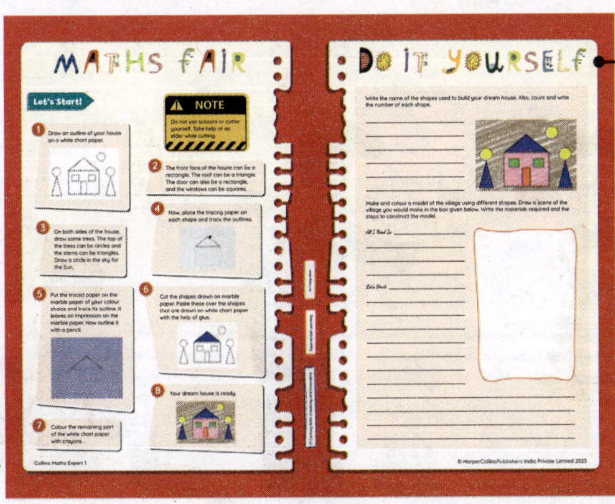

Poster:

Hands-on/STEAM-based activities to develop 21st Century Skills

Contents

Let's Recap!

1. Choose the correct option.

a. The simplest form of $\frac{64}{96}$ is

i. $\frac{1}{2}$ ii. $\frac{1}{3}$ iii. $\frac{2}{3}$ iv. $\frac{1}{4}$

b. Composite number that is not divisible by 6 is

i. 24 ii. 30 iii. 35 iv. 42

c. The sum of $\frac{3}{4}$ and $\frac{1}{5}$ is

i. $\frac{2}{20}$ ii. $\frac{4}{20}$ iii. $\frac{5}{20}$ iv. $\frac{19}{20}$

d. The number of lines of symmetry in the letter D is

i. 0 ii. 2 iii. 1 iv. 4

e. The next number in the given pattern is 5, 8, 11, 14, _____

i. 16 ii. 17 iii. 31 iv. 33

f. Twin prime numbers between 10 and 20 are

i. 11 and 13 ii. 11 and 17

iii. 17 and 19 iv. 13 and 19

2. Fill in the blanks.

a. The number 254675060 in the international system of numeration is read as ______________________________.

b. The place value of digit 4 in 74573081 is ______________.

c. The successor of 6,53,97,789 is ______________.

d. CLXIV is written as ______________ in Arabic numerals.

e. An isoceles triangle has ______________ line of symmetry.

3. Match the following.

a. A quadrilateral made up of 4 equal sides	i. Isosceles triangle
b. An angle that measures 180°	ii. Square
c. A 6-sided polygon	iii. Protractor
d. A triangle that has 2 equal sides and 2 equal angles	iv. Straight angle
e. It is used to measure angles	v. Hexagon

4. **Identify and continue the following patterns. What comes next?**

a.  , , , , ________

b. 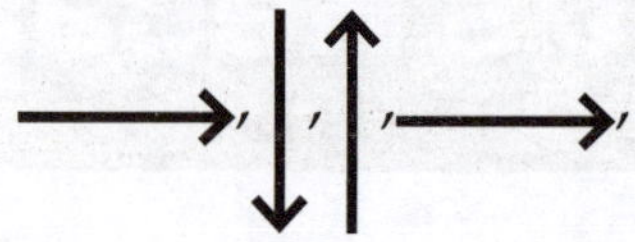 , , , , ________

5. **Answer the following.**

a. What is the LCM of 12, 15 and 20?

b. What is the measurement of each side of a square of perimeter 28 cm?

c. What is 15% of 3 kg?

d. What is the product of 26.8 and 1.2?

e. Convert 21.25 into a percentage.

f. Evaluate the following:

i. 235484 + 685724 − 574564 ii. 7234 × 2545 iii. 1564805 ÷ 115

6. **Study the pictograph and fill in the blanks.**

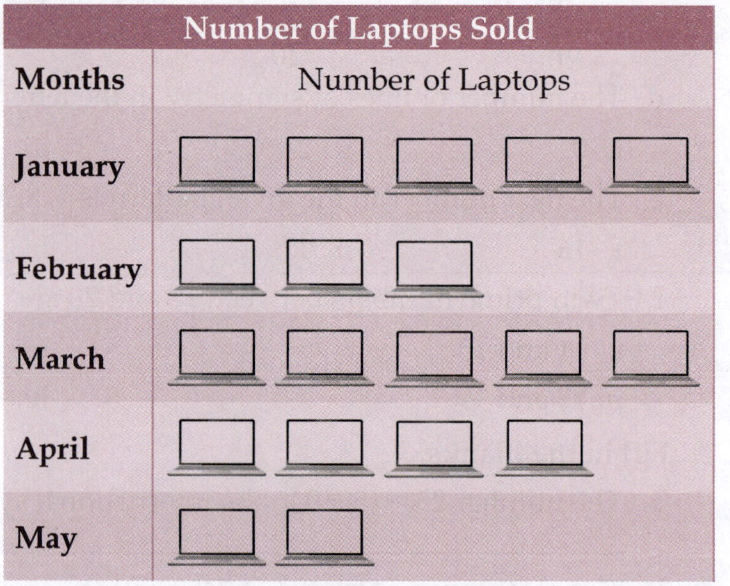

Scale:  = 10 laptops

a. The most number of laptops were sold in the month of ________.

b. The least number of laptops were sold in the month of ________.

c. The same number of laptops were sold in the month of March and ________.

d. The difference between the number of laptops sold in the month of February and April is ________.

e. ________ laptops were sold in all from January to May.

7. **Solve the following word problems.**

a. Ishan had ₹5000 with him, out of which he spent ₹2400 to buy clothes and ₹1300 to buy a pair of shoes. How much money is left with Ishan?

b. There are 18 houses in a street. If there are 3 vehicles in each house, then how many vehicles are there in 4 such similar streets?

c. A brick kiln produces 250650 bricks in a month. Each day, 105 bricks are damaged, and the left-over bricks are sold in 33 loads. Each load has the same number of bricks. Find the number of bricks sold in each load if there are 30 days in this month.

d. A train left Mumbai at 9:30 a.m. and reached Pune at 2 p.m. On the way, it stopped for 45 minutes. For how long was the train moving?

e. The population in a city is 85,065,450. If 34,548,120 are men and 29,875,490 are women, find the number of children in the city.

1 Large Numbers

Prior Knowledge

- 5-digit numbers
- Finding place value and face value of digits
- Comparing and ordering 5-digit numbers
- Operations on 5-digit numbers

Learning Objectives

- Comparing numbers up to 8-digits
- Comparing and ordering large numbers
- Forming large numbers
- Conversion of units
- Performing arithmetic operations on large numbers
- Solving word problems involving large numbers
- Estimating sum, difference, product and quotient
- Estimating large numbers to the nearest tens, hundreds, thousands, and ten-thousands

Let's Get Started

The distance between Delhi and Mysore is 2,296 km.

The distance between Delhi and Ooty is 2,470 km.

The distance between Delhi and Kodaikanal is 2,639 km.

The distance between Delhi and Kanyakumari is 2,838 km.

Compare the distances and find out which place is nearest to Delhi and which place is farthest from Delhi among the four places.

The place nearest to Delhi is ____________.

The place farthest from Delhi is ____________.

Let us study more about large numbers, their comparisons and performing arithmetic operations on them.

INTRODUCTION TO NUMBERS

Let us recall some of the basic terminologies related to numbers.

Digits

The ten basic symbols, 0, 1, 2, 3, 4, 5, 6, 7, 8 and 9, used to represent numbers are known as **digits**.

Number

A **number** is a value in mathematics used for measuring or counting a certain quantity. Numbers are represented using a combination of digits from 0 to 9.

Numeral and Numeration

A number written in figures is called a **numeral.** 6, 24, 536 are examples of numerals.

Numeration means to write a number in words or symbols. Six, twenty-four, five hundred thirty-six are examples of numeration.

The largest 5-digit number is 99,999. On adding 1 to it, we get the smallest 6-digit number 1,00,000.

The largest 6-digit number is 9,99,999.

Similarly, we can find the largest and the smallest 7-digit numbers, 8-digit numbers and so on.

Example 1: How many 6-digit numbers are there in all?

Solution: The largest 6-digit number is 9,99,999.

The smallest 6-digit number is 1,00,000.

So, the number of 6-digit numbers is

9,99,999 – 1,00,000 + 1 = 9,00,000.

The two commonly used systems of numeration are the Indian system of numeration and the International system of numeration.

INDIAN SYSTEM OF NUMERATION

In the Indian system of numeration, the places are ones, tens, hundreds, thousands, ten thousands, lakhs, ten lakhs, etc.

The first three places from the right (ones, tens and hundreds) are grouped into one category called 'Ones period'. Then, as we move to the left from the ones period, every two places are grouped to form different periods.

The following table gives the details of the periods and their place values.

Indian System of Numeration									
Periods	**Crores**		**Lakhs**		**Thousands**		**Ones**		
Places	Ten Crores	Crores	Ten Lakhs	Lakhs	Ten Thousands	Thousands	Hundreds	Tens	Ones
Numbers	10,00,00,000	1,00,00,000	10,00,000	1,00,000	10,000	1000	100	10	1

Commas are used after each period while writing a number. This helps us to read the numbers easily and to understand the place value of each digit in the number.

The table given below shows the short forms for different places (O for ones, T for tens, H for hundreds, Th for thousands, TTh for ten thousands, L for lakhs, TL for ten lakhs, C for crores and TC for ten crores).

Indian Place Value Chart									Number	Number Name
Crores		**Lakhs**		**Thousands**		**Ones**				
TC	**C**	**TL**	**L**	**TTh**	**Th**	**H**	**T**	**O**		
			1	3	7	5	0	6	1,37,506	One lakh thirty-seven thousand five hundred six
		5	2	0	5	3	9	8	52,05,398	Fifty-two lakh five thousand three hundred ninety-eight
	6	1	8	7	3	0	0	2	6,18,73,002	Six crore eighteen lakh seventy-three thousand two

Place Value, Face Value, and Expanded Form

The **place value** is the value of the place or position, of a digit in a number or series.

The **face value** is the value of the digit itself (on the face of it).

> Place value of a digit = Digit itself or face value × Value of the place

The **expanded form** of a number is a way of representation where the number is expressed as the sum of the place values of its digits.

Example 2: Insert commas to rewrite 7523864 as per the Indian place value system. Also write the number in words and in its expanded form. What is the place value of 2 in this number?

Solution: Number: 75,23,864

In words: Seventy-five lakh twenty-three thousand eight hundred sixty-four

Expanded form: 70,00,000 + 5,00,000 + 20,000 + 3,000 + 800 + 60 + 4

Place value of 2 is 20,000.

Example 3: Write the number corresponding to four crore seventy-three lakh two thousand nine hundred one. Also, write the number in its expanded form.

Solution: Number: 4,73,02,901

Expanded form: 4,00,00,000 + 70,00,000 + 3,00,000 + 2,000 + 900 + 1

INTERNATIONAL SYSTEM OF NUMERATION

In this system, the places are ones, tens, hundreds, thousands, ten thousands, hundred thousands, millions, ten millions, hundred millions, etc. Also, every three places are grouped into one period. The following table gives the details of the periods and their place values.

Millions			Thousands			Hundreds		
Hundred Millions	Ten Millions	Millions	Hundred Thousands	Ten Thousands	Thousands	Hundreds	Tens	Ones
100,000,000	10,000,000	1,000,000	100,000	10,000	1,000	100	10	1

REMEMBER

Place Value of a digit in a number is the digit multiplied by the value of its place. For example: Place value of 6 in 6,45,000 is 6,00,000.

Face Value of a digit is the actual value of the digit in a number. For example: Face value of 5 in 1,57,90,980 is 5.

Let us consider the examples given in the following table.

Number	Use of Commas	Number Name
65321	65,321	Sixty-five thousand three hundred twenty-one
803640	803,640	Eight hundred three thousand six hundred forty
9538542	9,538,542	Nine million five hundred thirty-eight thousand five hundred forty-two
81256307	81,256,307	Eighty-one million two hundred fifty-six thousand three hundred seven

Example 4: Express the following numbers in expanded form:

a. 6,422,891 b. 60,240,012

Solution: a. 6,422,891 = 6,000,000 + 400,000 + 20,000 + 2,000 + 800 + 90 + 1

b. 60,240,012 = 60,000,000 + 200,000 + 40,000 + 10 + 2

Example 5: Find the sum of the place value of two 7s and the face value of the two 9s in the number 7,394,709.

Solution: The place value of two 7s in the given number is

$7 \times 1{,}000{,}000 = 7{,}000{,}000$

$7 \times 100 = 700$

The face value of two 9s in the given number is 9.

Thus, the required sum is 7,000,000 + 700 + 9 + 9 = 7,000,718.

EXERCISE 1.1

1. **Write the number names of the following numbers in both Indian and International place value systems.**

   a. 135204 b. 9052020 c. 52147683 d. 50412565

   e. 25386125 f. 50263050 g. 52010509 h. 24502012

2. **Write the place value and face value of the underlined digits in each number. Also, write the numbers in the expanded form.**

   a. $5\underline{7},4\underline{9}5,702$ b. $\underline{7}5,\underline{5}0,293$ c. $\underline{1}40,8\underline{4}9,021$ d. $7\underline{5},\underline{9}5,008$

   e. $1\underline{7},00\underline{3},004$ f. $\underline{2}3,45,\underline{8}92$ g. $6,\underline{8}0,\underline{3}6,203$ h. $2,\underline{3}5,67,\underline{8}90$

3. **Write the numbers corresponding to the following number names in the Indian place value system.**

   a. Three crore seventy lakh forty thousand two hundred five

   b. Nine crore one lakh thirty-three thousand eight hundred seven

   c. Ninety-nine lakh forty-one thousand five hundred ninety

   d. Sixty-seven lakh four

   e. Two crore

4. **Write the numbers corresponding to the following number names in the International place value system.**

   a. Thirty-seven million fifty thousand two hundred five

   b. Thirty-four million seven hundred thousand six

   c. Five million four

   d. Seven million sixty

   e. Four million four

5. **Write the following expanded forms in the standard form:**

   a. 80,00,000 + 70,000 + 3,000 + 400 + 1

   b. 9,00,000 + 5,000 + 200 + 80

   c. 40,00,00,000 + 5,00,000 + 6,000 + 700 + 80 + 9

COMPARING AND ORDERING OF NUMBERS

Recall the symbols used for comparing numbers.

Symbol	Meaning
>	Greater than
<	Less than
=	Equal to

To compare numbers, that is, to find which number is greater/smaller or whether the numbers are equal, follow the rules given below.

Rule 1: Compare the number of digits in both the numbers.
If the number of digits is not equal, then the number with more digits is bigger than the other number.

For example, 30,245,879 > 9,856,784

Rule 2: If the number of digits in both the numbers is equal, then start comparing the digits starting from the extreme left.

For example, consider the numbers 9,09,15,327 and 8,97,65,379.

Both the numbers have 8 digits. So, we start comparing the digits from the extreme left, that is, we compare the digits at the crores place.

	C	TL	L	T Th	Th	H	T	O
9 > 8	9	0	9	1	5	3	2	7
	8	9	7	6	5	3	7	9

We see that the digit at the crores place in 9,09,15,327 is greater than that in 8,97,65,379.

Therefore, 9,09,15,327 > 8,97,65,379.

But what if the digits at the leftmost place are same in both the numbers?

In such a case, we compare the digits on the immediate right of the leftmost digits. We continue this process till we find two unequal digits at the corresponding places.

Ordering Numbers

Numbers can be arranged in two ways:

Ascending order: The order in which numbers are arranged from the smallest to the largest is called ascending order or increasing order.

Descending order: The order in which numbers are arranged from the largest to the smallest is called descending or decreasing order.

Example 6: Arrange the following numbers in ascending order.

7862578, 9009852, 8521456, 9109999, 7872599

Solution: First, let us insert commas in the numbers according to the Indian system of numeration.

78,62,578; 90,09,852; 85,21,456; 91,09,999; 78,72,599

Now, on arranging the numbers in ascending order, we get

78,62,578 < 78,72,599 < 85,21,456 < 90,09,852 < 91,09,999

Example 7: Arrange the following numbers in descending order.

99999999, 80009980, 52056800, 75600985, 5007990

Solution: First, let us insert commas in the numbers according to the Indian system of numeration.

9,99,99,999; 8,00,09,980; 5,20,56,800; 7,56,00,985; 50,07,990

Now, on arranging the numbers in descending order, we get

9,99,99,999 > 8,00,09,980 > 7,56,00,985 > 5,20,56,800 > 50,07,990

FORMING NUMBERS

The formation of the greatest and smallest number by using the given digits can be done in two ways:

1. Without repetition of the given digits and

2. With repetition of the given digits.

Without Repetition of the Given Digits

In this case, to form the greatest and smallest numbers by using the given digits, we arrange the given digits in descending and ascending order, respectively.

Example 8: Write the greatest and smallest number that can be formed by using the digits 6, 9, 5, 0, 4, 8 and 2 without repetition of the digits.

Solution: Given digits are 6, 9, 5, 0, 4, 8 and 2.

The smallest digit other than 0 is 2.

so, the smallest number is 20,45,689.

The greatest digit is 9.

So, the greatest number is 98,65,420.

REMEMBER

If the given digits contain '0', then write the smallest digit other than 0 at the extreme left followed by a 0 and after that arrange the remaining digits in the ascending order of the values.

With Repetition of the Given Digits

In this case, to form the greatest and smallest numbers, we select the greatest and the smallest digits from the given digits and then repeat these digits to form the numbers.

Example 9: Form the smallest and greatest 6-digit numbers using the digits 5, 1, 8, 6, and 7 with repetition of digits at least once.

Solution: In the given digits, the greatest and the smallest digits are 8 and 1, respectively.

Thus, with repetition of digits at least once, we get

The greatest 6-digit number is 8,87,651 and the smallest 6-digit number is 1,15,678.

Therefore, the smallest and greatest 6-digit numbers formed using the digits 5, 1, 8, 6, and 7 are 1,15,678 and 8,87,651.

EXERCISE 1.2

1. **Compare the following numbers and fill in the blanks with > or <.**

a. 12568958 ________ 12560998 b. 99999999 ________ 99999990

c. 89567426 ________ 90050580 d. 10000001 ________ 20000002

e. 45612300 ________ 45632100 f. 23578246 ________ 2357842

g. 72400578 ________ 72450306 h. 98765421 ________ 12345678

2. **Arrange the following numbers in ascending order.**
   a. 4345608, 3350720, 21007891, 3052608, 72456218
   b. 2000123, 20607812, 10200123, 20450012, 9999901, 1112222
   c. 12043015, 12010214, 23015670, 10206789, 1243015
   d. 70050236, 10024005, 79050510, 1000245, 70522369, 78045123
   e. 2344988, 2344889, 2344898, 2345888
3. **Arrange the following numbers in descending order.**
   a. 1205679, 7856824, 5067891, 5026078, 1262187
   b. 81110203, 20104712, 28902823, 20450023, 20801503, 22102183
   c. 70130114, 70130110, 70130600, 70130112, 70130350
   d. 31010230, 31250202, 43551012, 25020245, 31251236, 31278451
   e. 10130123, 60131485, 50890600, 90174442, 60376990
4. **Write the greatest and smallest number that can be formed by the digits 2, 8, 9, 7 and 5 without repetition. Also, write the number names of these numbers.**
5. **Find the difference between the greatest and smallest 7-digit numbers that can be formed by the digits 8, 1, 4 and 3 if repetition of digits is allowed.**

CONVERSION OF UNITS

To convert a number from a bigger unit to a smaller unit, multiply the number by 10, 100, 1000,... To convert a number from a smaller unit to a bigger unit, divide the number by 10, 100, 1000,...

Kilometre, hectometre, decametre, metre, decimetre, centimetre and millimetre are the units in descending order used for measuring length.

	Unit	Symbol
Multiples	**Kilo**metre	km
	Hectometre	hm
	Decametre	dam
→	Metre	m
Sub-multiples	**Deci**metre	dm
	Centimetre	cm
	Millimetre	mm

REMEMBER

As we move down in the table, the units of length become smaller. From a particular unit when we move down one level for conversion, we multiply by 10. If we move down two levels, we multiply by 100 and so on. If we move up one level, we divide by 10. If we move up two levels, we divide by 100 and so on.

Example 10: Convert 9,000 cm into a. decimetre b. metre c. hectometre.

Solution: a. $1\text{ cm} = \frac{1}{10}\text{ dm}$

$9{,}000\text{ cm} = \frac{9{,}000}{10} = 900\text{ dm}$

b. $1\text{ cm} = \frac{1}{100}\text{ m}$

$9{,}000\text{ cm} = \frac{9{,}000}{100} = 90\text{ m}$

c. $1\text{ cm} = \frac{1}{10{,}000}\text{ hm}$

$9{,}000\text{ cm} = \frac{9{,}000}{10{,}000} = \frac{9}{10}\text{ hm}$

WORD PROBLEMS INVOLVING LARGE NUMBERS

Example 11: I ordered two tables for my home. The first table weighs 11 kg 200 g and the second table weighs 14 kg 102 g. What is the total weight of the two tables in grams?

Solution:

Weight of the first table	=	11 kg 200 g
Weight of the second table	=	+ 14 kg 102 g
Total weight of two tables	=	25 kg 302 g

As 25 kg 302 g $= (25 \times 1{,}000)$ g + 302 g

= 25,000 g + 302 g

= 25,302 g

The total weight of the two tables is 25,302 g.

Example 12: Raju stays in USA and his monthly income is $22,450. Find his income in rupees, if each dollar is equal to ₹79.

Solution: Raju's monthly income (in rupees) = 22,450 × 79

$$\begin{array}{r} 2\,2\,4\,5\,0 \\ \times\ 7\,9 \\ \hline 2\,0\,2\,0\,5\,0 \\ +\ 1\,5\,7\,1\,5\,0\,0 \\ \hline 1\,7\,7\,3\,5\,5\,0 \end{array}$$

Thus, Raju's monthly income in rupees is ₹17,73,550.

Example 13: A rocket travelled a distance of 65,75,294 km in 169 hours. It travelled equal distance, in the first 168 hours and some additional distance in the 169th hour. Find the distance covered by the rocket in the first 168 hours and also in the 169th hour.

Solution: The total distance travelled = 65,75,294 km

In the first 168 hours, the rocket travelled equal distances every hour, so divide 65,75,294 by 168.

Quotient will be the distance covered in the first 168 hours and remainder will be the distance covered in the 169th hour.

$$\begin{array}{r} 0039138 \\ 168\overline{)6575294} \\ -0 \\ \hline 65 \\ -0 \\ \hline 657 \\ -504 \\ \hline 1535 \\ -1512 \\ \hline 232 \\ -168 \\ \hline 649 \\ -504 \\ \hline 1454 \\ -1344 \\ \hline 110 \end{array}$$

Thus, distance covered in the first 168 hours is 39,138 km.

And, distance covered in the 169th hour is 110 km.

Example 14: A sugar manufacturing factory had a stock of 12,50,000 kg of sugar at the beginning of the year. During the year, the factory produced 35,67,000 kg of sugar and could export 45,28,000 kg of sugar. Find the remaining stock of sugar in the factory.

Solution: Remaining stock of sugar in the factory = stock + production of sugar in the year – quantity of sugar exported in the year

Stock	=	1	^{1}2	5	0	0	0	0
Production	= +	3	5	6	7	0	0	0
Total amount of sugar	=	4	$\overset{7}{\not 8}$	$\overset{10}{\not 1}$	$\overset{17}{\not 7}$	0	0	0
Exported sugar	= –	4	5	2	8	0	0	0
		0	2	8	9	0	0	0

Thus, a stock of 2,89,000 kg of sugar remains in the factory.

Exercise 1.3

1. The diameter of Mars is 67,79,000 m and the diameter of Earth is 1,27,42,000 m. Find the difference between the diameter of Earth and Mars.
2. During the festival season, a baker sold 1,86,295 boxes each containing 250 g of savouries and 175 g of sweets. Find the total amount of sweets and the total amount of savouries sold by the baker.
3. A person needs 4,500 mL of water per day for drinking. Find the amount of water needed by 275 people for 45 days. (Assume that each person needs the same amount of water.)
4. An entrepreneur made a profit of ₹4,56,98,641 in the first year and ₹25,67,894 more in the second year. Find the total profit made by him in both the years.
5. Radha purchased gold worth ₹8,60,61,250. Find the amount of gold purchased by her, if each gram of gold is worth ₹3025.
6. Sum of two numbers is 4,56,81,200. If one of the numbers is 45,290, find the other.
7. There are 450 books in each shelf in a library. If there are 205 shelves in the library, what is the total number of books in the library?
8. Ria earned a profit of ₹4,52,56,800 in a year. If she distributes the profit equally to 400 of her employees, how much profit did each employee get?
9. Adil invested ₹2,50,000 and his sister invested 1,85,000 more than him in the share of a company. How much did Adil's sister invest?
10. What must 689 be multiplied by to give 10,76,907?

ESTIMATION OF NUMBERS

The word estimation is used to represent an approximate value of certain things. You can estimate things by rounding off. As you know, numbers can be rounded off to different place values, such as tens, hundreds, thousands and so on. Let us recall rounding off of numbers to different place values.

Less than 5					5 and more than 5				
0	1	2	3	4	5	6	7	8	9
0					1				
Rounding down ←					→ Rounding up				

In order to round off a number to a certain place, you need to check whether the digit immediately to the right of that place is less than, greater than or equal to 5.

Rounding off to the nearest ten

Let us round off 53 to the nearest tens. Note that the digit at the ones place is 3 and it is less than 5. So, make it 0.

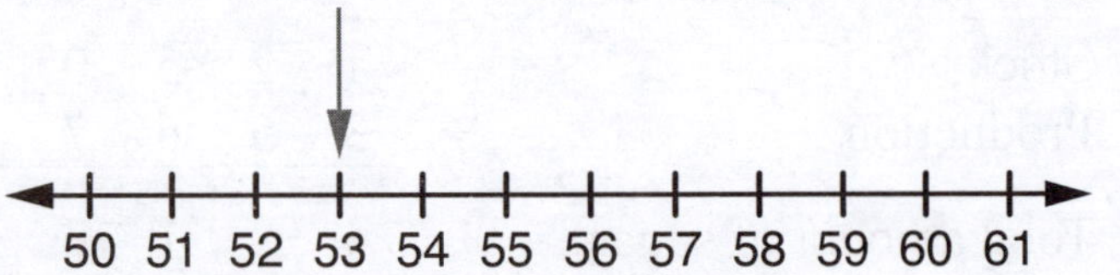

Hence, 50 is the answer.

Consider another number 78. Note that the digit at the ones place is 8 and is more than 5. So, change 8 into 0 and add 1 to the digit at the tens place, that is, 7 + 1 = 8.

Hence, 80 is the answer.

Examples: 142 → 140   578 → 580   1,079 → 1,080   87,142 → 87,140

Rounding off to the nearest hundred

Consider the number 423. Note that the digit at the tens place is 2 and is less than 5. So, change 2 and 3 into 0. In other words, 423 is closer to 400 than 500. So, 400 is the answer.

Examples: 938 → 900   2,558 → 2,600   51,079 → 51,100

Rounding off to the nearest thousand

Consider the number 1,623. Note that the digit at the hundreds place is 6 and is greater than 5. So, change 6, 2 and 3 into 0. Also, add 1 to the digit at the thousands place, that is, 2. In other words, 1,623 is closer to 2,000. So, 2,000 is the answer.

Examples: 3,178 → 3,000   4,938 → 5,000   17,258 → 17,000   68,579 → 69,000

Rounding off to the nearest ten thousand

Consider the number 71,245. Note that the digit at the thousands place is 1 and is less than 5. So, it can be rounded off to 70000.

Examples: 13,178 → 10,000   47,938 → 50,000   85,258 → 90,000   20,579 → 20,000

Estimation of Sum

Estimate the augend and addend individually and add them to get the estimated sum. Study the examples given below.

Estimation	Nearest Ten	Nearest Hundred	Nearest Thousand	Nearest Ten Thousand
Problem	57 + 42	248 + 391	2,856 + 7,123	55,268 + 72,045
Numbers	57 → 60 42 → 40	248 → 200 391 → 400	2,856 → 3,000 7,123 → 7,000	55,268 → 60,000 72,045 → 70,000
Estimated Sum	60 + 40 = 100	200 + 400 = 600	3,000 + 7,000 = 10,000	60,000 + 70,000 = 1,30,000

Estimation of Difference

Estimate the subtrahend and minuend individually and subtract them to get the estimated difference. Study the examples given below.

Estimation	Nearest Ten	Nearest Hundred	Nearest Thousand	Nearest Ten Thousand
Problem	57 – 42	391 – 248	7,123 – 2,856	72,045 – 55,268
Numbers	57 → 60 42 → 40	248 → 200 391 → 400	2,856 → 3,000 7,123 → 7,000	55,268 → 60,000 72,045 → 70,000
Estimated Difference	60 – 40 = 20	400 – 200 = 200	7000 – 3000 = 4000	70,000 – 60,000 = 10,000

Estimation of Product

Estimate the multiplier and the multiplicand individually and multiply them to get the estimated product. Study the examples given below.

Estimation	Nearest Ten	Nearest Hundred	Nearest Thousand
Problem	57 × 42	391 × 248	7,123 × 2,856
Numbers	57 ⟶ 60 42 ⟶ 40	248 ⟶ 200 391 ⟶ 400	2,856 ⟶ 3,000 7,123 ⟶ 7,000
Estimated Product	60 × 40 = 2,400	400 × 200 = 80,000	7,000 × 3,000 = 2,10,00,000

Estimation of Quotients

In order to estimate the quotient of a division problem, you need to round off the dividend and the divisor, and then carry out the division.

Examples: a. 589 ÷ 34 589 ⟶ 600 34 ⟶ 30 (rounding off to the nearest hundred and ten)

600 ÷ 30 = 20

Actual answer: 589 ÷ 34 = 17.32

It is very close to estimated value.

b. 1,489 ÷ 18 1,489 ⟶ 1,000 18 ⟶ 20 (rounding off to the nearest thousand and ten)

1,000 ÷ 20 = 50

Actual answer: 1,489 ÷ 18 = 82.72

It is not close to estimated value.

Exercise 1.4

1. **Round off the following numbers and fill in the table.**

Number	Nearest Ten	Nearest Hundred	Nearest Thousand	Nearest Ten Thousand
7243				
50,421				
21,897				
12,05,392				

2. **Estimate the following.**

a. 786 − 421 b. 384 + 236 c. 28 × 41 d. 412 ÷ 36

e. 2,378 + 5,601 f. 89,014 − 52,478 g. 129 × 387 h. 76 × 501

3. **Estimate the value of 31,528 + 63,82,543 + 74,52,548 to the nearest ten thousands and then compare it with the actual sum.**
4. **Nikhil paints portraits and sells each for ₹3,674. Estimate his earnings if he has sold 18 portraits by rounding off the numbers to nearest tens.**
5. **Rahul travelled 1,973 km to go from place A to B and then he went to place C after travelling 1,687 km. Estimate the distance between A and C, to the nearest thousands.**

KEY CONCEPTS

LARGE NUMBERS

Indian Number System (Hindu-Arabic Number System)

Crores		Lakhs		Thousands		Ones		
TC	C	TL	L	T Th	Th	H	T	O

Expanded form
Example: 8,45,36,786
8,00,00,000 + 40,00,000 + 5,00,000 + 30,000 + 6,000 + 700 + 80 + 6

International Number System

Billions			Millions			Thousands			Ones		
Hundred Billions	Ten Billions	Billions	Hundred Millions	Ten Millions	Millions	Hundred Thousands	Ten Thousands	Thousands	Hundreds	Tens	Ones

Expanded form
Example: 84,536,786
80,000,000 + 4,000,000 + 500,000 + 30,000 + 6,000 + 700 + 80 + 6

1 hundred thousand = 1 lakh
1 million = 10 lakh
10 million = 1 crore
100 million = 10 crore
1 billion = 100 crore

Numbers have:

Face value
It is the value of the digit itself irrespective of its position.

Place value
It is the product of place and the digit.

Estimation → **Rounding off**

Example: 4,56,87,642 rounded off to nearest
Ten = 4,56,87,640
Hundred = 4,56,87,600
Thousand = 4,56,88,000
Ten thousand = 4,56,90,000

Arithmetic Operations

Addition — Example

```
   1 1
 7 3 4 8 5 6 1
+2 5 4 9 6 3 8
 9 8 9 8 1 9 9
```

Subtraction — Example

```
  7 15 13 17 15
 5 8 6 4 8 5 7
-2 5 6 8 9 7 5
 3 2 9 5 8 8 2
```

Multiplication — Example

```
      5 2 6 8 6
          × 8 4
    2 1 0 7 4 4
+ 4 2 1 4 8 8 0
  4 4 2 5 6 2 4
```

Division — Example

```
     17126
15 ) 256894
    -0
     25
    -15
     106
    -105
       18
      -15
        39
       -30
         94
        -90
          4
```

Comparison and Order

Ascending order
From smallest to greatest number

Descending order
From greatest to smallest number

Revision Exercise

1. **Choose the correct option.**

   a. The place value of 3 in 35460678 is

   i. 30 crores ii. 3 lakhs iii. 30 million iv. 3 million

   b. The estimated sum of 3,54,52,879 and 7,689 is

   i. 30,008,000 ii. 4,00,07,000 iii. 3,00,07,000 iv. 4,00,08,000

   c. What should be added to 2,45,000 to get 23,50,000?

   i. 2,10,500 ii. 21,05,000 ii. 1,00,000 iii. 10,00,000

   d. Sum of the place values of 8 in 8,970,467 and 489,034 is

   i. 1,010,000 ii. 808,000 iii. 8,080,000 iv. 80,080,000

   e. A printing press prints 23,450 copies per day. How many copies are printed in 30 days?

   i. 7,03,500 ii. 73,500 iii. 70,03,500 iv. 7,03,000

2. **Write the numbers corresponding to the following number names. Also, arrange the numbers in ascending order.**

   a. Nine crore ninety-two lakh four thousand two hundred six

   b. Nineteen million seventy-one thousand nine hundred thirty-eight

   c. Seven crore thirteen lakh twenty-four thousand nine hundred nine

   d. Two million four thousand two hundred eleven

   e. Eight crore seventy-five lakh forty thousand one hundred fifty

   f. Four million fourteen thousand nine hundred five

3. **Write the following numbers in both Indian and International place value systems. Also, write the number names and identify the largest number and the smallest number among the given numbers.**

   a. 6045896 b. 20456087 c. 20850135 d. 5021369

   e. 90001009 f. 10302410 g. 10238001 h. 68759087

4. **Arrange the following in descending order.**

   a. 1,825,790; 1,825,970; 185,297; 1,089,201; 1,825,901

   b. 78,52,015; 7,85,43,012; 99,85,214; 7,85,96,541; 78,52,016

   c. 9,85,62,104; 9,85,62,140; 9,85,68,025; 9,85,62,001; 9,85,62,875

   d. 90,085,602; 90,085,609; 90,086,001; 98,752,149; 90,085,637

   e. 8,345,600; 8,343,450; 8,344,450; 8,434,422; 8,434,550

5. **Compare the numbers and fill in the blanks with > or <.**

   a. 50,400,825 ______ 50,501,099 d. 12,002,891 ______ 12,002,059

   b. 46,709,021 ______ 46,221,036 e. 45,66,78,330 ______ 45,66,87,330

   c. 11,14,520 ______ 20,15,57,025

6. **Write the smallest and greatest 7-digit numbers having three different digits.**

7. **Round off the numbers as mentioned in each case.**

   a. The radius of the planet Venus is 6,052 km. (nearest thousand)

   b. The height of the Mount Everest is 29,029 ft. (nearest ten thousand)

   c. The number of foreign tourists who visited India in 2021 was 8,37,574. (nearest lakh)

   d. The current population of Goa in 2022 is 15,42,750. (nearest ten lakh)

   e. The population of Haryana in 2022 was is 2,73,88,008. (nearest crore)

8. **Evaluate the following by rounding to the greatest place:**

   a. 4769832 + 22557788

   b. 9136008 - 3054999

   c. 45602 × 24

   d. 16675830 ÷ 645

   e. 165 + 674

   f. 5888 - 2033

   g. 91 × 55

   h. 4800 ÷ 43

9. **Find the sum of all possible 3-digits numbers that can be formed by using 0, 2 and 7, where the repetition of digits is not allowed.**

10. **Solve the following word problems.**

    a. There were 34,555 people watching hockey and 53,400 people watching cricket. Find the product of place value of the digit 3 in both the numbers.

    b. The number of people watching a tennis match was 67,809 and the number of people watching a cricket match was 67,980. Subtract the smaller number from the bigger number.

    c. The deepest trench in the Pacific Ocean is Mariana Trench measuring 35,994 feet. The deepest Arctic trench, the Litke Deep, measures 17,881 feet. Find the difference between the two trenches.

    d. If the annual earnings of Bhuvan is ₹5,48,060 and that of Raman is ₹5,34,679, then find their total earnings.

    e. A car weighs about 1087 kg. What will be the weight of 100 such cars?

    f. A cargo plane can carry around 39,780 kg of weight. How many such boxes can it carry if each box weighs 3060 kg?

2 Whole Numbers

Prior Knowledge

- Bigger numbers in Indian and International number system
- Place value and expanded form
- Comparing and ordering numbers
- Forming numbers

Learning Objectives

- Natural numbers and whole numbers
- Predecessor and successor
- Representation of whole numbers on the number line
- Properties of whole numbers
- Division algorithm
- Identifying patterns

Let's Get Started

Answer the following questions:

1. *How many students are there in your class?*
2. *How many ears do we have?*
3. *How many months are there in a year?*

To answer these questions, we need to count beginning from 1. The numbers 1, 2, 3, 4, ... are called counting numbers. These numbers are also called natural numbers. Hence, the numbers 1, 2, 3, ..., 1000, ..., 10,00,000, ..., etc. are called **natural** or **counting numbers**.

When 0 is added in the collection of natural numbers then, it becomes the collection of **whole numbers**, i.e. W = {0, 1, 2, 3, 4, 5,...}. Every natural number is a whole number but, there exists a whole number '0' which is not a natural number.

From above, we find that:

- There is no largest number in the number system.
- Zero is a whole number.
- The only difference between whole numbers and the natural numbers is 0.

Whole Numbers (W)

Natural Numbers (N)

0, 1, 2, 3, 4, 5, 6, 7, 8, ...

Which set of numbers has more numbers: whole numbers or natural numbers?

PREDECESSOR AND SUCCESSOR

The number that comes just before a particular number is called its **predecessor**.

Predecessor = Number – 1

The number that comes just after a particular number is called its **successor**.

Successor = Number + 1

Example 1: Write the predecessor of 258.

Solution: The predecessor of 258 is 258 – 1 = 257

Example 2: Write the successor of 49,999

Solution: The successor 49,999 is 49,999 + 1 = 50,000

REMEMBER

1. There is always a number next to the given number irrespective of its value.
2. All natural numbers except 1 have both a successor and a predecessor.

REPRESENTING WHOLE NUMBERS ON THE NUMBER LINE

To represent whole numbers on a number line, we follow the given steps.

1. Draw a straight line and mark a point O on it.
2. Mark another point A to the right of O. The distance between O and A denotes one unit.
3. Now mark more points to the right of A at every unit distance. Label these points as B, C, D, E, …
4. Write 0 below point O. Similarly, write 1, 2, 3, 4, … below the points A, B, C, D, … respectively as shown in the figure below.

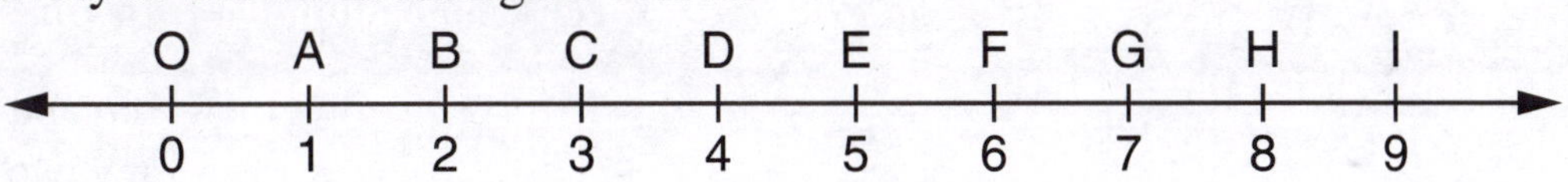

Let OA = 1 unit

Then, AB = BC = CD = DE = EF = FG = GH = 1 unit

OB = OA + AB = (1 + 1) units = 2 units

OC = OB + BC = (2 + 1) units = 3 units

OD = OC + CD = (3 + 1) units = 4 units, and so on

Here O corresponds to the whole number 0, and points A, B, C, D, … correspond to the whole numbers 1, 2, 3, 4, … respectively.

- Every whole number is smaller than the whole numbers lying to the right of it on a number line.
- There is no whole number between two consecutive whole numbers.
- All whole numbers (except 0) lie to the right of 0 on a number line. Hence, 0 is the smallest whole number.
- All natural numbers (except 1) lie to the right of 1 on a number line. Hence, 1 is the smallest natural number.

EXERCISE 2.1

1. **Write the successors of the following numbers:**

   a. 5,84,345   b. 7,87,601   c. 47,89,236   d. 99,81,349

2. **Write the predecessors of the following numbers:**

   a. 8,44,360   b. 42,57,333   c. 87,40,023   d. 46,02,286

3. **Write the two whole numbers that come just after 54,39,258.**
4. **How many numbers are there between 3,487 and 3,585?**
5. **How many numbers are there between 9,834 and 12,550?**

PROPERTIES OF WHOLE NUMBERS

There are four fundamental operations that can be performed on whole numbers: addition, subtraction, multiplication and division. There are some basic properties of all the operations on whole numbers.

Under Addition

Look at the following table showing the properties of the whole numbers under addition. Fill in the blanks where required.

Closure Property	a	b	$a + b$	**Is $a + b$ a whole number?**		**Observation**
	5	4	$5 + 4 = 9$	Yes		If a and b are any two whole numbers, then $(a + b)$ is also a whole number.
	64	0	$64 + 0 = 64$	______		
	45	4	______	______		
Commutative Property	a	b	$a + b$	$b + a$	**Is $a + b = b + a$?**	If a and b are any two whole numbers, then $a + b = b + a$.
	8	5	$8 + 5 = 13$	$5 + 8 = 13$	Yes	
	0	80	______	______	______	
	50	12	______	______	______	
Additive Identity	a	$a + 0$	$0 + a$	**Is $a + 0 = 0 + a = a$?**		If a is any whole number, then $a + 0 = 0 + a = a$. 0 is the additive identity of whole numbers.
	5	$5 + 0 = 5$	$0 + 5 = 5$	Yes		
	452	______	______	______		
	87	______	______	______		
Associative Property	a, b, c	$(a + b) + c$		$a + (b + c)$	**Is $(a + b) + c = a + (b + c)$?**	If a, b and c are any three whole numbers, then $(a + b) + c = a + (b + c)$.
	1, 3, 5	$(1 + 3) + 5 = 4 + 5 = 9$		$1 + (3 + 5) = 1 + 8 = 9$	Yes	
	3, 0, 8	______		______	______	

Example 3: Verify the following and name the property satisfied.

a. 7077 + 1023 = 1023 + 7077

Solution: LHS RHS

7077 + 1023 = 8100 1023 + 7077 = 8100

LHS = RHS and the property satisfied is the commutative property of addition.

b. (3657 + 3043) + 980 = 3657 + (3043 + 980)

Solution: LHS RHS

LHS	RHS
(3657 + 3043) + 980	3657 + (3043 + 980)
= 6700 + 980	= 3657 + 4023
= 7680	= 7680

LHS = RHS and the property satisfied is the associative property.

Under Subtraction

Look at the following table showing the properties of whole numbers under subtraction. Fill in the blanks where required.

Closure Property	a	b	$a - b$	Is $a - b$ a whole number?	Observation
	5	4	5 – 4 = 9	Yes	$(a - b)$ is a whole number, if $a > b$ and $(a - b)$ is not a whole number, if $b > a$. Thus, difference $(a - b)$ may or may not be a whole number. **Conclusion:** Closure property does not hold true for subtraction.
	4	5	4 – 5 is not a whole number.	No	
	523	752	______	______	

Commutative Property	a	b	$a - b$	$b - a$	Is $a - b = b - a$?	Observation
	5	4	5 – 4 = 1	4 – 5 is not a whole number.	No	If a and b are any two unequal whole numbers, then $a - b \neq b - a$. **Conclusion:** Commutative property does not hold true for subtraction.
	0	708	______	______	______	

Subtraction Property of 0	a	$a - 0 = a$	$0 - a$ is not a whole number.	Observation
	5	5 – 0 = 5	0 – 5 is not a whole number.	If a is any whole number, then $a - 0 = a$, but $0 - a$ is not a whole number. **Conclusion:** 0 is not an identity element for subtraction.
	801	______	______	

Associative Property	a, b, c	$(a-b)-c$	$a-(b-c)$	Is $(a-b)-c = a-(b-c)$?	
	7, 6, 5	$(7-6)-5 =$ $1-5$ is a whole number.	$7-(6-5)$ $=7-(1)$ $=6$	No	If a, b and c are three unequal whole numbers, then $(a-b)-c \neq a-(b-c)$. **Conclusion:** Associative property does not hold true for subtraction.
	8, 5, 2	______	______	______	
	6, 1, 0	______	______	______	

Exercise 2.2

1. **Complete the following.**
   a. 6107 + 3049 = ______ + 6107 b. 7021 + ______ = 90,333 + 7021
   c. 48,026 + ______ = 48,026 d. 6031 + 0 = ______
2. **Verify the following.**
   a. 72,091 + 30,054 = 30,054 + 72,091 b. 43,001 + 362 = 362 + 43,001
   c. 3003 + (80,251 + 6007) = (3003 + 6007) + 80,251
   d. (50,106 + 4084) + 33,707 = 50,106 + (4084 + 33,707)
3. **Verify the associative property under subtraction for each of the following groups of whole numbers.**
   a. 25, 8, 0 b. 45, 8, 21 c. 317, 312, 50 d. 87, 82, 2018

Under Multiplication and Division

Look at the following table showing the properties of whole numbers under multiplication and division. Fill in the blanks where required.

Closure Property	a	b	$a \times b$	Is $a \times b$ a whole number?	Observation
Under Multiplication	15	2	$15 \times 2 = 30$	Yes	If a and b are any two whole numbers, then $(a \times b)$ is also a whole number.
	0	201	______	______	
	124	2	______	______	
	a	b	$a \div b$	Is $a \div b$ a whole number?	If a and b are any two non-zero whole numbers, then $a \div b$ is not always a whole number. **Conclusion:** Closure property is true for multiplication but it does not hold true for division.
Under division	50	2	$50 \div 2 = 25$	Yes	
	0	201	$0 \div 201 = 0$	Yes	
	3	2	$3 \div 2 = \frac{3}{2}$	No	
	150	0	$150 \div 0$	Not defined	

Commutative Property	a	b	$a \times b$	$b \times a$	Is $a \times b = b \times a$?	
Under multiplication	15	4	$15 \times 4 = 60$	$4 \times 15 = 60$	Yes	If a and b are any two whole numbers, then $a \times b = b \times a$.
	0	821	______	______	______	

	a	b	$a \div b$	$b \div a$	Is $a \div b = b \div a$?	
Under division	15	3	$15 \div 3 = 5$	$3 \div 15 = \frac{1}{5}$	No	If a and b are any two non-zero unequal whole numbers, then $a \div b \neq b \div a$.
	0	482	$0 \div 482 = 0$	$482 \div 0$ is not defined	No	**Conclusion:** Commutative property is true for multiplication but it does not hold true for division.
	785	5	______	______	______	

Multiplicative Identity	a	$a \times 1$	$1 \times a$	Is $a \times 1 = 1 \times a = a$?	
	5	$5 \times 1 = 5$	$1 \times 5 = 5$	Yes	If a is any whole number, then $a \times 1 = 1 \times a = a$. 1 is the multiplicative identity of whole numbers.
	452	______	______	______	

Associative Property	a, b, c	$(a \times b) \times c$	$a \times (b \times c)$	Is $(a \times b) \times c = a \times (b \times c)$?	
Under multiplication	2, 3, 5	$(2 \times 3) \times 5 = 6 \times 5 = 30$	$2 \times (3 \times 5) = 2 \times 15 = 30$	Yes	If a, b and c are any three whole numbers, then $(a \times b) \times c = a \times (b \times c)$.
	0, 5, 9	______	______	______	

	a, b, c	$(a \div b) \div c$	$a \div (b \div c)$	Is $(a \div b) \div c = a \div (b \div c)$?	
Under division	24, 6, 3	$(24 \div 6) \div 3 = 4 \div 3 = \frac{4}{3}$	$24 \div (6 \div 3) = 24 \div 2 = 12$	No	If a, b and c are any three unequal whole numbers, then $(a \div b) \div c \neq a \div (b \div c)$.
	16, 8, 2	______	______	______	**Conclusion:** Associative property is true for multiplication but it does not hold true for division.

Distributive Law of Multiplication Over Addition

Complete the table given below.

a, b, c	$a \times (b + c)$	$(a \times b) + (a \times c)$	Is $a \times (b + c) = (a \times b) + (a \times c)$?
2, 4, 3	$2 \times (4 + 3) = 2 \times 7 = 14$	$(2 \times 4) + (2 \times 3) = 8 + 6 = 14$	Yes
12, 18, 20	______	______	______

If a, b and c are any three whole numbers, then $a \times (b + c) = (a \times b) + (a \times c)$.

Distributive Law of Multiplication Over Subtraction

Complete the table given below.

a, b, c	$a \times (b - c)$	$(a \times b) - (a \times c)$	Is $a \times (b - c) = (a \times b) - (a \times c)$?
18, 12, 0	$18 \times (12 - 0)$ $= 18 \times 12 = 216$	$(18 \times 12) - (18 \times 0)$ $= 216 - 0 = 216$	Yes
120, 15, 14	________	________	________

If a, b and c are any three whole numbers, then $a \times (b - c) = (a \times b) - (a \times c)$.

SPECIAL PROPERTIES

1. If a is a whole number, then $a \times 0 = 0$.

   Examples: $15 \times 0 = 0$; $234 \times 0 = 0$

2. If a is a non-zero whole number, then $0 \div a = 0$.

   Examples: $0 \div 1505 = 0$; $0 \div 54,788 = 0$

3. If a is a whole number, then $a \div 0$ is not defined.

   Example: $45 \div 0 =$ Not defined

4. If a is any whole number, then $a \div 1 = a$.

   Examples: $110 \div 1 = 110$; $55 \div 1 = 55$

Example 4: Find the product by suitably arranging the numbers.

a. $50 \times 204 \times 20$

Solution: $(50 \times 20) \times 204 = 1000 \times 204 = 2,04,000$

b. $375 \times 24 - 375 \times 4$

Solution: $375 \times (24 - 4) = 375 \times 20 = 7500$

Example 5: Find the product using distributive laws.

a. 9×102

Solution: By the distributive law of addition,

$9 \times (100 + 2) = 9 \times 100 + 9 \times 2$

$= 900 + 18$

$= 918$

b. 21×97

Solution: By the distributive law of subtraction,

$21 \times (100 - 3) = 21 \times 100 - 21 \times 3$

$= 2100 - 63$

$= 2037$

DIVISION ALGORITHM

Dividend = (Divisor × Quotient) + Remainder

On dividing 601 by 18, we get 33 as the quotient and 7 as the remainder.

$\therefore 601 = (18 \times 33) + 7$

```
    33
18)601
  - 54
    61
   -54
    07
```

If a and b are two whole numbers such that $a > b$, and if a is divided by b, then $a = bq + r$, where q is the quotient and r is the remainder, where $0 \leq r < b$. This result is known as **division algorithm**.

Example 6: Find the number which when divided by 5 gives 45 as the quotient and 3 as the remainder.

Solution: Given: Divisor = 5, Quotient = 45, Remainder = 3

By division algorithm,

Dividend = (Divisor × Quotient) + Remainder

$= (5 \times 45) + 3 = 225 + 3 = 228$

Therefore, the number is 228.

IDENTIFYING PATTERNS

A pattern is a repeated arrangement of numbers or shapes. Patterns are formed when numbers or combination of numbers are repeated in a regular manner.

Some elementary shapes can be formed using a combination of dots or by rearranging few dots in a specific pattern.

Line segment: A line segment can be drawn using a minimum of two points. Every whole number greater than or equal to 2 can be expressed by a combination of dots arranged as a line segment to represent the number.

2 3 4 5

Triangles: A triangle can be drawn using a minimum of 3 points.

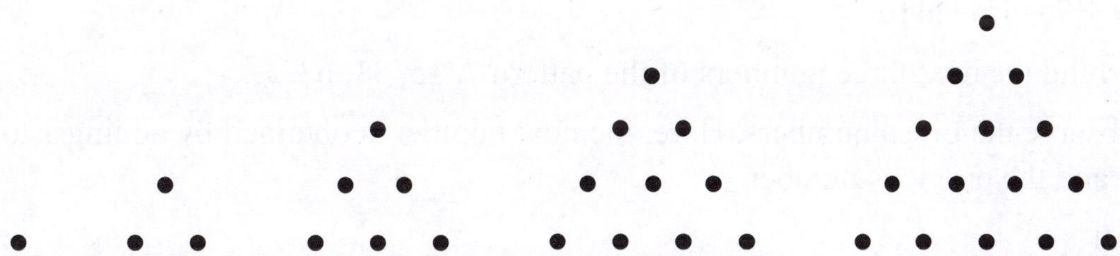

1 3 6 10 15

The number of dots used to form the above triangles are 1, 3, 6, 10, 15, 21, and so on. These numbers are called **triangular numbers**.

Rectangle/Square: A rectangle or square can be drawn using a minimum of 4 points.

4 6

Number Patterns in Whole Number or Natural Number

Number patterns in whole number or natural number is a set of numbers that are related to each other with a specific rule. There are several patterns of whole numbers or natural numbers like even numbers, odd numbers, square numbers, cube numbers, sum or difference or multiple or division of two numbers, etc.

We can find the missing number in the pattern by identifying the rule used in the pattern.

Example 7: Find the next three numbers in the pattern: 3, 8, 13, 18, ….

Solution: The given pattern is 3, 8, 13, 18, …

Here, $8 - 3 = 5$, $13 - 8 = 5$, $18 - 13 = 5$

Hence, the next number is obtained by adding 5 to the previous number.

$18 + 5 = 23$, $23 + 5 = 28$ and $28 + 5 = 33$

Therefore, the pattern is 3, 8, 13, 18, 23, 28 and 33.

Example 8: Write the next three steps of the pattern given below.

$1 \times 9 + 1 = 10$

$12 \times 9 + 2 = 110$

$123 \times 9 + 3 = 1110$

$1234 \times 9 + 4 = 11110$

Solution: Observe the pattern. Here, 10 is obtained by adding 1 to the product of 1 and 9, 110 is obtained by adding 2 to the product of 12 and 9, 1110 is obtained by adding 3 to the product of 123 and 9 and 11110 is obtained by adding 4 to the product of 1234 and 9.

Hence, the next 3 steps are:

$12345 \times 9 + 5 = 111110$

$123456 \times 9 + 6 = 1111110$

$1234567 \times 9 + 7 = 11111110$

Example 9: Find the next three numbers of the pattern 7, 15, 31, 63, ….

Solution: Observe the given numbers. Here, the next number is obtained by adding 1 to the product of 2 and the previous number.

$3 \times 2 + 1 = 7$

$7 \times 2 + 1 = 15$

$15 \times 2 + 1 = 31$

$31 \times 2 + 1 = 63$

$63 \times 2 + 1 = 127$

$127 \times 2 + 1 = 255$

$255 \times 2 + 1 = 511$

Hence, the next three numbers in the pattern are 7, 15, 31, 63, **127, 255, 511.**

Example 10: Draw the next two figures with respect to the pattern given below.

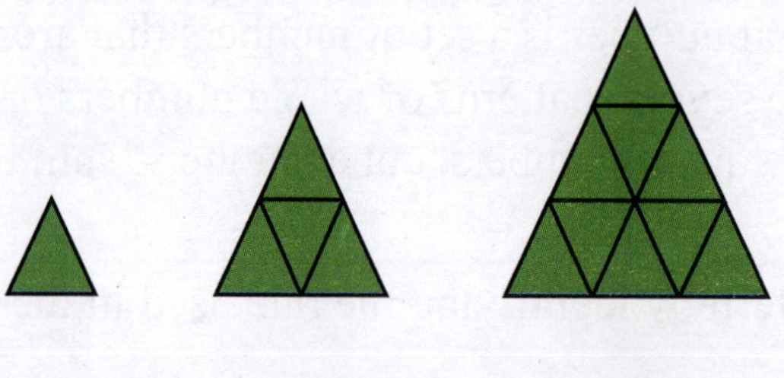

Solution: Observe the given figures. The first figure contains one triangle, the second one is a combination of four triangles and the third one is a combination of nine small triangles.

Hence, the next two figures should be a combination of 16 and 25 triangles.

Therefore, the given pattern becomes:

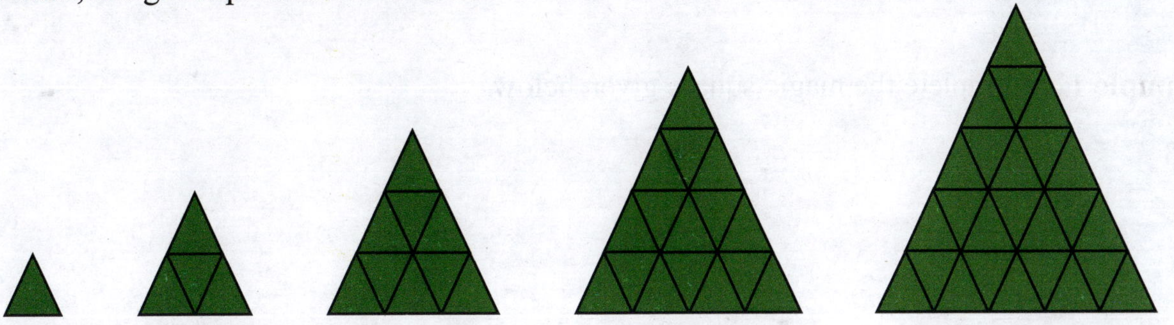

MAGIC SQUARES

A magic square is a square which is divided into cells and the sum of elements of any row, column or diagonal in the square is the same.

Steps to find the missing numbers in a magic square:

- Add the numbers in the column or row or diagonal to find the sum.
- Fill the remaining cells by making the sum of any row or column or diagonal the same.

Example 11: Complete the magic squares given below.

2		4
	5	
6		

Solution: Let us denote the missing numbers with any letter of the alphabet.

2	p	4
q	5	r
6	s	t

In the given magic square, on adding the elements at the given diagonal, we get 15.

That is, $6 + 5 + 4 = 15$

Hence, the sum of numbers in any row or column or diagonal should be equal to 15.

That is, $2 + p + 4 = 15 \Rightarrow p = 15 - 6 = 9$

$2 + q + 6 = 15 \Rightarrow q = 15 - 8 = 7$

$2 + 5 + t = 15 \Rightarrow t = 15 - 7 = 8$

$4 + r + t = 15 \Rightarrow 4 + r + 8 = 15 \Rightarrow r = 15 - 12 = 3$

$6 + s + t = 15 \Rightarrow 6 + s + 8 = 15 \Rightarrow s = 15 - 14 = 1$

Therefore, the magic square is:

2	9	4
7	5	3
6	1	8

Example 12: Complete the magic square given below.

13		
	12	
9		11

Solution: Let us denote the missing numbers in the given magic square as follows.

13	p	q
r	12	s
9	t	11

Observe the given magic square. Here, one diagonal is given completely.

That is, 13 + 12 + 11 = 36

Hence, the sum of numbers in any row or column or diagonal should be equal to 36.

$13 + r + 9 = 36 \Rightarrow r = 36 - 13 - 9 = 14$

$9 + t + 11 = 36 \Rightarrow t = 36 - 9 - 11 = 16$

$9 + 12 + q = 36 \Rightarrow q = 36 - 9 - 12 = 15$

$13 + p + q = 36 \Rightarrow 13 + p + 15 = 36 \Rightarrow p = 36 - 13 - 15 = 8$

$11 + s + q = 36 \Rightarrow 11 + s + 15 = 36 \Rightarrow s = 36 - 11 - 15 = 10$

Therefore, the magic square is:

13	8	15
14	12	10
9	16	11

Exercise 2.3

1. **Complete the following statements.**

   a. 604 × 3081 = 3081 × ________

   b. 70,704 × ________ = 0

   c. 673 × ________ = 673

   d. 4090 × (806 × 31) = ________ × (4090 × 31)

   e. 802 × 205 + 802 × 705 = 802 × (________ + ________)

2. **State the property in each of the following.**

a. 20,340 × 10,030 = 10,030 × 20,340
b. 302 × (604 × 7090) = (302 × 604) × 7090
c. 7,01,080 × 0 = 0
d. 90,200 × 1 = 90,200

3. **Find the products by suitably arranging the numbers.**

a. 400 × 2037 × 25
b. 2000 × 4305 × 5
c. 50 × 10,042 × 20
d. 4000 × 2009 × 25
e. 25 × 6025 × 80
f. 400 × 50 × 1025

4. **Solve the following.**

a. 555 ÷ 15
b. 1326 ÷ 13
c. 9036 ÷ 18
d. 2109 ÷ 19
e. 4,58,942 ÷ 11

5. **Find the quotient and the remainder by actual division and check the answer by the division algorithm.**

a. 742 ÷ 23
b. 1005 ÷ 101
c. 773 ÷ 30
d. 4909 ÷ 22
e. 557 ÷ 5
f. 88404 ÷ 23

6. **The product of two numbers is 1,41,705. If one of the numbers is 705, find the other.**

7. **Find the missing term in the following using the division algorithm.**

a. 459 = (________ × 38) + 3
b. ________ = (22 × 305) + 18
c. 33333 = (22 × 1515) + ________
d. 4,24,284 = (42 × ________) + 0

8. **Find the next figure in the pattern given below.**

a.

b.
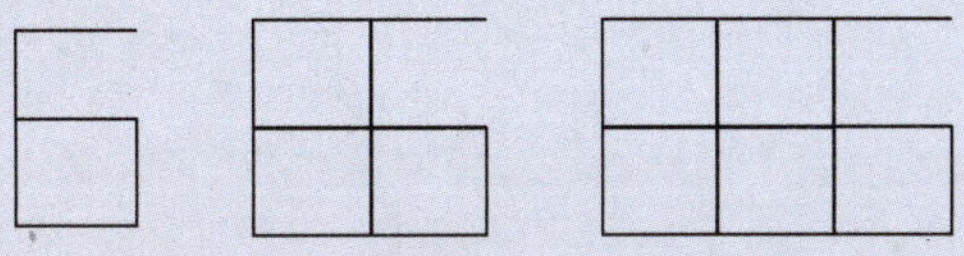

c.
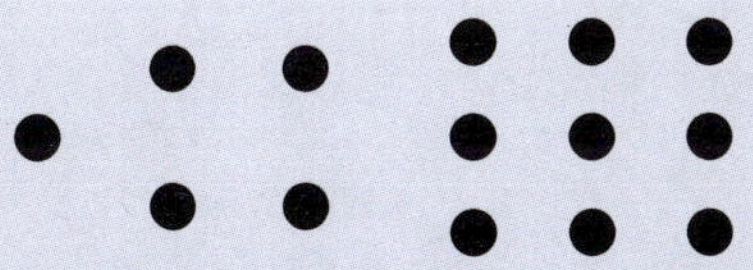

d.
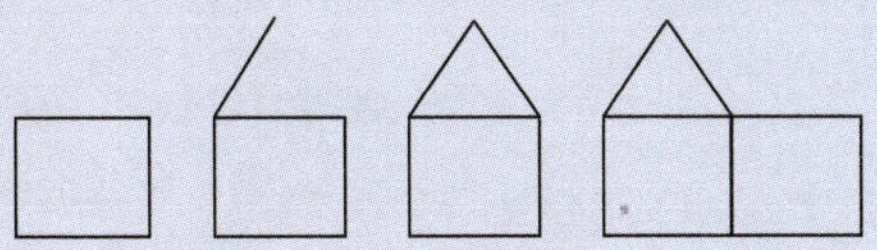

9. **Complete the following magic squares.**

a.

2		6
	5	
		8

b.

		7
4		8
		3

c.

		12
	15	27
18		

d.

		23
17	24	19

Key Concepts

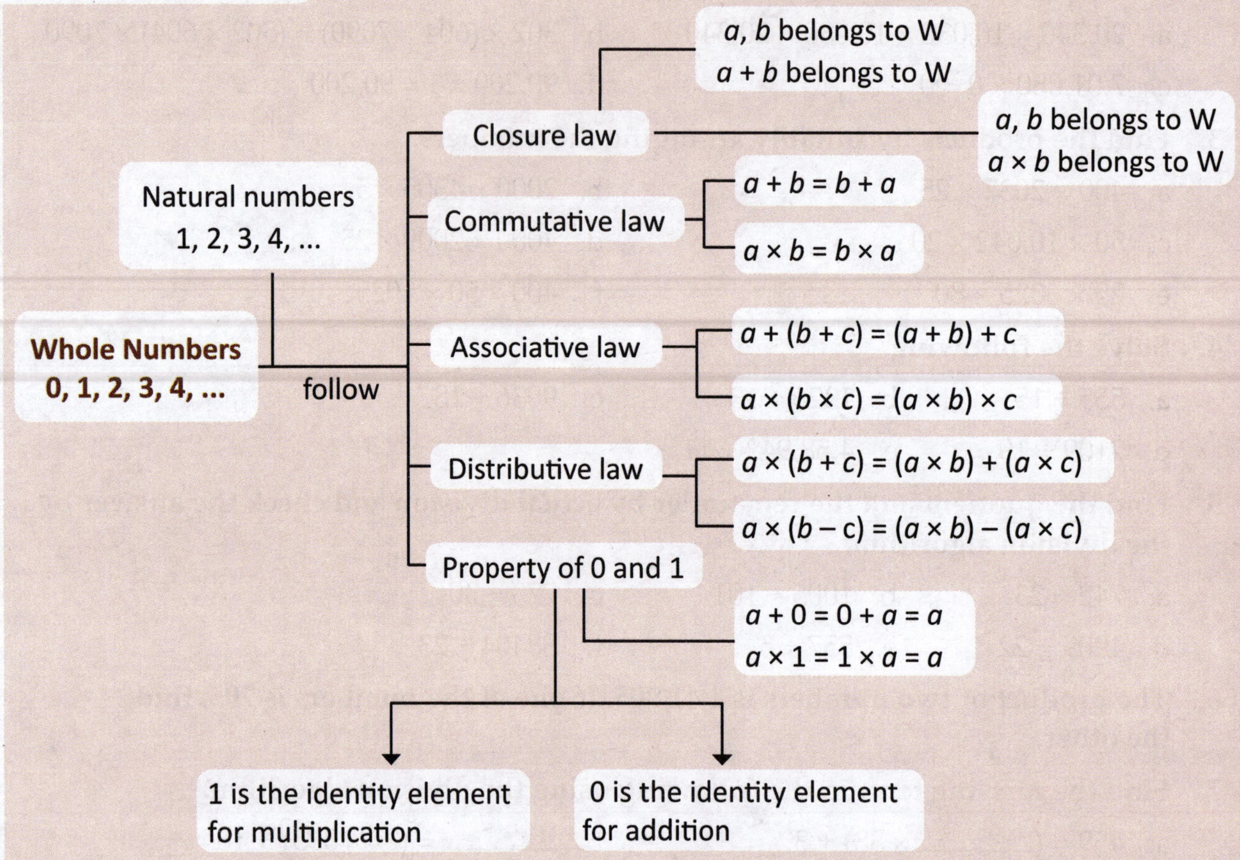

REVISION EXERCISE

1. Choose the correct option.

a. Commutative property of whole numbers for multiplication is

i. $a + b = b + a$ ii. $a(b + c) = ab + ac$

iii. $a \times b = b \times a$ iv. $a \times (b \times c) = (a \times b) \times c$

b. Distributive property of multiplication over addition is

i. $a(b - c) = ab - ac$ ii. $a(b + c) = ab + ac$

iii. $a + b = b + a$ iv. $a + (b + c) = (a + b) + c$

c. The product of the smallest whole number and the smallest natural number is

i. 0 ii. 1 iii. 2 iv. 10

d. Closure property for whole numbers holds good for

i. addition ii. multiplication iii. subtraction iv. both (i) and (ii)

e. Associative property for whole numbers holds good for

i. multiplication ii. subtraction iii. division iv. both (i) and (ii)

2. Fill in the blanks.

a. 206 + ______ = 206

b. 874 × 0 = ______

c. 22,584 × ______ = 22,584

d. 77,859 × 105 = 77,859 × (100 + ______)

e. 2335 × 98 = ______ × (100 − 2)

3. Solve the following using suitable rearrangement.

a. 7082 + 30,033 + 2018

b. 9091 + 9092 + 9093 + 9097 + 9098 + 9099

c. 500 × 451 × 18

d. 104 × 106 × 250 × 4

4. Solve the following using properties of whole numbers.

a. 1004 × 555

b. 98 × 6023

c. 70,641 × 93 + 70,641 × 2 + 70,641

d. 88,765 × 1005 − 88,765 × 5

5. Find the product using distributive laws.

a. 32 × 105 b. 44 × 99

6. Find the missing term in the following using the division algorithm.

a. 666 = (______ × 60) + 6

b. 874 = (9 × 97) + ______

c. 1295 = (10 × ______) + 5

d. 2763 = (12 × ______) + 3

7. Find the missing numbers in the following patterns.

a. 1, 4, 9, ____, 25, ____, 64

b. 12, 24, ____, 96, 192, ____

c. 38, 63, ____, ______, 138, 163

d. 115, ______, 99, 91, ____, 75

e. 64, 97, ____, ______, 196, 229

8. Solve the following word problems.

a. Find the number which when divided by 35 gives 202 as the quotient and 3 as the remainder.

b. Verify distributive property of multiplication over subtraction for the set of the numbers 2, 4 and 1.

c. Verify associative property of subtraction for the set of the numbers 3, 5 and 2.

d. Distributive property of addition over multiplication is not true. Show this with the help of an example.

e. Find the sum of the following numbers using suitable rearrangement: 237, 840, 180, 263, 320 and 160.

3 Integers

Prior Knowledge

- Natural numbers and whole numbers
- Representation of whole numbers on a number line
- Operations on numbers

Learning Objectives

- Absolute value of an integer
- Comparing and ordering integers
- Addition of integers
- Subtraction of integers

Let's Get Started

We often come across opposite quantities like height and depth, increase and decrease, deposit and withdrawal, above and below freezing point, above and below sea level, etc.

These pairs of opposites can be represented by using positive and negative numbers.

Write the numbers given in each of the following statements using appropriate signs.

1. A mountain peak has an altitude of 11,560 ft above sea level. ________
2. A desert location has an altitude of 185 ft below sea level. ________
3. The temperature of Kolkata is 28°C more than 0°C. ________
4. A deposit of ₹10,000 ________

What do we call the collection of numbers that do not have fractional values and may be negative, positive or zero?

INTEGERS

Integers are the whole numbers and their opposites. There is either positive, zero, or negative.

In the previous example, we observe that 1200, 0, and –1200 are **integers**.

The set of integers can be written as {. . . , –4, –3, –2, –1, 0, 1, 2, 3, 4, . . .}, where ". . ." means that the numbers go on indefinitely. The set of integers contains:

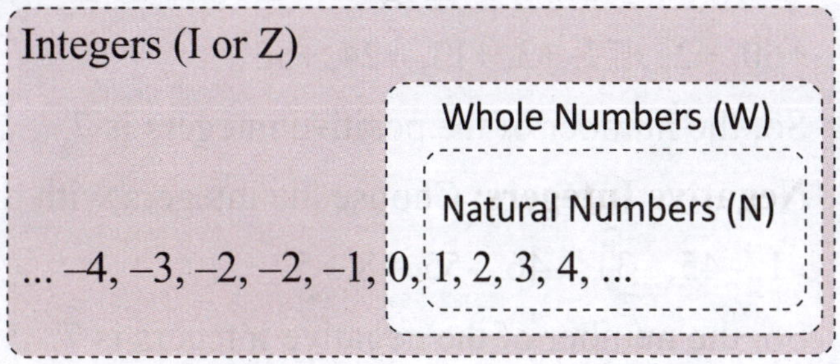

- the set of natural numbers, {1, 2, 3, 4, . . .}.
- the set of whole numbers, {0, 1, 2, 3, 4, . . .}.
- the set of opposites of natural numbers, {. . . , –4, –3, –2, –1}.

Representing Integers on a Number Line

The opposite of an integer is the integer that is the same distance from 0 on a number line but is located on the opposite side of 0.

To plot an integer on a number line, draw a dot to locate the point on the number line that corresponds to the integer.

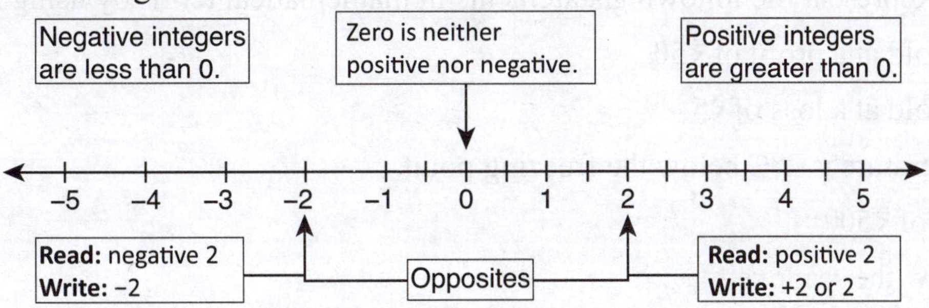

Numbers –1, –2, –3, –4, ... are called **negative integers** and numbers 1, 2, 3, 4,... are called **positive integers**. Number '0' is considered neither positive nor negative.

On a number line, when we move right from 0, we get positive integers and when we move left from 0, we get negative integers.

> **REMEMBER**
>
> Conventionally, we do not write the + sign before a positive number. However, it is necessary to write the – sign before a negative number.

Use of Integers as Directed Numbers

Integers can be used in the real life for the following purposes:

Use of Integers (Z)	Positive Integers (Z^+)	Negative Integers (Z^-)
Business	Profit	Loss
Banks	Credited amount	Debited amount
Height with respect to sea level	Above sea level	Below sea level
Temperature in thermometers	Temperature above 0°	Temperature below 0°

Example 1: List out the positive and negative integers among the following collection of integers.

–1, +60, –45, –31, +2, –46, –55, +77, –8, +3, –5, +13, +24, +32

Solution: Positive Integers: Choose the integers with the positive (+) sign.

+60, +2, +77, +3, +13, +24, +32

So, the number of the positive integers is 7.

Negative Integers: Choose the integers with the negative (–) sign.

–1, –45, –31, –46, –55, –8, –5

So, the number of the negative integers is 7.

Example 2: For each lettered point on the number line below, name the integer and its opposite.

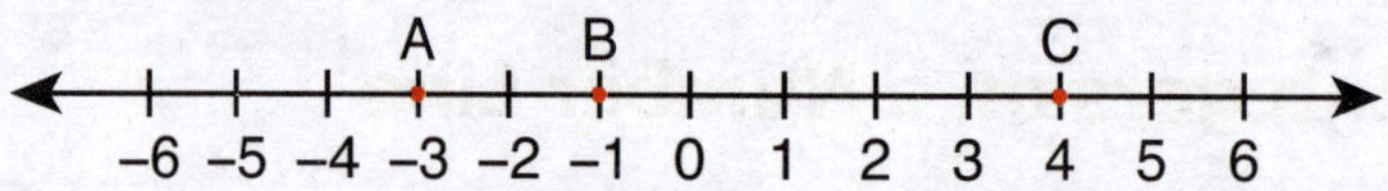

Solution: Point A is at –3. Opposites: –(–3) = 3 | Point B is at –1. –(–1) = 1 | Point C is at 4. –(4) = –4

Example 3: Represent the following statements in mathematical terms by using integers:

a. A bag is sold at a profit of ₹50.

b. A pen is sold at a loss of ₹5.

c. The temperature is 2°C below the freezing point.

d. A deposit of ₹500

e. 30 m below the sea level

Solution: a. Profit is represented with a positive sign. So, profit of ₹50 is represented as + ₹50.

b. Loss is represented with a negative sign. So, loss of ₹5 is represented as – ₹5.

c. Temperature below 0°C is represented with a negative sign. So, the given temperature is represented as –2°C.

d. Deposit is represented with a positive sign. So, deposit of ₹500 is represented as + ₹500.

e. Distance below the sea level is represented with a negative sign. So, 30 m below the sea level is represented as –30 m.

Absolute Value of an Integer

Observe the given number line.

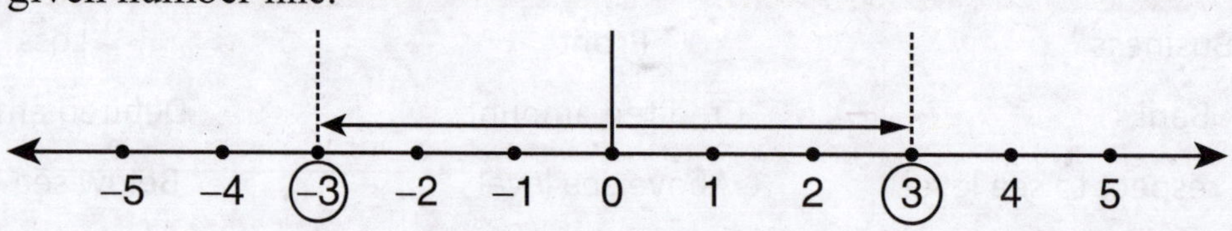

On the number line, –3 and 3 are on the opposite sides of 0 and are equidistant from it. So the absolute value of +3 is 3 and the absolute value of –3 is also 3.

Thus, the **absolute value** of an integer is the numerical value of the integer regardless of its sign. The symbol for absolute value is two vertical bars on either side of the number. For example, the absolute value of 10 is represented as |10|.

REMEMBER

1. The absolute value of 0 is 0, that is, |0| = 0.
2. The absolute value of a number is never negative.

Examples:

The absolute value of 4 is 4, that is, |4| = 4.

The absolute value of –4 is 4, that is, |–4| = 4.

COMPARING AND ORDERING INTEGERS

We can use a number line to compare and order integers. The following facts are used to compare and order integers.

1. All positive integers are greater than negative integers.
2. Zero is less than every positive integer and greater than every negative integer.
3. If a natural number is greater than another natural number, its negative is less than the negative of the other number and vice versa. For example, as 7 > 4, we have –7 < –4; as 3 < 5, we have –3 > – 5.
4. The greatest negative integer is –1.
5. The smallest positive integer is 1.

Example 4: Compare –|5| and |–5|.

Solution: The absolute value of 5 is 5. That is, |5| = 5 ⇒ –|5| = –5

The absolute value of –5 is 5. That is, |–5| = 5

–5 < 5 (Since a negative integer is always less than a positive integer.)

Therefore, –|5| < |–5|.

Example 5: Compare the following pairs of integers using the symbol '>' or '<'.

a. 3 and –5

Solution: First, let us represent 3 and –5 on the number line.

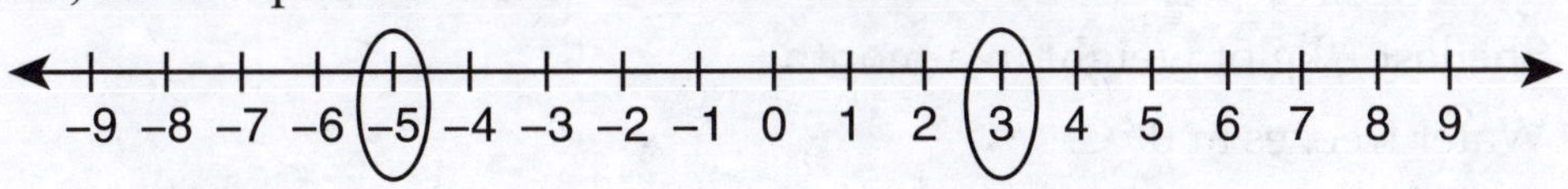

3 is on the right of zero and –5 is on the left of zero. So, 3 is greater than – 5. Therefore, 3 > –5.

b. –10 and –8

Solution: First, let us represent –10 and – 8 on the number line.

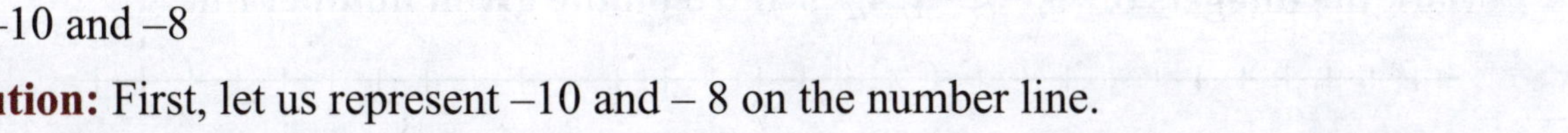

–10 is on the left of –8 on the number line. Therefore, –10 < –8.

Example 6: Arrange the following set of integers in ascending order.

4, –7, 0, 2, –1, –13

Solution: Let us represent the integers on a number line. Then, order the integers from the smallest to the greatest.

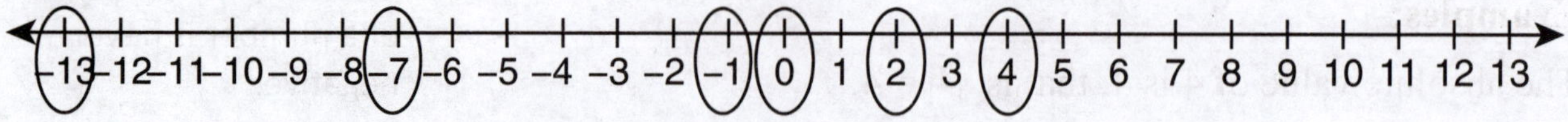

Numbers in ascending order: –13 < –7 < –1 < 0 < 2 < 4

Example 7: Arrange the following set of integers in descending order.

0, –4, 13, –11, –5, 6, 1

Solution: Represent the numbers on a number line. Then, order the integers from the greatest to the smallest.

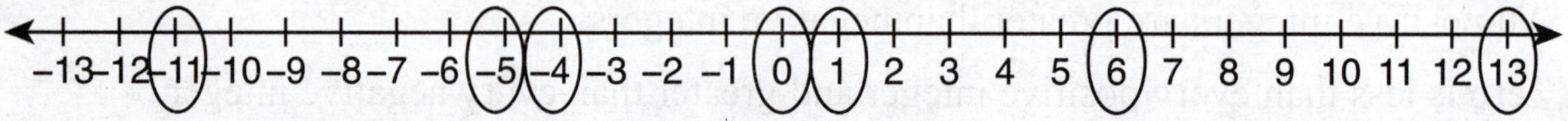

Numbers in descending order: 13 > 6 > 1 > 0 > –4 > –5 > –11

Example 8: Using a number line, find all the integers from −5 to −1. State which of them is the greatest and the smallest integer.

Solution: Let us represent the numbers on a number line.

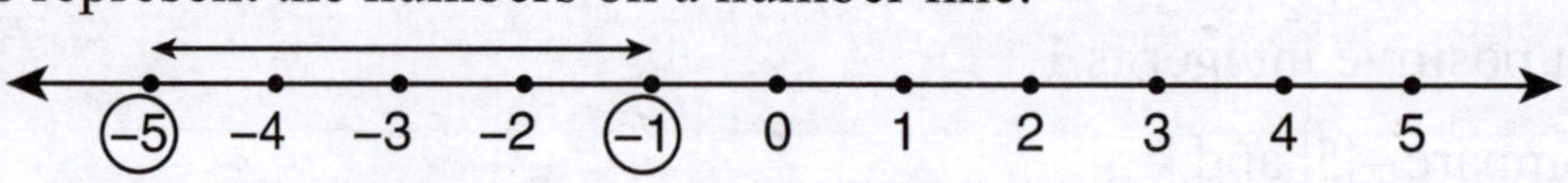

The integers are –5, –4, –3, –2 and –1.

The greatest integer is –1 and the smallest integer is –5.

Exercise 3.1

1. **Read the statements and write the numbers with appropriate signs (+ or –).**
   a. A bird is flying at a height of 25 m above sea level.
   b. The average temperature at Mount Everest in January is 36 °C below 0 °C.
   c. She lost 2 kg of weight in a month.
   d. Water freezes at 0 °C.
   e. The fish is swimming 10 m below the water surface.
   f. He deposited ₹1000 in my bank account.
2. **Mark the integers 6, −3, −7, −1, 4, −5 and 3 on the given number line.**

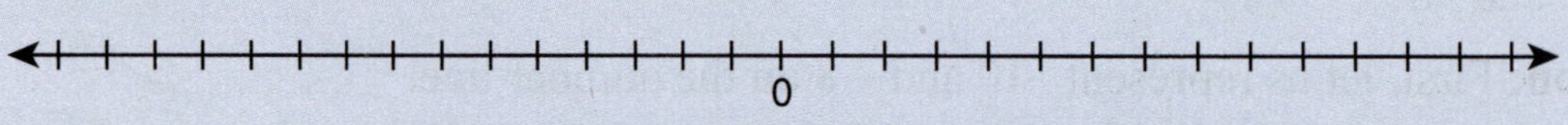

3. **Put the appropriate symbol '<' or '>' in the blanks below.**
   a. –2 ____ 20 b. 3 ____ –50 c. |–4| ____ –5
   d. 0 ____ –10 e. 0 ____ 40 f. 100 ____ –100

4. **Write the following sets of integers in the ascending order.**

   a. –4, 0, –10, 1, –2, 4, 5 b. –9, –11, 3, –2, –24, 8, –5

   c. –1, 6, –8, 11, 13, 0, –13 d. 2, 5, –6, 9, 1, –2, –5, –40

   e. 4, 7, –9, 0, –2, –3, 1

5. **Write the following sets of integers in the descending order.**

   a. –3, 4, –10, 10, –5, 7, –13 b. –9, –11, 3, –2, –24, 8, 0

   c. 5, –8, –2, –3, 11, 19, –36 d. 11, –3, –6, –9, 12, 16, –2

   e. 11, 0, 7, –2, –5, –7, 4, –11

6. **Find all the integers that lie between the given two integers.**

   a. –5 and 3 b. –11 and –3 c. –4 and 0

   d. –3 and 1 e. –2 and 2

7. **Write the absolute value for each of the following.**

   a. $|-3|$ b. $|232|$ c. $|0|$

   d. $-|3|$ e. $-|-3|$ f. $-|0|$

8. **Evaluate the following:**

   a. $|16-7|$ b. $|5|+|-3|$ c. $|-6|+|-16|$ d. $|-12|-|+7|$

   e. $|+86|-|-57|$ f. $|327-269|$ g. $|-456|-|-389|$

ADDITION AND SUBTRACTION OF INTEGERS

In this section, we will learn how to add and subtract integers.

Addition of Integers

We move towards the right to add a positive integer and move towards the left to add a negative integer on the number line.

Example 9: Add (–4) and (+2).

Solution: Starting from –4, move 2 units towards the right to get –2.

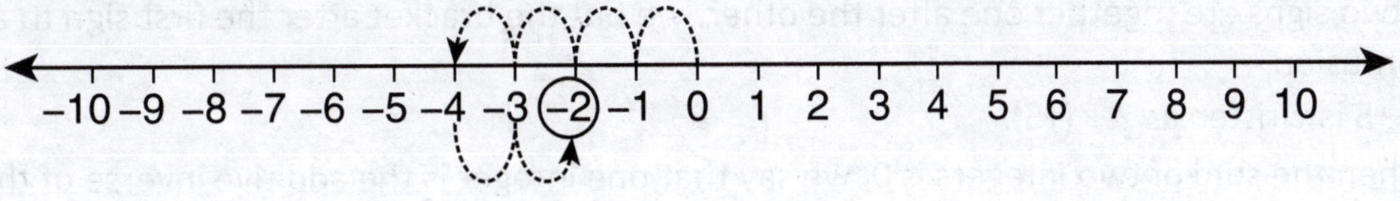

∴ (–4) + (+2) = (–2)

Example 10: Add (+4) and (–3).

Solution: Starting from +4, move 3 units towards the left to get (+1).

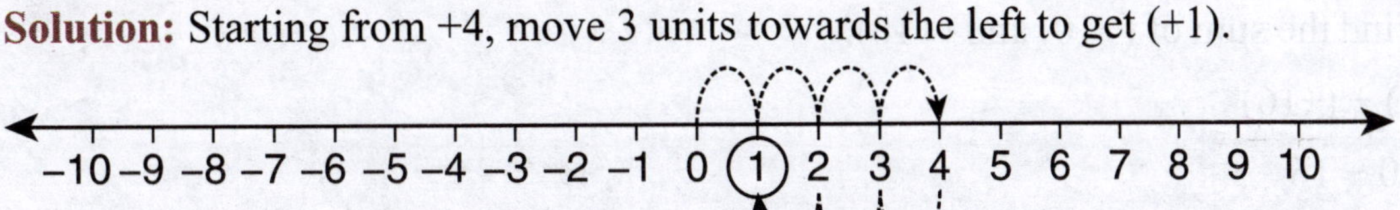

∴ (+4) + (–3) = (+1)

Example 11: Add the following:

a. 4 and 3 b. (–4) and (–3)

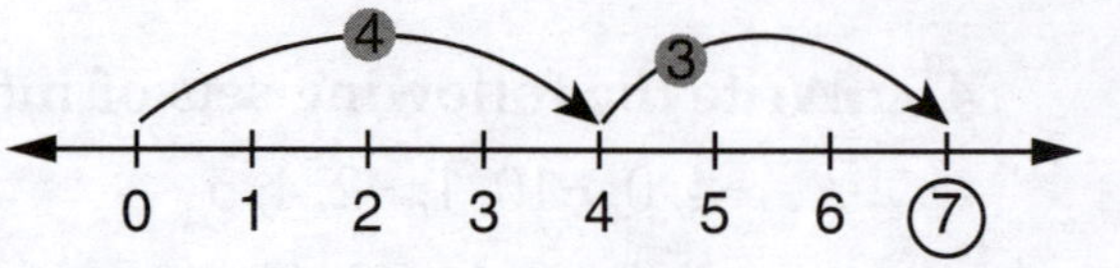

4 + 3 = 7

Solution: a. First move 4 steps to the right from 0 to reach 4. Then, move 3 steps to the right of 4 to reach 7.

$\therefore\ 4 + 3 = 7$

b. First move 4 steps to the left from 0 to reach –4. Then, move 3 steps to the left of –4 to reach –7.

$\therefore\ (-4) + (-3) = (-7)$

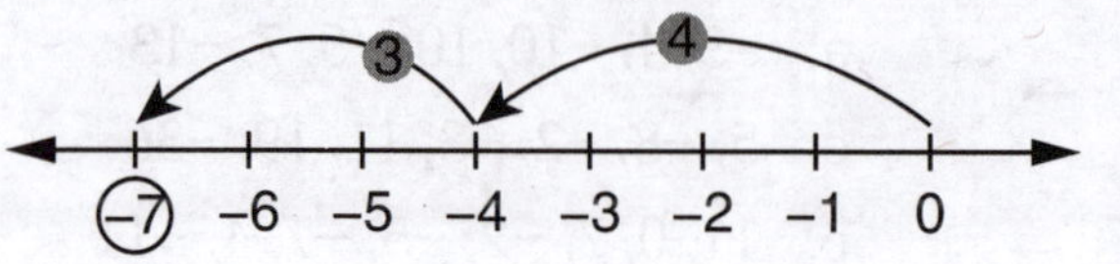

(–4) + (–3) = –7

Thus, from the above examples, we can conclude that:

- The sum of two positive integers is always positive and the resulting integer is greater than the given integers.
- The sum of two negative integers is always negative and the resulting integer is lesser than the given integers.

Addition of Integers Without Using Number Line

1. If two integers have the same sign, we
   - add them (without the signs) and
   - then put their sign
2. If two integers have different signs, ignoring the signs, we
   - subtract the smaller number from the bigger number (without the signs) and
   - then put the sign of the bigger number

REMEMBER

- If we have the '+' sign outside a bracket and we remove the bracket, the sign of the number inside the bracket is taken.
  +(+3) = 3 and +(–3) = –3
- If two signs are together one after the other, we put the bracket after the first sign to avoid confusion.
  2++5 is written as 2 + (+5).
- When the sum of two integers is 0, we say that one integer is the additive inverse of the other. We write the additive inverse of a as $-a$ and vice versa.
  For any integer a, $a + (-a) = (-a) + a = 0$.

Example 12: Find the sum of (+10) and (+16).

Solution: (+10) + (+16)

= +10 + 16

= +26

Example 13: Find the sum of (–11) and (–22).

Solution: (–11) + (–22)

= –11 – 22

= –33

Example 14: Find the sum of (–72) and (+49).

Solution: (–72) + (+49) = –72 + 49 = –23

Subtraction of Integers

To subtract an integer from another integer, we add the additive inverse of the integer to be subtracted.

Example 15: Subtract (–3) from (–1).

Solution: The additive inverse of –3 is +3.

Instead of solving it as (–1) – (–3), we can solve it as (–1) + (+3).

Starting from –1, move 3 units towards right on the number line.

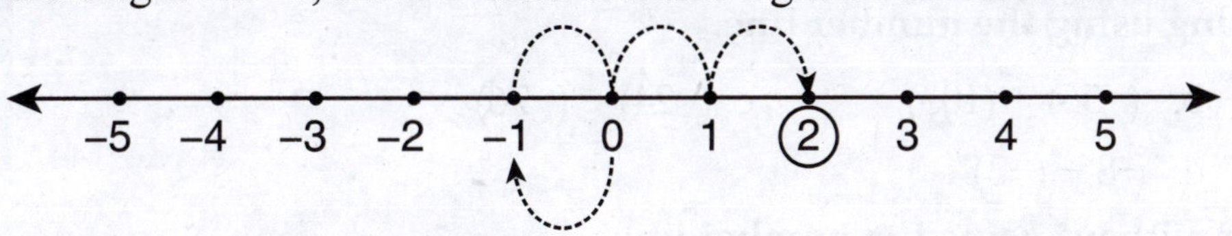

∴ (–1) – (–3) = 2

Example 16: Subtract (+4) from (–1).

Solution: The additive inverse of +4 is –4.

Instead of solving it as (–1) – (+4), we can solve it as (–1) + (– 4).

Starting from –1, move 4 units towards left on the number line.

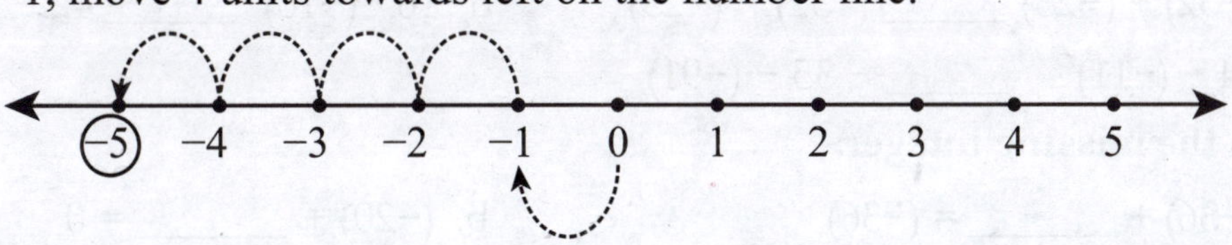

∴ (–1) – (+4) = –5

Subtraction of Integers without using Number Line

We subtract integers in a way similar to the way we add them. The only difference is that if we have the '–' sign outside a bracket, when we remove the bracket, the sign of the number inside the bracket changes. –(+3) = –3; –(–3) = +3

Example 17: Subtract 5 from 2.

Solution: 2 – 5 = –3

Example 18: Subtract (–2) from (–6).

Solution: (–6) – (–2) = –6 + 2 = –4

Example 19: Subtract –5 from (–58).

Solution: (–58) – (–5) = – 58 + 5

= – 53

Example 20: Subtract (–3215) from 6787.

Solution: 6787 – (–3215) = 6787 + 3215

= 10,002

Example 21: Subtract the sum of –68 and 36 from the sum of 56 and –82.

Solution: Sum of –68 and 36 is –68 + 36 = –32

Sum of 56 and –82 is 56 + (–82) = –26

Now, –26 – (–32) = –26 + 32 = 6.

Exercise 3.2

1. **Add the following using the number line.**

   a. 7 + 4   b. 5 + (−8)   c. (−3) + 6

   d. (−4) + (−7)   e. −2 + 2

2. **Solve the following without using the number line.**

   a. 37 + 107   b. (−7) − (+3)   c. 3 − (−2)

   d. 49 + (−54)   e. 17 + (−16)

3. **Subtract the following using the number line.**

   a. (−7) − (−3)   b. (−56) − (103)   c. (−24) − (−76)

   d. 8 − 3   e. −8 − (−3)

4. **Solve the following without using the number line.**

   a. (−19) − (+21)   b. 35 − (−18)   c. (−17) − (+15)

   d. 0 − (+120)   e. −11 − (+86)

5. **Fill in the blanks with <, >, or =.**

   a. (−3) + (−7) ______ (−7) − (−3)   b. 55 − (−22) ______ 0 − (−77)

   c. (−32) + (−23) ______ (−32) − (−23)   d. 16 −(−16) ______ 42 − 10

   e. 44 − (−11) ______ − 35 − (−91)

6. **Fill in the missing integer.**

   a. (−36) + ______ = (−36)   b. (−20) + ______ = 0

   c. (−14) − ______ = −28   d. ______ − (−15) = +10

   e. −11 − ______ = −18

7. **What number should be added to −14 to get −68?**

8. **The sum of two integers is 68. If one of them is −68, find the other.**

9. **The temperature on a particular morning is 14 °C, but by midnight it falls to −2 °C due to rain. By how many degrees does the temperature fall?**

10. **A bus travels 523 km north from Bangalore and then 201 km south on the same route. How far is the bus from Bangalore now?**

Key Concepts

Integers

Negative: {..., −3, −2, −1}
Zero: {0}
Positive: {1, 2, 3, ...}

Absolute value (numerical value of the integer without sign)

Example: |−3| = |−3| = 3
|3| = 3

Compare and Order

Order 2, −5, and 0 from least to greatest.
The order from least to greatest is: −5, 0, 2.
The order from greatest to least is: 2, 0, −5.

undergo

Addition

Subtraction

Add integer with same signs.
Subtract integer with different signs.

can be done

Using a number line

Without using a number line

Example: 75 + (−11) = 75 − 11 = 64

Example: −4 + 2

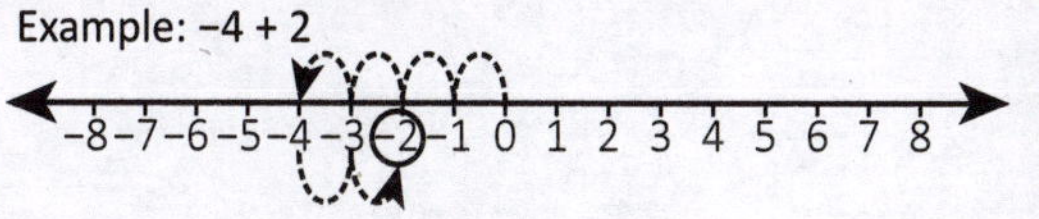

So, (−4) + 2 = (−2)

can be done

Using a number line

Without using a number line

Example:
34 − (−6) = 34 + 6 = 40

Example: −1 − (− 3)

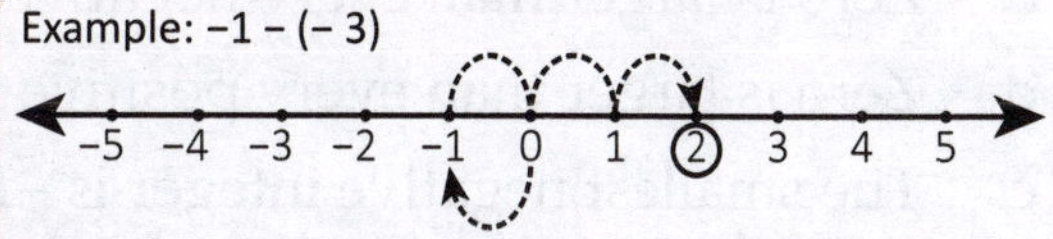

So, (−1) − (−3) = 2

Revision Exercise

1. **Write the positive and negative signs for the following statements.**

   a. Depth of an ocean
   b. Deposit in a bank account
   c. Height of a mountain
   d. Spending money on shopping
   e. Lift button indicating basement level

2. **Choose the correct integer from the given options and fill in the blanks.**

   +7, +3, +5, –5, –3

   a. Integer to the immediate right of –6: ____________
   b. Integer that is six places to the left of 3: ____________
   c. Integer that is 5 places to the right of –2: ____________
   d. Integer that is 5 more than 0: ____________
   e. Integer that is 10 places to the right of –3: ____________

3. **State whether the following statements are true or false.**

   a. Every positive integer is larger than every negative integer.
   b. The farther a number from zero towards the right, the smaller is its value.
   c. Zero is larger than every negative integer.
   d. Zero is larger than every positive integer.
   e. The smallest negative integer is –1.

4. **Compare the integers and write '<' or '>'.**

   a. (–22) ☐ (–13) b. 100 ☐ (–101) c. –142 ☐ –143
   d. 23 ☐ 32 e. –130 ☐ 15 f. 100 ☐ 99

5. **Write any four integers that are smaller than –2 and greater than –23.**

6. **Write all the integers (in the ascending order) between the given pairs of integers.**

   a. –6 and 1 b. 4 and –4 c. 7 and 2
   d. –2 and –9 e. –5 and 5

7. **Represent the following integers on the number line.**

   a. 4 b. –7 c. –1
   d. 6 e. –5 f. 7

8. **Simplify the following expressions.**

   a. (–15) + 8 b. (–110) + (–32) c. –215 + (+150)
   d. (–10) + (–19) e. 56 + (–11) f. 70 + (–25)
   g. 67 – (–5) h. (–25) – (–75) i. –29 – (+14)
   j. –15 – (–12) k. –9 + 7 + 6 – 4 l. 9 + 8 – 6 – 5 – 4 + 3
   m. 4 + 0 + 9 – 7 + 1 n. 1 + 9 – 2 – 2 + 1 o. –6 + 4 – 3 – 11 – 5 + 31

4 Sets

Prior Knowledge

- Grouping or collection of objects
- Types of numbers

Learning Objectives

- Concept of sets
- Representation of sets in descriptive, roster and set-builder forms
- Properties of a set
- Cardinal number of a set
- Different types of sets

Let's Get Started

Circle the name that does not belong to the collection.

1.	Soccer	Play	Volleyball	Tennis
2.	Monday	Wednesday	January	Friday
3.	Banana	Apple	Orange	Pulses
4.	Teacher	Father	Mother	Brother
5.	Listen	Music	Eat	Watch

In the above shown questions, one out of the four elements does not have common characteristics or property as the remaining three.

The elements which possess a common characteristics or property make a **collection**.

Find the element which does not belong to each collection and give reason. Give each of the above collections an appropriate name.

SET

In everyday life, we come across collections of objects, numbers and people that share a common characteristic or property. It is easy to say whether a particular object does or does not belong to it. Such collections are **well-defined collections**.

Example 1: Observe the pictures and state whether they are well-defined collections or not.

Group of best singers of India | Group of people whose name starts with R | Group of dangerous animals | Group of planets in the solar system

Solution: 1. Group of best singers of India is not a well-defined collection because the criterion of choosing the best singer varies from person to person.

2. Group of people whose name starts with R is a well-defined collection because we can identify the person whose name starts with the letter R.

3. Group of dangerous animals is not a well-defined collection because the criteria of determining dangerous animals can vary from person to person.

4. Group of planets in the solar system is a well-defined collection because we can identify the planets of our solar system.

A well-defined collection of objects is called a **set**, and if it is not a well-defined collection, then that collection is not a set. We usually denote a set by a capital letter.

Elements of a Set

The objects in a set are called **elements** or **members** of the set.

Consider the set of the first 5 whole numbers. In this set, the elements are 0, 1, 2, 3 and 4.

The elements of a set are written within a pair of curly braces { }. They are separated using commas.

Therefore, the set of the first 5 whole numbers can be written as W = {0, 1, 2, 3, 4}.

Example 2: Write the set of all even numbers between 9 and 15. Also state whether A is a well-defined object or not.

Solution: The even numbers between 9 and 15 are 10, 12 and 14.

Let the set be named as A.

Then, A = {10, 12, 14}

In the above example, 10 is an element of set A, that is, 10 belongs to A. This is written as $10 \in A$.

13 is not an element of this set, so it is written as $13 \notin A$.

> **REMEMBER**
> We usually denote sets by capital letters and their elements by small letters of the English alphabet.

In this example, it is possible to identify clearly whether an element belongs to A or not. Therefore, A is a collection of well-defined objects.

Example 3: State whether the following collections are sets.

a. Collection of all the schools in Kolkata

b. Collection of intelligent girls in a school

Solution: a. Clearly, the given collection will contain the names of all the schools in Kolkata, which may be known. Hence, the given collection is a set.

b. The term 'intelligent' can be interpreted differently by different people, so the elements are not well-defined. Hence, the given collection is not a set.

Example 4: A is the set of letters of the word TUBELIGHT. Fill in the blanks with $\in$ or $\notin$.

a. u ___ A   b. l ___ A   c. k ___ A

d. n ___ A   e. p ___ A   f. t, e ___ A

Solution: A = {t, u, b, e, l, i, g, h}

a. u $\in$ A   b. l $\in$ A   c. k $\notin$ A

d. n $\notin$ A   e. p $\notin$ A   f. t, e $\in$ A

Exercise 4.1

1. **State which of the following collections are sets. Justify your answer.**
   a. Collection of beautiful birds in India
   b. Collection of all the students in a school
   c. Collection of all the letters in your name
   d. Collection of all whole numbers
   e. Collection of roses in a basket
   f. Collection of polygons having three sides
2. **State true or false.**
   a. d $\notin$ {set of consonants}
   b. 2 $\in$ {3, 5, 2, 7}
   c. {2, 7} $\in$ {1, 2, 5, 7}
   d. 1, 7 $\in$ {1, 3, 6, 7}

Properties of a Set

1. The elements of a set can be written in any order, that is, change in the order of the elements does not change the set. For example, sets A = {1, 2, 3, 4, 5} and B = {4, 5, 3, 1, 2} are the same as they contain the same elements.

2. If one or many elements of a set are repeated, the set remains the same. For example, sets A = {1, 2, 3, 4, 5, 5, 5, 6, 7, 8} and B = {1, 2, 3, 4, 5, 6, 7, 8} are the same. This is because in a set, even if an element is repeated, we consider it once.

REPRESENTATION OF SETS

A set can be represented by three methods.

1. Description method
2. Roster method or tabular form
3. Rule method or set-builder form

Description Method

In this method, a set can be defined by describing the elements clearly in words.

Examples:

1. The set of integers between –5 and 9 is written as
   A is the set of all integers between –5 and 9.
2. The set of natural numbers less than 20 is written as
   B is the set of all natural numbers less than 20.

Example 5: Write these sets in the description method.

a. {2, 4, 6, 8, 10, 12}

b. {2, 3, 5, 7, 11, 13}

c. {. . . , – 4, –2, 0, 2, 4, 6, . . .}

d. {1, 2, 3, 6, 9, 18}

Solution: a. Set of all even natural numbers less than 13.

b. Set of all prime numbers less than 14.

c. Set of all integers divisible by 2.

d. Set of all factors of 18.

Roster Method or Tabular Form

In the **tabular form**, all the members of a set are written distinctly within curly brackets and are separated by commas. It is also known as the list method or the roster method.

Example 6: Write the following sets in roster form.

a. The collection of integers between −10 and 10 that are divisible by 3

b. The collection of even numbers between 10 and 100

Solution: a. D = {−9, −6, −3, 0, 3, 6, 9}

b. E = {12, 14, 16, …, 96, 98}

Rule Method or Set-Builder Form

In this method, we write a variable (say y) representing an element of the set, followed by a colon (:) or (|) and then we write the defining property of each element of the set and enclose the whole description in curly brackets.

If A is the set of elements x, where x is a day in the week, we write A = {x : x is a day of the week}.

This is read as, A is the set of elements x, such that x is a day of the week.

Example 7: Represent the following sets in the set-builder form.

a. A = {3, 6, 9, 12, 15, 18, 21}

b. F = {1, 3, 5, 15}

c. The collection of all the integers between 10 and 20

REMEMBER

The symbol ':' stands for 'such that'. At times '|' is also used in place of ':'.

Solution: a. A = {x | x is a natural number, x is a multiple of 3 and $x < 24$}

b. F = {x | x is a natural number and a factor of 15}

c. S = {x | x is an integer, $10 < x < 20$}

Example 8: Identify the methods by which the following sets have been represented.

a. A = {2, 4, 6, 8, 10, 12}

b. B = {x | x is a month of the year}

c. x is an even natural number less than 30 and greater than 10

Solution: a. Roster method

b. Rule method

c. Descriptive method

Example 9: Write set A = {y : $y = 2x + 1$, $x \in$ W and $x < 5$} in the roster form and also in descriptive form.

Solution: Given A = {y : $y = 2x + 1$, $x \in$ W and $x < 5$}

Whole numbers less than 5 are 0, 1, 2, 3, 4.

Putting $x = 0, 1, 2, 3, 4$ respectively in $y = 2x + 1$, we get:

when $x = 0, y = 2 \times 0 + 1 = 0 + 1 = 1$;

when $x = 1, y = 2 \times 1 + 1 = 2 + 1 = 3$;

when $x = 2, y = 2 \times 2 + 1 = 4 + 1 = 5$;

when $x = 3, y = 2 \times 3 + 1 = 6 + 1 = 7$ and

when $x = 4, y = 2 \times 4 + 1 = 8 + 1 = 9$.

$\therefore$ A = {1, 3, 5, 7, 9} is in roaster form.

The descriptive form is A = odd natural numbers less than 10

ALERT !

The set A = {1, 2, 3, 4, 5} is written in the set-builder form as

A = {x : x is a natural number} ×

A = {x : x is a natural number, $x < 6$} ✓

Standard Sets of Numbers

1. The set of natural numbers is denoted by N, that is, N = {1, 2, 3, 4, ...}.
2. The set of whole numbers is denoted by W, that is, W = {0, 1, 2, 3, 4, 5, ...}.
3. The set of integers is denoted by I or Z, that is, Z/I = {..., −3, −2, −1, 0, 1, 2, 3, 4, ...}.
4. The set of even natural numbers is denoted by E = {2, 4, 6, 8, ...}.
5. The set of odd natural numbers is denoted by O = {1, 3, 5, 7, 9, ...}.

CARDINAL NUMBER OF A SET

The number of distinct elements of a set A is called the **cardinal number** of A, which is denoted by n(A).

Consider the following examples.

1. Set X = $\{a, b, c, d, e, f, g\}$ has 7 distinct elements.
2. Set Y = {1, 1, 2, 3, 4, 4, 5, 6} has 6 distinct elements although it has 8 elements.

REMEMBER

While counting the distinct elements of a set to find its cardinal number, we consider the repeated elements only once.

Example 10: What is the cardinal number of set C = $\{m, n, o, m, p, q, r, s, p, t, u, v, w, x, y, z\}$?

Solution: Set C has 14 distinct elements. Therefore, its cardinal number is 14. This is written as n(C) = 14.

Example 11: Find the cardinal number for the given sets

a. M = {2, 4, 7, 11, 13, 15, 17}

b. P = $\{a, b, c, d, e, f\}$

Solution: a. In set M = {2, 4, 7, 11, 13, 15, 17}, there are 7 distinct elements. Therefore, n(M) = 7

b. In set P = $\{a, b, c, d, e, f\}$, there are 6 distinct elements. Therefore, n(P) = 6

Example 12: Write the cardinal number of a set E = { }.

Solution: Set E has no element. Therefore, its cardinal number is 0. So, n(E) = 0.

EXERCISE 4.2

1. **Express the following sets in roster form.**

   a. Set of all integers between −20 and −5

   b. Set of all 2-digit numbers greater than 79

   c. Set of all the multiples of 8 that are less than 80

   d. Set of the first 5 odd numbers that are divisible by 7

   e. Set of all consonants in the word KARNATAKA

2. **Represent the following sets in set-builder form.**

   a. D = {52, 54, 56, 58, 60, 62, 64, 66}

   b. P = {101, 103, 107, 109, 113, 127, 131, 137, 139, 149}

   c. M = {September, October, November, December}

   d. F = {2, 3, 5, 7, 11}

   e. S = {Mercury, Venus, Earth, Mars}

3. **Write these sets in the set-builder form as well as in the descriptive method.**

   a. {2, 3, 5, 7, 11, 13, 17, 19, 23}

   b. {5, 10, 15, 20, 25, 30, 35}

   c. {0, 1, 2, 3, 4, ..., 10}

   d. {–16, –12, – 8, – 4, 0, 4, 8, 12}

4. **Write the cardinal numbers of the following sets.**

   a. A = {p, q, r, s, t}

   b. B = {2, 2, 3, 5, 15, 15, 16, 17}

   c. C = {x | $x - 3 = 2$}

   d. D = {x | x is a prime factor of 20}

   e. E = {x | x is a 1-digit prime number}

   f. F = {100, 101, 102, 103, 104}

TYPES OF SETS

Let us learn about different types of sets.

Equivalent sets

If two sets have equal number of elements, then those sets are called **equivalent sets.**

Consider the following two sets.

A = {a, b, c, d} B = {3, 6, 9, 12}

What can you say about the number of elements in each set?

We notice that both the sets have equal number of elements. So, they are equivalent sets.

Thus, set A $\leftrightarrow$ set B if n(A) = n(B).

Example 13: Identify if the given pairs of sets are equivalent sets.

a. A = {x | x is a multiple of 4, $x < 24$} and B = {x | x is a multiple of 5, $x < 30$}

b. S = {1, 2, 3, 6} and T = {1, 2, 3, 4, 6, 12}

Solution: a. A = {4, 8, 12, 16, 20} and B = {5, 10, 15, 20, 25}

As n(A) = 5 = n(B), the sets A and B are equivalent sets.

b. As n(S) = 4 and n(T) = 6, the sets S and T are not equivalent sets.

Equal Sets

If two sets have the same elements, then the sets are called **equal sets**.

Consider the following sets.

P = $\{x \mid x$ is an even natural number, $x < 20\}$ and Q = $\{x \mid x$ is a multiple of 2, $x < 20\}$

Here, P = {2, 4, 6, 8, 10, 12, 14, 16, 18} and Q = {2, 4, 6, 8, 10, 12, 14, 16, 18}

Here, both the sets have the same elements. So, they are equal sets.

Example 14: Identify if the given pairs of sets are equal.

a. A = $\{x \mid x$ is a multiple of 3, $x < 15\}$ and B = $\{x \mid x$ is an odd number, $x < 8\}$

b. C = $\{x \mid x$ is a natural number, $x < 8\}$ and D = $\{x \mid x$ is an integer, $0 < x < 8\}$

Solution: a. A = {3, 6, 9, 12} and B = {1, 3, 5, 7}

Here, all the elements of set A are not elements of set B, so the sets are not equal.

b. C = {1, 2, 3, 4, 5, 6, 7} and D = {1, 2, 3, 4, 5, 6, 7}

Here, the sets C and D have the same elements. Therefore, they are equal sets.

Finite Set

If the elements of a set can be counted, then the set is a **finite set**.

Consider set A = $\{x \mid x$ is a multiple of 10, $0 < x < 100\}$.

Here, $n(\text{A}) = 9$. So, it is a finite set.

Infinite Set

If the number of elements of a set cannot be counted, then the set is an **infinite set**.

Consider set N = {1, 2, 3, 4, 5, 6, …}

Here, the counting does not stop and the number of elements is not finite.
Therefore, N is an infinite set.

Example 15: Classify the following as finite and infinite sets.

a. A = {10, 20, 30, 40, 50, …}

b. B = $\{x \mid x$ is a factor of 35$\}$

c. C = {2, 4, 6, 8, 10, 12, ...}

d. D = $\{x \mid x$ is a multiple of 3$\}$

Solution: a. Infinite set

b. Finite set

c. Infinite set

d. Here D = $\{x \mid x$ is a multiple of 3$\}$
= {3, 6, 9, 12, ……..}

Hence, D is an infinite set.

Singleton Set

A set that contains only one element is known as a **singleton set**.

Consider the set A = {2}.

This set has only one element in it, so it is a singleton set.

Similarly, set F = $\{x \mid x$ is the smallest even number$\}$ is a singleton set.

Example 16: Identify if the following are singleton sets.

a. A = {100000}

b. C = {x | x is a month of the year}

Solution: a. It is a singleton set.

b. It is not a singleton set.

Empty Set

A set that contains no element is called an **empty** or **null** or **void set**.

Consider the set E = { }. This set has no element, so it is an empty set.

For example, consider the set W of negative whole numbers.

Set W = { }

This is an empty set since there are no negative whole numbers.

Example 17: Identify if the following are empty sets.

a. A = {x | x is an even prime number}

b. B = {x | x is a month having 33 days}

Solution: a. It is not an empty set.

b. It is an empty set.

Disjoint Sets

Consider the sets A = {1, 3, 5, 7} and B = {2, 4, 6, 8}.

Do they have any elements in common? No

Such sets that have no common elements between them are known as **disjoint sets**.

Overlapping Sets or Intersecting Sets

Consider the sets A = {2, 4, 6, 8, 10} and B = {4, 8, 12, 16, 20}.

The elements 4 and 8 are common to both the sets.

Such sets that have at least one common element are called **overlapping** or **intersecting sets**.

Example 18: Classify the following as disjoint and overlapping sets.

a. P = {1, 3, 5, 7, 9}, Q = {2, 3, 5, 7, 11}

b. R = {a, e, i, o, u}, S = {v, w, x, y, z}

Solution:

a. In sets P = {1, 3, 5, 7, 9} and Q = {2, 3, 5, 7, 11}

Elements 3, 5, 7 are common. Hence, they are overlapping sets.

b. In sets R = {a, e, i, o, u} and S = {v, w, x, y, z}

There are no common elements. Hence, they are disjoint sets.

EXERCISE 4.3

1. **Identify if the following pairs of sets are equivalent.**
   a. A = {11, 13, 15, 17, 19} and B = {10, 12, 14, 16}
   b. C = {*p, q, r, s, t*} and D = {*d, e, f, g*}
   c. E = {x | x is a prime factor of 20} and F = {x | x is a multiple of 5, $x < 40$}
   d. G = {x | x is a letter in the word SOCIAL} and H = {x | x is a letter in the word SCIENCE}
   e. I = {2, 3, 5, 7} and J = {2, 4, 6, 8}
2. **Identify if the following pairs of sets are equal.**
   a. A = {*a, b, c, d, e*} and B = {*e, d, c, b, a*}
   b. C = {x | x is a vowel in the word COUNT} and D = {x | x is a vowel in the word WRITE}
   c. E = {x | x is an odd number, $5 < x < 15$} and F = {x | x is an even number, $5 < x < 15$}
   d. G = {1, 2, 3, 4, 5} and H = {0, 1, 2, 3, 4, 5}
   e. The set of the first 5 positive integers and the set of the first 5 negative integers
3. **Classify the following sets as singleton or empty sets.**
   a. The set of all negative natural numbers
   b. The set of all whole numbers less than 1
   c. A = {n}
   d. B = {x | x is a month having 27 days}
   e. C = {x | x is a natural number, $10 < x < 11$}
4. **Classify the following as finite and infinite sets.**
   a. The set of all the factors of 100
   b. The set of all the multiples of 4
   c. The set of all the integers between –1000 and 1000
   d. The set of all the points on a given line
   e. The set of all the states of India
5. **Classify the following as disjoint and overlapping sets.**
   a. A = {1, 3, 5, 7} B = {First 5 prime numbers}
   b. K = {a, b, c, d, e} L = {x | x is a vowel in the English alphabet}
   c. P = {pink, brown, maroon} Q = {x | x is a colour of the rainbow}
   d. S = {x | x is a whole number} T = {x | x is a natural number}
   e. X = {10, 20, 30, 40, 50} Y = {15, 25, 35, 45, 60}

KEY CONCEPTS

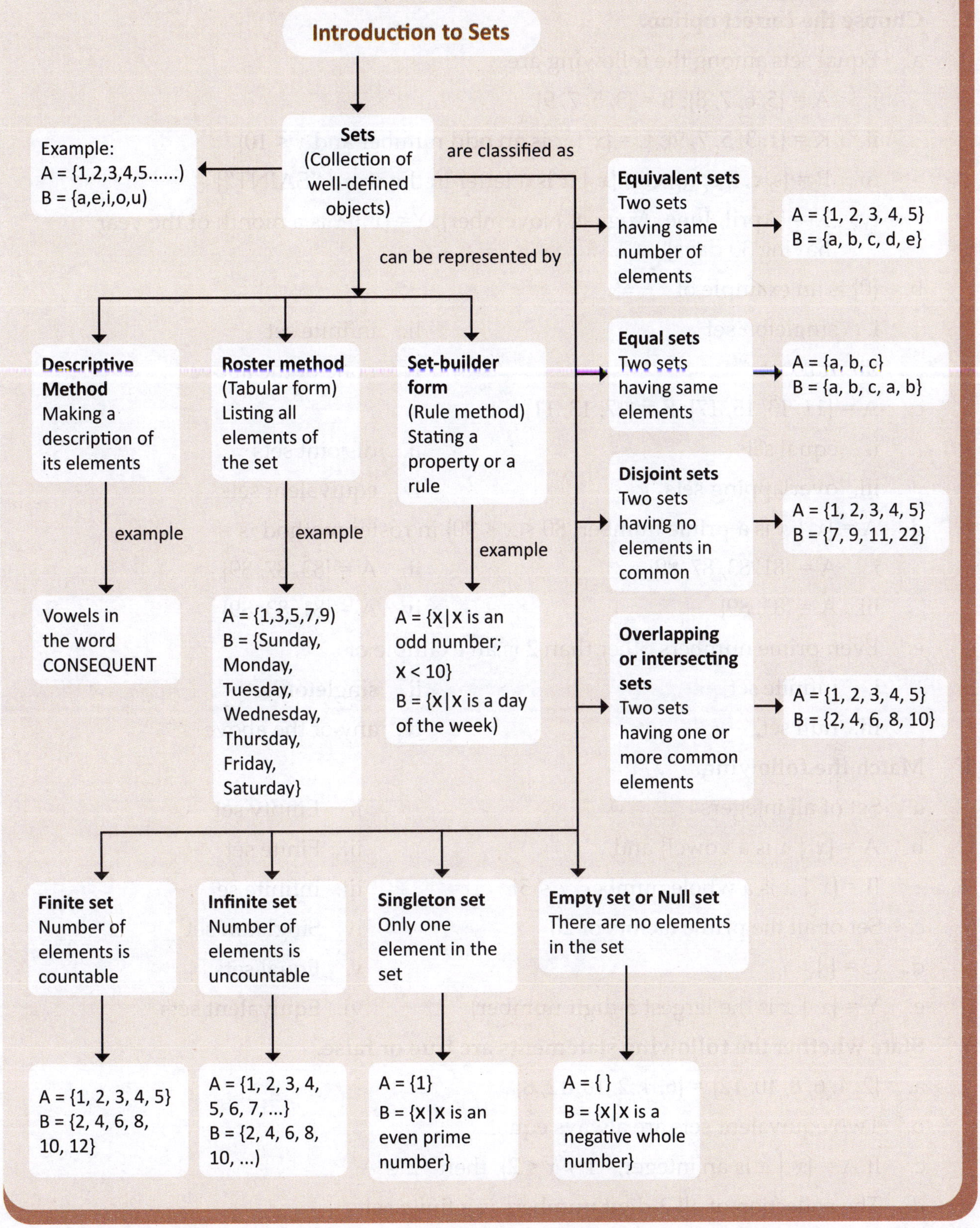

REVISION EXERCISE

1. Choose the correct option.

a. Equal sets among the following are

i. A = {5, 6, 7, 8}; B = {3, 5, 7, 9}

ii. K = {1, 3, 5, 7, 9}; L = {x | x is an odd number and x < 10}

iii. P = {s, c, i, e, n}; Q = {x | x is a letter in the word "SAINT"}

iv. X = {April, June, August, November}; Y= {x | x is a month of the year having 30 days}

b. {0} is an example of

i. singleton set
ii. infinite set
iii. null set
iv. none of the above

c. A = {11, 13, 15, 17}; B = {17, 13, 11} are

i. equal sets
ii. disjoint sets
iii. overlapping sets
iv. equivalent sets

d. A = {x | x is a prime number; $80 < x < 90$} in roster method is

i. A = {81, 83, 87, 89}
ii. A = {83, 87, 89}
iii. A = {83, 89}
iv. A = {81, 83, 89}

e. Even prime numbers other than 2 is an example of

i. infinite set
ii. singleton set
iii. null set
iv. any of the above

2. Match the following.

a.	Set of all integers	i.	Empty set
b.	A = {x | x is a vowel} and B = {x | x is a whole number, $x < 5$}	ii.	Finite set
		iii.	Infinite set
c.	Set of all the prime factors of 20	iv.	Singleton set
d.	C = { }	v.	Equal sets
e.	Y = {x | x is the largest 5-digit number}	vi.	Equivalent sets

3. State whether the following statements are true or false.

a. {2, 4, 6, 8, 10, 12} = {6, 4, 2, 10, 12, 8}

b. Two equivalent sets are always equal.

c. If A = {x | x is an integer, $-1 < x < 2$}, then $-2 \in$ A.

d. The collection of all 2-digit numbers is a finite set.

e. If B = {x | x is a factor of 28}, then n(B) = 6.

4. **State which of the following are sets. Justify your answer.**

a. The collection of tigers in India

b. The set of prime numbers

c. The set of beautiful flowers in a garden

d. The set of fast-flying birds

e. The collection of computers in the computer lab of a school

5. **Represent the following sets in roster form and write the cardinal number of each set.**

a. A = $\{x \mid x$ is a prime factor of $48\}$

b. B = Set of all the letters in the word COURAGE

c. C = $\{x \mid x$ is a multiple of 6, $x < 40\}$

d. D = $\{x \mid x$ is a composite number, $10 < x < 12\}$

e. E = $\{x \mid x$ is an odd prime number, $x < 20\}$

6. **Represent the following sets in set-builder form:**

a. A = {2, 3, 5, 7, 11, 13}

b. B = {January, March, May, July, August, October, December}

c. C = {5, 10, 15, 20, 25, 30}

d. D = {m, a, t, h, e, i, c, s}

e. E = { 2, 4, 6, 8, 10,....}

7. **Identify the finite sets, empty sets, and infinite sets from among the following:**

a. U = $\{x : x$ is an integer, $x > 20\}$

b. V = $\{x : x$ is a whole number, $x < 1\}$

c. W = $\{x : x$ is a natural number, $x < 1\}$

d. X = $\{x : x$ is a point on the circumference of a circle$\}$

e. Y = $\{x : x$ is an even prime number, $x > 8\}$

f. Z = $\{x : x$ is a negative integer greater than $-2\}$

5 Fractions and Decimals

Prior Knowledge

- Number system
- Part or whole
- Addition of whole numbers
- Subtraction of whole numbers
- Multiplication of whole numbers
- Division of whole numbers

Learning Objectives

- Fractions
- Solve problems on real-life application of fractions
- Decimal numbers
- Conversion of decimals into fractions and vice versa
- Perform basic operations on decimal numbers
- Solve word problems on decimals

Let's Get Started

Look at the glass of milk.

_____________ of the glass is full.

Kiansh and Advith shared a chocolate equally.

Each of them got ___________ of the chocolate.

Do you remember how to write 'half' as a number?

'Half' is written as ______________________.

Can you express the following in number form?

Two-third = _________________

One-fourth = __________________

Three-seventh = __________________

One-tenth = _____________________

Numbers which are expressed in the form of $\frac{\text{Numerator}}{\text{Denominator}}$ are called **fractions**.

Let us learn more about real life applications of fractions and decimal fractions in this chapter.

FRACTION AS A PART OF A WHOLE

Fraction means part of a whole.

A whole can either be a region or a collection.

When the whole object is one, it is called a **region**.

Example 1: Look at the given shapes.

Solution: Each shape is divided into 2 equal parts.

One part is shaded in each shape.

Each shaded part of the shape is **one-half of the whole**. It is written as $\frac{1}{2}$.

That is, $\frac{\text{Number of shaded parts}}{\text{Total number of parts in the whole}} = \frac{1}{2}$

Example 2: Look at the shapes given below. Each shape is divided into 3 equal parts. One out of the 3 parts is shaded.

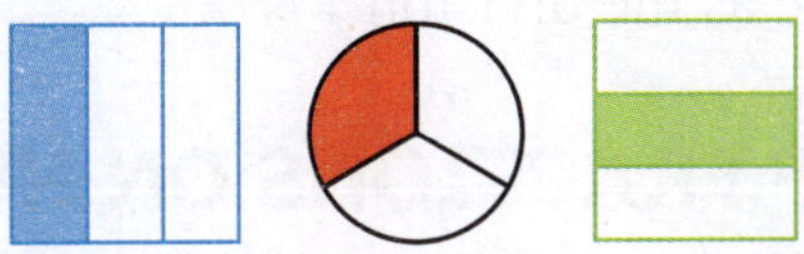

Solution: Each shaded part of the shape is **one-third of the whole**. It is written as $\frac{1}{3}$.

That is, $\frac{\text{Number of shaded parts}}{\text{Total number of parts in the whole}} = \frac{1}{3}$

Example 3: Look at the shapes given below. Each shape is divided into 4 equal parts. One out of the 4 parts is shaded.

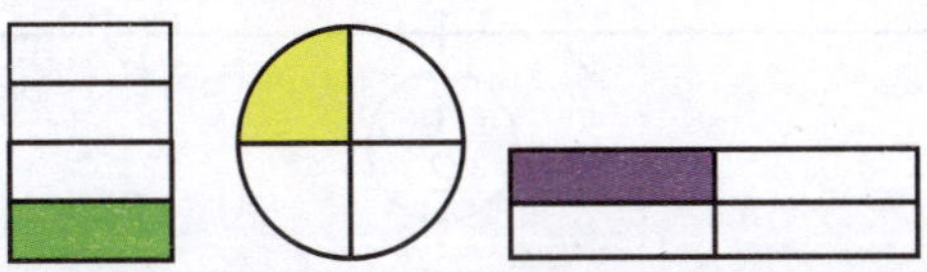

Solution: Each shaded part of the shape is **one-fourth of the whole**. It is written as $\frac{1}{4}$.

That is, $\frac{\text{Number of shaded parts}}{\text{Total number of parts in the whole}} = \frac{1}{4}$

Numerator and Denominator

Look at this figure.

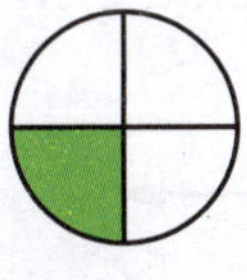

It is written as $\frac{1}{4} = \frac{\text{Numerator}}{\text{Denominator}}$

Numerator: It shows the number of equal parts which have been shaded.

Denominator: It shows the number of equal parts into which the whole has been divided.

FRACTION AS A DIVISION

We know that multiplication and division are reverse processes.

For example, $2 \times 3 = 6 \Rightarrow 6 \div 3 = 2$ or $6 \div 2 = 3$

We can extend the same idea to fractions.

Consider the fraction $\frac{1}{4}$. It is represented as 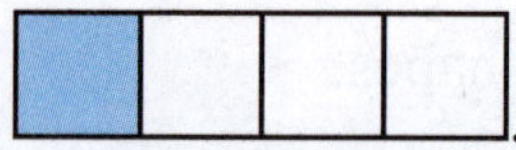.

Let us now consider $4 \times \frac{1}{4}$. It is represented as 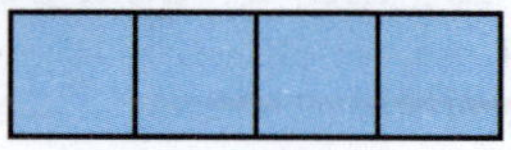 which is nothing but the whole, that is, 1. That is, $4 \times \frac{1}{4} = 1$

Using the above idea, we can write: $4 \times \frac{1}{4} = 1 \Rightarrow 1 \div 4 = \frac{1}{4}$

Therefore, the fraction $\frac{1}{4}$ is same as the division $1 \div 4$.

REPRESENTATION OF FRACTIONS ON NUMBER LINE

A **number line** is a line having numbers that are placed at equal distances on it.

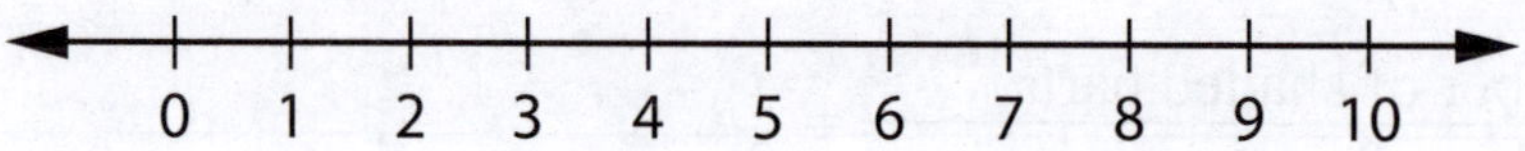

Let us represent $\frac{1}{2}$ on the given number line.

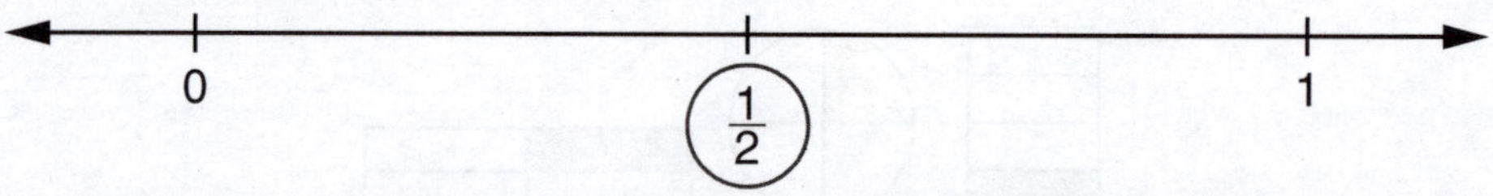

In the given number line, the distance between two consecutive numbers is one unit. Divide the distance between 0 and 1 into two equal parts. $\frac{1}{2}$ shows that one out of two parts is taken.

Therefore, $\frac{1}{2}$ lies between 0 and 1.

Example 4: Represent $\frac{1}{3}$ on the given number line.

Solution: Draw a number line from 0 to 1. Let the distance between the two consecutive numbers be one unit. Divide the unit into three equal parts.

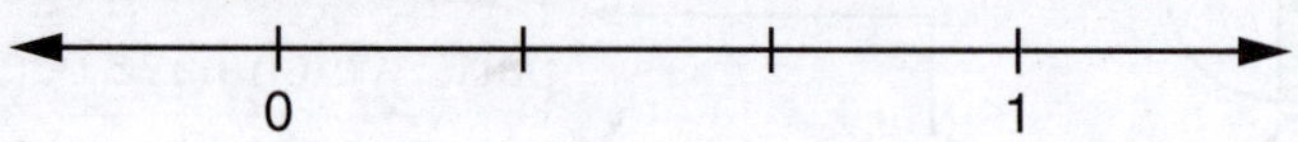

Now, show $\frac{1}{3}$ on the given number line.

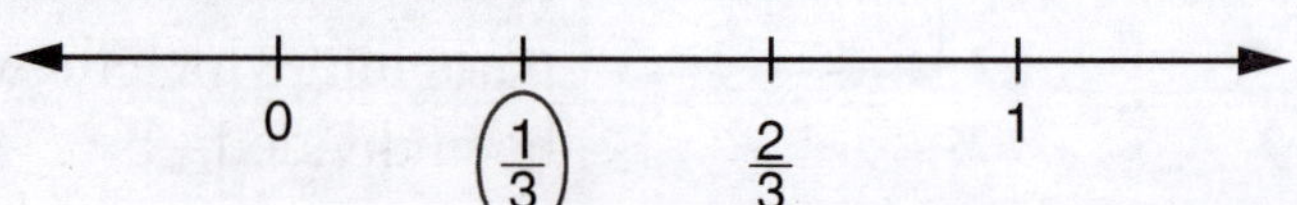

Example 5: Represent $\frac{2}{5}$ on the given number line.

Solution: Draw a number line from 0 to 1. Divide the unit into five equal parts and show $\frac{2}{5}$ on the number line.

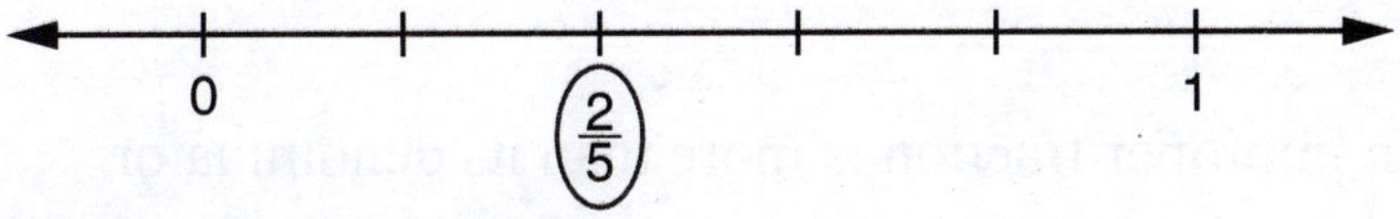

> **REMEMBER**
>
> A unit on the number line is divided into *n* equal parts where *n* is the value of the denominator.

EXERCISE 5.1

1. **Write the fraction for the coloured parts. The first one has been done for you.**

Figure	Fraction	Figure	Fraction
a. 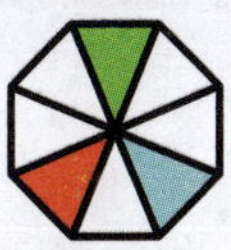	$\frac{3}{8}$	b. 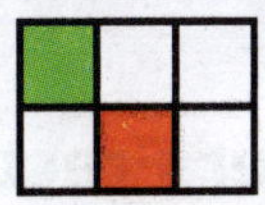	___
c. 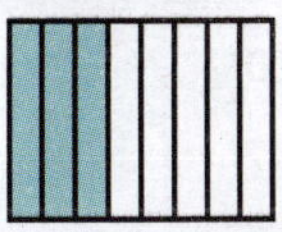	___	d. 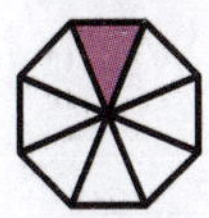	___

2. **Represent the following fractions on the given number lines.**

a. $\frac{3}{4}$ 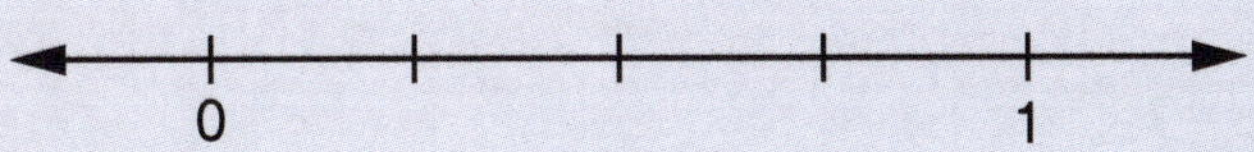

b. $\frac{1}{5}$ 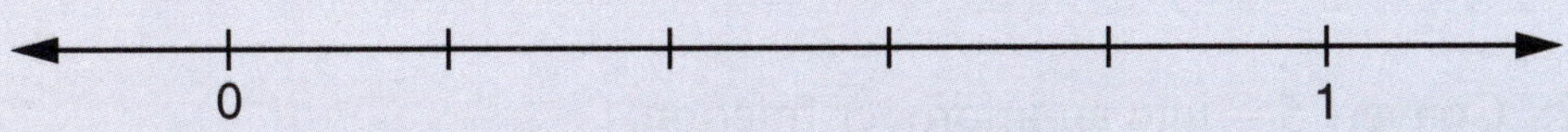

c. $\frac{5}{2}$ 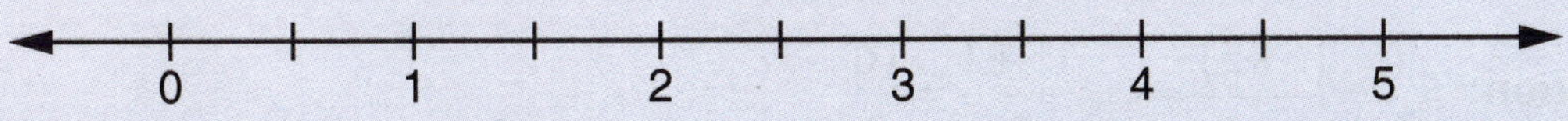

d. $\frac{4}{3}$ 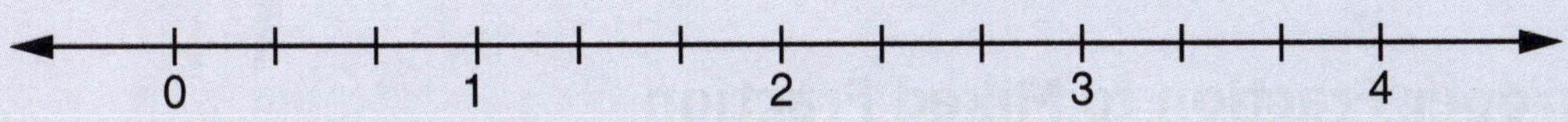

Types of Fractions

Like Fractions: Like fractions have the same denominator.

Examples: $\frac{1}{6}, \frac{2}{6}, \frac{3}{6}, \frac{4}{6}$ and $\frac{5}{6}$

Proper Fractions: The numerator of a proper fraction is less than its denominator.

Examples: $\frac{5}{6}, \frac{2}{7}, \frac{1}{8}, \frac{2}{3}$ and $\frac{9}{10}$

Unlike Fractions: Unlike fractions have different denominators.

Examples: $\frac{1}{2}, \frac{3}{4}, \frac{2}{5}, \frac{3}{7}$ and $\frac{6}{10}$

Unit Fractions: Unit fractions have 1 as their numerator.

Examples: $\frac{1}{2}, \frac{1}{3}, \frac{1}{4}, \frac{1}{6}$ and $\frac{1}{10}$

Improper Fractions: The numerator of an improper fraction is more than its denominator.

Examples: $\frac{3}{2}, \frac{5}{4}, \frac{9}{7}, \frac{8}{3}$ and $\frac{10}{6}$

Mixed Fractions: Combination of a whole number and a proper fraction is a mixed fraction.

Examples: $1\frac{1}{3}, 2\frac{3}{7}, 4\frac{5}{8}, 4\frac{2}{3}$ and $1\frac{7}{10}$

Conversion of Fractions

Mixed Fraction to Improper Fraction

$$\text{Improper fraction} = \frac{(\text{Whole number} \times \text{Denominator})\frac{1}{2} + \text{Numerator}}{\text{Denominator}}$$

Example 6: Convert $3\frac{1}{2}$ into an improper fraction.

Solution: $3\frac{1}{2} = \frac{(3 \times 2)+1}{2} = \frac{6+1}{2} = \frac{7}{2}$

Example 7: Convert $5\frac{1}{3}$ into an improper fraction.

Solution: $5\frac{1}{3} = \frac{(5 \times 3)+1}{3} = \frac{15+1}{3} = \frac{16}{3}$

Improper Fraction to Mixed Fraction

Divide the numerator by the denominator, then

$$\text{Mixed fraction} = \text{Quotient}\ \frac{\text{Remainder}}{\text{Divisor}}$$

Example 8: Convert $\frac{5}{2}$ into a mixed fraction.

Solution: $\frac{5}{2} = 2\frac{1}{2}$

$$\begin{array}{r|l} & 2 \rightarrow \text{Quotient} \\ 2) & 5 \\ & -4 \\ \hline & 1 \rightarrow \text{Remainder} \end{array}$$

EXERCISE 5.2

1. **Classify the following fractions into proper, improper and mixed fractions.**

$$\frac{1}{4}, \frac{7}{3}, 1\frac{8}{9}, 2\frac{3}{5}, \frac{13}{7}, \frac{14}{5}, 2\frac{4}{7}, \frac{9}{11}, \frac{7}{10}, \frac{1}{8}, 5\frac{1}{7}, \frac{12}{11}$$

2. **Classify the following pairs into like and unlike fractions.**

a. $\frac{1}{2}$ and $\frac{5}{2}$ b. $\frac{5}{6}$ and $\frac{1}{6}$ c. $\frac{7}{8}$ and $\frac{8}{7}$ d. $\frac{6}{10}$ and $\frac{7}{10}$ e. $\frac{4}{9}$ and $\frac{4}{7}$

3. **Convert the following into mixed fractions.**

a. $\frac{11}{6}$ b. $\frac{9}{2}$ c. $\frac{17}{10}$ d. $\frac{8}{3}$ e. $\frac{21}{11}$

4. **Convert the following into improper fractions.**

a. $2\frac{2}{5}$ b. $4\frac{2}{3}$ c. $1\frac{5}{7}$ d. $2\frac{3}{4}$ e. $3\frac{3}{5}$

EQUIVALENT FRACTIONS

Equivalent fractions have the same value.

Examples:

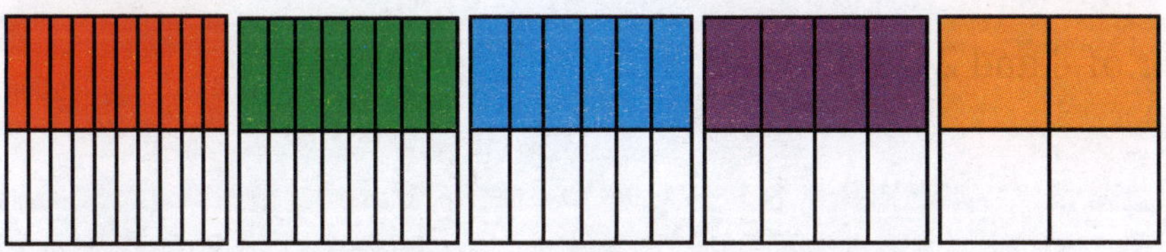

$\frac{10}{20}$ $\frac{8}{16}$ $\frac{6}{12}$ $\frac{4}{8}$ $\frac{2}{4}$

REMEMBER

To get an equivalent fraction, multiply or divide the numerator and the denominator of the fraction by the same number.

These fractions represent the same part of the whole.

That is, $\frac{10}{20} = \frac{8}{16} = \frac{6}{12} = \frac{4}{8} = \frac{2}{4} = \frac{1}{2}$

Example 9: Find the equivalent fractions of $\frac{3}{10}$.

Solution: Multiply both the numerator and the denominator of $\frac{3}{10}$ by the same number.

$$\frac{3}{10} = \frac{3\times2}{10\times2} = \frac{6}{20}; \frac{3\times3}{10\times3} = \frac{9}{30}; \frac{3\times4}{10\times4} = \frac{12}{40}$$

$$\frac{3}{10} = \frac{6}{20} = \frac{9}{30} = \frac{12}{40} = \ldots$$

Therefore, three equivalent fractions of $\frac{3}{10}$ are $\frac{6}{20}, \frac{9}{30}$ and $\frac{12}{40}$.

Let $\frac{a}{b}$ and $\frac{c}{d}$ be any two fractions. By cross multiplying the fractions, we get ad and bc. The given fractions are equivalent if the cross products are equal.

That is, $\frac{a}{b} = \frac{c}{d}$, if $ad = bc$.

Example 10: Find if the given fractions are equivalent or not.

a. $\frac{4}{25}$ and $\frac{8}{50}$

Solution: The cross products of $\frac{4}{25}$ and $\frac{8}{50}$ are $4 \times 50 = 200$ and $25 \times 8 = 200$.

Since the cross products are equal, the fractions are equivalent.

b. $\frac{3}{6}$ and $\frac{8}{12}$

Solution: The cross products of $\frac{3}{6}$ and $\frac{8}{12}$ are $3 \times 12 = 36$ and $6 \times 8 = 48$.

Since the cross products are not equal, the fractions are not equivalent.

Simplification of Fractions

A fraction is said to be in the simplest form if its numerator and denominator have no common factor except 1.

Example 11: Reduce $\frac{8}{24}$ to its simplest form.

Solution: Highest common factor of 8 and 24 is 8.

So, $\frac{8}{24} = \frac{8 \div 8}{24 \div 8} = \frac{1}{3}$

Now, 1 and 3 have no common factor except 1. Hence, $\frac{1}{3}$ is the simplest form of $\frac{8}{24}$.

Verification: Cross products of $\frac{8}{24}$ and $\frac{1}{3}$ are $8 \times 3 = 24$ and $24 \times 1 = 24$.

Since these are equal, the fractions are equivalent.

Example 12: Reduce $\frac{15}{25}$ to its simplest form.

Solution: The HCF of 15 and 25 is 5.

So, $\frac{15}{25} = \frac{15 \div 5}{25 \div 5} = \frac{3}{5}$

Now, 3 and 5 have no common factor except 1. Hence, $\frac{3}{5}$ is in the simplest form.

Verification: Cross products of $\frac{15}{25}$ and $\frac{3}{5}$ are $15 \times 5 = 75$ and $25 \times 3 = 75$.

Since these are equal, the fractions are equivalent.

Exercise 5.3

1. **Write four equivalent fractions for the given fractions.**

   a. $\frac{4}{5}$ b. $\frac{6}{7}$ c. $\frac{3}{4}$ d. $\frac{5}{8}$

2. **Check whether the given fractions are equivalent or not.**

   a. $\frac{5}{8}$ and $\frac{8}{12}$ b. $\frac{1}{8}$ and $\frac{6}{10}$ c. $\frac{4}{9}$ and $\frac{12}{27}$ d. $\frac{5}{13}$ and $\frac{6}{14}$

3. **Reduce each of the given fractions into its simplest form.**

   a. $\frac{16}{24}$ b. $\frac{10}{50}$ c. $\frac{18}{72}$ d. $\frac{36}{54}$

COMPARISON OF FRACTIONS

Comparison of two fractions

- **When their denominators are same,** the fraction with the greater numerator is greater than the other fraction.
- **When their numerators are same,** the fraction with the greater denominator is smaller than the other fraction.
- **When their denominators are different,** we make the denominators equal by taking LCM and then compare the numerators.

Example 13: Compare $\frac{5}{8}$ and $\frac{3}{8}$.

Solution: $\frac{5}{8} > \frac{3}{8}$ (Since the denominators are same and $5 > 3$)

Example 14: Compare $\frac{4}{9}$ and $\frac{4}{7}$

Solution: $\frac{4}{9} < \frac{4}{7}$ (Since the numerators are same and $7 < 9$)

Example 15: Compare $\frac{1}{5}$ and $\frac{2}{3}$.

Solution: Make the denominators equal and compare the numerators.

$\frac{1\times3}{5\times3} = \frac{3}{15}$ and $\frac{2\times5}{3\times5} = \frac{10}{15}$ (LCM of 5 and 3 is 15.)

$\therefore \frac{10}{15} > \frac{3}{15}$ (Since the denominators are same and $10 > 3$)

So, $\frac{2}{3} > \frac{1}{5}$.

ORDERING OF FRACTIONS

Example 16: Nisha, Deepa, Megha, Deeksha and Sanjana knitted the shawls measuring $\frac{1}{6}$ m, $\frac{1}{2}$ m, $\frac{1}{4}$ m, $\frac{1}{3}$ m and $\frac{1}{10}$ m, respectively. Arrange the given measurements in ascending order.

Solution: Since the numerators are same, arrange the denominators in order.

$$\frac{1}{10} < \frac{1}{6} < \frac{1}{4} < \frac{1}{3} < \frac{1}{2}$$

Example 17: Arrange these fractions in descending order.

$$\frac{4}{9}, \frac{2}{3}, \frac{5}{9}, \frac{1}{3}, \frac{8}{9}$$

Solution: Make the denominators equal $\frac{4}{9}, \frac{2\times3}{3\times3} = \frac{6}{9}, \frac{5}{9}, \frac{1\times3}{3\times3} = \frac{3}{9}, \frac{8}{9}$ (LCM of 9 and 3 is 9.)

Since the denominators are same, arrange the numerators in order.

$\frac{8}{9}, \frac{6}{9}, \frac{5}{9}, \frac{4}{9}, \frac{3}{9}$

That is, $\frac{8}{9} > \frac{2}{3} > \frac{5}{9} > \frac{4}{9} > \frac{1}{3}$

EXERCISE 5.4

1. **Compare the fractions and insert the symbol '>' or '<'.**

   a. $\frac{3}{6} \square \frac{3}{4}$ b. $\frac{2}{3} \square \frac{4}{7}$ c. $\frac{1}{5} \square \frac{4}{5}$

   d. $\frac{7}{9} \square \frac{1}{3}$ e. $\frac{2}{3} \square \frac{1}{4}$ f. $\frac{3}{7} \square \frac{5}{7}$

2. **Arrange the following in ascending order.**

   a. $\frac{3}{10}, \frac{3}{7}, \frac{3}{11}, \frac{3}{4}, \frac{3}{5}$ b. $\frac{6}{7}, \frac{4}{7}, \frac{3}{14}, \frac{9}{14}, \frac{3}{7}$

   c. $\frac{4}{5}, \frac{3}{5}, \frac{1}{5}, \frac{2}{5}, \frac{5}{5}$ d. $\frac{1}{2}, \frac{2}{3}, \frac{5}{6}, \frac{1}{3}, \frac{1}{6}$

3. **Arrange the following in descending order.**

   a. $\frac{4}{9}, \frac{4}{5}, \frac{4}{8}, \frac{4}{7}, \frac{4}{10}$ b. $\frac{2}{3}, \frac{1}{5}, \frac{2}{5}, \frac{1}{3}, \frac{4}{5}$

   c. $\frac{8}{10}, \frac{4}{10}, \frac{9}{10}, \frac{3}{10}, \frac{7}{10}$ d. $\frac{1}{8}, \frac{1}{2}, \frac{5}{8}, \frac{3}{4}, \frac{1}{4}$

BASIC OPERATIONS ON FRACTIONS

Addition and Subtraction of Like Fractions

The sum of like fractions is found by adding their numerators. Similarly, the difference is found by subtracting their numerators.

Example 18: Find the sum of $\frac{5}{9}$ and $\frac{1}{9}$.

Solution: $\frac{5}{9}+\frac{1}{9}=\frac{6}{9}=\frac{2}{3}$

Therefore, the sum of $\frac{5}{9}$ and $\frac{1}{9}$ is $\frac{6}{9}=\frac{2}{3}$.

Example 19: Find the difference between $\frac{4}{5}$ and $\frac{1}{5}$.

Solution: $\frac{4}{5}-\frac{1}{5}=\frac{3}{5}$

Therefore, the difference between $\frac{4}{5}$ and $\frac{1}{5}$ is $\frac{3}{5}$.

Addition and Subtraction of Unlike Fractions

The sum of unlike fractions is found by making the denominators equal and then adding the numerators. Similarly, the difference is found by making the denominators equal before subtracting the numerators.

Example 20: Find the sum of $\frac{2}{3}$ and $\frac{1}{4}$.

Solution: $\frac{2}{3}+\frac{1}{4}=\frac{2\times 4}{3\times 4}+\frac{1\times 3}{4\times 3}$

$$=\frac{8}{12}+\frac{3}{12}=\frac{11}{12}$$

Therefore, the sum of $\frac{2}{3}$ and $\frac{1}{4}$ is $\frac{11}{12}$.

Example 21: Find the difference between $\frac{1}{2}$ and $\frac{1}{7}$.

Solution: $\frac{1}{2}-\frac{1}{7}=\frac{1\times 7}{2\times 7}-\frac{1\times 2}{7\times 2}$

$$=\frac{7}{14}-\frac{2}{14}=\frac{5}{14}$$

Therefore, the difference between $\frac{1}{2}$ and $\frac{1}{7}$ is $\frac{5}{14}$.

Addition and Subtraction of Mixed Fractions

The sum or the difference of mixed fractions is found by converting them into improper fractions. Retain the answer in its simplest form always.

Example 22: Find the sum of $1\frac{1}{5}$ and $2\frac{1}{10}$.

Solution: $1\frac{1}{5} + 2\frac{1}{10}$

$= \frac{6}{5} + \frac{21}{10}$

$= \frac{6 \times 2}{5 \times 2} + \frac{21}{10}$

$= \frac{12}{10} + \frac{21}{10} = \frac{33}{10} = 3\frac{3}{10}$

Therefore, the sum of $1\frac{1}{5}$ and $2\frac{1}{10}$ is $3\frac{3}{10}$.

Example 23: Find the difference between $2\frac{2}{3}$ and $1\frac{1}{2}$.

Solution: $2\frac{2}{3} - 1\frac{1}{2}$

$= \frac{8}{3} - \frac{3}{2}$

$= \frac{8 \times 2}{3 \times 2} - \frac{3 \times 3}{2 \times 3}$

$= \frac{16}{6} - \frac{9}{6} = \frac{7}{6} = 1\frac{1}{6}$

Therefore, the difference between $2\frac{2}{3}$ and $1\frac{1}{2}$ is $1\frac{1}{6}$.

Example 24: What should be added to $2\frac{1}{2}$ to get $4\frac{1}{4}$?

Solution: Let the number to be added be x.

$2\frac{1}{2} + x = 4\frac{1}{4}$

$x = 4\frac{1}{4} - 2\frac{1}{2}$

$= \frac{17}{4} - \frac{5}{2}$

$= \frac{17}{4} - \frac{5 \times 2}{2 \times 2} = \frac{17}{4} - \frac{10}{4} = \frac{7}{4} = 1\frac{3}{4}$

Therefore, $1\frac{3}{4}$ should be added to $2\frac{1}{2}$ to get $4\frac{1}{4}$.

REMEMBER

Shortcut for addition of mixed fractions:

1. Add the whole parts separately.
2. Add the fractional parts separately.
3. Combine answers of steps (1) and (2) and write the answer.

For example, $3\frac{1}{2} + 1\frac{1}{2} = 3 + 1 + \frac{1}{2} + \frac{1}{2} = 4 + 1 = 5$

Example 25: What should be subtracted from $6\frac{1}{4}$ to get $2\frac{1}{3}$?

Solution: Let the number to be subtracted be x.

$$6\frac{1}{4} - x = 2\frac{1}{3}$$

$$x = 6\frac{1}{4} - 2\frac{1}{3}$$

$$= \frac{25}{4} - \frac{7}{3}$$

$$= \frac{25\times3}{4\times3} - \frac{7\times4}{3\times4} = \frac{75}{12} - \frac{28}{12}$$

$$= \frac{47}{12} = 3\frac{11}{12}$$

Therefore, $3\frac{11}{12}$ should be subtracted from $6\frac{1}{4}$ to get $2\frac{1}{3}$.

EXERCISE 5.5

1. **Find the sum of the following.**

   a. $\frac{1}{9}$ and $\frac{4}{9}$ b. $\frac{2}{3}$ and $\frac{1}{6}$ c. $\frac{4}{5}$ and $\frac{1}{3}$ d. $1\frac{1}{2}$ and $5\frac{2}{7}$

2. **Find the difference between the following.**

   a. $\frac{4}{9}$ and $\frac{7}{9}$ b. $\frac{4}{5}$ and $\frac{3}{10}$ c. $\frac{3}{4}$ and $\frac{2}{3}$ d. $2\frac{1}{3}$ and $1\frac{3}{4}$

3. **What should be added to $1\frac{1}{5}$ to get $4\frac{2}{3}$?**

4. **What should be subtracted from $6\frac{4}{7}$ to get $2\frac{1}{4}$?**

MULTIPLICATION OF FRACTIONS

$$\text{Product of fractions} = \frac{\text{Product of the numerators}}{\text{Product of the denominators}}$$

REMEMBER

Mixed fractions are converted into improper fractions before multiplying.

Example 26: Find the product of $\frac{2}{3}$ and 15.

Solution: $\frac{2}{\cancel{3}_1} \times \frac{\cancel{15}^5}{1} = 10$

Example 27: Find the product of $\frac{4}{5}$ and $\frac{3}{8}$.

Solution: $\frac{\cancel{4}^1}{5} \times \frac{3}{\cancel{8}_2} = \frac{3}{10}$.

Example 28: Find the product of $2\frac{5}{8}$ and 24.

Solution: $2\frac{5}{8}=\frac{21}{8}$ and $24=\frac{24}{1}$

$$\frac{21\times\cancel{24}^{3}}{\cancel{8}_{1}\times1}=\frac{21\times3}{1\times1}=\frac{63}{1}=63$$

Example 29: Find the product of $1\frac{3}{4}$ and $2\frac{8}{9}$.

Solution: $1\frac{3}{4}=\frac{7}{4}$ and $2\frac{8}{9}=\frac{26}{9}$

$$\frac{7\times\cancel{26}^{13}}{\cancel{4}_{2}\times9}=\frac{7\times13}{2\times9}=\frac{91}{18}=5\frac{1}{18}$$

DIVISION OF FRACTIONS

To divide a fraction by another fraction, we multiply the first fraction by the reciprocal of the second fraction. Note that we always retain the answer in its simplest form.

Example 30: $10\div\frac{2}{3}$

Solution: $\frac{10}{1}\div\frac{2}{3}=\frac{^{5}\cancel{10}}{1}\times\frac{3}{\cancel{2}_{1}}=15$

Example 31: $1\frac{5}{6}\div2\frac{3}{4}$

Solution: $1\frac{5}{6}\div2\frac{3}{4}=\frac{11}{6}\div\frac{11}{4}=\frac{\cancel{11}}{\cancel{6}_{3}}\times\frac{\cancel{4}^{2}}{\cancel{11}}=\frac{2}{3}$

Example 32: $1\frac{6}{7}\div26$

Solution: $1\frac{6}{7}\div26=\frac{^{1}\cancel{13}}{7}\times\frac{1}{\cancel{26}_{2}}=\frac{1}{14}$

Example 33: What should be multiplied by $3\frac{1}{9}$ to get $5\frac{4}{9}$ as a product?

Solution: $5\frac{4}{9}=3\frac{1}{9}\times x$

$$x=5\frac{4}{9}\div3\frac{1}{9}=\frac{49}{9}\div\frac{28}{9}$$

$$x=\frac{\cancel{49}^{7}}{\cancel{9}}\times\frac{\cancel{9}}{\cancel{28}_{4}}=\frac{7}{4}=1\frac{3}{4}$$

Example 34: $\frac{4}{9}\div\frac{1}{6}$

Solution: $\frac{4}{9}\div\frac{1}{6}=\frac{4}{9}\times\frac{6}{1}=\frac{4}{\cancel{9}_{3}}\times\frac{\cancel{6}^{2}}{1}=\frac{8}{3}$

$$=2\frac{2}{3}$$

EXERCISE 5.6

1. Find the product of the following.

a. $\frac{1}{5}\times45$ b. $\frac{5}{6}\times\frac{7}{11}$ c. $2\frac{1}{3}\times3\frac{3}{5}$

d. $5\frac{3}{5}\times\frac{4}{7}$ e. $2\frac{1}{2}\times15$ f. $\frac{1}{4}\times\frac{5}{8}$

2. Solve the following.

a. $9\div\frac{2}{3}$ b. $\frac{4}{15}\div6$ c. $\frac{3}{15}\div\frac{6}{20}$

d. $\frac{14}{15}\div1\frac{1}{6}$ e. $2\frac{1}{4}\div1\frac{1}{3}$ f. $2\frac{2}{3}\div\frac{8}{11}$

REAL-LIFE APPLICATIONS OF FRACTIONS

Example 35: If $\frac{1}{4}$ of an audience are women while $\frac{1}{3}$ are children, what part of the audience are men?

Solution: Fraction of men = Total of fractions − (Fraction of women + Fraction of children)

$$= 1-\left(\frac{1}{4}+\frac{1}{3}\right) = 1-\left(\frac{3+4}{12}\right) = 1-\left(\frac{7}{12}\right) = \frac{12-7}{12} = \frac{5}{12}$$

Thus, $\frac{5}{12}$ of the audience are men.

Example 36: A mug can hold $\frac{1}{2}$ L of water. How many mugs of water will be needed to fill up an empty bucket of capacity $4\frac{1}{2}$ L?

Solution: Capacity of bucket = $4\frac{1}{2}$ L Capacity of mug = $\frac{1}{2}$ L

Number of mugs of water needed to fill the bucket = $4\frac{1}{2} \div \frac{1}{2} = \frac{9}{\cancel{2}} \times \frac{\cancel{2}^1}{\cancel{1}} = 9$

Thus, 9 mugs of water will be needed to fill up the bucket.

Example 37: A man gave $\frac{5}{8}$ of his money to his daughter, $\frac{2}{3}$ of the remaining to his son and the remaining to his wife. If his wife gets ₹8,500, what is the total amount?

Solution: Part of the money given to the daughter = $\frac{5}{8}$

Part of the money given to the son = $\frac{2}{3}$ of $\left(1-\frac{5}{8}\right) = \frac{2}{3}$ of $\frac{3}{8} = \frac{\cancel{2}}{\cancel{3}} \times \frac{\cancel{3}}{\cancel{8}_4} = \frac{1}{4}$

Part of the money given to the wife = $1-\left(\frac{5}{8}+\frac{1}{4}\right) = 1-\left(\frac{5+2}{8}\right) = 1-\frac{7}{8} = \frac{8-7}{8} = \frac{1}{8}$

If $\frac{1}{8}$ of the amount is ₹8,500, then the total amount is 8,500 × 8 = ₹68,000.

Example 38: There are 150 members in a committee. In a meeting, $\frac{7}{10}$ of them are present. How many members are absent?

Solution: Number of members present = $\frac{7}{10}$ of 150 = $\frac{7}{1\cancel{0}} \times 15\cancel{0} = 7 \times 15 = 105$

Number of members absent = 150 – 105 = 45

Thus, 45 members are absent.

Exercise 5.7

1. In a school, $\frac{3}{8}$ of the number of students are boys while the girls are 850 in number. Find the number of boys in the school.
2. A sum of money was divided between Anil and Karan. If Karan got $\frac{4}{9}$ of the whole amount and his share was ₹3500, find the total amount and Anil's share.
3. A drum of water was $\frac{2}{3}$ full. When 20 litres were drawn from it, it became half full. What was the capacity of the drum and how much water did the drum contain when it was $\frac{2}{3}$ full?
4. Three ballpoint pens cost ₹$22\frac{1}{2}$ and five sketch pens cost ₹$58\frac{3}{4}$. How much more does each sketch pen cost than each ballpoint pen?
5. An iceberg of total height 66 m is floating in the sea. $\frac{5}{6}$ part of the iceberg is under water. How many metres of the iceberg can be seen above the level of water?

DECIMAL FRACTIONS

The fractions in which the denominators are 10, 100, 1000 and so on are known as **decimal fractions**. We already know how to represent tenths and hundredths in the pictorial form. Look at the following.

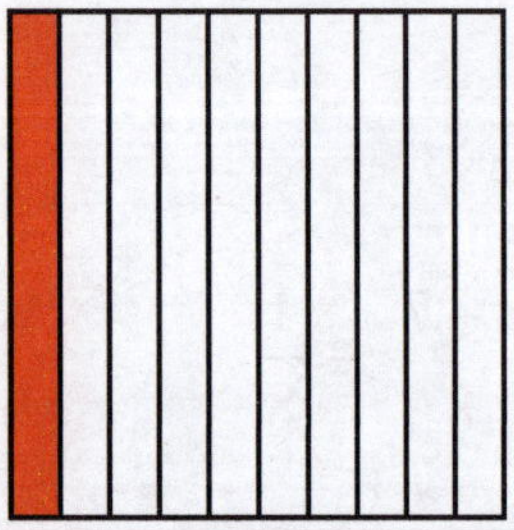

$\frac{1}{10} = 0.1$

$\frac{1}{10}$ represents one-tenth of the figure and is written as 0.1. It is read as 'zero point one'.

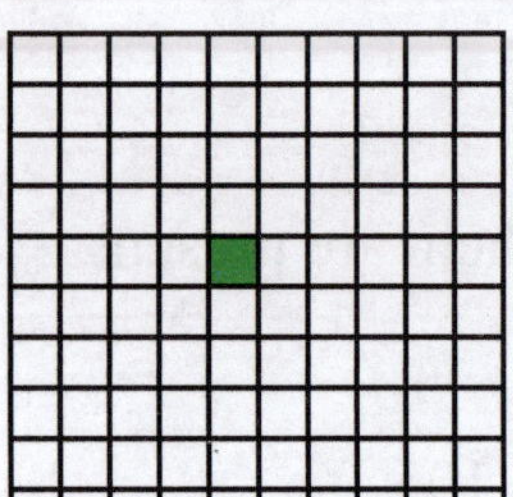

$\frac{1}{100} = 0.01$

Similarly, $\frac{1}{100}$ represents one-hundredth and is written as 0.01. It is read as 'zero point zero one'.

Now, let us learn about thousandths.

When one whole is divided into 1000 equal parts, each part represents $\frac{1}{1000}$. It is written as 0.001 and read as 'one thousandths' or 'zero point zero zero one'.

Decimal Place Value Chart

In a decimal place value chart, as we move towards left by one place, the place value increases by 10 times and as we move towards right by one place, the place value becomes one-tenth.

Place Value Chart for Decimals

Whole Number Part				Decimal Number Part		
Thousands	Hundreds	Tens	Ones	Tenths	Hundredths	Thousandths
1000	100	10	1	$\frac{1}{10}$	$\frac{1}{100}$	$\frac{1}{1000}$

Now, let us see how to write the place value of each digit in a place value chart for a decimal number 3,618.925.

Thousands	Hundreds	Tens	Ones	Decimal Point	Tenths	Hundredths	Thousandths
3×1000	6×100	1×10	8×1	.	$9 \times \frac{1}{10} = \frac{9}{10}$	$2 \times \frac{1}{100} = \frac{2}{100}$	$5 \times \frac{1}{1000} = \frac{5}{1000}$

In the decimal notation, a dot or a point separates a number into two parts. This dot is also known as a decimal point. The number to the left of the decimal point is the whole number part, and the number to the right of the decimal point is the fractional part. Thus, the number 3,618.925 is read as 'three thousand six hundred eighteen point nine two five'.

The number of digits in the decimal part of a decimal number gives the number of **decimal places**.

For example, 6.06 is a decimal number with two decimal places and 7,168.543 is a decimal number with three decimal places.

Example 39: Write the place value of each digit in the following.

a. 23.62

Solution:

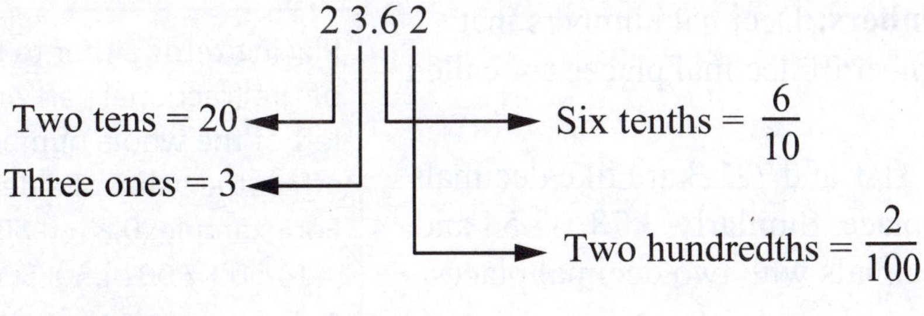

b. 5240.101

Solution:

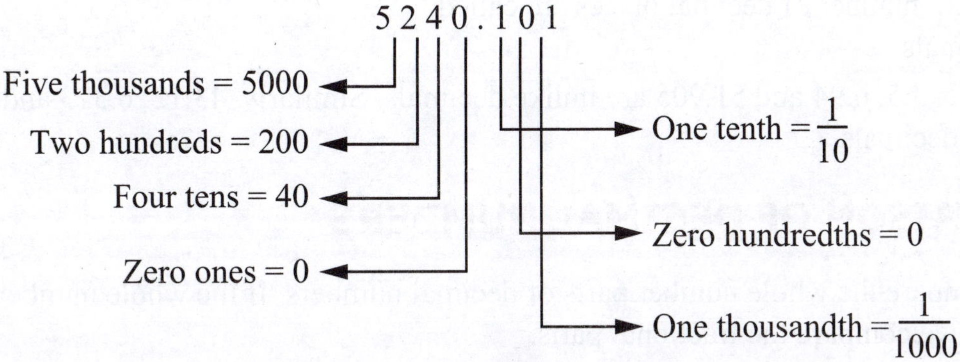

Example 40: Write the place value of the underlined digit.

a. 34.5<u>6</u>

Solution: The place value of 6 in the number 34.56 is six hundredths or $\frac{6}{100}$.

b. 432.76<u>5</u>

Solution: The place value of 5 in the number 432.765 is five thousandths or $\frac{5}{1000}$.

Example 42: Write the following numbers in the place value table. Also, write their expanded forms.

a. 12.43 b. 947.526

Solution: a. 12.43

$$= 1 \times 10 + 2 \times 1 + 4 \times \frac{1}{10} + 3 \times \frac{1}{100}$$

$$= 10 + 2 + \frac{4}{10} + \frac{3}{100}$$

$$= 10 + 2 + 0.4 + 0.03$$

b. 947.526

$$= 9 \times 100 + 4 \times 10 + 7 \times 1 + 5 \times \frac{1}{10} + 2 \times \frac{1}{100} + 6 \times \frac{1}{1000}$$

$$= 900 + 40 + 7 + \frac{5}{10} + \frac{2}{100} + \frac{6}{1000}$$

$$= 900 + 40 + 7 + 0.5 + 0.02 + 0.006$$

TYPES OF DECIMAL NUMBERS

Like decimal numbers: Decimal numbers that have the same number of decimal places are called like decimals.

For example, 0.2, 31.1 and 721.3 are like decimals with one decimal place. Similarly, 3.78, 32.54 and 144.06 are like decimals with two decimal places.

Unlike decimal numbers: Decimal numbers that have different number of decimal places are called unlike decimals.

Placing zeros either to the extreme right of the fractional part or to the extreme left of the whole number part does not affect the value of a decimal number. For example, 0.8 = 0.80 = 0.800 and 14.5 = 14.500 = 0014.50. Such decimals are called **equivalent decimals**.

For example, 3.5, 6.94 and 51.905 are unlike decimals. Similarly, 43.12, 6.323 and 1.9 are also unlike decimals.

COMPARISON OF DECIMAL NUMBERS

We first compare the whole number parts of decimal numbers. If the whole number parts are equal, then we compare the fractional parts.

- The decimal number with the greater whole number part is greater.

  For example, 63.734 > 59.805.
- We begin by converting the given numbers into like decimals by putting the required number of zeros to the right of the decimal point. Then we start comparing from the tenths place. The decimal number with the greater digit in the same place is greater.

  For example, for comparing the two numbers 9.1 and 9.008, we first convert them into like decimals.

That is, 9.1 = 9.100. Now, 9.100 and 9.008 are like decimals.

On comparing, we get 9.100 > 9.008.

EXERCISE 5.8

Which is greater?

1. 0.12 or 0.21	**2.** 0.11 or 0.111	**3.** 4.1 or 4.8
4. 0.55 or 5.5	**5.** 1.23 or 0.123	**6.** 0.099 or 0.19

CONVERTING FRACTIONS INTO DECIMALS

Let us now try to find the decimal representations of some more fractions.

Case 1: When denominators are 10, 100, 1000 and so on

Example 42: Convert $\frac{501}{10}, \frac{501}{100}$ and $\frac{501}{1000}$ into decimal numbers.

Solution: The decimal form of $\frac{501}{10}$ is 50.1.

The decimal form of $\frac{501}{100}$ is 5.01.

And the decimal form of $\frac{501}{1000}$ is 0.501.

Case 2: When denominators are not powers of 10

If the denominator of a fraction is not a power of ten, then we multiply both the numerator and the denominator by a whole number that makes the denominator a power of 10.

Example 43: Convert $\frac{25}{500}$ into a decimal number.

Solution: Multiply the numerator and the denominator by the same number to make the denominator a power of 10.

That is, $\frac{25}{500} = \frac{25 \times 2}{500 \times 2} = \frac{50}{1000} = 0.050 = 0.05$

> 0.050 is same as 0.05 because there is no value for zero that is on the right of the decimal number after significant digit.

Example 44: Convert $1\frac{3}{4}$ into a decimal number.

Solution: To convert $1\frac{3}{4}$ into a decimal number, we need to find an equivalent fraction whose denominator is a power of 10.

That is, $1 + \frac{3}{4} = 1 + \frac{3 \times 25}{4 \times 25} = 1 + \frac{75}{100} = 1 + 0.75 = 1.75$

Fractions can also be converted into decimal numbers by the long division process.

Example 45: Convert $\frac{3}{25}$ into a decimal number using the long division process.

Solution: Convert $\frac{3}{25}$ into decimal form by making the denominator a multiple of 10 and verify the answer.

$$\begin{array}{r} 0.12 \\ 25\overline{)3.00} \\ -2\,5 \\ \hline 50 \\ -50 \\ \hline 0 \\ \hline \end{array}$$

$\therefore \frac{3}{25} = 0.12$

REMEMBER

Once we have put the decimal, each time we divide, we can add one zero on our own.

CONVERTING DECIMALS INTO FRACTIONS

Now, let us learn how to convert decimal numbers like 0.7, 0.5 and 0.4 into fractions.

For example, $0.7 = 0 + \frac{7}{10} = \frac{7}{10}$

Steps to add unlike fractions

1. Find the LCM of the denominators.
2. Convert the unlike fractions into like fractions.
3. Add the like fractions.
4. Keep the sum in the simplest form.

Example 46: Convert 4.3 into a fraction and write the answer in the simplest form.

Solution: $4.3 = \frac{4}{1} + \frac{3}{10} = \frac{40+3}{10} = \frac{43}{10} = 4\frac{3}{10}$

Example 47: Convert 1.25 into a fraction and write the answer in the simplest form.

Solution: $1.25 = 1 + \frac{25}{100} = 1 + \frac{1}{4} = \frac{4+1}{4} = \frac{5}{4} = 1\frac{1}{4}$

REMEMBER

To convert money, length, mass, etc. from one unit into another, we often use decimals. Given below are a few examples.

5 p = ₹$\frac{5}{100}$ = ₹0.05 (₹1 = 100 p)

220 g = $\frac{220}{1000}$ kg = 0.220 kg (1 kg = 1000 g)

25 cm = $\frac{25}{100}$ m = 0.25 m (1 m = 100 cm)

REPRESENTATION OF DECIMALS ON A NUMBER LINE

We have learnt to convert fractions into decimals. These decimals occupy the same position on the number line as their corresponding fractions. Let us look at the following examples.

Example 48: Represent 0.3 on a number line.

Solution: $0.3 = \frac{3}{10}$

So, divide one unit of the segment into ten equal parts and take 3 parts to the right of 0 to represent 0.3 on the number line as shown below.

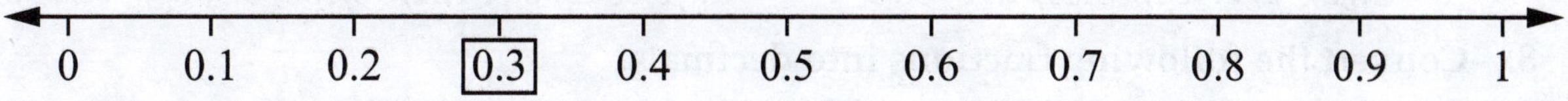

Example 49: Represent 1.4 on a number line.

Solution: $1.4 = \frac{14}{10}$

The whole number part is 1. So, divide the length between 1 and 2 into ten equal parts. And take 4 parts to represent 1.4 on the number line as shown below.

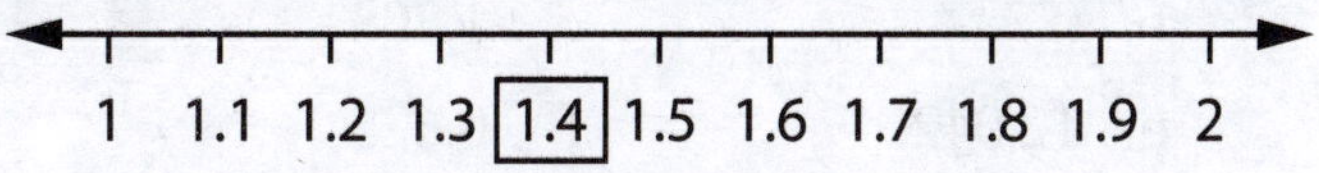

EXERCISE 5.9

1. **Express the following decimals as numerals.**
   a. Five point five
   b. Eighty-three point one seven
   c. Two hundred sixty-seven point zero zero three
   d. Fourteen point two zero three
   e. Ten point zero eight seven
2. **Write the place value of 7 in the following decimal numbers.**
   a. 9.746 b. 97.46 c. 671.009 d. 394.007 e. 3.071 f. 745.069
3. **Write the expanded form of the following decimal numbers.**
   a. 495.6 b. 23.18 c. 14.087 d. 3527.17 e. 505.505 f. 7654.321
4. **Write whether the following sets of decimal numbers are like or unlike decimals.**
   a. 3.56, 16.95, 780.54
   b. 12.76, 16.7, 9.865
   c. 1.1, 42.43, 435.768
   d. 43.60, 47.8, 56.9
   e. 0.81, 1.18, 23.45
   f. 12.33, 0.97, 345.245
5. **Compare the decimals and fill in the blanks with ‘<’, ‘>’ or ‘=’.**
   a. 29.1 ☐ 291.1 b. 0.98 ☐ 9.08 c. 3.06 ☐ 3.006
   d. 8.76 ☐ 8.706 e. 32.5 ☐ 32.500 f. 0.195 ☐ 0.19

6. **Arrange the following groups of decimal numbers in ascending order.**
   a. 0.3, 0.003, 0.03, 3.3, 3.03, 0.33
   b. 1.463, 4.643, 4.436, 4.346, 4.364
   c. 2.45, 0, –4.25, –3.05, –1, 2.05, 3.92, 0.13
   d. 1.7564, 1.5467, 1.4576, 1.8927
7. **Arrange the following groups of decimal numbers in descending order.**
   a. 5.5, 5.05, 0.55, 55.5, 0.505, 50.5
   b. 3.617, 3.712, 3.434, 3.279, 3.999
   c. –1.75, –2, 0.404, –3.45, 1.78, 6.75
   d. 0.6312, 0.63121, –0.936, 0.9366, –0.93661
8. **Convert the following fractions into decimals.**
   a. $\frac{7}{100}$ b. $\frac{2}{5}$ c. $6\frac{18}{100}$
   d. $\frac{52}{40}$ e. $65\frac{76}{1000}$ f. $\frac{16}{125}$
9. **Convert the following decimals into fractions.**
   a. 0.58 b. 0.7 c. 1.308
   d. 0.02 e. 12.042 f. 0.625
10. **Represent the following decimals on a number line.**
    a. 0.2 b. 0.5 c. 1.9 d. 2.5

ADDITION AND SUBTRACTION OF DECIMALS

Addition of Decimals

To add/subtract decimal numbers, arrange the decimal numbers in a column according to the place value of the digits such that the decimal points come one below the other. Then add or subtract the numbers and place the decimal point in the answer exactly below the decimal points of the given numbers.

Example 50: Add 9.38, 3.895, 109.5, 72.87 and 0.005.

Solution:

	H	T	O		Tths	Hths	Thths
		2	2		2	1	
			9	.	3	8	0
			3	.	8	9	5
	1	0	9	.	5	0	0
		7	2	.	8	7	0
+			0	.	0	0	5
	1	9	5	.	6	5	0

$\therefore$ 9.38 + 3.895 + 109.5 + 72.87 + 0.005 = 195.65

Example 51: Ramesh went to the market to buy vegetables. He bought 3 kg 250 g tomatoes, 7 kg 500 g potatoes, 750 g beans and 100 g green chillies. What was the total mass of the vegetables Ramesh bought? Express the answer in kg.

Solution: Mass of tomatoes = 3 kg 250 g = 3.250 kg

Mass of potatoes = 7 kg 500 g = 7.500 kg

Mass of beans = 750 g = 0.750 kg

Mass of green chillies = 100 g = 0.100 kg

Therefore, total mass of the vegetables Ramesh bought was 11.6 kg.

	T	O		Tths	Hths	Thths
	1	1		1		
		3	.	2	5	0
		7	.	5	0	0
		0	.	7	5	0
+		0	.	1	0	0
	1	1	.	6	0	0

Subtraction of Decimals

Example 52: Find the difference between 218.302 and 34.111.

Solution:

	H	T	O		Tths	Hths	Thths
	1	11			2	10	
	~~2~~	~~1~~	8	.	~~3~~	~~0~~	2
–		3	4	.	1	1	1
	1	8	4	.	1	9	1

∴ 218.302 – 34.111 = 184.191

Example 53: Marina bought 2.025 m of dress material for her elder daughter and 1.75 m for the younger one. What is the difference in the lengths of the two dress materials?

Solution: Length of the cloth bought for the elder daughter = 2.025 m

Length of the cloth bought for the younger daughter = 1.75 m

Therefore, the difference in the lengths of the two dress materials bought by Marina for her daughters is 0.275 m.

	T	O		Tths	Hths	Thths
		1		~~10~~ 9	12	
		~~2~~	.	~~0~~	~~2~~	5
–		1	.	7	5	0
		0	.	2	7	5

EXERCISE 5.10

1. **Solve the following.**

   a. 97.71 + 1.3 b. 28.93 + 43.12 c. 77.5 + 71.615

   d. 40.917 + 75.85 e. 71.92 + 3.963 + 55.5 f. 325.7 + 98.079 + 0.87 + 263.86

2. **Eqvaute the following.**

   a. 61.92 – 25.19 b. 99.61 – 30.3 c. 26.809 – 5.232

   d. 100 – 0.001 e. 436.2 – 128.107 f. 55.5 – 5.777 – 7.55

3. **Fill in the blanks.**

a. 48.4 – 19.32 – 5 = ______ b. 7.4 – 3.6 + 2.82 = ______

c. 0.7 + 0.007 + 3.447 – 2.181 = ______ d. 127.5 – 84.1 – 13 + 4.39 = ______

e. 45.8 – ______ + 23.772 = 56.802

f. 82.672 – 30.54 – 10.012 + ______ = 107.535

4. What should be added to 67 to get 70.751?

5. What should be added to the difference of 3.14 and 1.674 to get 10?

6. Anil has ₹230.65 and Bhaskar has ₹125.35. How much money do they have altogether?

7. Tom and Tony were running a relay race. The distance to be run was 33.03 km in total. If Tom ran 16.93 km, how far did Tony run?

WORD PROBLEMS INVOLVING ADDITION AND SUBTRACTION OF DECIMALS

Example 54: Deepa bought balloons for ₹25.50 and decorative papers for ₹37.25. If she gives ₹100 to the shopkeeper, how much money should she get back?

Solution:

		₹		P
Cost of balloons =		25	.	50
Cost of decorative papers =	+	37	.	25
Total cost =		62	.	75

		₹		P
Amount given to shopkeeper =		100	.	00
Total cost =	–	62	.	75
Change to be taken =		37	.	25

Deepa should get back ₹37.25 from the shopkeeper.

Example 55: A vendor bought 12.5 kg onions from the market in the morning and 8.25 kg in the afternoon. By the end of the day, he could sell 18.9 kg onions in his locality. Find the amount of onions left with the vendor.

Solution:

		kg		g
Onions bought in the morning =		12	.	50
Onions bought in the afternoon =	+	8	.	25
Total weight of onion =		20	.	75

		kg		g
Total weight of onion =		20	.	75
Onions sold in a day =	–	18	.	90
Onion left with the vendor =		1	.	85

Therefore, 1.85 kg onions were left with the vendor.

Example 56: Navya travels 29.7 km every day, of which she walks 2.9 km in the morning, 3.8 km in the evening and travels the rest in a bus. Find the distance travelled by Navya by bus.

Solution:

	km		m
Travelled in the morning =	2	.	9
Travelled in the evening =	+ 3	.	8
Distance covered by walking =	6	.	7

	km		m
Total distance travelled =	29	.	7
Distance covered by walking =	– 6	.	7
Distance travelled by bus =	23	.	0

Therefore, Navya travels a distance of 23 km by bus.

Example 57: Early morning, the temperature of a city was 18.6°C. It came down by 1.2°C at 8 a.m. and by afternoon, it shot up by 4.3°C. Find the temperature of the city in the afternoon.

Solution:

Temperature in the morning =	18	.	6
Decrease in temperature =	– 1	.	2
Temperature at 8 a.m. =	17	.	4
Increase in temperature =	+ 4	.	3
Temperature in the afternoon =	21	.	7

Therefore, the temperature was 21.7°C in the afternoon.

Exercise 5.11

1. Sudha had ₹75.50 with her. If she spends ₹35.25 and ₹6.75 on breakfast and tea, respectively, how much money is left with her?
2. A vendor brings 68.55 kg fruits from the market, out of which 3.05 kg was rotten. He sells 51.25 kg by evening. Find the amount of fruits left with the vendor by the end of the day.
3. Sheela brings 10 m cloth and uses 6.9 m out of it to stitch her dresses. Finally, she finds that only 1.2 m cloth was left with her. Find the measurement of the cloth wasted during stitching.
4. A shopkeeper has 30 L 700 mL milk. If he used 5 L 300 mL milk to prepare tea and 15 L 450 mL milk to prepare sweets, how much milk is left?

MULTIPLICATION OF DECIMALS

When we multiply a decimal number by 10, 100, 1000, etc, the decimal point in the resultant number is shifted to the right by the same number of places as the number of zeroes in the multiplier.

Example 58: Find the product of 34.52 and 1000.

Solution: Number of zeroes in 1000 are three.

So, shift the decimal point three places to the right i.e., $\therefore$ 34.520 × 1000 = 34520.0 = 34520

Multiplying a Decimal Number by a Whole Number

Ignoring the decimal point, we multiply decimal numbers as whole numbers. After that we place a decimal point in the product such that the product has as many decimal digits as the number of decimal places in the given decimal numbers.

Example 59: Find the product of 1.19 and 2.

Solution: Write 1.19 without decimal and multiply by 2, to get 238.

$$\begin{array}{r} 1\ 1\ 9 \\ \times \quad\ \ 2 \\ \hline 2\ 3\ 8 \\ \hline \end{array}$$

Number of decimal places in 1.19 is 2.

So, insert a decimal point in the product at 2 places to the left from the end of the number.

$\therefore$ 1.19 × 2 = 2.38

Multiplying a Decimal Number by Another Decimal Number

We can multiply decimals as whole numbers without decimal point and then place the decimal point in the product such that there are equal number of decimal places in the products as the sum of the decimal places in the given decimal number.

Example 60: Multiply 1.7 by 0.6.

Solution: First, multiply the decimal numbers as whole numbers, ignoring the decimal point.

17 × 6 = 102

Now, decimal places in multiplicand (1.7) = 1

Decimal places in multiplier (0.6) = 1

Sum of decimal places = 1 + 1 = 2

So, insert a decimal point after 2 digits from right.

$\therefore$ 1.7 × 0.6 = 1.02

Example 61: 1 kg multigrain atta costs ₹53.75. Find the cost of 17 kg of atta.

Solution: Cost of 1 kg of atta = ₹53.75

Cost of 17 kg of atta = 53.75 × 17

Now, to multiply 53.75 by 17, we multiply them as whole numbers and then put decimal point two places from right in the resultant numbers.

5375 × 17 = 91375

Therefore, the cost of 17 kg of atta is ₹913.75.

DIVISION OF DECIMALS

The process of dividing decimal numbers is the same as multiplying decimal numbers but the decimal point will be moved to the left.

For example, 34.52 ÷ 10 = 3.452 (The decimal 'jumps over' 1 digit to the left)

034.52 ÷ 100 = 0.3452 (The decimal 'jumps over' 2 digit to the left)

0034.520 ÷ 1000 = 0.03452 (The decimal 'jumps over' 3 digit to the left)

Dividing Decimal Numbers by a Non-zero Whole Number

We can divide a decimal number number by a non-zero by following the given steps of division.

Step 1: To divide a decimal by a whole number, divide like whole numbers and place a decimal point in the quotient as soon as the decimal point is crossed over in the dividend.

Step 2: If after division you have a remainder, add a zero to the dividend and continue to divide until there is zero remainder or till the desired number of decimal points is reached in the quotient.

Example 62: Divide 4.48 by 4.

Solution: Divide 4.48 by 4 as whole numbers. Place the decimal point in the quotient as soon as the decimal point is crossed over in the dividend.

$$\begin{array}{r|l} & 1.12 \\ \hline 4 & 4.48 \\ & -4 \\ \hline & 04 \\ & -4 \\ \hline & 08 \\ & -8 \\ \hline & 0 \end{array}$$

$\therefore$ 4.48 ÷ 4 = 1.12

Dividing Decimal Numbers by Decimal Numbers

We can divide a decimal number by another decimal number by following the given steps.

Step 1: Convert the divisor into a whole number by multiplying the dividend and the divisor by a suitable multiple of 10.

Step 2: Now, divide the new dividend by the whole number as discussed earlier.

Example 63: Evaluate 0.039 ÷ 0.03.

Solution: $\dfrac{0.039 \times 100}{0.03 \times 100} = \dfrac{3.9}{3}$

$$\begin{array}{r|l} & 1.3 \\ \hline 3 & 3.9 \\ & -3 \\ \hline & 9 \\ & -9 \\ \hline & 0 \end{array}$$

Hence, 0.039 ÷ 0.03 = 1.3.

Example 64: Mohan packed 24.4 kg pulses equally in 5 bags. Find the quantity of pulses in each bag?

Solution: Quantity of pulses in 5 bags = 24.4 kg

Quantity of pulses in 1 bag = $\frac{24.4}{5}$ kg

= 4.88 kg

$$\begin{array}{r|l} & 4.88 \\ \hline 5 & 24.40 \\ & -\ 20 \\ \hline & 44 \\ & -\ 40 \\ \hline & 40 \\ & -\ 40 \\ \hline & 0 \end{array}$$

EXERCISE 5.12

1. **Find the following.**

   a. 3 × 0.45 b. 3.5 × 1.4 c. 1.23 × 2 d. 0.09 × 8

   e. 3 ÷ 2.4 f. 5.68 ÷ 0.4 g. 1.3 ÷ 100 h. 0.25 ÷ 0.05

2. **The sides of a square are of 54.3 cm each. What is the perimeter of the square?**
3. **Benjamin weighs 4 times the weight of his younger brother. His brother's weight is 10.6 kg. What is Benjamin's weight?**
4. **Sangeeta wants to make a suit for herself. She purchased 4 m of fabric at the rate of ₹45.35. How much money did she spend?**
5. **Five runners complete a marathon relay race. Each runner covers 3.75 km. How much distance got covered in the marathon?**
6. **Ravi can walk 3.5 km in one hour. How long will it take him to walk to the market which is 10.5 km from his home?**
7. **For a class party, students of Class VII bought sweets for ₹740.25 and cold drink for ₹70. If 35 students contributed equally for this, what amount was contributed by each student?**

Key Concepts

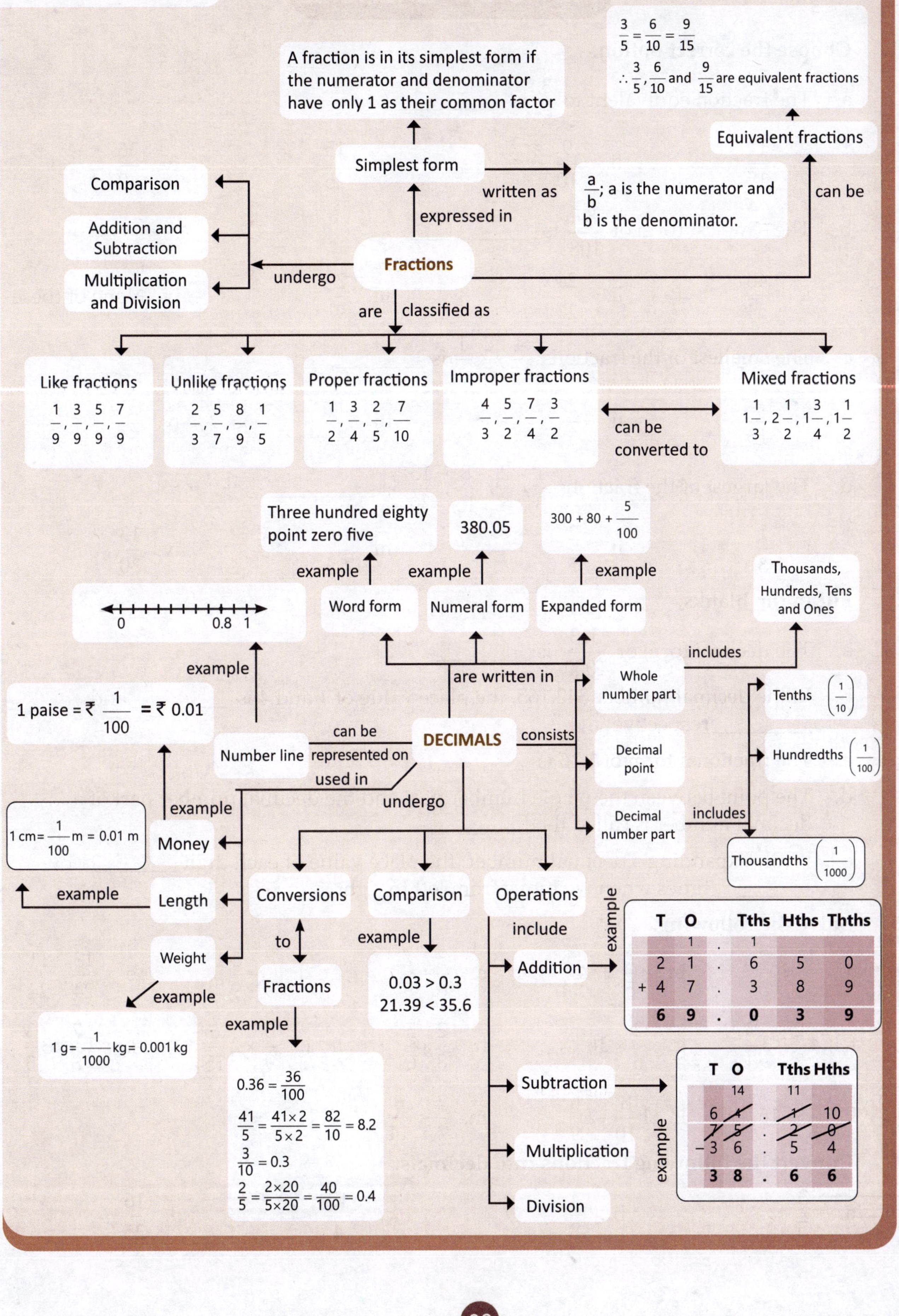

Fractions

- Fractions are expressed in **Simplest form** — A fraction is in its simplest form if the numerator and denominator have only 1 as their common factor
- Simplest form written as $\frac{a}{b}$; a is the numerator and b is the denominator.
- Fractions can be **Equivalent fractions**: $\frac{3}{5} = \frac{6}{10} = \frac{9}{15}$ $\therefore \frac{3}{5}, \frac{6}{10}$ and $\frac{9}{15}$ are equivalent fractions
- Fractions undergo:
  - Comparison
  - Addition and Subtraction
  - Multiplication and Division
- Fractions are classified as:
  - Like fractions: $\frac{1}{9}, \frac{3}{9}, \frac{5}{9}, \frac{7}{9}$
  - Unlike fractions: $\frac{2}{3}, \frac{5}{7}, \frac{8}{9}, \frac{1}{5}$
  - Proper fractions: $\frac{1}{2}, \frac{3}{4}, \frac{2}{5}, \frac{7}{10}$
  - Improper fractions: $\frac{4}{3}, \frac{5}{2}, \frac{7}{4}, \frac{3}{2}$ — can be converted to Mixed fractions
  - Mixed fractions: $1\frac{1}{3}, 2\frac{1}{2}, 1\frac{3}{4}, 1\frac{1}{2}$

DECIMALS

- Decimals are written in:
  - Word form — example: Three hundred eighty point zero five
  - Numeral form — example: 380.05
  - Expanded form — example: $300 + 80 + \frac{5}{100}$
- Decimals consists:
  - Whole number part — includes Thousands, Hundreds, Tens and Ones
  - Decimal point
  - Decimal number part — includes Tenths $\left(\frac{1}{10}\right)$, Hundredths $\left(\frac{1}{100}\right)$, Thousandths $\left(\frac{1}{1000}\right)$
- Decimals can be represented on Number line — example: number line from 0 to 1 showing 0.8
- Decimals used in:
  - Money — example: 1 paise = ₹ $\frac{1}{100}$ = ₹ 0.01
  - Length — example: 1 cm = $\frac{1}{100}$ m = 0.01 m
  - Weight — example: 1 g = $\frac{1}{1000}$ kg = 0.001 kg
- Decimals undergo:
  - Conversions to Fractions — example:
    - $0.36 = \frac{36}{100}$
    - $\frac{41}{5} = \frac{41 \times 2}{5 \times 2} = \frac{82}{10} = 8.2$
    - $\frac{3}{10} = 0.3$
    - $\frac{2}{5} = \frac{2 \times 20}{5 \times 20} = \frac{40}{100} = 0.4$
  - Comparison — example: 0.03 > 0.3; 21.39 < 35.6
  - Operations include:
    - Addition — example:

	T	O		Tths	Hths	Thths
		1	.	1		
	2	1	.	6	5	0
+	4	7	.	3	8	9
	6	**9**	**.**	**0**	**3**	**9**

    - Subtraction — example:

	T	O		Tths	Hths
		14		11	
	6	~~4~~	.	~~1~~	10
	~~7~~	~~5~~	.	~~2~~	~~0~~
−	3	6	.	5	4
	3	**8**	**.**	**6**	**6**

    - Multiplication
    - Division

REVISION EXERCISE

1. Choose the correct option.

a. The fraction equivalent to $\frac{3}{5}$ is ________.

i. $\frac{12}{15}$ ii. $\frac{9}{10}$ iii. $\frac{15}{25}$ iv. $\frac{36}{40}$

b. The simplest form of $\frac{84}{108}$ is ________.

i. $\frac{48}{54}$ ii. $\frac{24}{27}$ iii. $\frac{7}{9}$ iv. None of these

c. The smallest of the fractions $\frac{4}{15}, \frac{2}{5}, \frac{1}{3}$ is ________.

i. $\frac{4}{15}$ ii. $\frac{2}{5}$ iii. $\frac{1}{3}$ iv. $\frac{3}{5}$

d. The largest of the fractions $\frac{1}{3}, \frac{2}{5}, \frac{8}{15}, \frac{13}{30}$ is ________.

i. $\frac{1}{3}$ ii. $\frac{2}{5}$ iii. $\frac{8}{15}$ iv. $\frac{13}{30}$

2. Fill in the blanks.

a. The decimal form of $\frac{513}{1000}$ is ________.

b. In the decimal number 342.165, the place value of 1 and 4 is ________ and ________ respectively.

c. The fractional form of 1.16 is ________.

d. The point between the whole number part and the decimal number part of a decimal number is called the ________.

e. While expanding a decimal number, the place value of each digit ________ by ________ times when we move from left to right.

3. Solve the following.

a. $\frac{4}{5}+\frac{2}{5}$ b. $6\frac{2}{5}+4\frac{3}{4}$ c. $\frac{3}{6}+\frac{7}{9}$ d. $\frac{7}{9}-\frac{5}{9}$ e. $\frac{13}{24}-\frac{11}{24}$

f. $4\frac{2}{3}-3\frac{3}{4}$ g. $\frac{2}{6}\times 36$ h. $\frac{2}{8}\times\frac{5}{6}$ i. $\frac{5}{9}\times 2\frac{6}{15}$ j. $1\frac{7}{8}\times 3\frac{3}{5}$

k. $\frac{2}{5}\div 16$ l. $1\frac{8}{10}\div 1\frac{6}{9}$ m. $\frac{2}{7}\div\frac{6}{14}$

4. Convert the following fractions into decimals.

a. $\frac{3}{5}$ b. $\frac{4}{8}$ c. $\frac{12}{4}$ d. $\frac{16}{25}$

5. **Convert the following decimals into fractions.**

a. 0.5 b. 1.5 c. 0.123 d. 12.23

6. **Answer the following questions.**

a. Write the expanded forms of 12.2, 32.44 and 644.368.

b. Write the decimal forms of the following.

i. $4 + \frac{3}{10}$ ii. $30 + 2 + \frac{7}{10} + \frac{8}{100}$ iii. $100 + 20 + 1 + \frac{1}{10} + \frac{4}{1000}$

c. Write the place value of the underlined digit in each decimal.

i. $23.6\underline{4}$ ii. $12.\underline{5}46$ iii. $214.98\underline{7}$

7. **Evaluate the following.**

a. 80.5 + 72.10 b. 1.85 + 74.19

c. 0.024 x 100 d. 201.3 + 13.64 + 6.751

e. 89.7 – 34.44 f. 9.99 ÷ 6.6

g. 0.25 ÷ 0.05 h. 68.2 – 41.71 – 24.541

8. **Evaluate the following.**

a. $1\frac{1}{2} \div 1\frac{1}{5} \times 2\frac{6}{7}$ b. $1\frac{1}{5} \div \left(1\frac{9}{15} \text{ of } 2\frac{1}{3}\right) \div \frac{1}{2}$

c. $1\frac{6}{8} \div \left(\frac{5}{8} \text{ of } 1\frac{2}{14}\right) + \frac{7}{10}$ d. $\frac{17}{20} \div \left(\frac{5}{8} - \frac{1}{5}\right) - \frac{1}{4}$

9. **Compare the following decimals and write '<' or '>'in the given boxes.**

a. 93.390 ☐ 93.039 b. 44.89 ☐ 43.580

c. 23.7 ☐ 27.3 d. 5.371 ☐ 5.731

10. **Solve the following word problems.**

a. Megha bought $1\frac{1}{5}$ kg of grapes and $2\frac{3}{4}$ kg of mangoes. What was the total weight of the fruits that Megha bought?

b. A petrol tank is filled with $4\frac{1}{4}$ litres of petrol. If $\frac{1}{8}$ of the petrol leaks out, then how many litres of petrol would be left?

c. There are 180 members of a committee. In a meeting, $\frac{3}{5}$ of them were present. How many members were absent?

d. A carpenter wants to make a table top measuring 25 square metres. If one square metre of wood costs ₹20.50, how much money will he spend to purchase the wood for the table top?

e. Radhika spent $\frac{4}{7}$ part of her holidays completing her homework, $\frac{2}{7}$ part on a holiday trip and the rest with her grandparents. If she spent 4 days with her grandparents, then what is the total duration of the holidays?

6 Playing with Numbers

Prior Knowledge

- Number system
- Performing basic operations on numbers

Learning Objectives

- Factors and multiples
- Classification of natural numbers (prime triplet, perfect number)
- Divisibility test, properties of divisibility
- Prime factorisation
- Highest Common Factor (HCF)
- Least Common Multiple (LCM)
- Relationship between HCF and LCM
- Order of performing operations

Let's Get Started

For a workshop, 8 chairs are to be arranged in rows and columns in a room. Which of the following arrangements would you prefer and why?

If the number of chairs was 50, how would you find out the possible combinations for arranging the chairs in rows and columns?

Let us learn how to solve this kind of situation.

FACTORS AND MULTIPLES

From the arrangements of chairs given on the previous page, we observe that 8 can be written as a product of two numbers in different ways as:

$8 = 1 \times 8$ $\quad$ $8 = 2 \times 4$ $\quad$ $8 = 4 \times 2$ $\quad$ $8 = 8 \times 1$

We can say that 1, 2, 4 and 8 exactly divide 8.

Thus, 1, 2, 4 and 8 are exact divisors of 8.

They are called the **factors** of 8.

So, the factors of 8 are 1, 2, 4, and 8.

Also, the product is the **multiple** of the factors—that is, 8 is a multiple of 1, 2, 4, and 8.

A **factor** of a number is a number that divides the number exactly without leaving any remainder.

Examples: The factors of 15 are 1, 3, 5 and 15.

The factors of 20 are 1, 2, 4, 5, 10 and 20.

Properties of Factors

- 1 is a factor of every number.
- Every number is a factor of itself.
- Number of factors of a number is finite.
- Every factor of a number is less than or equal to the given number.
- Every factor of a number is an exact divisor of that number.

A **multiple** of a number is obtained by multiplying that number by a natural number.

Examples: The multiples of 7 are 7, 14, 21, 28, 35,...

The multiples of 10 are 10, 20, 30, 40...

Properties of Multiples

- Every number is a multiple of itself.
- Every multiple of a number is greater than or equal to that number.
- Number of multiples of a number is infinite.

Common Factors and Common Multiples

A number that is a factor of two or more numbers is called a **common factor** of those numbers.

Example 1: Find the common factors of 12, 48 and 100.

Solution: Factors of 12 are 1, 2, 3, 4, 6 and 12.

Factors of 48 are 1, 2, 3, 4, 6, 8, 12, 16, 24 and 48.

Factors of 100 are 1, 2, 4, 5, 10, 20, 25, 50 and 100.

The common factors of 12, 48 and 100 are 1, 2, and 4.

Example 2: Find the first two common multiples of 6 and 15.

Solution: Multiples of 6 are: 6, 12, 18, 24, 30, 36, 42, 48, 54, 60,...

Multiples of 15 are: 15, 30, 45, 60, 75, 90,...

The first two common multiples of 6 and 15 are 30 and 60.

The multiples that are common to a set of numbers are called the **common multiples**.

Exercise 6.1

1. **State whether the following statements are correct or incorrect.**
   a. 6 is a factor of 42.
   b. 24 is not a multiple of 5.
   c. 20 is a multiple of 3.
   d. 3 and 15 are factors of 54.
   e. 1 is a factor of 20
2. **Write all the possible factors of the following numbers.**
   a. 40 b. 65 c. 90 d. 150 e. 200
3. **Write the first 6 multiples of the following numbers.**
   a. 3 b. 11 c. 8 d. 4 e. 7
4. **Answer the following.**
   a. The smallest factor of 55 other than 1
   b. The largest factor of 10
   c. The 5th multiple of 9
   d. All the factors of 24
   e. Common factor of 18 and 60.
5. **Check whether 351 is a multiple of 13.**

CLASSIFICATION OF NATURAL NUMBERS

The numbers 1, 2, 3, 4, … are called natural numbers. Natural numbers are denoted by the letter **N**.

All natural numbers that are divisible by 2 are **even numbers**. Even numbers end with the digits 0, 2, 4, 6 and 8.

All natural numbers that are not divisible by 2 are **odd numbers**. Odd numbers end with the digits 1, 3, 5, 7 and 9.

Natural numbers are classified into prime and composite numbers based on the number of factors.

Remember

- The number 1 is neither prime nor composite.
- The number 2 is the only even prime number. All other even numbers are composite.
- Co-prime numbers need not be prime numbers.
  Examples: 13 and 15, 16 and 25

Natural Numbers

Prime Numbers
A prime number has only two factors, that is, 1 and the number itself. The smallest prime number is 2.
Examples: 2, 3, 5, 7, 11, ...

Composite Numbers
A composite number has more than two factors, that is, it has factors other than 1 and the number itself. The smallest composite number is 4.
Examples: 4, 6, 9, 10, 12, ...

Twin Prime Numbers
If the difference between two prime numbers is 2, then they are said to be twin primes.
Examples: 3 and 5, 11 and 13

Co-prime Numbers
Two numbers are said to be co-prime or relatively prime if their common factor is only 1.
Examples: 2 and 5, 3 and 8

Prime Numbers Up To 100

There is a simple method to identify prime numbers up to a given limit. The method is known as the **Sieve of Eratosthenes**. It was given by a Greek mathematician Eratosthenes. The numbers that remain after identifying prime numbers are composite numbers.

Let us identify prime numbers up to 100. For this, arrange all the natural numbers from 2 to 100 in ascending order in a grid. Circle the prime numbers up to 10—that is, 2, 3, 5, and 7. Cross-out the multiples of 2, 3, 5, and 7 in the grid. Then circle the numbers that are not crossed out.

The circled numbers are prime numbers. The numbers that are crossed out are composite numbers.

	2	3	4	5	6	7	8	9	10
11	12	13	14	15	16	17	18	19	20
21	22	23	24	25	26	27	28	29	30
31	32	33	34	35	36	37	38	39	40
41	42	43	44	45	46	47	48	49	50
51	52	53	54	55	56	57	58	59	60
61	62	63	64	65	66	67	68	69	70
71	72	73	74	75	76	77	78	79	80
81	82	83	84	85	86	87	88	89	90
91	92	93	94	95	96	97	98	99	100

Exercise 6.2

1. **Identify the composite numbers from the given numbers.**
   a. 17 b. 15 c. 23 d. 91 e. 137
2. **Write the prime numbers between each of the following pairs of numbers.**
   a. 3 and 21 b. 15 and 50 c. 64 and 87
   d. 21 and 79 e. 110 and 130
3. **State whether the following statements are true or false and justify your answers.**
   a. All odd numbers are prime numbers.
   b. All even numbers are composite numbers.
   c. Two consecutive odd prime numbers are twin primes.
   d. 2 is the only even prime number.
   e. All co-primes are prime numbers, but all prime numbers need not be co-primes.
4. **Find the even numbers between 168 and 242.**
5. **Find the odd numbers between 1,387 and 1,492.**

DIVISIBILITY RULES

The test of divisibility helps to identify whether a number is a prime number or a composite number. We can check the divisibility by using the following divisibility rules:

Test	Rule	Example
Divisibility by 2	All even numbers are divisible by 2.	52, 68 and 304 are even numbers; therefore, they are divisible by 2. 47, 67 and 307 are odd numbers; therefore, they are not divisible by 2.
Divisibility by 3	If the sum of the digits of a number is divisible by 3, then the number is divisible by 3.	396 $3 + 9 + 6 = 18$ 18 is divisible by 3; therefore, 396 is divisible by 3.
Divisibility by 4	If the last two digits of a number is divisible by 4, then the number is divisible by 4.	852 52 is divisible by 4; therefore, 852 is divisible by 4.
Divisibility by 5	If the digit in the ones place of a number is 0 or 5, then the number is divisible by 5.	230, 595, 120 and 765 have the digit 0 or 5 in their units place; therefore, they are divisible by 5. 459, 567, 602 and 703 do not have the digit 0 or 5 in their units place; therefore, they are not divisible by 5.
Divisibility by 6	If a number is divisible by both 2 and 3, then it is divisible by 6.	204 204 is an even number; therefore, it is divisible by 2. $2 + 0 + 4 = 6$ 6 is divisible by 3. 204 is divisible by both 2 and 3; therefore, it is divisible by 6.
Divisibility by 8	If the last 3 digits of a number is divisible by 8, then the number is divisible by 8.	9864 864 is divisible by 8; therefore, 9864 is divisible by 8.
Divisibility by 9	If the sum of the digits of a number is a multiple of 9, then the number is divisible by 9.	684 $6 + 8 + 4 = 18$ 18 is divisible by 9; therefore, 684 is divisible by 9.
Divisibility by 10	If the ones digit of a number is 0, then the number is divisible by 10.	560, 2510, 3500 and 4050 have the digit 0 in the ones place; therefore, they are divisible by 10.
Divisibility by 11	If the difference between the sum of the digits in the even places and the sum of the digits in the odd places is 0 or a multiple of 11, then the number is divisible by 11.	9328 $(9 + 2) - (3 + 8) = 11 - 11 = 0$ 0 is divisible by 11; therefore, 9328 is divisible by 11.

Properties of Divisibility of Numbers

- If *a* is divisible by *b*, then *a* is divisible by all the factors of *b*.

  For example, 48 is divisible by 12, and it is divisible by all the factors of 12. That is, 48 is divisible by 1, 2, 3, 4, 6 and 12.
- If a number is divisible by each of the co-prime numbers, then it is divisible by the product of the co-prime numbers.

  For example, 108 is divisible by the co-prime numbers 3 and 4. 108 is also divisible by the product of 3 and 4, that is, 12.
- If a pair of numbers is divisible by a number, then the sum of or the difference between the given pair of numbers is also divisible by the same number.

  For example, 65 and 35 are divisible by 5. The sum of 65 and 35, that is, 100 is also divisible by 5. Similarly, the difference between them, that is, 30 is also divisible by 5.

Exercise 6.3

1. **Complete the following table.**

Number	Divisible by									
	2	3	4	5	6	7	8	9	10	11
7020	Yes									
11,456					No					
7,31,541				No						
97,240		No							Yes	

2. **State whether the following statements are true or false and justify your answers.**
   a. All numbers that are divisible by 9 are not necessarily divisible by 3.
   b. If two given numbers are divisible by a number, then their difference/sum is also divisible by that number.
   c. If a number is divisible by 2 and not by 3, then it is divisible by 6.
   d. If a number is divisible by 2 and 5, then it is also divisible by the sum of 2 and 5, that is, 7.
   e. 84 is divisible by 4 and also by the multiples of 4.
3. **Replace the * by the smallest digit, so that:**
   a. 78*964 is divisible by 9   b. 75* is divisible by 4   c. 2*345 is divisible by 3

PRIME FACTORISATION

A prime number that divides a number completely is a **prime factor** of that number.

For example, the factors of 48 are 1, 2, 3, 4, 6, 8, 12, 16, 24 and 48. Thus, the prime factors of 48 are 2 and 3. Similarly, the factors of 100 are 1, 2, 4, 5, 10, 20, 25, 50 and 100. So, the prime factors of 100 are 2 and 5.

Prime factorisation can be done either by the factor tree method or by the division method. We will call the division method of finding prime factors as the **prime factor method**.

REMEMBER

1 is not a prime factor of any number.

Example 3: Express 840 as the product of its prime factors.

Solution: Factor Tree Method

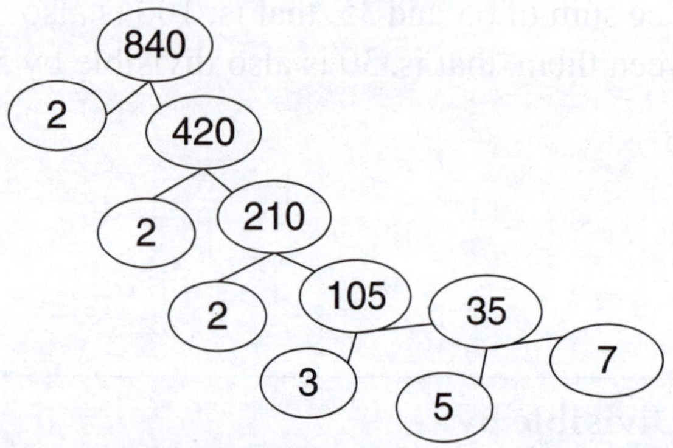

Division Method

2	840
2	420
2	210
3	105
5	35
	7

840 = 2 × 2 × 2 × 3 × 5 × 7

Exercise 6.4

1. **Express the following numbers as the product of their prime factors.**

   a. 136 b. 252 c. 9317 d. 1035 e. 13,915

2. **Find the smallest number having four different prime factors.**

3. **Find the smallest and the largest 4-digit numbers and express them in terms of their prime factors.**

HIGHEST COMMON FACTOR (HCF)

The **highest common factor (HCF)** of any two numbers is the highest among the common factors. It is also known as the **greatest common divisor** (GCD). There are different ways to find the HCF for a given set of numbers. Let us discuss them one by one.

Method 1 **Method of Common Factors**

Step 1: List the factors of each number.

Step 2: Mark the common factors.

Step 3: Identify the highest common factor among all the common factors.

Example 4: Find the HCF of 64 and 120.

Solution: The factors of 64 are 1, **2, 4, 8,** 16, 32 and 64.

The factors of 120 are 1, **2**, 3, **4**, 5, 6, **8**, 10, 12, 15, 20, 24, 30, 40, 60 and 120.

The common factors are 2, 4 and 8.

So, the HCF of 64 and 120 is 8.

Method 2 Prime Factorisation Method

Step 1: Factorise the given numbers into prime factors.

Step 2: Find the HCF by multiplying the common prime factors.

Example 5: Find the HCF of 45 and 108.

Solution:

3	45
3	15
5	5
	1

2	108
2	54
3	27
3	9
3	3
	1

Prime factors of 45 = **3** × **3** × 5

Prime factors of 108 = 2 × 2 × 3 × **3** × **3**

Therefore, the HCF of 45 and 108 is 3 × 3 = 9.

Method 3 Long Division Method

Step 1: Divide the greater number by the smaller number and then divide the previous divisor by the remainder.

Step 2: Repeat the process of division until the remainder is 0.

Step 3: The last divisor is the HCF of the numbers.

Example 6: Find the HCF of 144 and 84.

Solution:

$$84\,\overline{)144}\,(1 \quad -84 = 60;\qquad 60\,\overline{)84}\,(1 \quad -60 = 24;\qquad 24\,\overline{)60}\,(2 \quad -48 = 12;\qquad 12\,\overline{)24}\,(2 \quad -24 = 00$$

Therefore, the HCF of 144 and 84 is 12.

Example 7: Find the HCF of 936 and 864.

Solution:

$$864\,\overline{)936}\,(1 \quad -864 = 72;\qquad 72\,\overline{)864}\,(12 \quad -864 = 000$$

Therefore, the HCF of 936 and 864 is 72.

This answer can also be verified by the method of common factors as follows:

The factors of 144 are 1, 2, 3, 4, **6**, **12**, 24, 36, 48, 72 and 144.

The factors of 84 are 1, 2, 3, 4, **6**, 7, **12**, 14, 21, 28, 42 and 84.

So, the HCF is 12.

Example 8: A rectangular hall of dimensions 60 feet by 24 feet is to be tiled with square tiles of a certain dimension. All tiles have to be of the same dimensions. Find the largest square tile that can be used to cover the hall completely.

Solution:

```
     2
24 ) 60
    -48   2
    12 ) 24
        -24
         00
```

The HCF of 60 and 24 is 12.

Therefore, a square tile of dimension 12 feet would be the largest square tile that can be used to cover the hall completely.

Example 9: A library has 450 books on arts and 600 books on science. The librarian wants to arrange them in the shelves in such a way that each shelf contains the same number of books of the same subject with no books left. Find the greatest number of books that can be arranged in each shelf. Also, find the total number of shelves needed.

Solution:

```
       1
450 ) 600
     -450    3
     150 ) 450
          -450
           000
```

The HCF of 450 and 600 is 150.

The greatest number of books that can be arranged in each shelf is 150.

Total number of books = Number of books on arts + Number of books on science

$= 450 + 600 = 1050$

Number of shelves needed = $1050 \div 150 = 7$

Therefore, 7 shelves are needed to arrange all the books.

Exercise 6.5

1. **Find the HCF of each pair of numbers by listing the factors.**

   a. 12 and 28 b. 30 and 12 c. 24 and 48

   d. 45 and 72 e. 25 and 45

2. **Find the HCF of each pair of numbers using the prime factorisation method.**

   a. 12 and 28 b. 64 and 120 c. 36 and 12

   d. 40 and 88 e. 72 and 90

3. **Find the HCF of each pair of numbers using the long division method.**

   a. 13 and 65 b. 120 and 280 c. 582 and 372

   d. 658 and 770 e. 120 and 660

4. **A rectangular lawn of dimensions 168 m by 144 m is to be paved exactly with artificial square grass patches of the same size. All grass patches have to be of the same size. What is the largest size of grass patch that can be used to cover the lawn?**

5. **A total of 672 boys and 480 girls are on a national learning trip. The boys and the girls are to be divided into separate smaller groups such that each group has the same number of girls and boys. What is the maximum number of students in each group such that no student is left out?**

6. **Find the smallest number, which on being added to 5, is exactly divisible by 4, 6, 8 and 10.**

7. **In classes 8, 9 and 10, there are 60, 54 and 48 students, respectively. Groups of equal number of students have to be formed such that no student is left behind. What is the highest number of students in each group?**

8. **Clothes measuring 45 m, 63 m and 90 m are to be cut into small pieces of equal length. How many such equal pieces can be cut?**

LEAST COMMON MULTIPLE (LCM)

The **least common multiple (LCM)** of two numbers is the smallest among the common multiples of these numbers. There are different ways of finding the LCM of a given set of numbers. Let us learn them one by one.

Method 1 Common Multiple Method

Step 1: List the multiples of the given numbers.

Step 2: Identify the common multiples among them.

Step 3: Identify the least common multiple or LCM.

Example 10: Find the LCM of 5 and 6.

Solution: The multiples of 5 are 5, 10, 15, 20, 25, **30**, 35, 40, 45, 50, 55, **60**…

The multiples of 6 are 6, 12, 18, 24, **30**, 36, 42, 48, 54, **60**…

So, the common multiples of 5 and 6 are 30, 60….

Therefore, the LCM of 5 and 6 is 30.

Example 11: Find the LCM of 4 and 9.

Solution: The multiples of 4 are 4, 8, 12, 16, 20, 24, 28, 32, **36**, 40, 44, 48, 52, 56, 60, 64, 68, **72**…

The multiples of 9 are 9, 18, 27, **36**, 45, 54, 63, **72**…

The common multiples of 4 and 9 are 36, 72,…

Therefore, the LCM of 4 and 9 is 36.

Method 2 Prime Factorisation Method

In this method, prime factorise the numbers and then identify factors occurring maximum number of times in any of the numbers. Find their product to get the LCM.

Example 12: LCM of 20 and 30

Solution: 20 = **2 × 2 × 5**

30 = **2 × 3 × 5**

2	20
2	10
5	5
	1

2	30
3	15
5	5
	1

Note that 2 occurs two times in 20, 3 and 5 occur once in 30.

So, the product 2 × 2 × 3 × 5 is the LCM.

LCM of 20 and 30 = 2 × 2 × 3 × 5 = 60

Example 13: LCM of 18, 36 and 81

Solution: 18 = 2 × 3 × 3

36 = 2 × 2 × 3 × 3

81 = 3 × 3 × 3 × 3

2 occurs twice in 36, 3 occurs four times in 81.

LCM of 18, 36 and 81 = 2 × 2 × 3 × 3 × 3 × 3

= 324

Example 14: LCM of 40, 50 and 75

Solution: 40 = 2 × 2 × 2 × 5

50 = 2 × 5 × 5

75 = 3 × 5 × 5

LCM of 40, 50 and 75 = 2 × 2 × 2 × 5 × 5 × 3

= 600

Method 3 Common Division Method

Step 1: Arrange the given numbers in a row in any order.

Step 2: Identify a prime number that divides at least two of the given numbers. Write the quotients and the undivided numbers below it.

Step 3: Identify another prime number which divides at least two numbers in the second row. Write the quotients and the undivided numbers (if any) below it.

Step 4: Continue this until all the numbers in a row are 1.

Step 5: LCM is the product of all these divisors.

Example 15: Find the LCM of 42 and 86.

Solution:

2	42,	86
3	21,	43
7	7,	43
43	1,	43
	1,	1

Therefore, the LCM of 42 and 86 is $2 \times 3 \times 7 \times 43 = 1806$.

Example 16: Find the LCM of 210 and 250.

Solution:

2	210,	250
3	105,	125
5	35,	125
5	7,	25
5	7,	5
7	7,	1
	1,	1

Therefore, the LCM of 210 and 250 is $2 \times 3 \times 5 \times 5 \times 5 \times 7 = 5250$.

Example 17: If a patient is advised to take a cough syrup every 4 hours and pills for fever at every 5 hours, then after how many hours will the patient take both the cough syrup and the pills?

Solution: Cough syrup is to be taken at hours that are multiples of 4 and pills are to be taken at hours that are multiples of 5.

The multiples of 4 are 4, 8, 12, 16, 20, 24, 28, 32, 36, 40,…

The multiples of 5 are 5, 10, 15, 20, 25, 30, 35, 40, 45, 50,…

The common multiples of 4 and 5 are 20 and 40.

The LCM of 4 and 5 is 20.

So, after 20 hours, the patient will take both the cough syrup and the pills.

Example 18: Two measuring rods are of lengths 66 cm and 84 cm. Find the shortest length that can be measured exactly by each one of these rods.

Solution:

2	66,	84
2	33,	42
3	33,	21
7	11,	7
11	11,	1
	1,	1

The LCM of 66 and 84 is $2 \times 2 \times 3 \times 7 \times 11 = 924$.

Therefore, 924 m is the shortest length that can be measured exactly by each of the two rods.

Alternate Method For Finding HCF And LCM

Find the HCF and LCM of 36 and 60.

2	36
2	18
3	9
	3

2	60
2	30
3	15
	5

REMEMBER

Use the prime factorisation method when both HCF and LCM are to be found in the same sum.

$36 = 2 \times 2 \times 3 \times 3$

$60 = 2 \times 2 \times 3 \times 5$

HCF = $2 \times 2 \times 3 = 12$ (For HCF, find the product of all prime factors which are common in both the numbers).

LCM = $2 \times 2 \times 3 \times 3 \times 5 = 180$ (For LCM, multiply the common factors and the other factors also, that is, common and uncommon factors are to be multiplied).

RELATIONSHIP BETWEEN HCF AND LCM

We know HCF of 12 and 18 = 6 and LCM of 12 and 18 = 36

Product of HCF and LCM = $6 \times 36 = 216$

Product of the numbers = $12 \times 18 = 216$

This is true for all numbers.

Product of two numbers = HCF × LCM

Example 19: Can two numbers have 24 as their HCF and 440 as LCM?

Solution: The HCF of two numbers is a factor of their LCM. Here, 24 is not a factor of 440 as $440 \div 24 = 18$ remainder 8

Therefore, there can not be two numbers which have 24 as their HCF and 440 as LCM.

EXERCISE 6.6

1. **Find the LCM of each pair of numbers by the common multiple method.**
   a. 2 and 3 b. 4 and 7 c. 5 and 15
   d. 10 and 25 e. 15 and 25
2. **Find the LCM of each pair of numbers using the prime factorisation method.**
   a. 24 and 36 b. 24 and 80 c. 90 and 125
   d. 160 and 112 e. 150 and 360

3. **Find the LCM of each pair of numbers using the common division method.**

a. 80 and 90 b. 108 and 180 c. 120 and 350

d. 700 and 490 e. 48 and 120

4. **Rahul goes to the market every 20 days and Marian goes to the same market every 45 days. They met each other today. After how many days will they meet again at the same market?**

5. **Find the least number that when divided separately by 28 and 36 leaves 9 as the remainder in each case.**

6. **In a class, the students can be arranged in groups of 3, 4, 5 or 9 with no student left behind. Find the least number of students in the class.**

7. **A school bell rings at an interval of 40 minutes. Another school bell rings at an interval of 50 minutes. After how minutes will they ring together?**

8. **Vinay goes for swimming every 4th day of the week and Sara goes every 6th day of the week. If they start swimming on the same day, after how many days will they meet/ swim together?**

9. **Find the greatest 6-digit number which is exactly divisible by 1,050 and 1,925.**

10. **Find the LCM of two numbers, 12 and 16, if their HCF is 4.**

11. **Find the HCF of two numbers, 12 and 14, if their LCM is 84.**

12. **The HCF and LCM of two numbers are 24 and 240, respectively. If one of the numbers is 120, find the other number.**

ORDER OF PERFORMING OPERATIONS

You may come across some problems where more than one operation is used. Consider the example, [23 × {9 + 15} – (20 + 12 – 10)]. How do you simplify them? Which operation would you perform first?

In order to solve such problems, we have to follow certain rules.

BODMAS Rule

The rule we generally follow during simplification is the BODMAS rule. This rule tells us the order of operations that is to be followed.

B	O	D	M	A	S
Brackets	Of	Divide	Multiply	Add	Subtract

First, you need to look for brackets in a given problem and simplify them.

Types of Brackets

( ) are known as round brackets or parentheses.

{ } are known as curly brackets or braces.

[ ] are known as square brackets or box brackets.

When an expression is enclosed inside a bracket, we simplify it separately. This is called the removal of the brackets. The preferences for brackets are given as follows.

1. First, we remove ( ).
2. Next, we remove { }.
3. Finally, we remove [ ].

Some examples are given below for simplification according to the BODMAS rule.

Example 20: Simplify (–9) + 45 + {(–7) + (–4)} × 6 ÷ 3

Solution: (–9) + 45 + {(–7) + (–4)} × 6 ÷ 3

= (–9) + 45 + (–11) × 6 ÷ 3	**B**rackets
= (–9) + 45 – 11 × 2	**D**ivision (6 ÷ 3 = 2)
= (–9) + 45 – 22	**M**ultiplication (11 × 2 = 22)
= 45 – 9 – 22 = 45 – 31	**A**ddition (–9 – 22 = –31)
= 14	**S**ubtraction (45 – 31 = 14)

Example 21: 55 + 900 – [(34 – 7) × 2]

Solution: 55 + 900 – [(34 – 7) × 2]

= 55 + 900 – [27 × 2]

= 55 + 900 – 54 = 955 – 54 = 901

EXERCISE 6.7

1. Use the BODMAS rule to simplify the following.

a. {24 – (–3)} ÷ (–9) × 6
b. 12 – 36 ÷ (–9)
c. 7 – 3 × (–5)
d. (–18) ÷ {6 – (–3)} + 4
e. (–9) + 27 ÷ (–9)
f. (–5) × (–11) – 5 × 6
g. {9 × (–7)} ÷ 3 + 21
h. {9 – (–18)} ÷ 9 – (–2)

2. Solve the following:

a. 25 + 50 × 20 – (–14) + (33 ÷ 3)
b. {(90 + 50) – 22} + 4 × 25 – 20
c. 30 – [18 – {14 – (15 – 4 ÷ 2 × 2)}]
d. [50 – (–2) {6 – (7 – 3)}] ÷ [3 × {5 + 13}]

KEY CONCEPTS

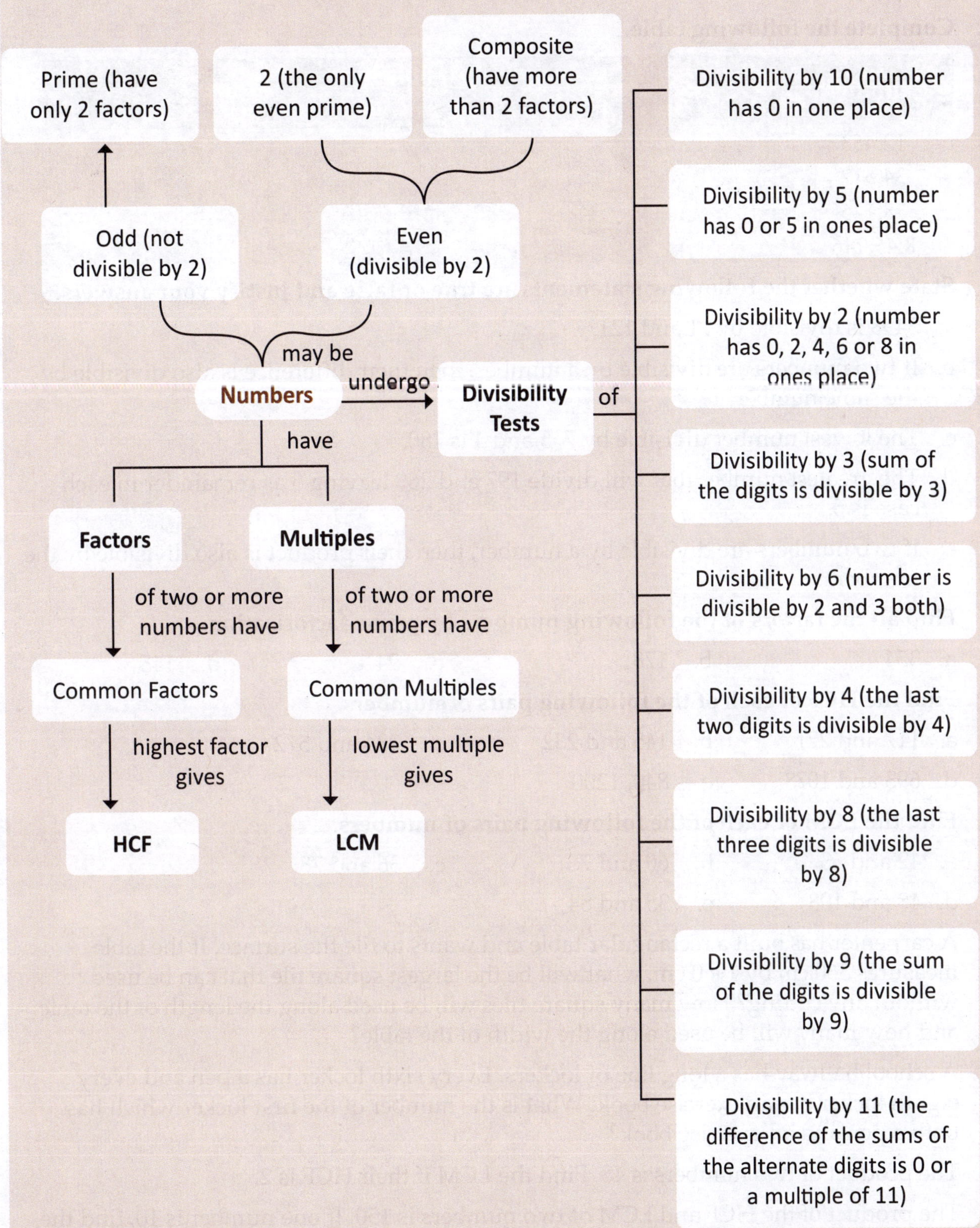

Revision Exercise

1. **Complete the following table.**

Number	Divisible by									
	2	3	4	5	6	7	8	9	10	11
12,453										
34,512										
78,145										
8,45,746										

2. **State whether the following statements are true or false and justify your answers.**
   a. 3498 is divisible by 11 and 121.
   b. If two numbers are divisible by a number, then their difference is also divisible by the same number.
   c. The lowest number divisible by 7, 5 and 4 is 180.
   d. The greatest number that will divide 197 and 269 leaving 5 as remainder in each case is 6.
   e. If two numbers are divisible by a number, then their product is also divisible by the number.
3. **Find all the factors of the following numbers by prime factorisation.**
   a. 354 b. 178 c. 24 d. 145
4. **Find the HCF of each of the following pairs of numbers.**
   a. 117 and 221 b. 145 and 232 c. 234 and 572
   d. 693 and 1078 e. 840, 1200
5. **Find the LCM of each of the following pairs of numbers.**
   a. 42 and 63 b. 60 and 75 c. 36 and 78
   d. 48 and 108 e. 35 and 84
6. A carpenter has built a rectangular table and wants to tile the surface. If the table measures 360 cm by 1960 cm, what will be the largest square tile that can be used without any cutting? How many square tiles will be used along the length of the table and how many will be used along the width of the table?
7. A school hallway has a long line of lockers. Every sixth locker has a pen and every eighth locker has an exercise book. What is the number of the first locker which has both a pen and an exercise book?
8. The product of two numbers is 48. Find the LCM if their HCF is 2.
9. The product of the HCF and LCM of two numbers is 150. If one number is 10, find the other number.
10. Find the greatest 5-digit number exactly divisible by 16, 18, 24, and 30.

7 Ratio and Proportion

Prior Knowledge

- Basic operations on numbers
- Fractions and their simplification

Learning Objectives

- Ratios
- Equivalent ratios
- Comparing ratios
- Concept of proportion
- Concept of unitary method
- Speed and its relationship with time and distance

Let's Get Started

The table given below shows the medals won by India in 2022 Commonwealth games.

S. No.	Games	Gold	Silver	Bronze
1.	Boxing	🥇🥇🥇	🥈	🥉🥉🥉
2.	Wrestling	🥇🥇🥇🥇🥇🥇	🥈	🥉🥉🥉🥉🥉
3.	Athletics	🥇	🥈🥈🥈🥈	🥉🥉🥉
4.	Weightlifting	🥇🥇🥇	🥈🥈🥈	🥉🥉🥉🥉
5.	Table tennis	🥇🥇🥇🥇	🥈	🥉🥉

Answer the following questions based on the above information. One is done for your reference.

S. No.			Fraction	Ratio
1.	Number of silver medals to number of gold medals in Boxing	:	$\frac{1}{3}$	1 : 3
2.	Number of gold medals in wrestling to that in weightlifting	:		
3.	Total medals in Athletics to weightlifting	:		
4.	Number of bronze medals in weightlifting to number of gold medals in wrestling	:		
5.	Number of gold medals in table tennis to that in wrestling	:		

RATIO

In our daily life, we compare quantities of same kind with one another by using subtraction or division operations. Generally, we use division method in ratios.

Akshay is 1 m 26 cm tall and her father is 1 m 89 cm tall.

We compare their heights by division.

$$\frac{\text{Height of Akshay}}{\text{Height of Father}} = \frac{126}{189} = \frac{2}{3}$$

So, Akshay's height is $\frac{2}{3}$ times his father's height.

We can also say that the ratio of Akshay's height to his father's height is 2 : 3.

Comparison of two or more quantities of the same kind by division is called **ratio**.

It is denoted by colon ':' and read as '**is to**'.

In the ratio 2 : 3, the first term (2) is called **antecedent** and the second term (3) is called **consequent**.

REMEMBER

- The order of terms in a ratio is important when we compare two quantities. For example, 2 : 3 is different from 3 : 2.
- The quantities to be compared must be in the same unit. A ratio is a pure number. So, it does not have a unit.

Ratio
2 : 3
Antecedent   Consequent

Example 1: Find the ratio of 30 min to 2 h.

Solution: Converting 2 hours into minutes, we get 2 h = 2 × 60 min = 120 min

$\therefore$ Required ratio $= 30 : 120 = \frac{30}{120} = \frac{1}{4} = 1 : 4$

Example 2: Find the ratio of 2.5 m to 50 cm.

Solution: We know that 1 m = 100 cm.

Converting 2.5 metres into centimetres, we get

2.5 × 100 cm = 250 cm

Therefore, the required ratio $= 250 : 50 = \frac{250}{50} = \frac{5}{1} = 5 : 1$

ALERT !

The ratio of 5 cm to 20 mm is
5 : 2 ✓   5 : 20 = 1 : 4 ×

Difference Between Fraction and Ratio

A fraction is a number that represents a part of a whole or a group, whereas a ratio is a comparison between two or more quantities of the same kind.

For example, there are 10 girls and 20 boys in a class.

The ratio of girls to the total number of students is $10 : 30 = 1 : 3 = \frac{1}{3}$. Here one-third of the total number of students is girls.

The ratio of boys to the total number of students is $20 : 30 = 2 : 3 = \frac{2}{3}$. Here two-third of the total is boys.

The ratio of girls to boys is $10 : 20 = 1 : 2 = \frac{1}{2}$. Here the number of girls is half the number of boys.

Example 3: If 75 g of a spice packet contains 45 g coriander powder and 30 g red chilli powder, what is the ratio of coriander powder to red chilli powder in the spice packet?

Solution: Ratio of coriander powder to red chilli powder

$$= \frac{\text{Quantity of coriander powder}}{\text{Quantity of red chilli powder}} = \frac{45\text{ g}}{30\text{ g}} = \frac{3}{2} = 3:2$$

EQUIVALENT RATIOS

We can find the equivalent ratios of a given ratio by multiplying or dividing the antecedent and the consequent of the given ratio by the same number.

Example 4: Find two equivalent ratios of 2 : 4.

Solution: $2:4 = \frac{2}{4} = \frac{2 \times 2}{4 \times 2} = \frac{4}{8}$

Therefore, 4 : 8 is an equivalent ratio of 2 : 4.

Similarly, $2:4 = \frac{2}{4} = \frac{2 \div 2}{4 \div 2} = \frac{1}{2}$

So, 1 : 2 is another equivalent ratio of 2 : 4.

Example 5: Are 1 : 5 and 2 : 10 equivalent ratios?

Solution: $2:10 = \frac{2}{10} = \frac{2 \div 2}{10 \div 2} = \frac{1}{5}$

Therefore, 1 : 5 and 2 : 10 are equivalent ratios.

Example 6: Diya earns ₹1,500 by working for 2 hours. If she works for 8 hours, how much money will she earn?

Solution: The ratio between the money Diya earns to the hours she works = $1500:2 = \frac{1500}{2}$.

Here, we have to find the equivalent ratio with the second term as 8.

Money she earns in 8 hours = $\frac{1,500}{2} \times \frac{?}{?} = \frac{1,500 \times 4}{2 \times 4} = \frac{6,000}{8}$

Therefore, she earns ₹6,000 in 8 hours.

RATIO IN SIMPLEST FORM

If the antecedent and the consequent of a ratio do not have any common factor except 1, then the ratio is said to be in its lowest terms or the simplest form.

For example: The ratios 3 : 5 and 5 : 8 are in their respective simplest forms.

(i) To convert a given ratio into its simplest form, find the HCF of its antecedent and consequent and divide both the terms by the HCF.

Example 7: Convert the ratio 100 : 625 into its lowest term.

Solution: The HCF of 100 and 625 is 25.

$$\frac{\cancel{100}^{4}}{\cancel{625}_{25}} = 4:25$$

Example 8: Convert the ratio 60 : 132 into its lowest term.

Solution: The HCF of 60 and 132 is 12.

$$\frac{\cancel{60}^{5}}{\cancel{132}_{11}} = 5:11$$

(ii) If the antecedent or the consequent or both the terms of a ratio are fractions, then we find the LCM of the denominators of the fractions and multiply both the terms of the ratio by this LCM. This will convert the fractional terms into natural numbers.

Example 9: Convert the ratio 510 : 690 into its simplest form.

Solution: HCF of 510 and 690 is 30.

Therefore, $\frac{510}{690} = \frac{510 \div 30}{690 \div 30} = \frac{17}{23} = 17 : 23$

Example 10: Simplify the ratio:

$\frac{1}{3}:\frac{3}{4}:\frac{4}{5}$

Solution: The LCM of 3, 4 and 5 is 60.

$\frac{1}{3}:\frac{3}{4}:\frac{4}{5} = \frac{1}{3}\times 60 : \frac{3}{4}\times 60 : \frac{4}{5}\times 60$

$= 20 : 3 \times 15 : 4 \times 12$

$= 20 : 45 : 48$

Example 11: Simplify each of the following ratios.

a. $1 : \frac{8}{3}$

Solution: $1 : \frac{8}{3} = 1 \times 3 : \frac{8}{3} \times 3 = 3 : 8$

b. $2 : \frac{7}{5}$

Solution: $2 : \frac{7}{5} = 2 \times 5 \; \frac{7}{5} \times 5 = 10 : 7$

c. $\frac{1}{15} : \frac{1}{10}$

Solution: The LCM of 15 and 10 is 30.

$\frac{1}{15} : \frac{1}{10} = \frac{1}{15} \times 30 : \frac{1}{10} \times 30 = 2 : 3$

d. $\frac{1}{6} : \frac{2}{3} : \frac{1}{2}$

Solution: The LCM of 6, 3 and 2 is 6.

$\frac{1}{6} : \frac{2}{3} : \frac{1}{2} = \frac{1}{6} \times 6 : \frac{2}{3} \times 6 : \frac{1}{2} \times 6 = 1 : 4 : 3$

COMPARISON OF RATIOS

We have already learned how to compare fractions. To compare ratios, we convert them into fractions and then compare. Look at the following examples.

REMEMBER

To compare two ratios, convert them into equivalent like fractions.

Example 12: Compare the following ratios:

a. 11 : 15 and 7 : 10

b. 7 : 9 and 11 : 12

Solution: a. 11 : 15 can be written as $\frac{11}{15}$ and 7 : 10 can be written as $\frac{7}{10}$.

Now, let us compare $\frac{11}{15}$ and $\frac{7}{10}$.

The LCM of 15 and 10 is 30.

Now, making the denominators of each fraction equal to 30, we get

$\frac{11}{15} = \frac{11 \times 2}{15 \times 2} = \frac{22}{30}$ and $\frac{7}{10} = \frac{7 \times 3}{10 \times 3} = \frac{21}{30}$

we have, $\frac{22}{30} > \frac{21}{30} \Rightarrow \frac{11}{15} > \frac{7}{10}$

Hence, 11 : 15 > 7 : 10.

b. 7 : 9 can be written as $\frac{7}{9}$ and 11 : 12 can be written as $\frac{11}{12}$.

LCM of 9 and 12 is 36.

Now, $\frac{7}{9} = \frac{7 \times 4}{9 \times 4} = \frac{28}{36}$ and $\frac{11}{12} = \frac{11 \times 3}{12 \times 3} = \frac{33}{36}$

We have, $\frac{33}{36} > \frac{28}{36} \Rightarrow \frac{11}{12} > \frac{7}{9}$

Hence, 11 : 12 > 7 : 9

Example 13: School A has 8 volleyball players and 10 football players. School B has 9 volleyball players and 4 football players. Which school has a higher ratio of volleyball players to football players?

Solution: Ratio of volleyball players to football players in School A = 8 : 10

Ratio of volleyball players to football players in School B = 9 : 4

Converting both the ratios into fractional form, we get $\frac{8}{10}$ and $\frac{9}{4}$.

$\frac{8 \times 2}{10 \times 2} = \frac{16}{20}, \frac{9 \times 5}{4 \times 5} = \frac{45}{20}$

On comparing these two ratios, we see that School B has a higher ratio of volley ball players to football players as compared to School A.

EXERCISE 7.1

1. **Express each of the following ratios into simplest form.**

   a. 24 : 72 b. 80 : 112 c. 130 : 160
   d. 629 : 407 e. 925 : 725

2. **Find the ratio of the first quantity to the second quantity in the simplest form.**

   a. ₹7, ₹1.75 b. 5 m, 150 cm c. 6 h, 1 h 50 min
   d. 6 ℓ, 625 mℓ e. 575 g : 2 kg

3. **Rewrite the following ratios with their terms as natural numbers.**

   a. $1 : \frac{6}{1}$ b. $\frac{7}{12} : 2$ c. $\frac{3}{4} : \frac{5}{6}$
   d. $5\frac{1}{2} : 3\frac{2}{3}$ e. $2\frac{3}{5} : 3\frac{1}{4}$

4. **Which of the following sets are equivalent ratios?**

a. 3 : 5, 27 : 45 b. 2 : 3, 30 : 20 c. 7 : 4, 126 : 64

d. 135 : 30, 9 : 2 e. 8 : 9, 32 : 45

5. **Compare the ratios in each of the following.**

a. 5 : 6, 6 : 7 b. 19 : 25, 37 : 50 c. 24 : 13, 12 : 7

d. 21 : 50, 43 : 100 e. 5 : 7, 9 : 11

PROPORTION

Observe the following table that provides the cost of different number of books.

Number of Books	1	5	10	15	18
Cost (in Rupees)	6	30	60	90	108

From the table, we see that the cost of 10 books is ₹60, and the cost of 18 books is ₹108.

Therefore, the ratio of the number of books = 10 : 18 = 5 : 9

Ratio of their costs = 60 : 108 = 5 : 9

The two ratios are equal, that is, 10 : 18 = 60 : 108.

If two ratios are equal, then the four numbers forming the two ratios, written in order, are said to be in **proportion**.

In general, a, b, c and d are said to be in proportion if $a : b = c : d$.
We write it as $a : b : : c : d$ and read it as 'a is to b is as c is to d'.

Here, :: is the symbol of proportionality and is read as 'is proportional to'.

The terms b and c are called the means, while the terms a and d are called the extremes of the proportion.

We can say that the terms 10, 18, 60, 108 are in proportion.

We write this as 10 : 18 : : 60 : 108.

Notice that 10 × 108 = 1080 and 18 × 60 = 1080

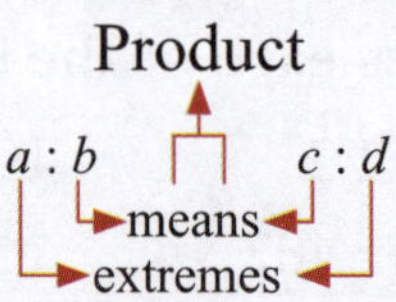

product of extremes = product of means
$ad = bc$

Example 14: Test whether the following sets of numbers are in proportion.

a. 3, 9, 5, 15

Solution: In the given numbers,

Product of the extremes = 3 × 15 = 45

Product of the means = 9 × 5 = 45

∴ Product of extremes = Product of means

Therefore, 3, 9, 5 and 15 are in proportion.

b. 10, 15, 24, 30

Solution: In the given numbers,

Product of the extremes = 10 × 30 = 300

Product of the means = 15 × 24 = 360

∴ Product of extremes ≠ Product of means

Therefore, 10, 15, 24 and 30 are not in proportion.

Example 15: Find the fourth proportional of 12, 20 and 3.

Solution: Let d be the fourth proportional of 12, 20 and 3.

Thus, 12, 20, 3 and d are in proportion.

Product of extremes = Product of means

$\therefore\ 12 \times d = 20 \times 3 \Rightarrow 12d = 60 \Rightarrow d = \frac{60}{12} \Rightarrow d = 5$

Therefore, the fourth proportional of 12, 20 and 3 is 5.

Example 16: If a car travels 138 km in 3 hours, then how much distance will it cover in 9 hours?

Solution: Let x be distance covered by a car in 9 hours.

Here quantities are in proportion.

Hence, 138 km : 3 hours :: Distance covered in 9 hours : 9 hours

That is $138 : 3 :: x : 9$

$138 \times 9 = 3x$

$x = 138 \times \frac{9}{3}$

$x = 414$

Therefore, the car covers 414 km in 9 hours.

Example 17: John bought 3 jars of tomato ketchup for ₹90. Jennifer bought 21 jars of tomato ketchup for ₹630. Check if the number of jars and the cost are in proportion.

Solution: If they are in proportion, then number of jars John bought : Cost paid by John : : Number of jars Jennifer bought : Cost paid by Jennifer. That is, 3 : 90 : : 21 : 630.

Product of the extremes = 3 × 630 = 1,890 and product of the means = 90 × 21 = 1,890

Hence, 3, 90, 21 and 630 are in proportion.

Therefore, the number of jars and the cost are in proportion.

Example 18: If the weight of 5 packs of fruits is 15 kg, then find the weight of 3 such packs.

Solution: Let 'a' be the weight of 3 packs of fruits.

If the given quantities are in proportion, then

5 packs : Weight of 5 packs :: 3 packs: Weight of 3 packs, that is, $5 : 15 :: 3 : a$

Product of extremes = Product of means

$5 \times a = 15 \times 3$

$a = \frac{15 \times 3}{5} = 3 \times 3 = 9$

Therefore, the weight of 3 packs of fruits is 9 kg.

Continued Proportion

If the second and the third terms are equal in proportion, then the proportion is called **continued proportion**.

$$a : b :: b : c$$

For example, if 4 : 6 :: 6 : 9, then we say that 4, 6, 9 are in continued proportion.

Mean Proportion

If the terms a, b and c are in continued proportion, then 'b' is called the **mean proportion** of a and c.

In general, if $a : b :: b : c$, then product of extremes = Product of means. We have, $a \times c = b \times b$.

Here, b is called the mean proportion.

Third Proportion

If the terms a, b, c are in continued proportion, then c is called the **third proportion**.

If a, b, c are in continued proportion, then

$a \times c = b \times b \Rightarrow b^2 = ac$

Example 19: Find the third proportion of 4 and 8.

Solution: Let the third proportional be c. We have

$4 \times c = 8 \times 8$

or $c = (8 \times 8) \div 4 = \dfrac{8 \times \cancel{8}^{2}}{\cancel{4}_{1}} = 8 \times 2 = 16$

So, the third proportion = 16.

Exercise 7.2

1. **Which of the following sets of numbers are in proportion?**

   a. 2, 3, 22, 33　b. 8, 6, 12, 9　c. 15, 30, 7, 14

   d. 15, 21, 25, 40　e. 21, 35, 15, 25

2. **Find the missing numbers in the following proportions.**

   a. 24 : 18 :: ________ : 9　b. 12 : 16 :: 9 : ________

   c. ________ : 20 :: 5 : $2\frac{1}{2}$　d. $10\frac{1}{2}$: ________ :: $5\frac{1}{2}$: $2\frac{3}{4}$

   e. $4\frac{1}{9}$: ________ :: $8\frac{3}{4}$: $6\frac{1}{4}$

3. **Find the fourth proportional in each of the following.**

   a. 16, 12, 4　b. 9, 10, 18　c. 10, 20, 15

   d. 24, 18, 12　e. 45, 24, 15

4. **If the numbers 18, 6 and a are in continued proportion, find the value of a.**

5. **Solve the following questions.**

   a. 250 mL of mango squash requires 2 L of water. Find the ratio of water to mango squash.

   b. The length of a line segment is 114 cm. If it is divided in the ratio 9 : 10, find the length of the two parts.

   c. A milkman mixes milk and water in the ratio 5 : 2. Find the amount of water mixed by him in 6.3 L of milk.

   d. If the ratio of the three angles of a triangle is 1 : 2 : 3, then find the measure of each angle of the triangle. (Hint: The sum of the three interior angles of any triangle is 180°.)

e. In a class of 30 students, the number of boys is 16 and the remaining students are girls. Find the ratio between:
   i. the number of girls and boys. ii. the number of girls and the whole class.

f. A man earns ₹5,000 and spends ₹3,000. Find the ratio of his expenditure to
   i. his saving ii. his total income.

UNITARY METHOD

In unitary method, first the price or value of one unit is calculated and then the price of many or a required number of units is calculated.

Steps to be followed:

- Divide to find the value of one unit.
- Multiply to find the value of larger quantities.

Example 20: A car can travel 145 km with 10 L of petrol. What is its mileage?

Solution: Distance travelled with 10 L of petrol = 145 km

Distance travelled with 1 L of petrol = 145 ÷ 10 = 14.5 km

Therefore, the mileage of the car is 14.5 km per litre.

Example 21: The cost of 1 pack of chocolates is ₹72. Find the price of 5 chocolates, if there are 12 chocolates in each pack.

Solution: Cost of 12 chocolates = ₹72

We divide the price of 1 pack by the number of chocolates in the pack to get the cost of 1 chocolate.

Price of one unit = Price of all the units ÷ Number of units
= 72 ÷ 12 = 6

REMEMBER

Cost of 1 $\xrightarrow{\times}$ Cost of many

Cost of many $\xrightarrow{\div}$ Cost of 1

Thus, the price of one chocolate is ₹6.

Now, we multiply the price of one chocolate with the required quantity of chocolates, that is, 5.

Cost of 5 chocolates = 5 × 6 = 30

So, the cost of 5 chocolates is ₹30.

Example 22: If a transport company charges ₹1,500 to carry 3 kg of weight, then what will be the charges to carry 8 kg?

Solution: Charges for 3 kg of weight = ₹1,500

Charges for transporting 1 kg of weight = 1,500 ÷ 3 = ₹500

Charges for transporting 8 kg of weight = 500 × 8 = ₹4000

Therefore, the transport company charges ₹4000 to carry 8 kg of weight.

Here, the total cost increases as the amount of weight increases.

So, the cost is **directly proportional** to the amount of weight.

Example 23: If Afzal walks 18 km in 5 hours, how long would he take to walk 10.8 km?

Solution: Time taken to walk 18 km = 5 hours

Time taken to walk 1 km = $5 \div 18 = \frac{5}{18}$ hours

Time taken to walk 10.8 km = $10.8 \times \frac{5}{18} = 3$ hours

Therefore, Afzal would take 3 hours to walk a distance of 10.8 km.

Example 24: If the cost of 8 kg apples is ₹680, then find the cost of 15 kg apples.

Solution: Cost of 8 kg apples = ₹680

Cost of 1 kg apple = ₹680 ÷ 8 = ₹85

Cost of 15 kg apples = ₹85 × 15 = ₹1275

Therefore, the cost of 15 kg apples is ₹1275.

EXERCISE 7.3

1. **Find the missing quantities or values in the following cases.**

Quantity	Value (in ₹)	Required Quantity	Value of Required Quantity (in ₹)
3 sets of pen	180	5 sets of pen	
5 kg flour	165		396
15 m of ribbon	105	8 m of ribbon	
2 dozen eggs	144		360
7 L of apple juice	525		675

2. **Answer the following.**

   a. If the total expenditure of 5 students who went for a picnic is ₹1000, find the total number of students who went for a picnic at the cost of ₹10,000.

   b. A car travels 120 km in 10 litres of petrol. What is its mileage?

   c. 56 books weigh 8 kg. How much will 70 books weigh?

   d. 987 bricks are required to build a 3 m high wall. How many bricks will be required to build a 5 m high wall?

   e. Sachin can read 270 pages in 6 hours. Find out how many pages can he read in 5 hours.

   f. Twelve ink pens cost ₹192, and 18 ball pens cost ₹216. Find the ratio of the cost of one ink pen to the cost of one ball pen.

SPEED, DISTANCE AND TIME

Before understanding more about speed, let us recall what we have learned about 'distance' and 'time'.

Distance

Distance is the length between two points or places.

Some of the units of length are millimetre (mm), centimetre (cm), decimetre (dm), metre (m), decametre (dam), hectometre (hm) and kilometre (km).

The standard unit of length is **metre**.

Example 25: Express 5 m in centimetres.

Solution: 1 m = 100 cm

5 m = 5 × 100 cm = 500 cm

Example 26: Express 3.2 km in metres.

Solution: 1 km = 1000 m

3.2 km = 3.2 × 1000 m = 3200 m

REMEMBER

1 cm = 10 mm
1 dm = 10 cm
1 m = 10 dm
1 dam = 10 m
1 hm = 10 dm
1 km = 10 hm

Time

Durations of events and the intervals between them are measured in units of **time**.

Some of the units of time are second, minute, hour, day, week, month, year and decade.

The standard unit of time is **second**.

Example 27: Express 2.5 hours in minutes.

Solution: 1 h = 60 min

2.5 h = 2.5 × 60 min = 150 min

Example 28: Express 75 minutes in hours.

Solution: 60 min = 1 h

75 min = 75 ÷ 60 = $1\frac{1}{4}$ h = 1 h 15 min

REMEMBER

1 minute = 60 seconds
1 hour = 60 minutes
1 day = 24 hours
1 week = 7 days
1 month = 4 weeks / 5 weeks
1 year = 12 months
1 decade = 10 years
1 century = 10 decades

Speed

The distance covered by an object in unit time is called its **speed**.

Speed is calculated as the ratio of the distance covered by an object to the time taken by the object to cover that distance.

$$\text{Speed} = \frac{\text{Distance covered}}{\text{Time taken}}$$

The unit of speed is given by $\frac{\text{unit of distance}}{\text{unit of time}}$.

Speed is usually expressed in $\frac{\text{metre}}{\text{second}}$ (m/s) or $\frac{\text{kilometre}}{\text{hour}}$ (km/h)

The following table shows the distance covered and the time taken by an athlete.

Distance Covered	Time Taken
0 m	0 s
5 m	1 s
10 m	2 s
25 m	5 s
50 m	10 s
75 m	15 s
100 m	20 s

The speed of the athlete can be calculated as $\frac{\text{distance covered}}{\text{time taken}} = \frac{100 \text{ m}}{20 \text{ s}} = 5 \text{ m/s}$

One needs more time to cover a greater distance and less time to cover a smaller distance when the speed is the same. Thus, if the speed is constant, then the time taken is directly proportional to the distance covered.

Similarly, if the time taken is constant, then the speed is directly proportional to the distance covered.

$$\text{Time taken} = \frac{\text{Distance covered}}{\text{Speed}}$$

Example 30: Find the time taken by a train if it travels 68,82,000 m with a speed of 55.5 km/h. Note: If the speed of the train is given in km/h, express the distance covered by the train in kilometres.

Solution: Distance covered by the train = 68,82,000 m

$$= \frac{6882000}{1000} \text{ km} \quad (\text{Since } 1 \text{ m} = \frac{1}{1000} \text{ km})$$

$$= 6882 \text{ km}$$

Speed = 55.5 km/h

$$\text{Time taken} = \frac{\text{Distance covered}}{\text{Speed}} = \frac{6882}{55.5} = 124 \text{ h} = 5 \text{ days } 4 \text{ hours (Since 1 day = 24 hours)}$$

Consider the following table with respect to speed, time taken and distance covered by different modes of transport.

Modes of Transport	Speed	Time Taken	Distance Covered
	840 km/h	30 min	420 km
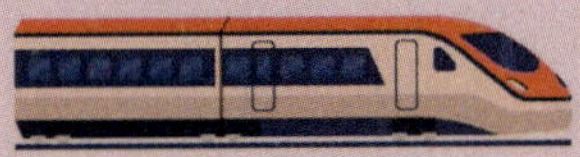	300 km/h	1 h 24 min	420 km
	70 km/h	6 h	420 km

As seen from the table, an object takes less time if the speed is more and more time if the speed is less to cover the same distance. Thus, if the distance covered is constant, then the speed is inversely proportional to the time taken.

Distance covered = Speed × Time taken

Example 31: How much distance does a helicopter cover if it travels at a constant speed of 226 km/h for 6.5 h?

Solution: Speed of the helicopter = 226 km/h

Time taken = 6.5 h

Distance covered = Speed × Time taken = 226 × 6.5 = 1469 km

Example 32: If the speed of a cycle is 18 km/h, find its speed in metres per second.

Solution: 18 km = 18 × 1000 m = 18,000 m (Since 1 km = 1000 m)

1 h = 60 min = 60 × 60 s = 3600 s

Therefore, the speed of the cycle in metres per second

$= \frac{18,000}{3,600}$ m/s = 5 m/s

REMEMBER

18 km/h = 5 m/s

1 km/h = $\frac{5}{18}$ m/s

1 m/s = $\frac{18}{5}$ km/h

Example 33: How much distance does a scooter travelling at a speed of 54 km/h cover in 5 min?

Solution:

Method 1

Distance travelled in 1 h (or 60 min) = 54 km = 54 × 1000 m

Distance travelled in 1 min = $\frac{54 \times 1000}{60}$ m = 900 m

Distance travelled in 5 min = 5 × 900 m = 4500 m = 4.5 km

Method 2

Speed of the scooter = 54 km/h = $54 \times \frac{5}{18}$ m/s = 3 × 5 m/s = 15 m/s

Time taken = 5 min = 5 × 60 s = 300 s

Distance covered = Speed × Time taken = 15 × 300 m = 4500 m = 4.5 km

Example 34: A car can finish a certain journey in 10 h at a speed of 56 km/h. By how many kilometres per hour must the speed of the car be increased to cover the same distance in 8 h?

Solution: Speed of the car = 56 km/h

Time taken = 10 h

Distance covered = Speed × Time taken = 56 × 10 = 560 km

Speed of the car required to travel 560 km in 8 hours = $\frac{\text{Distance covered}}{\text{Time taken}} = \frac{560}{8}$ km/h

= 70 km/h

Speed of the car should be increased by (70 – 56) km/h = 14 km/h

Example 35: Rahim jogs at a speed of $4\frac{1}{3}$ km/h in the morning. Running at the same speed, how much time will he take to cover 26 km?

Solution: Speed = $4\frac{1}{3}\text{ km/h} = \frac{13}{3}\text{ km/h}$

$$\text{Time} = \frac{\text{Distance}}{\text{Speed}} = \left(\frac{26}{\frac{13}{3}}\right)\text{h} = \left(26 \times \frac{3}{13}\right)\text{h} = 6\text{ h}$$

Hence, Rahim will cover 26 km in 6 hours.

Uniform Speed and Variable Speed

Uniform speed: An object is said to be moving with uniform speed if it covers equal distances in equal intervals of time.

For example, if a bus covers 40 km in the first hour and 40 km in the second hour and so on, then the bus is moving with a uniform speed of 40 km/h.

Variable speed: An object is said to be moving with a variable speed if it covers different distances in equal intervals of time.

For example, if a bus covers 45 km in the first hour and 40 km in the second hour, then the bus is moving with a variable speed.

Average Speed: Average speed of an object is the ratio of the total distance covered by the total time taken.

Example 35: If Praveen drives his car at a uniform speed of 55 km/h, then find the distance covered by him in 3 hour 15 minutes.

Solution: Given that speed of the car = 55 km/h

Time = 3 hour 15 minutes = 3 hours + 15 minutes

$$= 3 \text{ hours} + \frac{15}{60} \text{ hour} = 3 \text{ hours} + 0.25 \text{ hour} = 3.25 \text{ hours}$$

To find: Distance covered by Praveen in 3 hour 15 minutes

We know that Speed = $\frac{\text{Distance}}{\text{Time}}$

Hence, Distance = Speed × Time

$= 55 \times 3.25$

$= 178.75$ km

Therefore, Praveen covers 178.75 km in 3 hour 15 minutes.

Example 37: If a bike covers 120 km in 3 hours and 150 km in another 3 hours, then find the average speed of the bike.

Solution: Given that the bike covers 120 km in the first 3 hours and 150 km in another 3 hours.

Total distance covered = 120 km + 150 km = 270 km

Total time taken = 3 hours + 3 hours = 6 hours

Average speed = $\frac{\text{Total distance travelled}}{\text{Total time taken}}$

Hence, the average speed of the bike = $\frac{270}{6} = 45$ km/h

Exercise 7.4

1. **The speed 18 km/h is the same as 5 m/s. Using this result, answer the following questions:**
   a. Express the speeds 16.2 km/h, 45 km/h and 315 km/h in metres per second.
   b. Express the speeds 1.2 m/s, 35 m/s and 625 m/s in kilometres per hour.
2. **A train covers a distance of 10 km in 12 min. What is the speed of the train?**
3. **Karan rides a bike at a speed of 40 km/h. If his college is 900 m away from his home, find the time he takes to reach his college from home.**
4. **Find the distance covered by a man running at a speed of 5 m/s in one and a half minutes.**
5. **What is the distance covered by a bike racer in 5 min, if he rides at a speed of 90 km/h?**
6. **A train covers 14 km in 10 min. Find the time taken to cover the same distance, if the speed of the train is reduced by 4 km/h.**

7. Dilshad has travelled half of the 3.6 km distance to school when she realizes that she is getting late. At what speed must she cycle now to reach her school in another 5 min?
8. If Rohit can run 3 km in 15 minutes, then find the speed in km/h.
9. If Maya rides a car at a speed of 42 km/h, then find the time taken to reach a distance of 231 km.
10. If Abdul rides a bike at a speed of 55.5 km/h, then find the distance covered by him in 7 hours.
11. If a bus covers a certain distance at 50 km/h in 3 hours and comes back at 30 km/h and reached the initial position in 5 hours, then find the average speed of the bus.
12. A train travels at a uniform speed of 70 km/h. Find the distance covered by the train in 5 hour 30 minutes.
13. If Salman drives his car at a uniform speed and covers 220 km in 4 hours, then find the uniform speed.
14. In the first day of Kevin's riding, he covers 160 km in 5 hours and on the second day, he covers 130 km in 3 hours. Find the average speed of Kevin.

KEY CONCEPTS

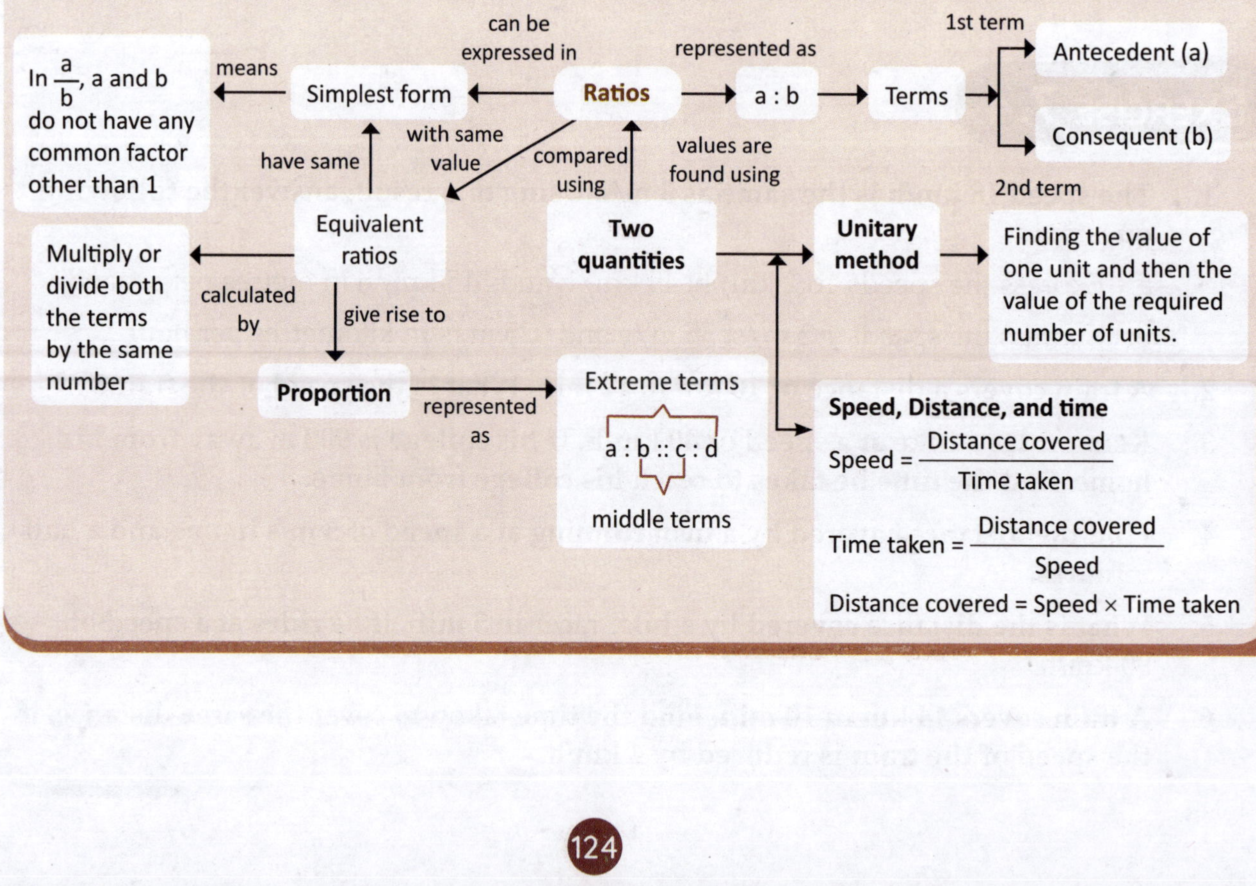

Revision Exercise

1. Choose the correct option.

a. In a box, there are 2 kg of fruits and 1 kg 600 g of vegetables. Find the ratio of vegetables to fruits.

i. 2 : 1,600 ii. 5 : 4 iii. 4 : 5 iv. 10 : 9

b. On simplifying the ratio $\frac{3}{5}:\frac{1}{2}$, we get ______.

i. 15 : 2 ii. 6 : 5 iii. 5 : 6 iv. 2 : 15

c. On converting the ratio 546: 378 to its simplest form, we get ______.

i. 13 : 9 ii. 14 : 9 iii. 9 : 13 iv. 9 : 14

d. If the weight of 15 books is 18.75 kg, then the weight of 25 books is ______.

i. 30.75 kg ii. 32.5 kg iii. 31.25 kg iv. 33.25 kg

e. If a car covers 476 km in 7 hours, then find the speed of the car.

i. 68 km/h ii. 72 km/h iii. 64 km/h iv. 78 km/h

2. State whether the following sentences are true (T) or false (F).

a. On converting 72 km/h into m/s, we get 25 m/s.

b. The quantities to be compared must be in the same unit.

c. The ratios 8:4 and 26:13 are in proportion.

d. The ratios 15: 17 and 85:75 are equivalent ratios.

e. If a car covers 272 km in 4 hours, then it covers 874 km in 13 hours.

3. Express each ratio in its simplest form.

a. 75 : 150 b. 37 : 47 c. 85 : 102

d. 425 : 750 e. 930 : 870

4. Which of the following sets of numbers are in proportion?

a. 5, 7, 15, 21 b. 5, 10, 16, 8 c. 16, 18, 8, 9

d. 24, 30, 10, 15 e. 45, 16, 25, 9

5. Complete the following table.

Speed	Distance	Time
	75 km	5 h
60 km/h		60 minutes
54 km/h	81,000 m	
	2.7 km	30 minutes
40 m/s		27 seconds
55 m/s	66 km	

6. **Express the following speeds in m/s.**

a. 32 km/h b. 90 km/h c. 162 km/h

d. 720 km/h e. 234 km/h

7. **Solve the following word problems.**

a. Two partners have invested in a business in the ratio 5 : 8. If they earn a profit of ₹1,04,000, then find the amount that each partner will receive as per their investment.

b. The ratio of the weights of two men is $\frac{1}{2} : \frac{1}{3}$. If the weight of the first person is $22\frac{1}{2}$ kg, then find the weight of the second person.

c. A certain type of basmati rice is available in 25 kg and 15 kg packs. If the 25 kg pack costs ₹1,250, then what will be the cost of the 15 kg pack?

d. Vikas is travelling in an auto at a speed of 54 km/h. How far will he go in 45 min?

e. A cab takes 50 min to reach the station if it travels at a speed of 54 km/h. What must be the speed of the cab to reach the station 10 min early?

f. Joseph jogs daily 5 times around a square park of width 90 m. At what speed should he jog if he wants to cover the entire distance in half an hour?

g. Mr Sharma sells a bag containing 12 kg of onions for ₹90, whereas Mr Verma sells a bag containing 15 kg of onions for ₹120. In whose shop are the onions cheaper and by how much?

h. The cost of 5 cups bought by Anil is ₹60 and the cost of 7 cups bought by Ankith is ₹84. Check if the cups and their cost are in proportion.

i. The distance travelled by Ashish is 210 km in a two-wheeler which consumed 7 litres of petrol and the distance travelled by him is 45 km in a car which consumed 3 litres of petrol. Check if the distance travelled and the fuel consumed are in proportion.

j. The quantity of sweets distributed by Aarav was 3 kg among 12 guests. Find the quantity of sweets distributed by Atharv among 16 guests if the quantity of sweets and guests are in proportion.

8 Percentage

Prior Knowledge

- Ratio and proportion
- Compare quantities
- Fraction
- Decimals
- Operations on fractions
- Decimals
- Operations on decimals

Learning Objectives

- Concept of percentage
- Express percentage as a fraction, decimal, and ratio and vice versa
- Find the given percentage of a quantity
- Express a quantity as a percentage of another quantity
- Express percentage as a measure of increase/decrease in a quantity
- Solve word problems based on percentage

Let's Get Started

Observe the pictures given below.

While going out for a shopping, you may see the posters like '70% Discount' or 'Sale Up to 90% off' etc. Also, while charging your smartphone, you may observe a notification like '50% completed'.

Similarly, while taking a loan from a bank, you may notice an interest rate of 5%, 10%, etc.

In all the above situations, we can see a symbol '%'.

What is this symbol called and what does it mean?

Let us learn more about this symbol in this chapter.

PERCENTAGE

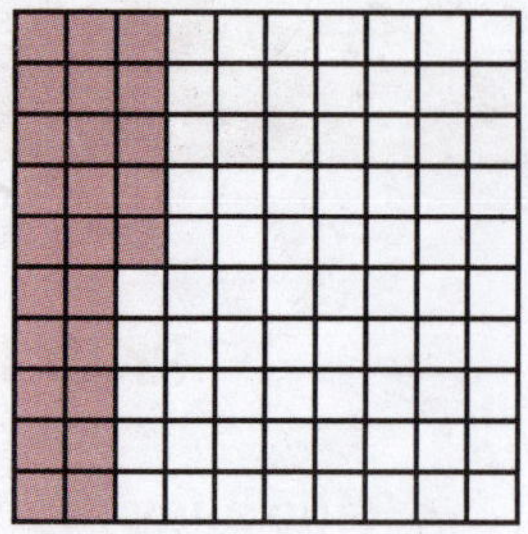

Percentage is a part of a whole that can be expressed as a fraction with denominator 100. It is denoted by the symbol %.

For example, 20% is 20 out of 100 or 20 hundredths and 5% is 5 out of 100 or 5 hundredths.

It means, $25\% = \frac{25}{100}$

Example 1: If out of 50 students in a class, 20 score more than 90 marks. Find the percentage of students, who scored more than 90 marks?

Solution: $\frac{\text{Number of students who scored more than 90 marks}}{\text{Total number of students}} = \frac{20}{50}$

Equivalent ratio of $\frac{20}{50}$ with 100 as the denominator $= \frac{20 \times 2}{50 \times 2} = \frac{40}{100}$

The numerator of equivalent ratio is 40.

So, the percentage of students who scored more than 90 marks = 40%

Conversion of Fraction Into Percentage

To convert a fraction (or decimal) into a percentage, multiply the fraction (or decimal) with 100 and write it with % symbol.

Similarly, to convert a percentage into a fraction (or decimal), divide the percentage by 100%, simplify and remove the % symbol.

Example 2: Convert the following fraction into percentage and percentage into fraction.

a. $\frac{1}{2}$ b. $\frac{13}{20}$ c. 40% d. 75%

Solution: a. To convert $\frac{1}{2}$ into percentage, multiply it with 100%.

That is, $\frac{1}{2} = \frac{1}{2} \times 100\ \% = 50\%$

b. To convert $\frac{13}{20}$ into fraction, multiply it with 100%.

We get $\frac{13}{20} = \frac{13}{20} \times 100\% = 65\%$

c. To convert 40% into percentage, divide by 100%.

We get $40\% = \frac{40}{100} = \frac{40 \div 20}{100 \div 20} = \frac{2}{5}$

d. To convert 75% into fraction, divide by 100%.

We get $75\% = \frac{75}{100} = \frac{75 \div 25}{100 \div 25} = \frac{3}{4}$

Conversion of Decimal Into Percentage

To convert a decimal into a percentage, multiply the decimal with 100 and write it with % symbol.

Similarly, to convert a percentage into a decimal, divide the percentage by 100%, simplify and remove the % symbol.

Example 3: Convert the following decimals into percentage and percentage into decimals.

a. 0.63 b. 0.015 c. 9% d. 125%

Solution: a. To convert 0.63 into percentage, multiply with 100%.

We get $0.63 = 0.63 \times 100\% = 63\%$

b. To convert 0.015 into percentage, multiply with 100%.

We get $0.015 = 0.015 \times 100\% = 1.5\%$

c. To convert 9% into decimal number, divide by 100%.

We get $9\% = \frac{9}{100} = 0.09$

d. To convert 125% into decimal number, divide by 100%.

We get $125\% = \frac{125}{100} = 1.25$

Conversion of Ratios to Percentages

We can convert a ratio to percentage in the same way as we convert a fraction.

$3:5 = \frac{3}{5} = 60\%$

Now, let's learn more about conversion of ratios to percentages.

Example 4: For making cookies, Rohini mixes the ingredients flour, sugar and baking powder in the ratio 3:2:1. What is the percentage of each ingredient in the mixture?

Solution: It is given that,

Flour: Sugar: Baking Powder = 3:2:1

Total parts of mixture = 3 + 2 + 1 = 6

Now, ratio of flour to total mixture = 3 : 6

Percentage of flour in the mixture $= \frac{3}{6} \times 100 = 50\%$

Similarly, we can find the percentage of sugar and baking powder in the mixture.

Percentage of sugar in mixture $= \frac{2}{6} \times 100 = 33.33\%$

Percentage of baking powder in the mixture $= \frac{1}{6} \times 100 = 16.66\%$

Conversion of Percentages into Ratios

To convert a percentage into a ratio, we divide the percentage by 100 and remove the % sign. Then, we simplify the resultant fraction and write it as a ratio.

Example 5: Express the following percentages as ratios:

a. 21% b. 1.5%

Solution: a. $21\% = \frac{21}{100} = 21:100$ b. $1.5\% = \frac{15}{1000} = \frac{3}{200} = 3 : 200$

EXERCISE 8.1

1. **Convert each of the following fractions into percentages.**

   a. $\frac{1}{4}$ b. $\frac{7}{10}$ c. $\frac{5}{8}$ d. $\frac{22}{25}$ e. $1\frac{17}{20}$

2. **Convert each of the following percentages into fractions.**

   a. 45% b. 132% c. 180% d. 95% e. 76%

3. **Convert each of the following decimals into percentages.**

   a. 0.06 b. 0.165 c. 2.35 d. 0.008 e. 0.6

4. **Convert each of the following percentages into decimals.**

   a. 105% b. 4% c. 0.1% d. 18% e. 60%

5. **Express the following ratios as percentages.**

   a. 4:10 b. 15:50 c. 130:200 d. 9:18 e. 45:180

ONE QUANTITY AS A PERCENTAGE OF ANOTHER QUANTITY

If a fruit seller sold 60 apples out of 200 apples, then to find the percentage of apples sold, we need to find what percent of 200 is 60.

That is, $\frac{60}{200} \times 100\% = 30\%$

Hence, the fruit seller sold 30% of the apples.

In general, to express one quantity x as a percentage of another quantity y,

- first write the fraction $\frac{x}{y}$
- then multiply that fraction with 100%

REMEMBER

Before expressing one quantity as a percentage of another, make sure that both the quantities are in the same unit.

Example 6: If Shalini scored 45 marks out of 50, then find the percentage of marks scored by Shalini.

Solution: Given that Shalini scored 45 marks out of 50 marks.

Fraction of marks scored $= \frac{45}{50} = \frac{9}{10}$

Percentage of marks scored $= \frac{9}{10} \times 100\% = 90\%$

Therefore, Shalini scored 90% marks.

Example 7: What percent of 2 m is 25 cm?

Solution: Here, both the quantities are in different units. On converting them into same units, we get 25 cm and 200 cm.

Hence, $\frac{25}{200} \times 100\% = 12.5\%$

Therefore, 25 cm is 12.5 % of 2 m.

FINDING PERCENTAGE OF A GIVEN QUANTITY

To find the percentage of a quantity, we need to follow the following steps:

- Convert the given percentage into fraction
- Multiply the fraction with the value of the quantity

Example 8: What is 52% of 6 kg? Express in grams.

Solution: We know that 1 kg = 1000 g

Hence, 6 kg = 6000 g

52% of 6 kg = $\frac{52}{100} \times 6000\ g = 3120$ g

Therefore, 52% of 6 kg is 3120 g.

Example 9: What is 40% of 1 hour?

Solution: 1 hour = 60 minutes

40% of 1 hour = $\frac{40}{100} \times 60 = 24$ minutes

Therefore, 40% of 1 hour is 24 minutes.

Example 10: If Arjun scored 78% in an exam conducted for 250 marks, then find the marks scored by Arjun.

Solution: Given: Total marks = 250

Percentage scored = 78%

Marks scored = $\frac{78}{100} \times 250 = 195$

Hence, Arjun scored 195 marks out of 250 marks.

INCREASE OR DECREASE PERCENT

Sometimes, we need to find the increase or decrease percentage of a given quantity. For example, if the cost of a book is increased from ₹40 to ₹60, then we can say the cost of the book is increased by 50%.

The following formula can be used to find the increase or decrease percent.

$$\text{Increase percentage} = \frac{\text{Increase in value}}{\text{Original value}} \times 100\%$$

$$\text{Decrease percentage} = \frac{\text{Decrease in value}}{\text{Original value}} \times 100\%$$

Example 11: The population of a village is 12,400. If the population of that village is reduced to 12,284, then what is the percentage decrease in the population?

Solution: Initial population of the village = 12,400

Decreased population = 12,284

Decrease in population = 116

Percentage decrease = $\frac{116}{12400} \times 100\% = 0.93\%$

Therefore, the population of the village is decreased by 0.93%.

Example 12: If the salary of an employee is increased from ₹40,250 to ₹51,520, then find the percentage increase in the salary.

Solution: Initial salary of the employee = ₹40,250

Final salary of the employee = ₹51,520

Increase in the salary of the employee = ₹11,270

Increase percentage = $\frac{11270}{40250} \times 100\% = 28\%$

Therefore, salary of the employee is increased by 28%.

Example 13: If the height of a plant increased from 3 m 60 cm to 5.85 m, then what is the percentage of increase in height?

Solution: Original height of the plant = 3 m 60 cm = 360 cm

Increased height of the plant = 5.85 m = 585 cm

Increase in height of the plant = 225 cm

Increased percentage = $\frac{225}{360} \times 100\% = 62.5\%$

Therefore, the height of the plant is increased by 62.5%.

EXERCISE 8.2

1. **What percent of 2 hours is 15 minutes?**
2. **What percent of 2 kg is 600 g?**
3. **What is 65% of 1 m 25 cm?**
4. **If Meera scored 81 marks out of 150 marks in an exam, then find the percentage of marks scored by Meera.**
5. **The monthly salary of Pooja is ₹28,500. If she saves 19% of her salary at the end of the month, then find the amount saved by Pooja.**
6. **If Diya scored 34% in an exam conducted for 150 marks and failed by 9 marks, then what is the passing marks of the exam?**
7. **If the cost of a television decreased from ₹21,850 to ₹19,228, then find the percentage decrease in the cost of television.**

8. If the salary of Aman increased from ₹34,250 to ₹39,730, then find the percentage increase in his salary.

9. In a class, the ratio of boys to girls is 4 : 5. What is the percentage of boys and girls in the class?

Key Concepts

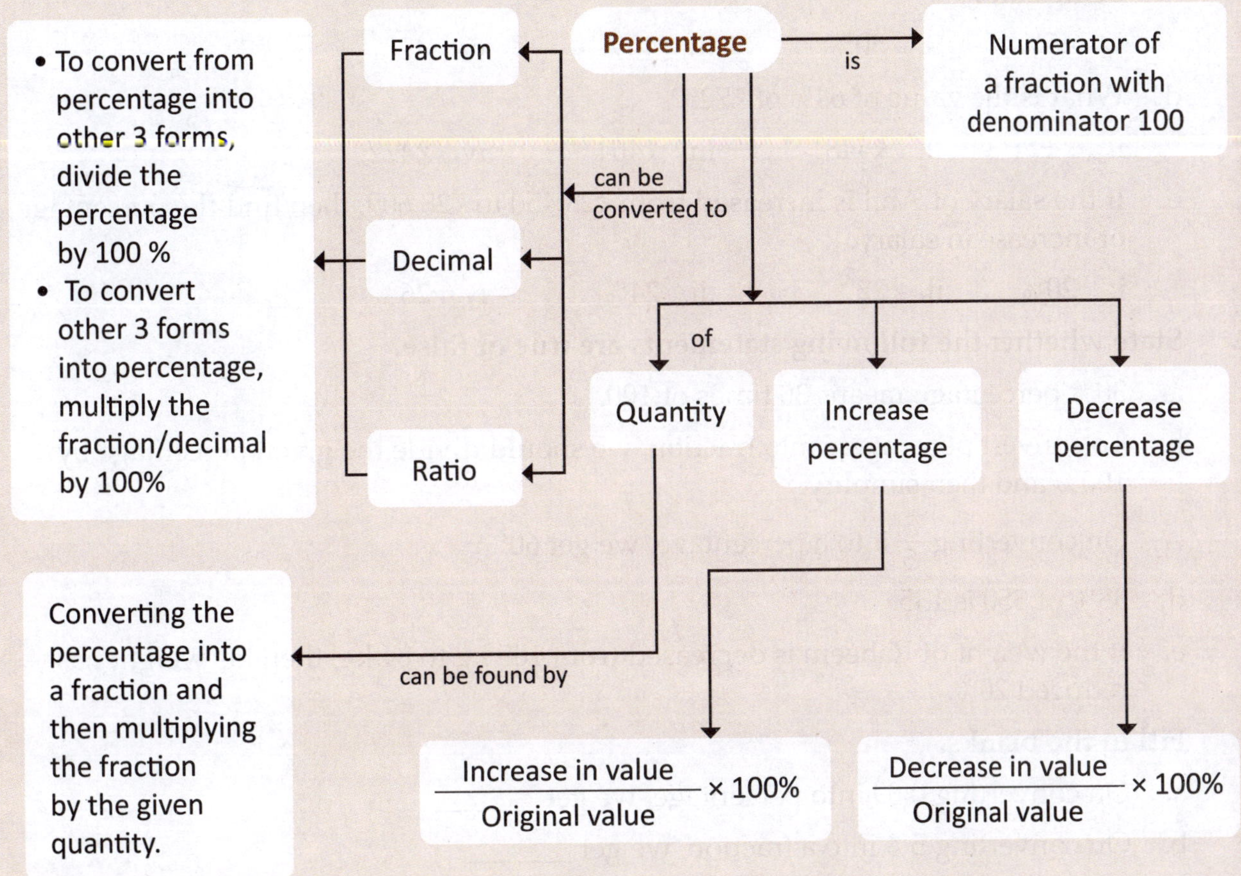

REVISION EXERCISE

1. **Choose the correct option.**

   a. On converting 35% into a decimal number, we get

   i. 3.5 ii. 0.35 iii. 0.035 iv. 35.0

   b. On converting $\frac{17}{20}$ into a percentage, we get

   i. 17% ii. 65% iii. 75% iv. 85%

   c. If a shopkeeper sold 18 kg out of 40 kg of fruits, then find the percentage of fruits being sold.

   i. 45% ii. 50% iii. 40% iv. 42%

   d. What is the value of 64% of ₹725?

   i. ₹424 ii. ₹448 iii. ₹464 iv. ₹472

   e. If the salary of Anil is increased from ₹23,450 to ₹28,609, then find the percentage of increase in salary.

   i. 20% ii. 22% iii. 24% iv. 26%

2. **State whether the following statements are true or false.**

   a. 30% percentage means 30 times of 100.

   b. To convert percentage into fraction, we should divide the given percentage by 100% and then simplify.

   c. On converting $\frac{3}{5}$ into a percentage, we get 60%.

   d. 38% of 350 is 135.

   e. If the weight of Raheem is decreased from 105 kg to 84 kg, then his weight has reduced 20%.

3. **Fill in the blanks.**

   a. On converting 0.09 into percentage, we get _______.

   b. On converting 5% into a fraction, we get _______.

   c. 36% of 1,050 km is _______ km.

   d. If the marks of a student increases from 75 to 87, then the increase in the percentage of marks is _______.

   e. On converting 65% into a fraction, we get _______.

4. **Answer the following questions.**

   a. Convert the following percentages into fractions and decimals.

   i. 45% ii. 60% iii. 8% iv. 115% v. 84%

   b. Convert the following decimals into percentages.

   i. 0.04 ii. 0.28 iii. 0.73 iv. 2.3 v. 1.05

c. Convert the following fractions into percentages.

i. $\frac{3}{8}$ ii. $\frac{7}{10}$ iii. $\frac{13}{25}$ iv. $\frac{19}{20}$ v. $\frac{4}{5}$

d. What percentage of 1 kg is 240 g?

e. Amar distributed 72 chocolates out of the 90 chocolates he had. Find the percentage of chocolates left with Amar.

f. The monthly expenditure of Aditya is 62%. If his monthly earnings amount to ₹37,650, then find his monthly expenditure and savings.

g. Ankita increased her weight from 36 kg to 45 kg. Find the increase in the percentage of weight.

h. If the monthly savings of Vikram is reduced from ₹7,650 to ₹7,038, then find the percentage of savings reduced.

i. Find the value of 25% of 50% of 12,600.

j. Out of 50 babies born in a hospital, 20 are boys and the rest are girls. What is the ratio of the number of girls to the total number of babies born in the hospital?

k. The population of rural people in a city went down from 50,000 to 40,000 in an year. What is the percentage decrease in rural population?

9 Introduction to Algebra

Prior Knowledge

- Number system
- Operations on numbers

Learning Objectives

- Introduction to variables and constants
- Generalising patterns
- Defining terminology associated with algebra
- Framing and evaluating algebraic expressions
- Substitution
- Operations on polynomials

Let's Get Started

Let us observe the pattern created by Divya using matchsticks.

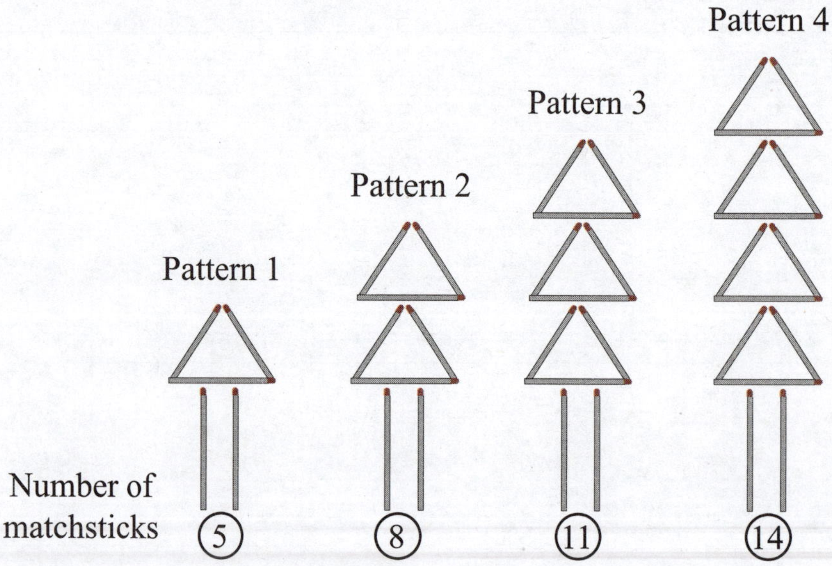

We can see that in the first pattern, she used 5 matchsticks, in the second, she used 8 matchsticks, then she used 11 matchsticks and lastly, she used 14 matchsticks.

Number of matchsticks required for the 5th pattern = ________.

Can you find the number of matchsticks required for the 25th pattern? What is it?

Yes, by writing a general rule using algebraic expressions for the pattern. Hence, we can find the unknowns for any number of patterns.

Let us learn more about algebraic expressions in this chapter.

INTRODUCTION TO VARIABLES AND CONSTANTS

In the previous question, we can see that the general rule followed in the patterns is $2 + 3k$, where k is the number of triangles.

Here k is the **variable** or **literal**. It does not have any fixed value. But 2 and 3 are **constants** as their value is fixed as two and three, respectively. The variable k can take any value, and the result will change accordingly.

k	$2 + 3k$
1	$5 = 2 + 3(1)$
2	$8 = 2 + 3(2)$
3	$11 = 2 + 3(3)$
4	$14 = 2 + 3(4)$

Example 1: Study the given pattern and complete the following table.

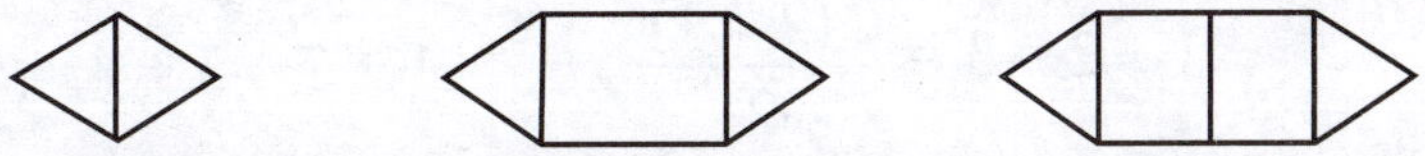

Shape 1 Shape 2 Shape 3

Shape number	1	2	3	4	5	6	9	12	15	20
Number of sticks	5	8	11							

Solution: The general rule for the given pattern is $3n + 2$, where n is the shape number.

The complete table for the given pattern is as follows:

Shape number	1	2	3	4	5	6	9	12	15	20
Number of sticks	5	8	11	14	17	20	29	38	47	62

GENERALISING PATTERNS

We have learnt about even and odd numbers in your previous grades. Let us see if we can write general statements for these numbers.

Look at the following tables of even and odd numbers.

Even Number	Pattern
2	$2 = 2 \times 1$
4	$4 = 2 \times 2$
6	$6 = 2 \times 3$
8	$8 = 2 \times 4$
⋮	⋮
	$2 \times n$; where n is a natural number

Odd Number	Pattern
1	$1 = 2(1) - 1$
3	$3 = 2(2) - 1$
5	$5 = 2(3) - 1$
7	$7 = 2(4) - 1$
⋮	⋮
	$2(\boldsymbol{n}) - 1$; where n is a natural number

We observe that an even number can be written as $\mathbf{2n}$ and an odd number can be written as $\mathbf{2n - 1}$.

Let us now look at a few number patterns and arrive at generalisations.

Pattern	Analysing the Pattern	Generalisation
4, 7, 10, 13, 16, . . .	$4 = 3(1) + 1$; $7 = 3(2) + 1$; $10 = 3(3) + 1$; $13 = 3(4) + 1$; $16 = 3(5) + 1$	$3k + 1$; where k is the number of terms
3, 8, 13, 18, 23, . . .	$3 = 5(1) - 2$; $8 = 5(2) - 2$; $13 = 5(3) - 2$; $18 = 5(4) - 2$; $23 = 5(5) - 2$	$5k - 2$; where k is the number of terms
$1 + 2 + 3 + 4 + \ldots + n$	$1 + 2 = 3 = \frac{2(2+1)}{2}$ $1 + 2 + 3 = 6 = \frac{3(3+1)}{2}$ $1 + 2 + 3 + 4 = 10 = \frac{4(4+1)}{2}$	$1 + 2 + 3 + 4 + \ldots + n = \frac{n(n+1)}{2}$; where n is the number of terms
$1 + 3 + 5 + 7 + \ldots + 2n - 1$	$1 + 3 = 4 = 2^2$ $1 + 3 + 5 = 9 = 3^2$ $1 + 3 + 5 + 7 = 16 = 4^2$	$1 + 3 + 5 + 7 + \ldots 2n - 1 = n^2$; where n is the number of terms

OPERATIONS IN ALGEBRA

Similar to numbers, different arithmetic operations can also be done with the combination of variables and numbers. The table below shows the four basic operations with numbers and the variable p.

Operation	Example	Statement
Addition	25 is added to p to get 30.	$25 + p = 30$
Subtraction	10 is subtracted from p to get 3.	$p - 10 = 3$
Multiplication	15 is multiplied by p to get 60.	$15p = 60$
Division	p is divided by 2 to get 9.	$\frac{p}{2} = 9$

The variable p represents different values in each of the above statements.

REMEMBER

The value of any non-zero number or variable raised to the power zero is always 1. For example, $y^0 = 1$, $x^0 y^0 = 1 \times 1 = 1$.

Power of a Variable

If a variable x is multiplied five times by itself, then it is written as

$x \times x \times x \times x \times x = x^5$ (read as x to the power 5)

Similarly,

$y \times y \times y = y^3$ (y to the power 3)

$a \times a \times a \times a = a^4$ (a to the power 4)

Here, x, y and a are bases and 5, 3 and 4 are called **exponents** or **powers**.

Now, let us look at some properties that are true for operations with variables.

Let a, b and c be any three variables.

Properties	Addition	Multiplication
Commutative property	$a + b = b + a$	$a \times b = b \times a$
Associative property	$a + (b + c) = (a + b) + c$	$a \times (b \times c) = (a \times b) \times c$
Additive/multiplicative identity	$a + 0 = 0 + a = a$	$a \times 1 = 1 \times a = a$
Distributive Property of Multiplication over Addition	$a \times (b + c) = (a \times b) + (a \times c)$	

Example 2: Rahman is 6 years older than his sister Sameera. Find an expression for Rahman's age in terms of Sameera's age.

Solution: Rahman's age is 6 years more than Sameera's age.

Let Sameera's age be p years.

Then, Rahman's age = $(p + 6)$ years

Example 3: An egg tray contains six eggs. Two egg trays contain 12 eggs. Three egg trays contain 18 eggs. How many eggs will be there in m number of trays?

Solution: Number of eggs in 1 tray = 6×1

Number of eggs in 2 trays = $12 = 6 \times 2$

Number of eggs in 3 trays = $18 = 6 \times 3$

We observe that number of eggs is equal to $6 \times$ number of trays.

Let m be the number of trays.

Therefore, number of eggs in m trays = $6 \times m = 6m$

The total number of eggs in m trays is equal to $6m$ and can take the value of 1, 2, 3, 4, 5, 6, ...

Example 4: There are 30 apples in a basket. How many apples will each child get, if the apples are shared equallly among the following?

a. 3 children b. 10 children c. n children

Solution: Total number of apples = 30. If apples are shared equally among:

a. 3 children

Then, each child will get $= \frac{30}{3} = 10$ apples

b. 10 children

Then each child will get $= \frac{30}{10} = 3$ apples

c. n children

Then each child will get $= \frac{30}{n}$ apples

EXERCISE 9.1

1. **Identify the rule and find the next term in the following patterns. Also, write the rule for the nth term of the pattern.**

a.

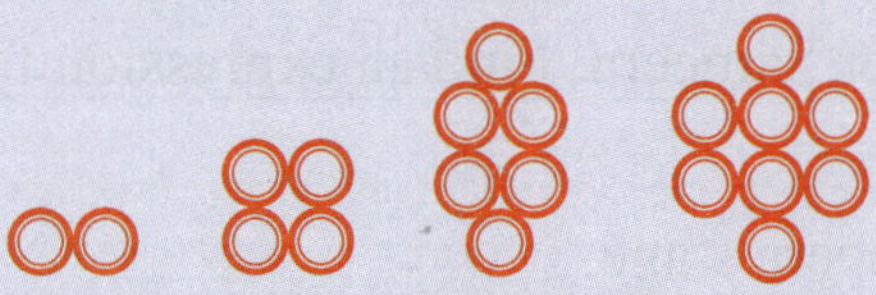

b.

2. **Answer the following questions.**
   a. A cheetah can run 29 metres per second. How much distance can it cover in t seconds?
   b. The cost of one *laddoo* is ₹12. What will be the cost of n *laddoos*?
   c. If there are 7 marbles in one box, find the number of marbles in 't' such boxes.
   d. Rahul can type 42 words in a minute. How many words can he type in 'l' minutes?
3. **Identify the variables and the constants in the following algebraic statements.**
   a. $5 - 6x$ b. $2 + m$ c. 100 d. $56l$ e. $39b$
4. **Find the rule of the following number pattern and then find its 15th term.**

   2, 4, 6, 8, 10
5. **Radha has p marbles. The number of marbles Sarita has is 10 times the number of marbles that Radha has. How many marbles does Sarita have?**
6. **A number is 6 times another number. If you write x as the smaller number, how will you write the larger number?**
7. **Mohan works for 2 hours less than John everyday. If John works for y hours, how many hours does Mohan work?**

USE OF VARIABLES IN WRITING FORMULAE

In geometry, variables are used in writing rules to find the perimeter and area of certain shapes.

Perimeter of a square: Let p be the perimeter of a square.

We know that the perimeter of a square = 4 × length of its side.

Let ℓ be the length of the side.

Therefore, $p = 4\ell$ gives the rule to find the perimeter of a square.

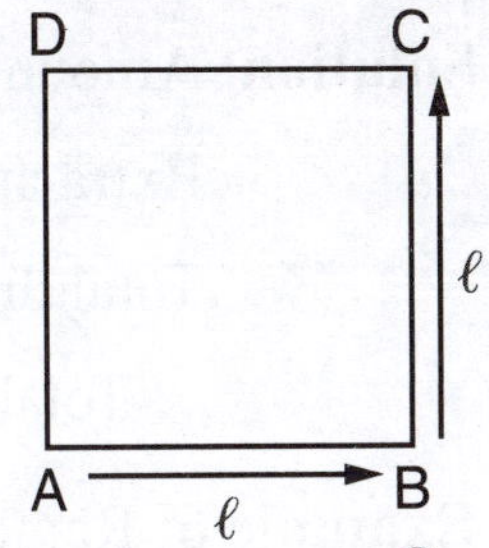

Area of a rectangle: Let A be the area of a rectangle.

We know that the area of a rectangle = length × breadth.

Let the length of the rectangle be ℓ and the breadth be b.

Then, the area of the rectangle = $\ell \times b$

Therefore, $A = \ell \times b$ gives the rule to find the area of a rectangle.

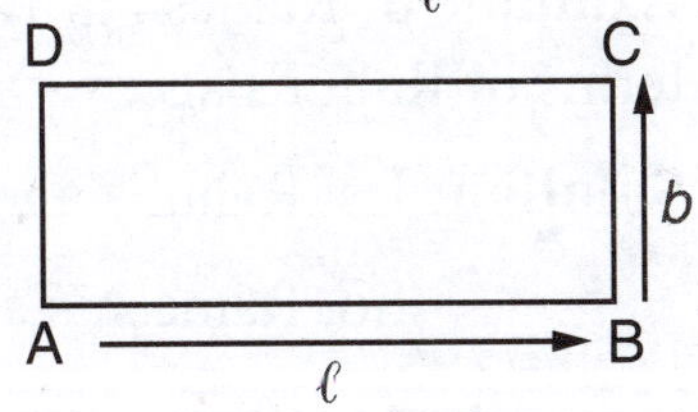

ALGEBRAIC EXPRESSIONS

Observe the following T-patterns formed with matchsticks.

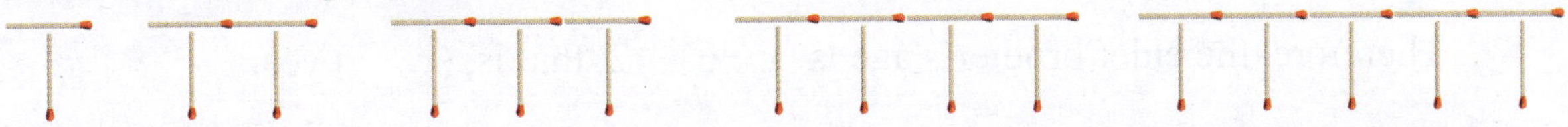

Here the number of matchsticks required is twice the number of shapes that are formed. It means, if $\boldsymbol{n}$ is the number of shapes formed, then the number of matchsticks required is $\mathbf{2 \times n}$.

Expressions like $2n$ and $2n + 2$ are algebraic expressions.

An **algebraic expression** is an expression that consists of variable(s) and constant(s) connected by arithmetic operators +, –, × and ÷. In the algebraic expression $2n + 2$, n is a variable, 2 is a constant and the arithmetic operations are multiplication and addition.

Let us understand how to frame an algebraic expression for a given situation.

25 subtracted from x	$x - 25$
Product of 3 and p added to 11	$11 + 3p$
17 reduced by $2x$	$17 - 2x$
$56m$ divided by 11 is increased by 6	$\frac{56m}{11} + 6$

Conversely, algebraic expression can be written in the form of statement forms too.

$2p - 15$	15 less than the product of 2 and p
$11 + 3p$	11 is added to the product of 3 and p
$17 - 2x$	$2x$ subtracted from 17
$\frac{x}{3} + 17$	one-third of x is increased by 17

Example 5: A taxi driver charges ₹20 for 1 km journey. He charges ₹2 extra for every additional kilometre journey. What will be the algebraic expression for the amount that Akhila would pay if she travelled p km?

Solution: Amount charged by the taxi driver for 1 km journey = ₹20

Extra amount charged per km = ₹2

Total distance travelled by Akhila = p

$\therefore$ Total amount to be paid by Akhila is $20 + 2(p - 1)$.

Example 6: Ramesh is 10 years younger than Rahul. Find an expression for Ramesh's age in terms of Rahul's age.

Solution: Let Rahul's age be x years. Ramesh's age is 10 years less than Rahul's age.

So, Ramesh's age is $x - 10$.

Example 7: The age of two brothers can be represented as consecutive odd integers. If the younger brother's age is $(x + 3)$ years, represent the age of the elder brother in terms of x.

Solution: Given that the age of two brothers are consecutive odd integers.

Younger brother's age is $(x + 3)$ years.

Therefore, the elder brother's age is $(x + 3) + 2$, that is, $(x + 5)$ years.

Exercise 9.2

1. **Write the algebraic expressions for the following statements.**
   a. 7 added to the product of 5 and x
   b. 13 added to the product of x and 4
   c. 10 times a number taken away from 7
   d. Half of the sum of $2x$ and $2y$
   e. A number t decreased by 3
   f. 4 divided by a
2. **Write the statements for the following algebraic expressions.**
   a. $25p + 10 = 60$
   b. $16m \div 2 = 24$
   c. $10x + 7y - 15$
   d. $100 - 15y$
   e. $11x + 5 = 27$
3. **Answer the following questions.**
   a. The length of the side of a regular heptagon is denoted by l. Express the perimeter p of the heptagon in terms of l.

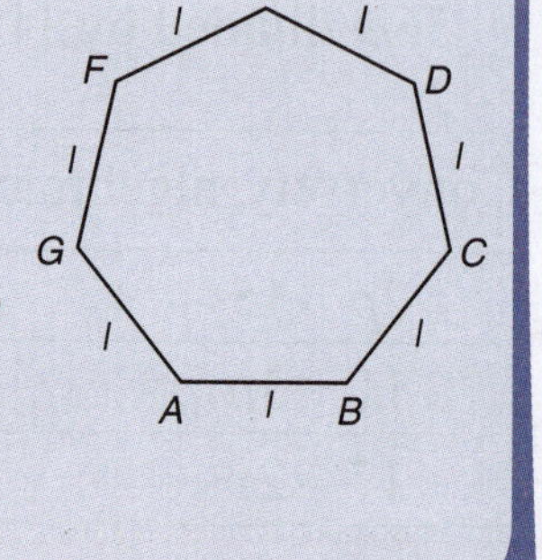

   b. Find the perimeter of a rectangle whose length and breadth are given as l and b, respectively.
   c. Find the perimeter of an equilateral triangle where each side is equal to s units.
   d. Express the perimeter of a regular hexagon using variables.

4. **Write the algebraic expressions representing the following situations.**

a. Reshmi earns ₹500 a day working at a supermarket. How much money will she earn in p days?

b. A hotel manager has to distribute ₹10,000 equally among the workers of the hotel as bonus. How much money will each worker get if there are k workers?

c. The length of a rectangle is 3 units more than twice its breadth. What is the perimeter of the rectangle?

d. The cost of apples is ₹100 per kg and the cost of oranges is ₹60 per kg. Find the total cost of p kg apples and q kg oranges.

e. The cost of an entry ticket to an exhibition is ₹25 for children and ₹50 for adults. Write an algebraic expression to find the total entry fee for x children and y adults.

f. An airplane goes 10 km in a minute. At the same speed, find the distance it covers in x minutes.

TERMS IN AN ALGEBRAIC EXPRESSION

Terms

The terms of an algebraic expression are the parts of the expression that are connected by '+' or '–' signs.

$$\underbrace{3x}_{\text{Term 1}} + \underbrace{4y}_{\text{Term 2}} + \underbrace{12}_{\text{Term 3}}$$

The above expression contains $3x$, $4y$ and 12 connected with '+' sign.

These are called **terms** of an algebraic expression.

Factors

When the numbers and variables are multiplied to form a term, then each quantity multiplied is called a **factor** of the term.

A constant factor is called the **numerical** factor, and the variable factor is called the **literal** factor.

$$6xy = 6 \times x \times y$$

Numerical factor ← 6; Literal factor → x, y

Example 8: Find the terms and factors of the expression: $6p - 4s$.

Solution:

Terms	Factors	Numerical Factor	Literal Factor
$6p$	$6, p$	6	p
$-4s$	$-4, s$	-4	s

Coefficients

A factor of a term is called the **coefficient** of the product of the remaining factors. Like factors, coefficients are also numerical and literal.

$$2ab = 2 \times a \times b$$

Numerical Coefficient ← 2 ; $a \times b$ → Literal Coefficient

Here, number of terms = 1

Coefficient of $a = 2b$; Coefficient of $b = 2a$; Coefficient of $ab = 2$

Like and Unlike Terms

Two or more terms with identical variables with powers are called **like terms**.

Two or more terms that are not like are called **unlike terms.**

For example,

Like Terms	Unlike Terms
$3x^2, -x^2$	$2x^2, 3y$
$ab, 3ab, -ab$	$a^2b, ab, -ab^2$
$xyz, -2xyz, 3xyz$	$2xy, -yz, 3zx$

TYPES OF ALGEBRAIC EXPRESSIONS

Consider the algebraic expressions $-6x$, $x + 2$ and $x + 7 + 4x^2$.

The first expression has one term, the second expression has two terms and the third expression has three terms. Based on the number of terms, algebraic expressions are classified as follows.

A **monomial** is an algebraic expression that has one term. For example, $2x$ and $5z$

A **binomial** is an algebraic expression that has two terms. For example, $2x + 1$ and $6d + 8$

A **trinomial** is an algebraic expression that has three terms. For example, $2x^2 + x + 1$ and $2x^2 + \frac{x}{y} + 1$

A polynomial is an algebraic expression with one or more terms. In a polynomial, the power of the variable cannot be negative or fractional.

In general, monomials, binomials, trinomials, etc. fall under the category of polynomials.

DEGREE OF ALGEBRAIC EXPRESSIONS

Degree of the term is the sum of the exponents of all the variables present in the term. For example, the degree of the term $7x^2y$ is 3.

Degree of an algebraic expression is the highest of all the degrees of the terms of that algebraic expression.

REMEMBER

A polynomial of degree 0 is called a constant. For example, –5 and 12

Let us understand with the help of following table.

Algebraic Expression	Degree of Each Term		Degree of the Algebraic Expression (Highest Degree)
$4x^2 + 5xy + 12x$	$4x^2$	2	2
	$5xy$	2	
	$12x$	1	
$3a^3bc + 2a^2b + 6abc$	$3a^3bc$	5	5
	$2a^2b$	3	
	$6abc$	3	

Exercise 9.3

1. **Identify the different terms (variable terms and constant terms) in the following algebraic expressions. Also identify the numerical coefficient and the power of the variable (exponent) in each term.**

   a. $-25x^3 + 2x^2 + x$ b. $4a^3b^2 - 2b^2 + 3a - 4$ c. $52z^2 + 19zx$

   d. $6x^4 + 4x^5 + 20x^3 - 6x^2 + 2$ e. $2l^3 + 24$ f. $(a + 4b + 5) \div 2$

2. **Identify the like terms in the following algebraic expressions.**

   a. $10p^2q - 4pq^2 + 12q^2p - 6qp^2$

   b. $5a - 8a + 12a^2 + 9a - 10a^2$

   c. $2x^2y^3 + 5x^3y^2 - 10x^3y^2 + 11x^3y^3 - 3x^2y^3$

   d. $24y^{10} + y^6 - 4y^{10} + 4y^2 + 7y^2 - 26y^6$

   e. $4yx + 5xy + 3xyz + 7z - 3z$

3. **Give reasons why the following groups of terms are unlike.**

   a. $-5x^3, 5x^2, 2x$ b. $2a, 2b, 2c$ c. $14m^3, 5m^2n, 10$

   d. $12p^2q, 11pq^2$ e. $4x, 5xy, 3xyz, 7$

4. **Classify the following algebraic expressions based on the number of terms.**

   a. $42b$ b. $0.5x^2$ c. $2p^2 + 2q^2$ d. $a^2 + 2ab + b^2$

   e. $4y^{10} + 6y^3x + 72y^3 + 20$ f. $12abc$ g. $24x^2 + 12y^2$

5. **State the degree of the following polynomials.**

   a. $2x + 1$ b. 5 c. 2

   d. $24x^2 + 12y^2$ e. $2xy + 5x + 1$

SUBSTITUTION

Monika wants to book a cab for sightseeing in Jaipur. She got the following information about the tariff.

Minimum distance to be travelled (in km)	Charge for distance up to 10 km (in ₹)	Charges per additional km (in ₹)	Driver charges for any trip (in ₹)
10	100	15	75

Let us write an expression to calculate the cab bill based on the number of kilometres travelled. Let the total distance travelled by Monika be x km.

Then, the amount to be paid is given by $100 + (x - 10)15 + 75 = 25 + 15x$

If she travels 15 km, then the bill would be $25 + 15(15) =$ ₹250.

If she travels 20 km, then the bill would be $25 + 15(20) =$ ₹325.

Example 9: Find the values of the following algebraic expressions for the given values of the variables.

a. $25x + 15y$ when $x = 2$ and $y = 3$ b. $(2m^2n) \div 4mn$ when $m = 4$ and $n = 2$

Solution: a. Substituting the values of x and y in the algebraic expression $25x + 15y$, we get

$25(2) + 15(3) = 50 + 45 = 95$

b. Substituting the values of m and n in the algebraic expression $(2m^2n) \div 4mn$, we get

$[2 \times (4)^2 \times 2] \div [4 \times (4) \times (2)] = 64 \div 32 = 2$

EXERCISE 9.4

1. **Find the values of the following algebraic expressions for the given values of the variables.**

   a. $2 + 3a + 6 - 7b$ when $a = -1$ and $b = 6$ b. $3(2x + 9)$ when $x = 10$

   c. $2xy + 6x - 9y$ when $x = -1$ and $y = 2$ d. $\frac{1}{x^2} \times 125 \times \frac{y}{125} \times 0$ when $x = 5$ and $y = -4$

2. **Evaluate each of the following expressions using the given values of the variables.**

   a. $-5p^3 + 2p^2 + p$ when $p = 6$

   b. $52z^2 + 19zq$ when $z = 3$ and $q = 2$

   c. $4a^3b^2 - 2b^2 + 3a - 4$ when $a = 4$ and $b = 3$

   d. $\frac{25 + x^2 + 5x}{5}$ when $x = 5$

3. **What is the value of the algebraic expression $10 + \frac{64}{x^2} + 6x$ when $x = 2, 4, 8$ and 11?**

4. **Find the value of algebraic expression $x^2 + xy + z$ when $x = 3, y = 4$ and $z = 6$.**

FUNDAMENTAL OPERATIONS

In addition and subtraction of like terms, we follow the same rule as we follow for addition and subtraction of integers. Let us see how to add or subtract like terms.

Addition of like terms: To add like terms, we should follow the following steps:

- If all the terms are positive, then add the coefficients of variables and keep the variables unchanged with a positive sign.
- If all the terms are negative, then add the coefficients of variables by neglecting the sign and keep the variables unchanged with a negative sign.
- If one term is positive and another is negative, then ignoring the signs, subtract the smaller coefficient from the larger coefficient and keep the variable unchanged with the sign of the larger coefficient.

Subtraction of like terms: In the subtraction of a like term from another like term, we always get a like term.

Addition or Subtraction of unlike terms: On adding or subtracting like terms, we get a single like term, but we cannot add or subtract two unlike terms together to get a single term.

Example 10: Add the following terms.

a. $2x$ and $6x$ b. $-5ab$ and $-12ab$ c. ax and $-5ax$

d. $4yz^3x^2$, $-7x^2yz^3$ and $11yx^2z^3$ e. $2a^2b$, $-5ba^2$, $9ba^2$ and $-6a^2b$

Solution: a. $2x$ and $6x$

$2x + 6x = (2 + 6)\,x = 8x$

b. $-5ab$ and $-12ab$

$-5ab + (-12ab) = (-5 - 12)\,ab$

$= -17ab$

c. ax and $-5ax$

$ax + (-5ax) = (1 - 5)\,ax = -4ax$

d. $4yz^3x^2$, $-7x^2yz^3$ and $11yx^2z^3$

$= (4yz^3x^2 + 11yx^2z^3) + (-7x^2yz^3)$

$= 15x^2yz^3 - 7x^2yz^3$

$= 8x^2yz^3$

e. $2a^2b$, $-5ba^2$, $9ba^2$ and $-6a^2b$

$(2a^2b + 9ba^2) + \{-5ba^2 + (-6a^2b)\}$

$= 11a^2b + (-11a^2b) = 0$

Example 11: Subtract the first term from the second term.

a. $12xy$ and $23xy$ b. $-x^2y^3$ and $-4y^3x^2$ c. $-7a$ and $5a$

d. $27a^2bc$ and $-15ca^2b$ e. $-12xy^2$ and y^2x

Solution: a. $12xy$ and $23xy$

$23xy - 12xy = 11xy$

b. $-x^2y^3$ and $-4y^3x^2$

$-4y^3x^2 - (-x^2y^3) = -4y^3x^2 + x^2y^3$

$= -3y^3x^2$

c. $-7a$ and $5a$

$5a - (-7a) = 5a + 7a = 12a$

d. $27a^2bc$ and $-15ca^2b$

$-15ca^2b - 27a^2bc = -42a^2bc$

e. $-12xy^2$ and y^2x

$y^2x - (-12xy^2) = y^2x + 12xy^2$

$= 13xy^2$

OPERATIONS ON POLYNOMIALS

Addition of polynomials: In addition, add the like terms separately and then write the result in the simplest form.

Row Method: To add the polynomials by row method, first write the polynomials in a row and group the like terms and add.

Example: Add $2a + b + c$ and $a + 5b - c$

$$\begin{aligned}(2a + b + c) + (a + 5b - c) &= (2a + a) + (b + 5b) + (c - c)\\ &= 3a + 6b + 0 = 3a + 6b\end{aligned}$$

Column Method: To add the polynomials using column method, write the given polynomials in a column in such a way that like terms are placed one below the other in vertical column.

Example: Add $3x + 2y + 4z$ and $2y + 2x + z$

$$\begin{array}{r} 3x + 2y + 4z \\ +\ 2x + 2y + \ \ z \\ \hline 5x + 4y + 5z \end{array}$$

Example 12: Find the sum of the following expressions using row method.

a. $3a + 5c - 2ab$, $3ca - 4b + 2c$ and $6bc + a - 3b$

b. $2xy^2 + yx^2 - 3x^2y^2$, $5x^2y - 4y^2x + 2x^2y^2$ and $xy - x^2y^2 - 2xy^2 + x^2y$

Solution:

a. $(3a + 5c - 2ab) + (3ca - 4b + 2c) + (6bc + a - 3b)$

$= (3a + a) + (5c + 2c) + (-4b - 3b) + (-2ab + 3ca + 6bc)$

$= 4a + 7c - 7b - 2ab + 3ca + 6bc$

b. $(2xy^2 + yx^2 - 3x^2y^2) + (5x^2y - 4y^2x + 2x^2y^2) + (xy - x^2y^2 - 2xy^2 + x^2y)$

$= (2xy^2 - 4y^2x - 2xy^2) + (yx^2 + 5x^2y + x^2y) + (-3x^2y^2 + 2x^2y^2 - x^2y^2) + xy$

$= (2xy^2 - 6y^2x) + 7x^2y + (-4x^2y^2 + 2x^2y^2) + xy$

$= -4y^2x + 7x^2y - 2x^2y^2 + xy$

Example 13: Find the sum of the following using column method.

a. $4x^3 - 7x^2 + 9x + 15$, $10x^3 - 6x - 20$ and $8x^2 + 3x + 3$

b. $2a^2 + 5ab^2 - 3a^2b$, $ab^2 + 2a^2b - b^2$ and $5a^2 + 6b^2 - 7ab^2$

Solution:

a.
$$\begin{array}{r} 4x^3 - 7x^2 + 9x + 15 \\ 10x^3 + 0 - 6x - 20 \\ +\ \ 0 + 8x^2 + 3x + 3 \\ \hline 14x^3 + x^2 + 6x - 2 \end{array}$$

b.
$$\begin{array}{r} 2a^2 + 5ab^2 - 3a^2b \qquad \\ 0\ +\ ab^2 + 2a^2b - b^2 \\ +\,5a^2 - 7ab^2 + \ 0\ + 6b^2 \\ \hline 7a^2 - ab^2 - a^2b + 5b^2 \end{array}$$

Subtraction of Polynomials: To subtract polynomials, follow the methods used in the addition of polynomials.

Row method: First, write the expression to be subtracted in brackets with a minus sign before the bracket and then remove the brackets by changing the sign of each term inside the bracket and then add or subtract the like terms.

Example: Subtract $5x - 4y + 3z$ from $9x + 5y - 2z$

$$(9x + 5y - 2z) - (5x - 4y + 3z) = 9x + 5y - 2z - 5x + 4y - 3z$$
$$= (9x - 5x) + (5y + 4y) + (-2z - 3z)$$
$$= 4x + 9y - 5z$$

Column Method: Write the polynomials one below the other such that the lower polynomial is the polynomial to be subtracted and then change the sign of each term of the polynomial to be subtracted and then add column-wise.

Example: Subtract $2a + 5b - 4c$ from $3c - 4b + 5a$

$$\begin{array}{l} 5a - 4b + 3c \\ 2a + 5b - 4c \\ - \quad - \quad + \\ \hline 3a - 9b + 7c \end{array}$$

Example 14: From the sum of $6x^2 - 5y^2 + 2z^2$ and $3y^2 - 2x^2 + 5z^2$, subtract $y^2 - 2z^2 + 3x^2$.

Solution: $(6x^2 - 5y^2 + 2z^2) + (3y^2 - 2x^2 + 5z^2) - (y^2 - 2z^2 + 3x^2)$

$= 6x^2 - 5y^2 + 2z^2 + 3y^2 - 2x^2 + 5z^2 - y^2 + 2z^2 - 3x^2$

$= (6x^2 - 2x^2 - 3x^2) + (3y^2 - 5y^2 - y^2) + (2z^2 + 5z^2 + 2z^2)$

$= x^2 - 3y^2 + 9z^2$

Example 15: Subtract $-4a^2 + 6a + 3$ from $6a^2 - 8a + 5$ by using column method.

Solution:

$$\begin{array}{l} 6a^2 - 8a + 5 \\ -4a^2 + 6a + 3 \\ + \quad - \quad - \\ \hline 10a^2 - 14a + 2 \end{array}$$

Example 16: Evaluate the following.

a. $3x^2y^3 - 6x^2y - 5x^2y^3 - 9x^2y$ b. $3ab - 5cb + 2ca - 7bc - ba + 6ac$

Solution:

a. $3x^2y^3 - 6x^2y - 5x^2y^3 - 9x^2y$

$= (3x^2y^3 - 5x^2y^3) + (-6x^2y - 9x^2y)$

$= (-2x^2y^3) + (-15x^2y)$

$= -2x^2y^3 - 15x^2y$

b. $3ab - 5cb + 2ca - 7bc - ba + 6ac$

$= (3ab - ba) + (-5cb - 7bc) + (2ca + 6ac)$

$= 2ab - 12bc + 8ac$

Multiplication of Polynomials

- **Multiplication of Monomials** = (Product of their coefficients) × (Product of their literals)

Example 18: Multiply $6a^2b^3$, $5ab^2$ and $4a^3b^2$

Solution: $6a^2b^3 \times 5ab^2 \times 4a^3b^2$

= (Product of their coefficients) × (Product of their literals)

$= (6 \times 5 \times 4) \times (a^2 \times a \times a^3) \times (b^3 \times b^2 \times b^2)$

$= 120 \times a^6 \times b^7$

$= 120a^6b^7$

- **Multiplication of a polynomial and a monomial:** Multiply each term of the polynomial by a monomial.

Example 19: Multiply $3x^2yz^3 - 4xy^2 - 5y^2z$ by xyz

Solution: $(3x^2yz^3 - 4xy^2 - 5y^2z) \times xyz$

$= (3x^2yz^3 \times xyz) - (4xy^2 \times xyz) - (5y^2z \times xyz)$

$= 3x^3y^2z^4 - 4x^2y^3z - 5xy^3z^2$

Example 20: Multiply $(4a^2 + 3b^3)$ and $5b^2$

Solution: $(4a^2 + 3b^3) \times 5b^2 = 4a^2 \times 5b^2 + 3b^3 \times 5b^2$

$= 20 \times a^2 \times b^2 + 15 \times b^3 \times b^2$

$= 20a^2b^2 + 15b^5$

REMEMBER

1. In multiplication, the powers of like terms are added.
   We know that $a^m \times a^n = a^{m+n}$
2. In division, use the quotient law: $a^m \div a^n = a^{m-n}$

Division of Polynomial

Division of a monomial by a monomial: To divide a monomial by a monomial, write both the terms in an expanded form and then cancel the common terms.

Example 21: Divide $42x^3y^5$ by $6x^2y^3$

Solution: $42x^3y^5 \div 6x^2y^3 = \dfrac{42x^3y^5}{6x^2y^3} = \dfrac{7 \times 6 \times x^2 \times x \times y^2 \times y^3}{6 \times x^2 \times y^3}$

$= 7xy^2$

Division of a polynomial by a monomial: Divide each term of the polynomial by the given monomial to find the quotient.

Example 22: Divide $18x^3 - 24x^5 - 30x^2 + 12x^2$ by $6x^2$

Solution: $18x^3 - 24x^5 - 30x^2 + 12x^2 \div 6x^2$

$= \dfrac{18x^3 - 24x^5 - 30x^2 + 12x^2}{6x^2}$

$= (\dfrac{18x^3}{6x^2}) + (\dfrac{-24x^5}{6x^2}) + (\dfrac{-30x^2}{6x^2}) + (\dfrac{12x^2}{6x^2})$

$= 3x - 4x^3 - 5 + 2$

$= 3x - 4x^3 - 3$

Exercise 9.5

1. **Add the following terms.**

   a. $5ab + 3b - 2a^2$, $2b^2 - 3ab - 5a$ and $2a + 4b + a^2 + b^2$

   b. $4a^2 - 5b^2 + 4ab - 6$ and $3a^2 - 7ab - 3 + b^2$

   c. $19y^2 - 15x^2 - 5xy$, $12x^2 - 7y^2 + 9xy$ and $11x^2 - 4y^2 - 5xy$

2. **Subtract the following terms.**

   a. $6x + 5y - 4z$ from $7x - 4y + 3z$

   b. $4ab + 2cd - 2ac - 4bd$ from $2ab + 4cd + 4ac + 2bd$

   c. $a^4 - 2b^3 + 2a$ from $2b^3 + 4a^4 - 6b - 4a$

3. **Multiply the following.**

   a. $-6x^2yz^3$, xy^3z and $2xyz$

   b. $(3xy^2 - 2yx^2)$ by $4xy$

   c. $(3a - 5b)$ by $3ab$

   d. $(5xy - 6x^2y - 7xy^2)$ by $-3x$

   e. $(12a - 15ab - 9c)$ by $2a$

4. **Divide the following.**

   a. $21a^5b^2$ by $3a^3b^2$

   b. $45x^7y^3$ by $(-9x^4y^3)$

   c. $(18a^3 + 24a^2 - 33a^4)$ by $3a^2$

   d. $(-21m^2 + 7m^3 - 49m^4)$ by $7m$

   e. $(35p^3 - 15p^5 - 65p^2)$ by $5p^2$

KEY CONCEPTS

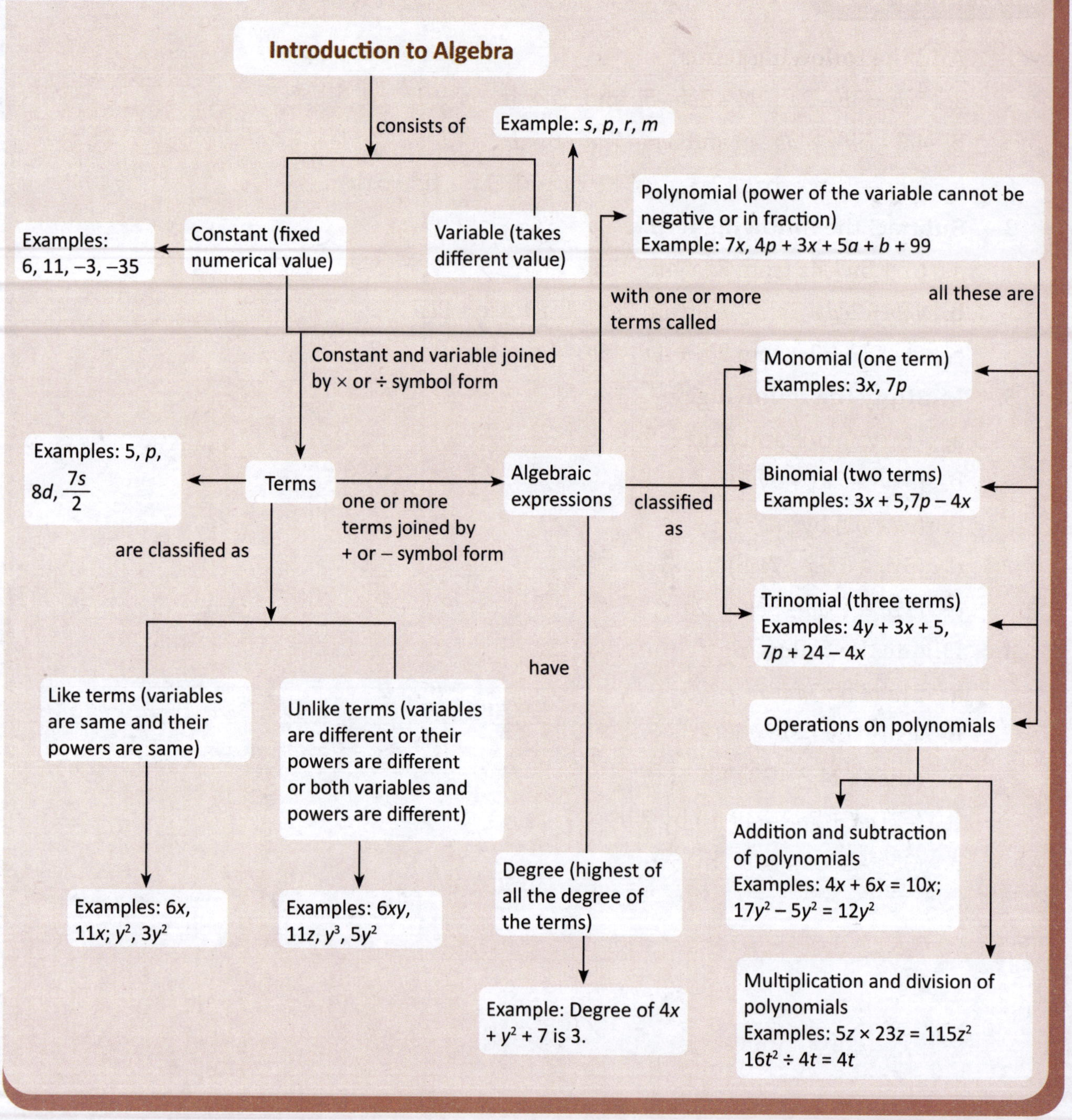

REVISION EXERCISE

1. Choose the correct option.

a. The general rule for the number pattern 2, 4, 6, 8.... is ____

i. n ii. $2n$ iii. $2n+1$ iv. $2n-1$

b. The literal coefficient of the term −7xy is

i. 7 ii. −7 iii. xy iv. $x+y$

c. The constant term of the algebraic expression $x^5y^2 + x^3 + 2$ is_____

i. 3 ii. 5 iii. 2 iv. 7

d. Length of a rectangle is 3 units more than its width. If width is 'x' units long, perimeter of the rectangle is

i. $6 + x$ units ii. $12 + x$ units iii. $2x + 6$ units iv. $4x + 6$ units

e. Which of the following is a trinomial?

i. $2x + x + 4$ ii. $2x + 3y + 4$ iii. $3x \times 4y \times 3z$ iv. All the above

f. The degree of the polynomial $x^5y^2 + x^3 + 2^9$ is ______.

i. 3 ii. 5 iii. 7 iv. 9

2. Fill in the blanks.

a. The numerical coefficient of the term $-4xy$ is ______

b. The next term in the pattern 12, 9, 6, 3, is ______

c. Thenth term of the set of odd numbers is given by ______

d. If one box can hold 80 marbles, the number of marbles in p such boxes is ______

e. The terms having same variable and same degree are called ______.

3. Write the following statements as true or false.

a. $2xy^2z^3$ and $-2xy^3z^2$ are like terms.

b. $3x + 5a + 7a$ is a binomial.

c. $8x$ is a polynomial.

d. The value of the algebraic expression $3x + 4y^2 - 35$ when $x = 2$ and $y = 3$ is 7.

4. Identify the constants and variables in the following.

a. $5x + 10$ b. $12y + 10$ c. $-7 + 16y + z$ d. $26a - 5$

5. Identify the rule and find the next term in the following pattern. Also, write the rule for the nth term of the pattern.

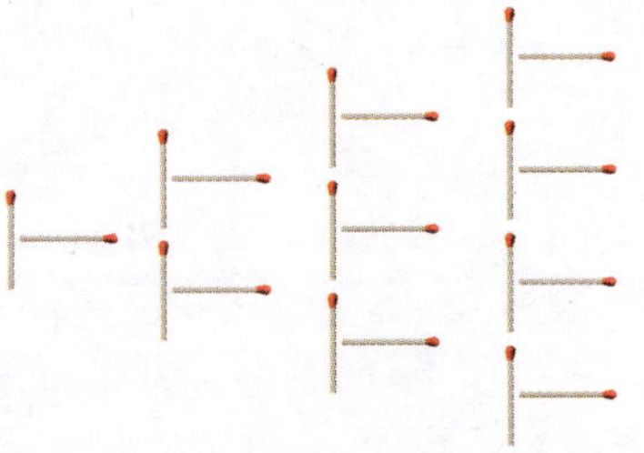

6. **Write the expressions using variables for the following situations.**

   a. The length of a football field is 110 metres more than its width. Express the length of the field in terms of its width.

   b. Ranjan's age is z years. Gita is 3 years older to him. Write Gita's age in terms of z.

   c. Find the rule for finding the perimeter of the square whose side is given by k.

   d. The diameter of a circle is twice the radius of the circle. Find the diameter of the circle whose radius is $15x$.

7. **Write the algebraic expressions for the following.**

   a. The sum of three consecutive whole numbers

   b. Four divided by a number reduced by 2

   c. The difference between d and 3

   d. Divide the product of 3 and x by 2

   e. The sum of $5x$ and 7

8. **Group the like terms together.**

   $14x^3$, $-26y^2$, $100x^2y$, $36a^3$, $42x^2$, $49y^2$, $-19a^2b^2$, $23a^3$, $-11x^3$, $-35a^2b$, $-12x^2$, $30x^2y$, $13a^2b^2$

9. **Find the value of $4a^3b^2c + 3a^2b - 12a$ when**

   a. $a = b = 1$ and $c = 2$ b. $a = 1$, $b = 2$ and $c = 3$ c. $a = -1$, $b = 1$ and $c = 2$

10. **State whether the following expressions are monomial, binomial or trinomial. Also, identify the degree of each of them.**

    a. $-2xy$ b. $4y^2$ c. $3x^3 + x^2 + 6$

    d. $3x^2 - 4x + 10$ e. $5x - 1$ f. $x^2 - 4x$

    g. $2x + 3y + 2$ h. $2a^2 + 3\,a^2b^2$

11. **The number of rose flowers is 8 more than the number of dahlias in a garden. Write an expression for this situation.**

12. **Hansita is x years old. Lisbeth is three times Hansita's age increased by 4 years. Write an expression for Lisbeth's age?**

10 Simple Linear Equations

Prior Knowledge

- Algebraic expressions
- Variables and constants
- Terms of algebraic expression
- Evaluation of expressions

Learning Objectives

- Algebraic equation
- Linear equation
- Trial and error method
- Balancing method
- Transposition method
- Forming and solving linear equations

Let's Get Started

Consider the information given below.

Diksha's age	Diksha's mother's age
3 years	35 years
5 years	37 years
10 years	42 years
After another 5 years	$42 + 5 = 47$ years
After another 15 years	$47 + 15 = 62$ years

What is the relation between Diksha and her mother's age?

If the age of Diksha's mother is 50 years, how will you find Diksha's age?

We know that,

Diksha's mother's age = $x + 32$ years

Also, her mother's age = 50 years

When we equate both the values, we get

$x + 32 = 50$

$x + 32 = 50$ is called an **equation**.

Every equation has a Left Hand Side (LHS) and a Right Hand Side (RHS). These two sides are separated by an equality sign (=). This shows that the LHS of an equation is always equal to the RHS of an equation.

LINEAR EQUATION

A **linear equation** is an equation with one or more variables and the power of the variables is always one.

For example, $2x + 1 = 5$, $5y - 3 = 2y + 6$, $\frac{2p}{3} + \frac{5}{6} = 3$, etc

Methods of Solving a Linear Equation

Solution of a linear equation is the value that satisfies the equation, that is, the value of the variable that makes RHS of the equation equal to LHS of the equation.

Example 1: Solve the following equations.

a. $x + 3 = 5$

b. $y - 2 = 7$

c. $4p = 12$

d. $\frac{m}{5} = 2$

Solution: a. $x + 3 = 5$

Subtract 3 from both sides

That is, $x + 3 - 3 = 5 - 3$

$x = 2$

b. $y - 2 = 7$

Adding 2 on both sides, we get

$y - 2 + 2 = 7 + 2$

$y = 9$

c. $4p = 12$

Dividing both sides of the equation by 4 we get $p = \frac{12}{4} = 3$

d. $\frac{m}{5} = 2$

Multiplying both terms by 5.

That is, $5 \times (\frac{m}{5}) = 5 \times 2$

$m = 10$

REMEMBER

The equation does not change if the same quantity is added or subtracted or multiplied or divided on both sides of the equation.

Example 2: Solve the following equations.

a. $\frac{x}{3} + 2 = 5$

b. $\frac{x}{4} - 3 = 2$

c. $\frac{3y}{5} = 6$

d. $3x - 5 = x + 11$

Solution: a. $\frac{x}{3} + 2 = 5$

Subtract 2 from both sides

$\frac{x}{3} + 2 - 2 = 5 - 2$

$\frac{x}{3} = 3$

Multiplying each term by 3

$3 \times (\frac{x}{3}) = 3 \times 3$

$\Rightarrow x = 9$

b. $\frac{x}{4} - 3 = 2$

Adding 3 on both sides

$\frac{x}{4} - 3 + 3 = 2 + 3$

$\Rightarrow \frac{x}{4} = 5$

Multiply sides of the equation by 4

$4 \times (\frac{x}{4}) = 4 \times 5$

$\Rightarrow x = 20$

c. $\frac{3y}{5} = 6$

Multiply each term by 5

$5 \times (\frac{3y}{5}) = 5 \times 6$

$\Rightarrow 3y = 30$

Dividing each term by 3

$\frac{3y}{3} = \frac{30}{3}$

$\Rightarrow y = 10$

d. $3x - 5 = x + 11$

Adding 5 on both sides

$3x - 5 + 5 = x + 11 + 5$

$3x = x + 16$

Subtract x from both sides

$3x - x = x + 16 - x$

$2x = 16$

Dividing each term by 2, we get

$x = 8$

Transposition Method

Transposition is the shifting of terms from one side of the equal sign to the other side. In transposition, positive terms become negative and negative terms become positive.

For example, $x + 3 = 5 \Rightarrow x = 5 - 3$ and $x - 2 = 6 \Rightarrow x = 6 + 2$

Example 3: Solve the following linear equations.

a. $1 + 2x = x + 9$

b. $3y - 3 = 2y + 4$

c. $2x - 3 = 7$

d. $\frac{x}{4} + 2 = 3$

Solution: a. $1 + 2x = x + 9$

Transposing + 1 to R.H.S., we get

$2x = x + 9 - 1$

$2x = x + 8$

Transposing + x to L.H.S., we get

$2x - x = 8$

$x = 8$

b. $3y - 3 = 2y + 4$

Transposing –3 to R.H.S., we get

$3y = 2y + 4 + 3$

$3y = 2y + 7$

Transposing + $2y$ to L.H.S., we get

$3y - 2y = 7$

$y = 7$

c. $2x - 3 = 7$

Transposing –3 to R.H.S., we get

$2x = 7 + 3$

$2x = 10$

Dividing each term by 2

$\frac{2x}{2} = \frac{10}{2}$

$x = 5$

d. $\frac{x}{4} + 2 = 3$

Transposing +2, we get

$\frac{x}{4} = 3 - 2$

$\frac{x}{4} = 1$

Multiply each term by 4

$\frac{x}{4} \times 4 = 1 \times 4$

$x = 4$

FORMING AND SOLVING WORD PROBLEMS

In solving word problems on linear equations, first read the statement and take the unknown quantity to be found as any letter and, then write the linear equation for the given statement and solve it. The solution of the linear equation is the value of the unknown quantity.

Example 4: When 15 is subtracted from a number, it becomes 37. Find the number.

Solution: Let the required number be x.

The given equation is $x - 15 = 37$

$x = 37 + 15$

$x = 52$

Therefore, the required number is 52.

Example 5: If after 8 years the age of Aliya is 24, then find the present age of Aliya.

Solution: Let the present age of Aliya be x years.

After 8 years, the age of Aliya is 24 years.

Hence the linear equation becomes $x + 8 = 24$.

$x = 24 - 8$

$x = 16$

Therefore, the present age of Aliya is 16 years.

Example 6: Rohan is 12 years older than his sister. After 2 years, his age will be twice the age of his sister. Find the present age of Rohan and his sister.

Solution: Let the present age of Rohan's sister = x

Hence, the present age of Rohan is $x + 12$.

From the given statement, $(x + 12) + 2 = 2\,(x + 2)$

Age of Rohan's sister after 2 years = $x + 2$

Age of Rohan after 2 years = $(x + 12) + 2$

$x + 14 = 2x + 4$

$\Rightarrow 2x - x + 4 = 14$

$\Rightarrow x + 4 = 14$

$\Rightarrow x = 10$

The present age of Rohan's sister is 10 years and Rohan's age $= x + 12 = 10 + 12 = 22$ years.

Therefore, the present age of Rohan is 22 years, and his sister's age is 10 years.

Exercise 10.1

1. **Identify the linear equations from the following.**

   a. $3y + 5 = 8$ b. $\frac{x}{3} + 2 = 4$

   c. $\frac{2}{x} + 5 = 10$ d. $2x^2 + 3 = 6$

   e. $x - 4 = 8 - 2x$

2. **Solve the following linear equations using balancing method.**

   a. $x + 26 = 2x + 4$ b. $7y - 7 = 4y + 2$

   c. $5x - 27 = 15 - 2x$ d. $\frac{3y}{5} + 4 = 13$

   e. $\frac{p}{3} - 2 = 3$ f. $6x - 3 = 2x + 17$

   g. $(60 - x) - 6 = 5(x - 6)$ h. $9x - 63 = 6x$

   i. $4x + 8 = \frac{5x}{2} + 20$ j. $9(5x + 3) = 11(4x + 3)$

3. **Solve the following linear equations using transposition.**

   a. $3x + 5 = 8$ b. $4m - 9 = 7$

   c. $5x - 21 = 4(6 - x)$ d. $\frac{p}{7} + 1 = 3$

   e. $7y + 2 = 22 + 3y$

4. **Answer the following questions.**

   a. **If the sum of two numbers is 68 and one of the numbers is 14 more than the other, then find the two numbers.**

   b. **The length of a rectangle is twice its breadth. If the perimeter is 144 cm, then find the length and the breadth of the rectangle.**

   c. **Aafsha is 5 years younger than Fathima. After 4 years, Fathima's age will be twice the age of Aafsha. Find the present age of Fathima and Aafsha.**

   d. **If the sum of three consecutive multiples of 3 is 45, then find the largest number.**

   e. **The cost of two tables and three chairs is ₹1500. If the cost of a table is ₹80 more than the cost of the chair, then find the cost of a table and a chair.**

   f. **If $\frac{4}{5}$ of a number is 6 more than $\frac{2}{3}$ of the same number, then find the number.**

Key Concepts

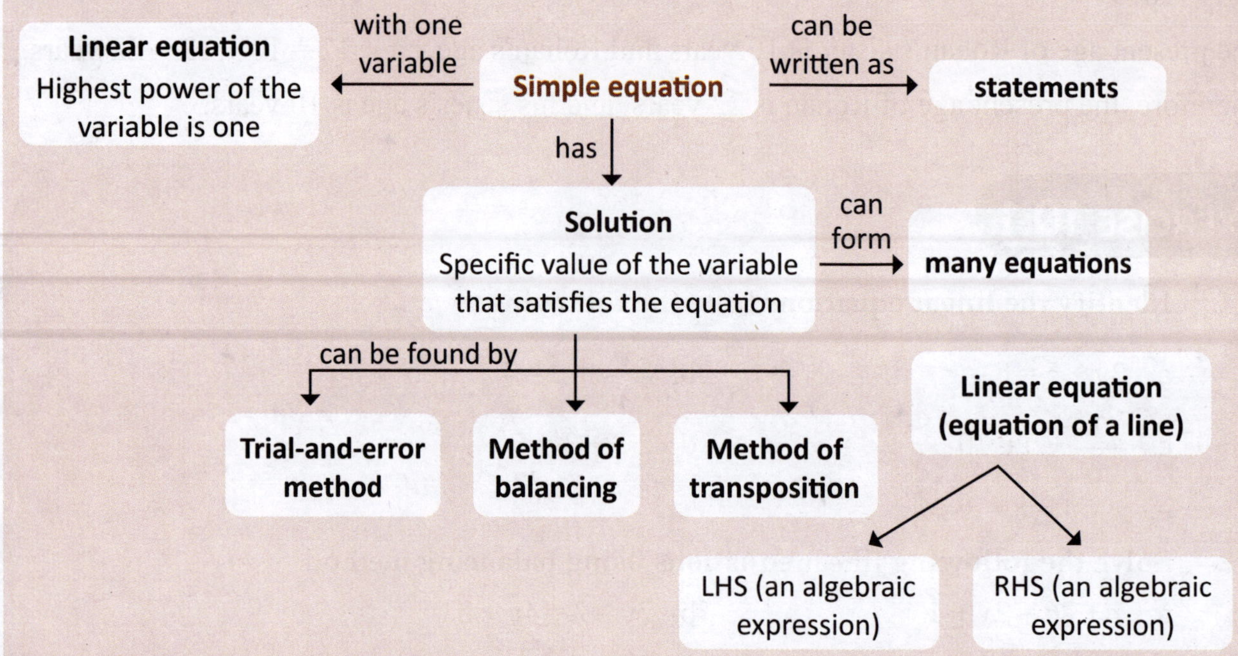

Revision Exercise

1. **Choose the correct option.**

   a. Which of the following is not a linear equation?

   i. $x + 2 = 5$ ii. $2x - x + 3 = 4$ iii. $\frac{2}{x} + 1 = 7$ iv. $\frac{2x}{3} - 3 = 6$

   b. The solution of the equation $5x - 75 = 2 - 6x$ is

   i. 9 ii. 7 iii. 11 iv. 8

   c. The solution of the linear equation $5x - 12x + 9 = 18 - 10x$ is

   i. 3 ii. 4 iii. 6 iv. 9

   d. If the sum of 3 consecutive multiples of 6 is 126, then find the largest number.

   i. 42 ii. 54 iii. 48 iv. 36

   e. The perimeter of a rectangular field is 154 m while its length is 2 m more than twice the breadth. Find the length of the field.

   i. 46 m ii. 54 m iii. 48 m iv. 52 m

2. **Fill in the blanks.**

   a. The degree of a linear equation is always ______.

   b. The solution of the equation $2x + 15 = 95$ is ______.

   c. The solution of the equation $\frac{5x}{3} - x + 6 = 14$ is ______.

   d. Amulya's age is 3 more than twice the age of Rajani. If the sum of ages of Rajani and Amulya is 33 years, then Amulya's age is ______.

   e. The sum of two numbers is 50. If one of the numbers is 18 more than the other, then the smaller number is ______.

3. **State which of the following are equations. Also identify linear equations and justify your answer.**

   a. $x + 6 = 14$ b. $x - 12 + 2 = -12$ c. $3y - 2 = 2$

   d. $4x + 5 < 8$ e. $2 \times 4x - 8 = 2$ f. $5x - 22 > 0$

4. **Solve the following questions.**

   a. Find the solution.

   i. $2y - 3 = y + \frac{21}{2}$. ii. $6x - 18 = x - (34 + 3x)$

   b. The difference between the ages of a mother and a son is 23 years and sum of their ages is 41 years. Find the age of the mother and son.

   c. In an examination, a student scores 4 marks for every correct answer and loses 1 mark for every wrong answer. If he/she attempts all 150 questions and scores 250 marks, find the number of questions he/she attempted correctly.

   d. If $\frac{3}{4}$ of a number is 21 more than half of the number, then find the number.

   e. Yashwant is three years elder to Monika. Five years ago, three-fifth of his age was equal to three-fourth of her age. What is the present age of Yashwant and Monika?

   f. The sum of the two digits of a two-digit number is 8. If the number obtained by interchanging the digits is 18 less than the original number, then find the original number.

11 Basic Geometrical Concepts

Prior Knowledge

- Plane
- Use of geometry boxes

Learning Objectives

- More about planes
- Types of lines
- Open and closed figures
- Linear and curvilinear boundaries
- Polygons

Let's Get Started

The term 'Geometry' is derived from an ancient Greek word where 'geo' means 'earth' and 'metron' means 'measurement'. Geometry originated when man felt the need to measure his land.

In ancient times, geometry was used to construct the pyramids in Egypt, canals in Rome and to measure the distance of ships from the shore.

Pyramids of Egypt

Ship Navigation

Today, geometry is used in various fields such as architecture, medicine and robotics.

List any three fields where geometry is used apart from those mentioned above.

____________ ____________ ____________

We will learn basic concepts of geometry in this chapter.

POINT

A small dot drawn using the tip of a pencil on a plane paper illustrates a point. It has only position but no length, breadth or thickness.

It is named by using a capital letter of the English alphabet.

Points A, B and C are shown in the adjacent figure.

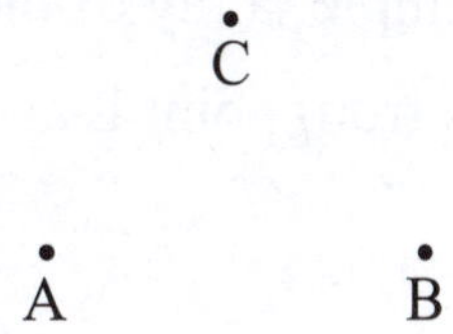

LINE

A line is a straight path that has no breadth and no thickness; it only has length.

Look at the image of a line given here, the arrows on both sides of the line signify that it can be extended indefinitely on both the sides.

$\overleftrightarrow{XY}$

Line XY Line *m*

There are infinite number of points on a line and infinite number of lines can be drawn through a single point on a line.

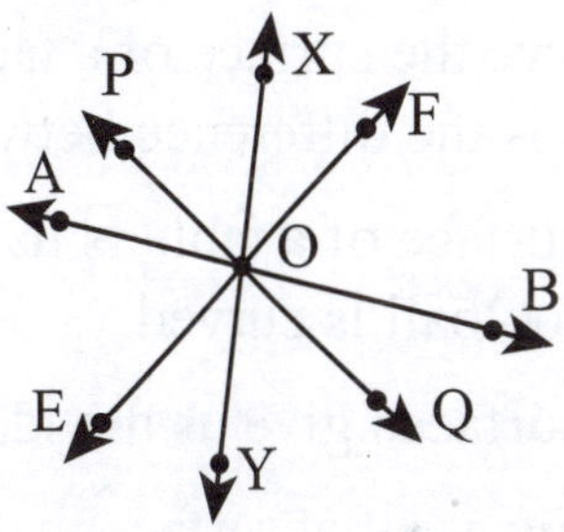

LINE SEGMENT

If we take two points on a line, then the two points and the part of the line between them is called a **line segment**. A line segment has two end points. It has length but no width and thickness. There are infinite number of points on a line segment.

REMEMBER

A line is a straight path that has no end points, no width and no breadth.

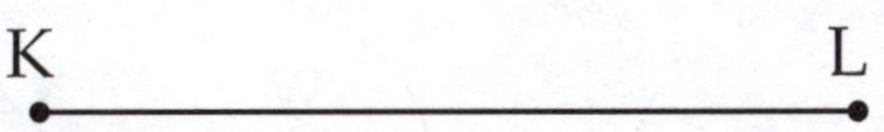

KL is a line segment that has K and L as its end points. It is written as $\overline{KL}$ or $\overrightarrow{LK}$.

Now, look at the figures given below.

Edge of a Rubik's cube

Edge of a notebook

Edge of a piece of paper

The sides or edges in the figures above show line segments in real-life objects.

Name one more object with line segments. ____________

RAY

A **ray** is a part of a line with one fixed endpoint and another that extends indefinitely in a direction. For example, a ray of the sun and a ray of light from a torch.

If a ray originates from point L and passes through point K, it extends endlessly from L to K.

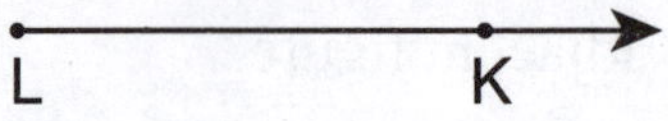

It is written as $\overrightarrow{LK}$ and read as ray LK. Here L is the initial point.

An infinite number of rays can be drawn from one initial point, or one endpoint.

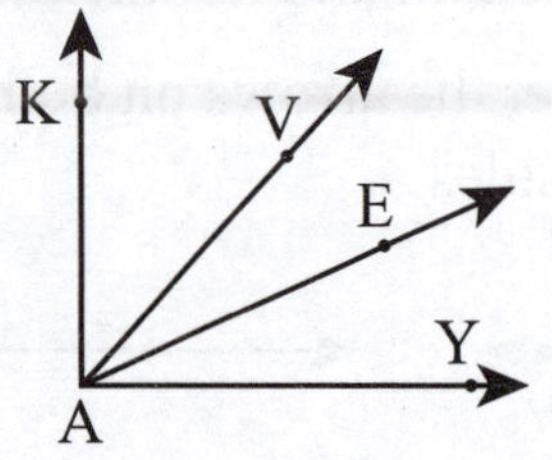

PLANE

Observe the surface of a table and a football. What is the difference between these surfaces?

The surface of a table is flat, whereas the surface of a football is curved.

Flat surfaces give us the idea of a plane.

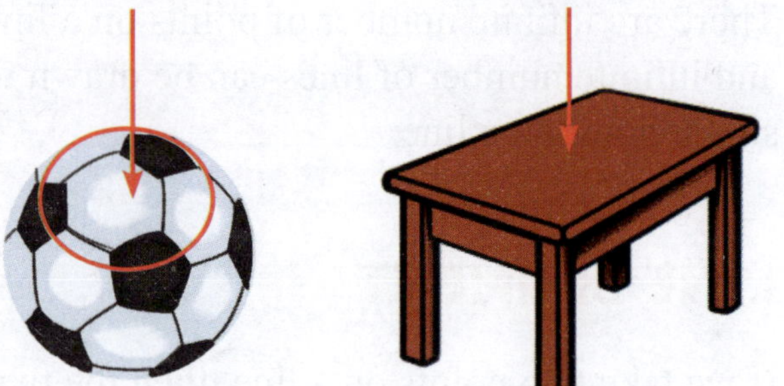

A **plane** is a flat surface that extends infinitely in all directions. A plane is a two-dimensional shape because it has length and breadth but no thickness.

It can be denoted by taking three or more points on it. The points should not lie on the same line.

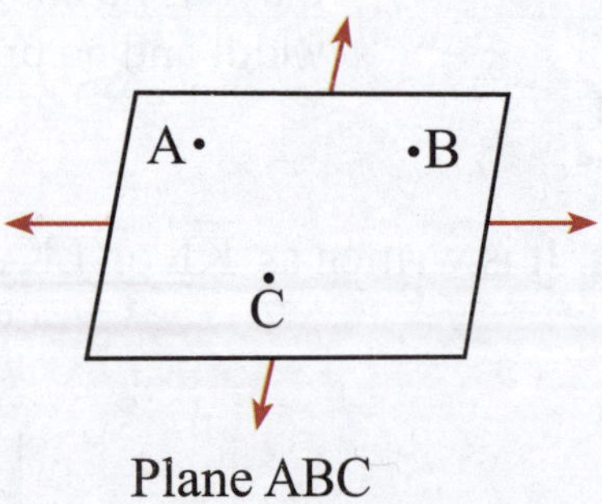

Plane ABC

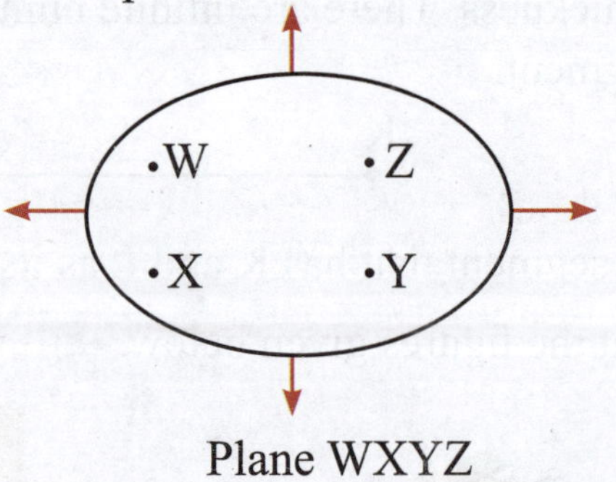

Plane WXYZ

Properties of A Plane

- Infinite number of lines can be drawn through any given point.
- Only one line can be drawn passing through two given points.

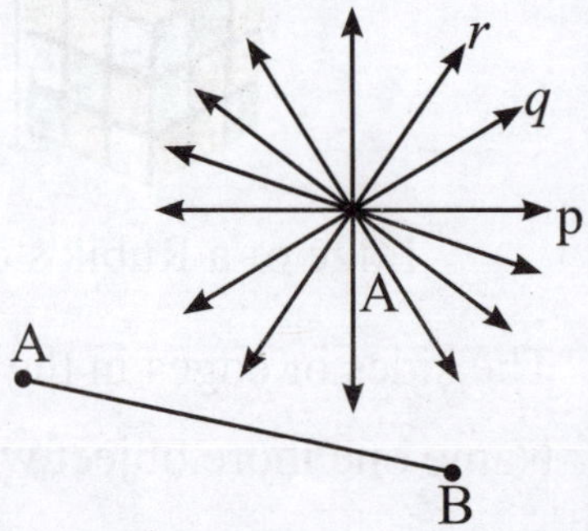

COLLINEAR AND NON-COLLINEAR POINTS

Through which points on the given plane can you draw a straight line?

A straight line can be drawn only through points A, B, C and D.

Three or more points that lie on a plane in a straight line are called **collinear points**.

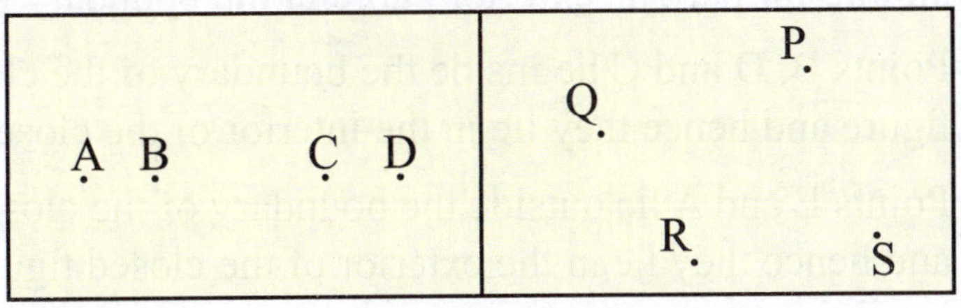

The line drawn through these points is called the **line of collinearity**. Here, line *l* is the line of collinearity.

Points P, Q, R and S are non-collinear points.

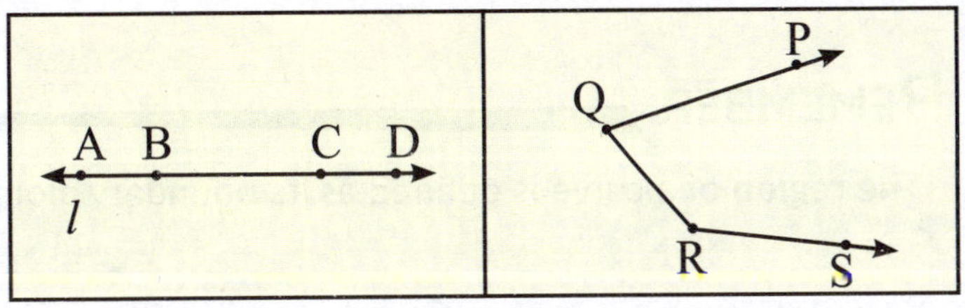

Example 1: Find the following from the given figure.

a. Line segments having one endpoint A

b. Line segments having one endpoint D

c. Collinear points

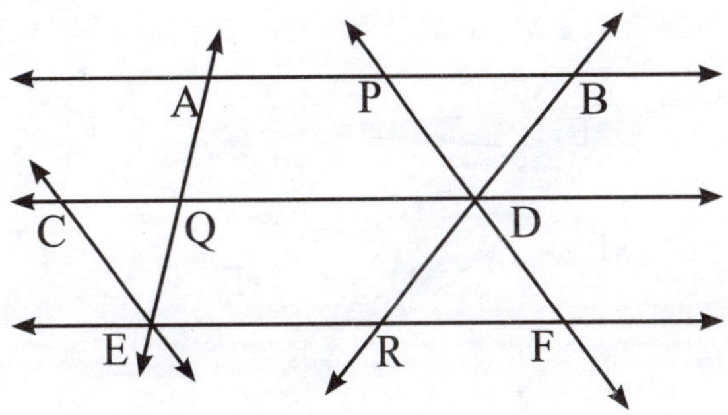

Solution: a. Line segment having one endpoint A:

AQ, AE, AP, AB

b. Line segment having one endpoint D:

DP, DB, DR, DF, DQ, DC

c. Collinear points:

A, Q, E; A, P, B; C, Q, D; P, D, F; B, D, R; E, R, F

OPEN AND CLOSED FIGURES

Definition	Illustration
Curves that do not cross themselves are known as **simple curves.**	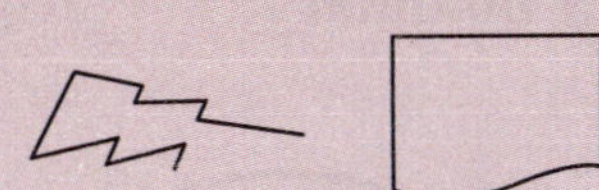
Simple curves that start and end at the same point are known as **closed curves.**	
Curves that do not start and end at the same point are known as **open curves.**	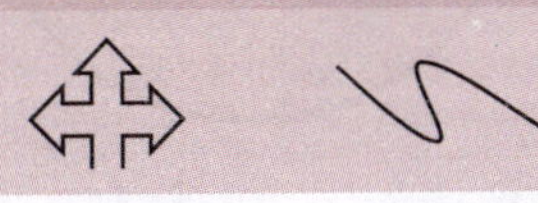

Interior and Exterior of a Closed Figure

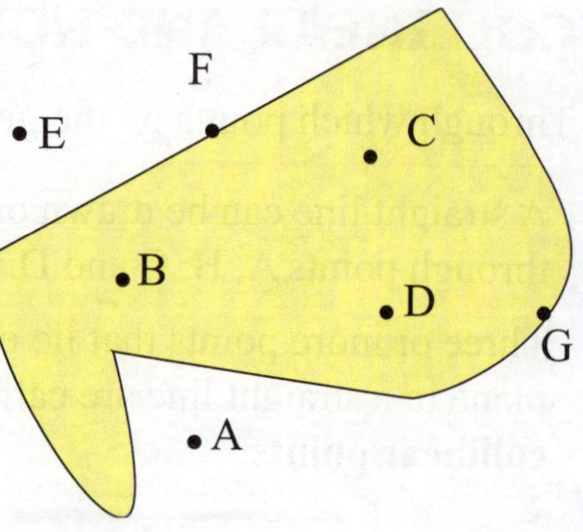

A simple closed curve divides a plane into three parts—an interior part, an exterior part and the boundary part.

Points B, D and C lie inside the boundary of the closed figure and hence they lie in the interior of the closed figure.

Points E and A lie outside the boundary of the closed figure and hence they lie in the exterior of the closed figure.

Points F and G lie on the boundary of the closed figure.

REMEMBER

The **region** of a curve is defined as its boundary along with its interior part

Example 2: Identify the points lying inside the boundary of the given figure.

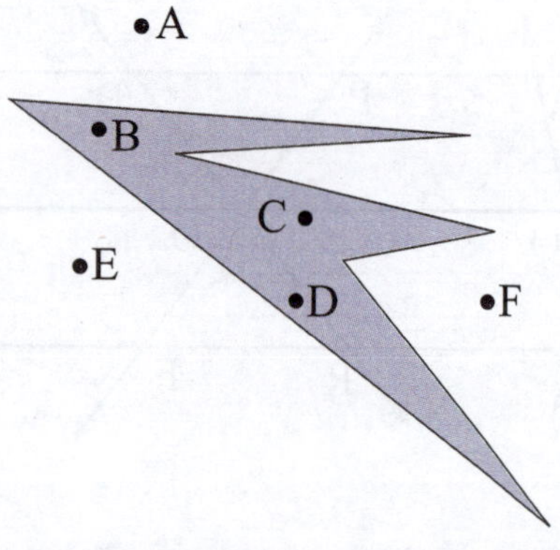

Solution: Points B, C and D lie inside the boundary of the figure.

Example 3: Identify the points lying outside the boundary of the given figure.

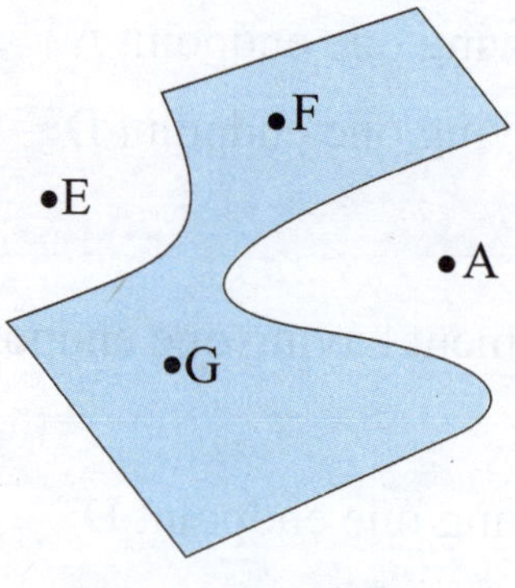

Solution: Points A and E lie outside the boundary of the figure.

Curvilinear and Linear Boundaries

Curvilinear means curved line. So, a boundary containing only curved lines is called a **curvilinear boundary**.

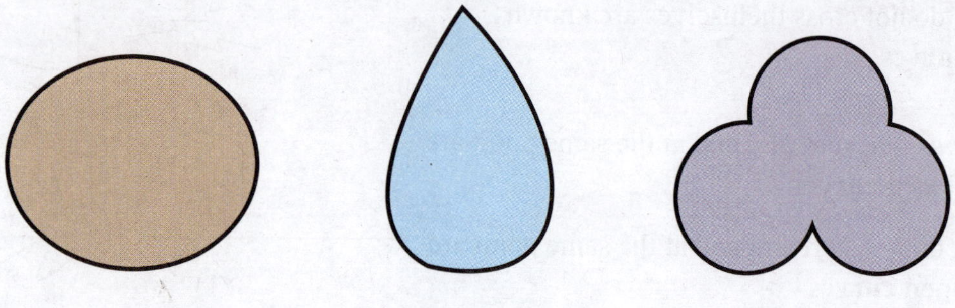

Linear means straight line. So, a boundary containing only straight lines is called a **linear boundary**.

Some figures have both curvilinear and linear boundaries.

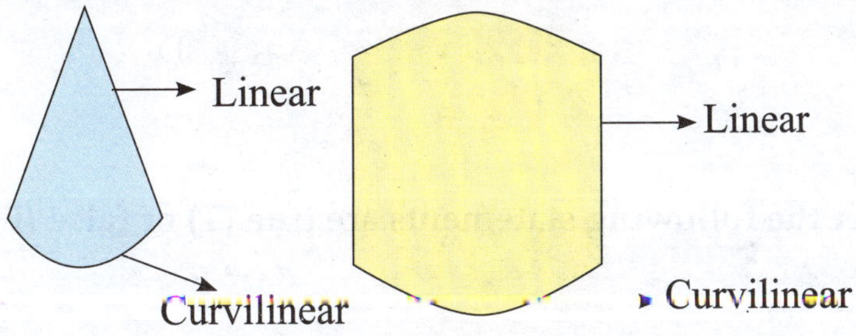

Exercise 11.1

1. **Identify the types of lines from the figure and answer the following questions.**

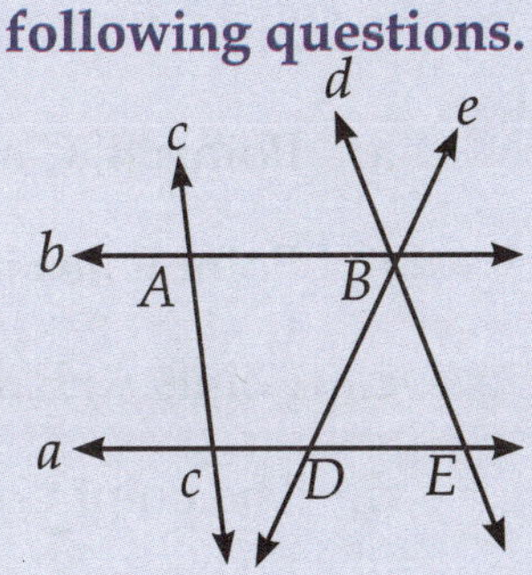

   a. Name line *c* in two other ways.

   b. Name line *d* in two other ways.

   c. Name three line segments on line *a*.

   d. Name two rays on line *b*.

   e. Name four rays on line *a*.

2. **Identify the points, lines, line segments and rays in the adjacent diagram and write them using the corresponding notation in the table.**

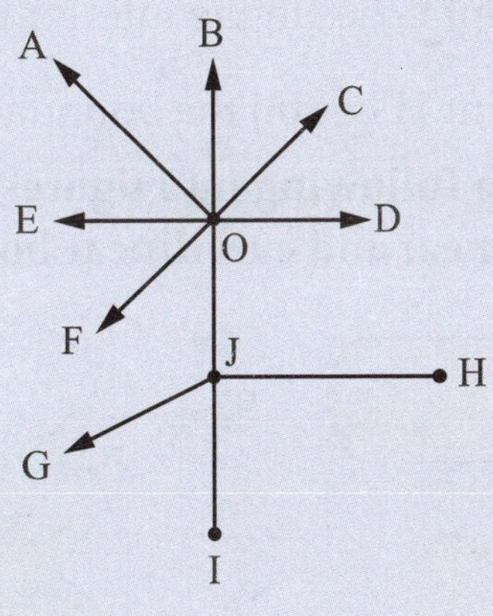

3. **Tick (✓) the simple closed curves among the following.**

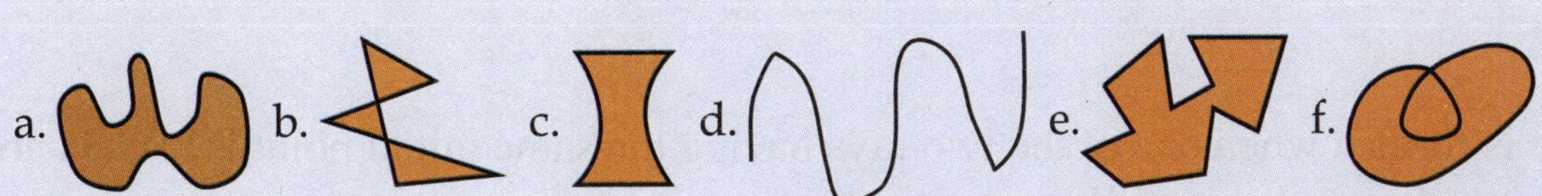

4. **Identify and list the points lying inside and outside the boundary of the figures given below.**

a.

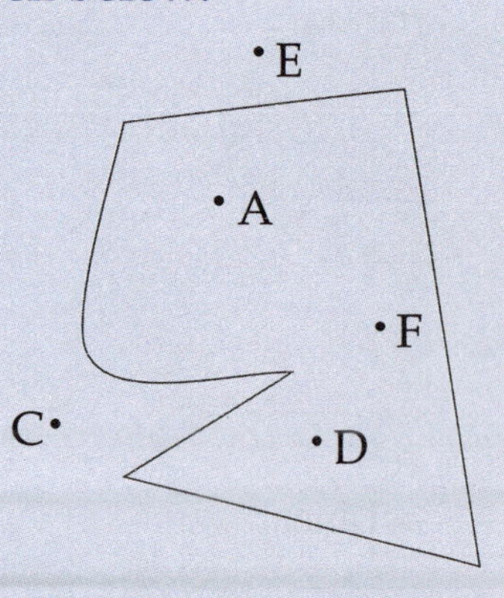

b.

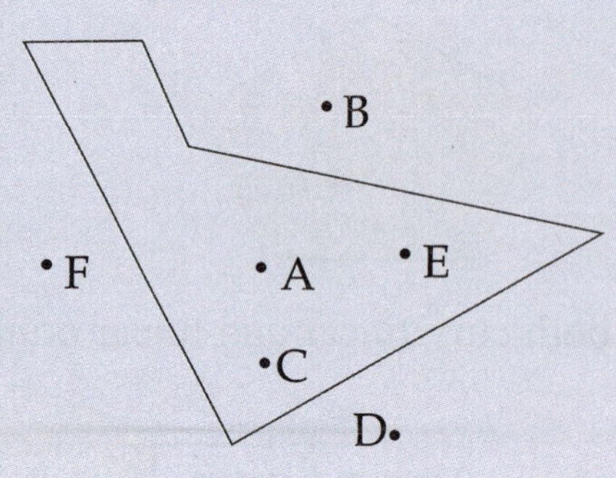

5. **State whether the following statements are true (T) or false (F).**

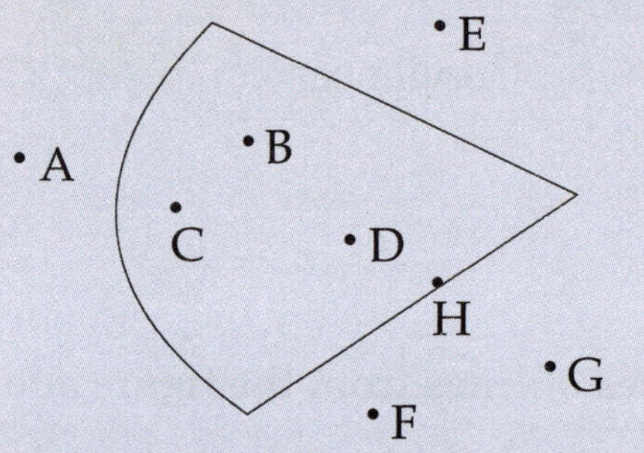

a. Points B, C and D lie in the interior of the closed figure. ☐

b. Point E lies in the exterior of the closed figure. ☐

c. Points A, E, F and G lie in the exterior of the open figure. ☐

d. The point G lies in the interior of the closed figure. ☐

e. The point H lies on the boundary of the closed figure. ☐

6. **Classify the following into figures with linear boundary, curvilinear boundary and both linear and curvilinear boundary.**

a. 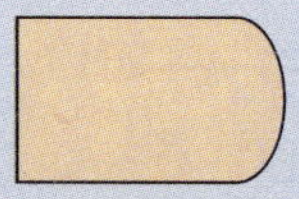 b. 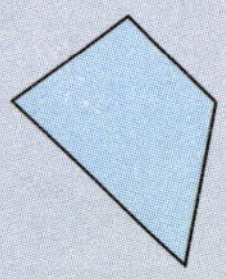 c. 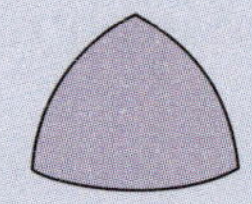

d. 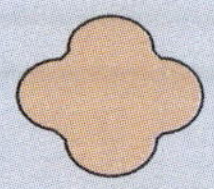 e. 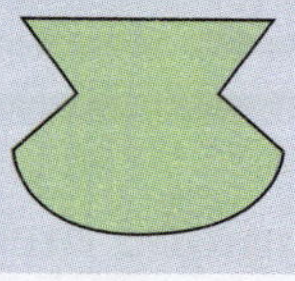 f. 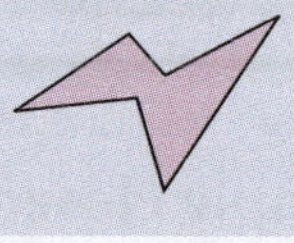

ANGLE

An **angle** is formed when one of the two rays having the same initial point is rotated about that point to take another position.

The two rays containing the angle are called its **arms** or **sides** and their common point of intersection is called the **vertex**.

An angle is denoted by '$\angle$'.

In the adjacent figure, the rays $\overrightarrow{BA}$ and $\overrightarrow{BC}$ are the arms, while the point B is the vertex.

We can name this angle as ∠ABC or ∠CBA or simply ∠B.

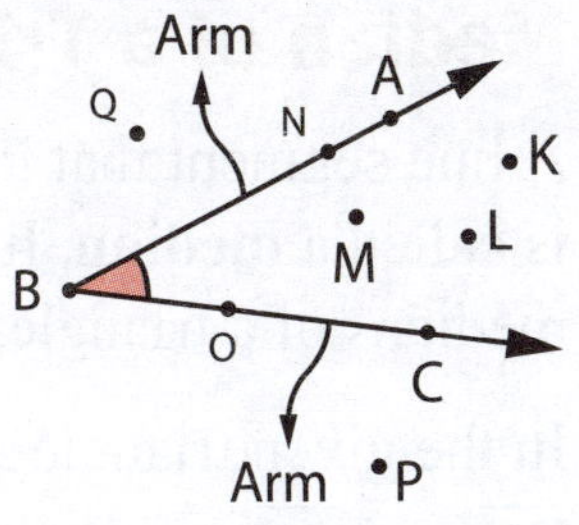

Interior and Exterior of an Angle

The region bounded by the arms of an angle extended indefinitely is called the **interior** of the angle.

In the given figure, the points K, L and M are in the interior of ∠ABC.

The region outside the arms of an angle extended indefinitely is called the **exterior** of the angle. Points P and Q are in the exterior of ∠ABC.

All the points on the arms of an angle are said to lie on the angle. In the given figure, the points N and O lie on ∠ABC.

The region in the interior of an angle alongwith its boundary is called its **angular region**.

TRIANGLE

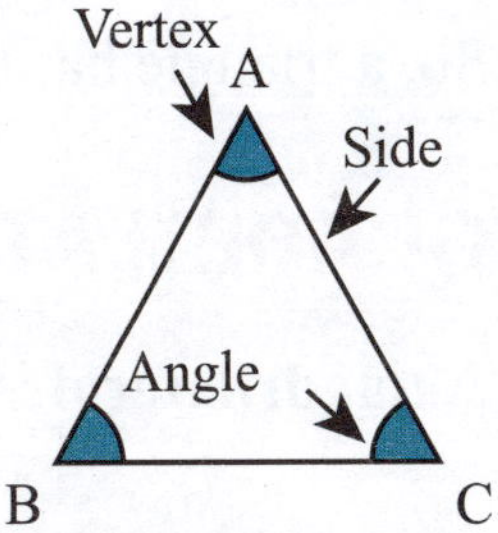

A closed figure formed by three line segments is called a **triangle**.

In other words, a plane figure formed by three non-parallel line segments is called a **triangle**.
It is denoted by 'Δ'. It can be named as ΔABC or ΔBCA or ΔCAB.

In triangle ABC,

- A, B and C are the vertices.
- Line segments AB, BC and CA are the sides.
- ∠A, ∠B and ∠C are the interior angles.
- ∠A lies opposite to side BC, ∠B lies opposite to side AC, ∠C lies opposite to side AB.

REMEMBER

1. While naming the angle, the vertex is always written in the middle.
2. The three sides and the three angles of a triangle are known as the **six parts or elements** of a triangle.

Interior and Exterior of a Triangle

A triangle divides a plane into three parts.

- The region inside the triangle is called its **interior**.
- The region outside the triangle is called its **exterior**.
- All the points that lie on the triangle form the **boundary** of the triangle.

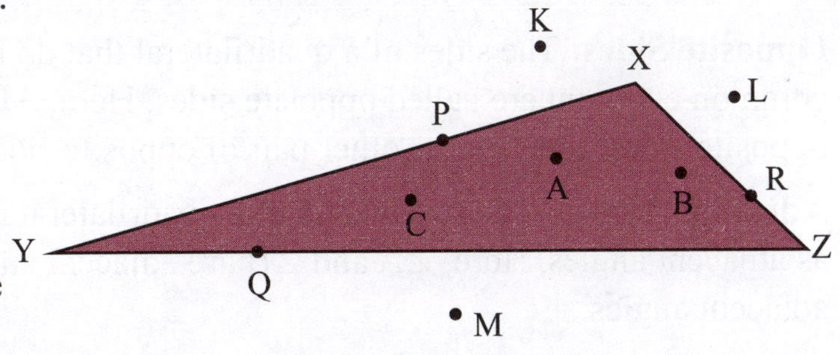

In the given figure, the points A, B and C are in the interior region, the points K, L and M are in the exterior region and the points P, Q and R are on the boundary of ΔXYZ.

The interior region along with the boundary is known as the **triangular region**.

Median of a Triangle

A line segment that joins a vertex to the midpoint of the opposite side is called a **median**. It divides the opposite side into halves. All the three medians of a triangle meet at a point called the **centroid**.

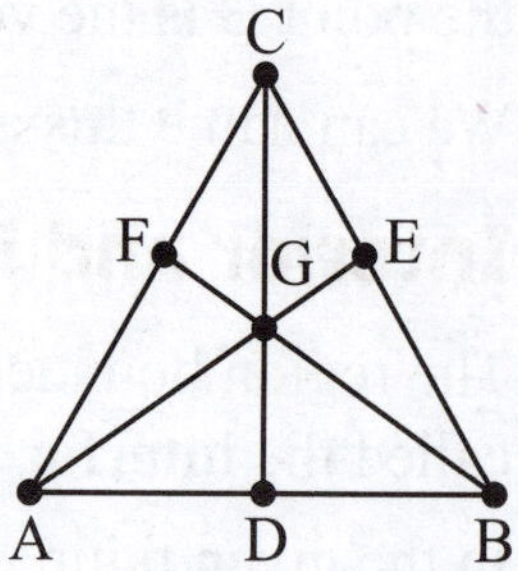

In the given triangle ABC, D, E and F are the midpoints of the sides $\overline{AB}$, $\overline{BC}$ and $\overline{AC}$, respectively. So, CD, AE and BF are the medians of ΔABC intersecting at point G. Thus, G is the centroid of ΔABC.

Altitude of a Triangle

In a triangle, **altitude** is the perpendicular drawn from a vertex to its opposite side. All the three altitudes of a triangle pass through a point called the **orthocentre**.

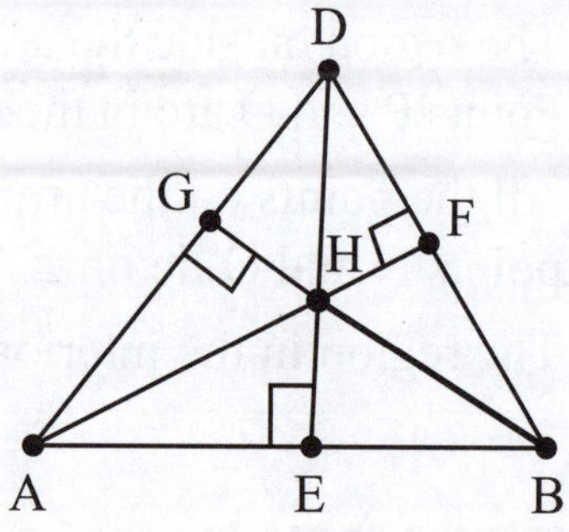

In the given triangle ADB, AF ⊥ $\overline{DB}$, DE ⊥ $\overline{AB}$ and BG ⊥ $\overline{AD}$. So, AF, DE and BG are the altitudes of ΔABD intersecting at point H. Thus, H is the orthocentre of ΔABD.

So, a triangle has three altitudes and three medians.

QUADRILATERAL

A **quadrilateral** is a simple closed figure bounded by four line segments.

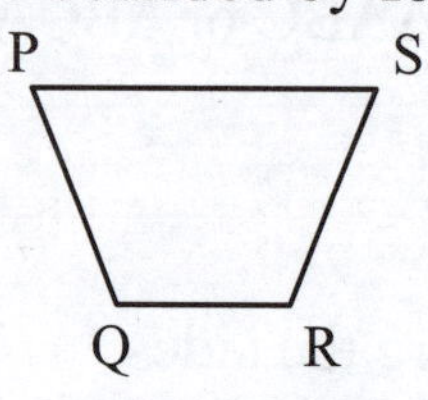

A quadrilateral PQRS has four sides, four vertices and four angles.

Elements of a Quadrilateral

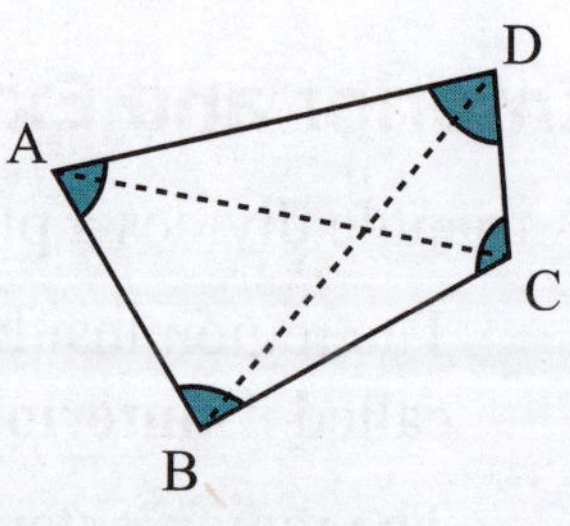

Adjacent Sides: The two sides of a quadrilateral that share a common endpoint are called adjacent sides. Here, $\overline{BC}$ and $\overline{CD}$ are adjacent sides. Identify the other pairs of adjacent sides.

Opposite Sides: The sides of a quadrilateral that do not share a common endpoint are called opposite sides. Here, $\overline{AB}$ and $\overline{DC}$ are opposite sides. Identify the other pair of opposite sides.

Adjacent Angles: The two angles of a quadrilateral that share a common arm are known as adjacent angles. Here, ∠A and ∠B are adjacent angles. Identify the other pairs of adjacent angles.

Opposite Angles: The two angles of a quadrilateral that do not share a common arm are known as opposite angles. Here, ∠A and ∠C are the opposite angles.

Identify the other pair of opposite angles.

Interior and Exterior of a Quadrilateral

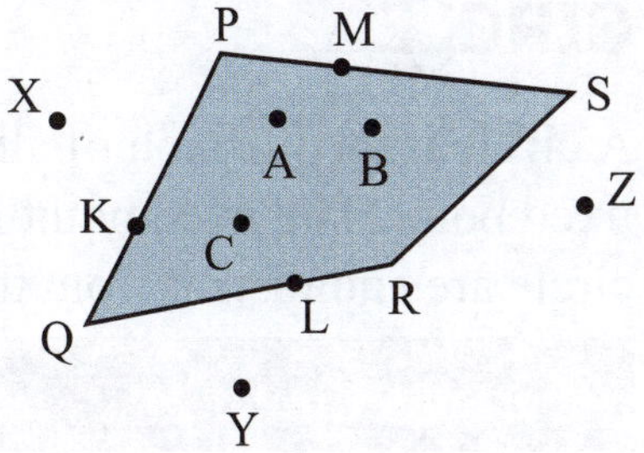

In the adjoining figure, the points A, B and C are in the interior, the points K, L and M are on the boundary and the points X, Y and Z are in the exterior of the quadrilateral PQRS.

The interior of the quadrilateral along with its boundary is known as the **quadrilateral region**.

EXERCISE 11.2

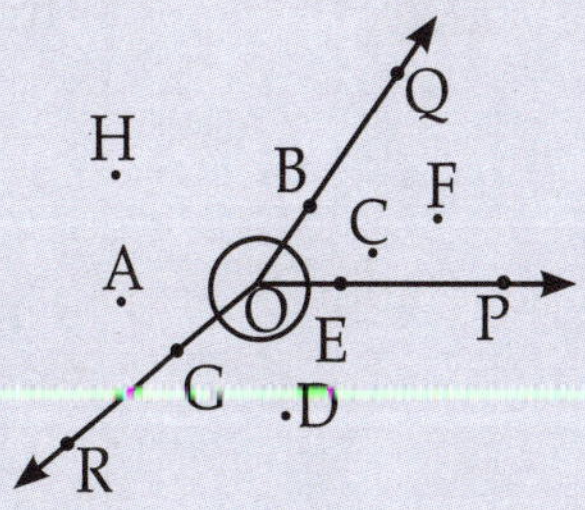

1. Answer the following questions.

a. How many angles are there in the figure?

b. Find the points in the interior, exterior and on the boundry of ∠QOR.

c. On the boundary of which angle(s) does point E lie?

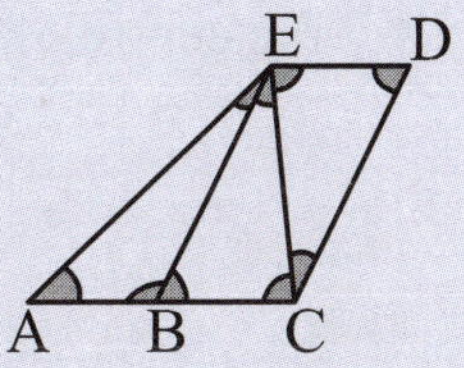

2. Identify all the triangles in the given figure. For each triangle, write its sides and angles.

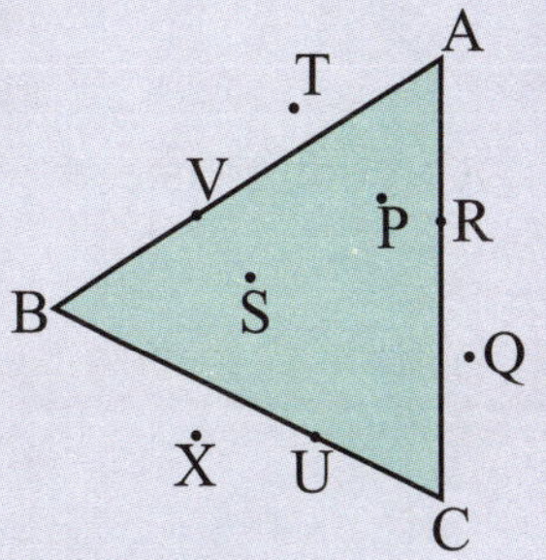

3. Study the given figure and and identify the points on the triangle, in the interior of the triangle and in the exterior of the triangle.

4. List all the interior points, exterior points and the points lying on the boundary of the given quadrilateral.

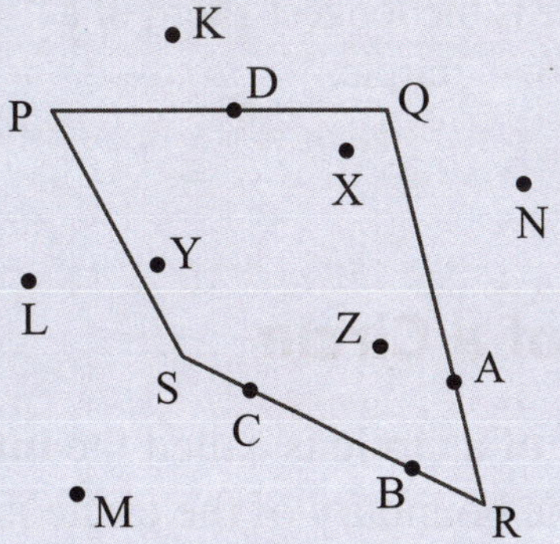

5. Write the opposite angles and the adjacent angles of the quadrilateral WXYZ.

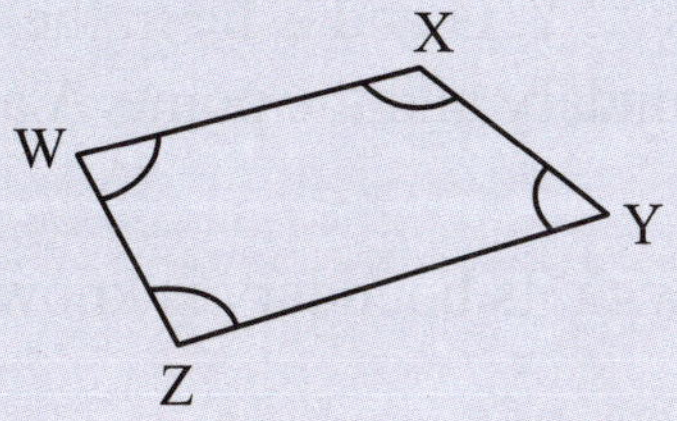

CIRCLE

A **circle** is a collection of all those points in a plane that are at the same distance from a fixed point. The fixed point is the centre and all points on the circumference of the circle are equidistant from the centre.

Part of a Circle	Definition	Illustration
Centre	The collection of all the points in a plane that are at the same distance from a fixed point. The fixed point is called the centre.	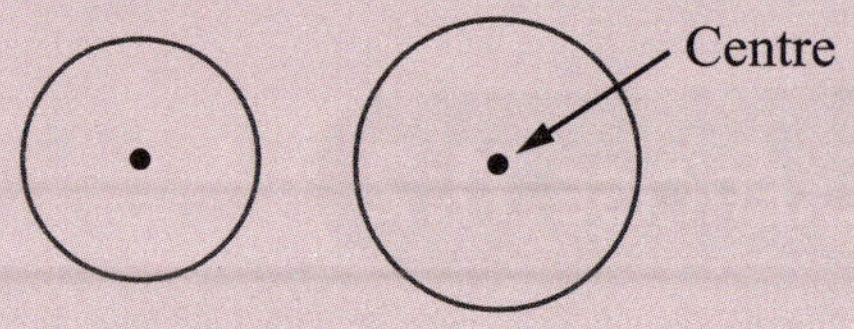
Radius	The distance from the centre of the circle to any point on the boundary is called the radius.	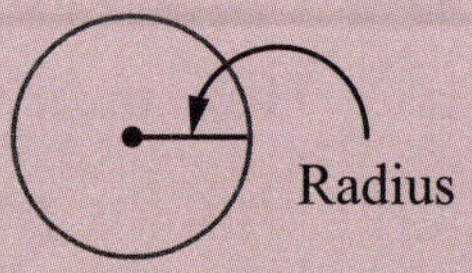
Diameter	A line segment whose endpoints lie on the circle and that passes through the centre of the circle is called its diameter.	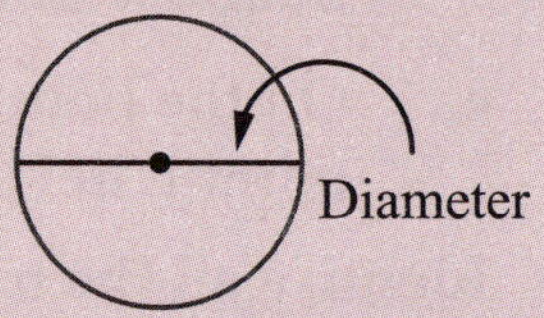
Circumference	The distance around the edge of a circle is called the circumference.	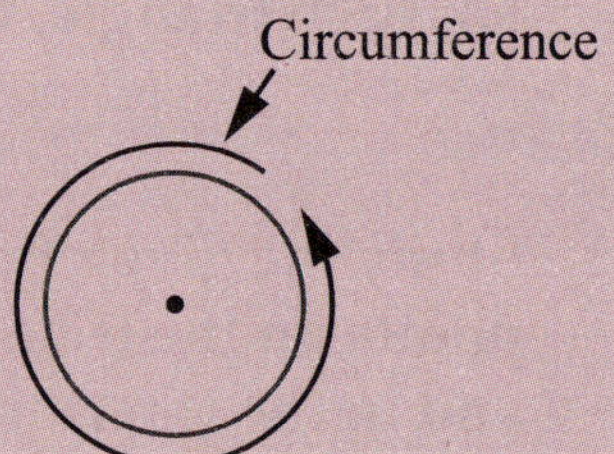
Chord	A line segment whose endpoints lie on the circle is called a chord. Diameter is the longest chord of a circle.	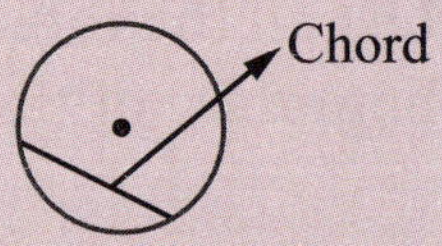

Interior and Exterior of a Circle

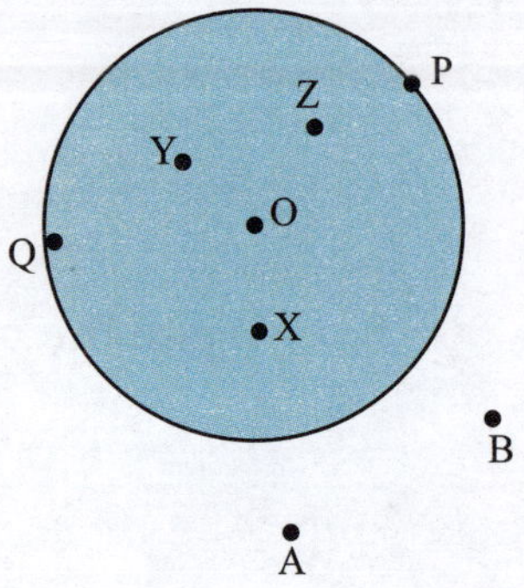

The region inside the boundary of a circle is called the **interior of the circle**, and the region outside the boundary of the circle is called the **exterior of the circle**.

In the adjacent figure, the points X, Y, O and Z lie in the interior, the points P and Q lie on the boundary and the points A and B lie in the exterior of the circle.

The interior of the circle along with its boundary is known as the **circular region**.

Semicircle: The end points of a diameter of a circle divide the circle into two equal parts; each part is called a **semicircle**.

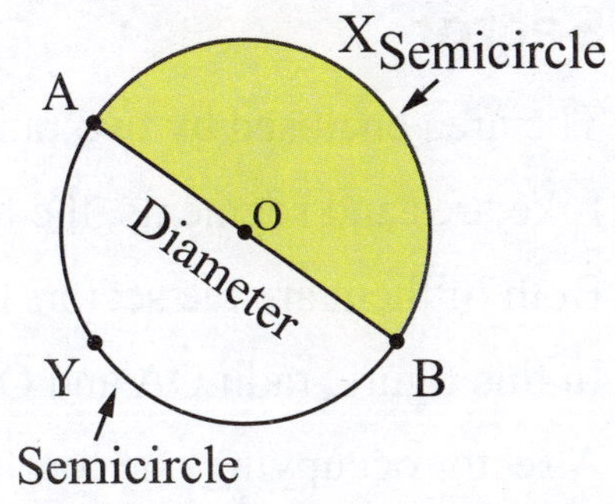

The diameter AB divides the given circle into two semicircles; AXB and AYB.

Secant: A line that passes through a circle and intersects the circle at two distinct points is known as a **secant**.

Tangent: A straight line touching a circle at one point only is known as **tangent**.

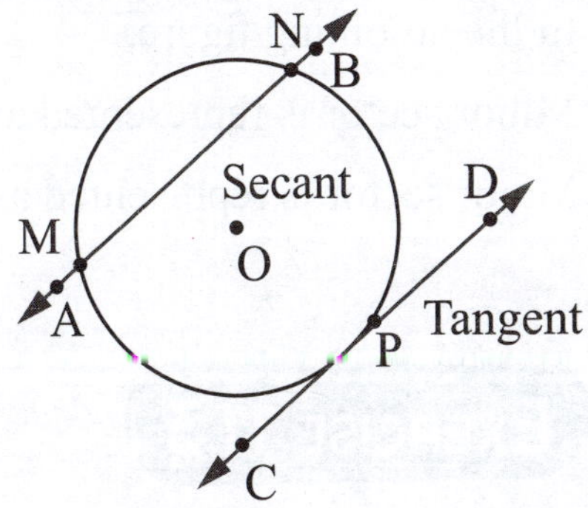

Here, AB is a secant and CD is a tangent. The point P, at which the tangent touches the circle is the point of contact.

Arc

An **arc** refers to the set of points on a circle that lie on the boundary of the circle.

In other words, an arc is a portion of the circumference of a circle.

In the given figure, AB is an arc of the circle.

It is represented by the symbol '⌒'.

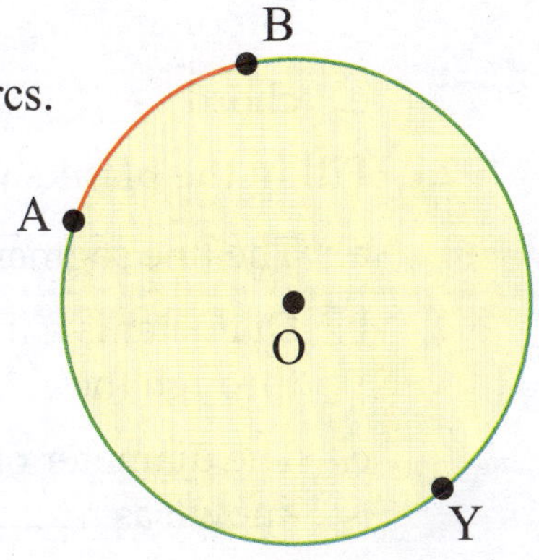

Two or three points lying on a circle actually define two types of arcs.

Minor Arc: Shortest distance between two points along the circumference.

Major Arc: Longest distance between two points on the circumference.

Here, the shorter arc is shown in red colour.

This is the minor arc. It is represented as $\overset{\frown}{AB}$.

The longer arc is shown in green colour.

This is the major arc. It is represented as $\overset{\frown}{AYB}$.

Segment

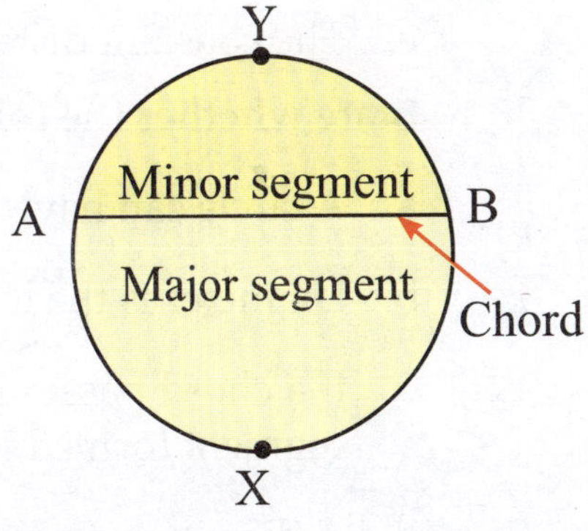

A chord of a circle divides it into two parts.

Each such part is called a segment of the circle.

Thus, the region enclosed by the chord and the arc of a circle is called a **segment**.

The segment containing the minor arc is called the **minor segment**, and the segment containing the major arc is called the **major segment** of the circle.

In the adjoining figure,

Minor segment is represented as $\overset{\frown}{AYB}$.

Major segment is represented as $\overset{\frown}{AXB}$.

Sector

The area enclosed by two radii of a circle and their connecting arc is called a **sector**.

Like arcs and segments, the two radii also divide the circle into two parts.

Both of them are the sectors of the circle.

In this figure, radii OA and OB divide the circle into two sectors.

A sector occupying one fourth of a circle is called a **quadrant**.

In the adjoining figure,

Minor sector is represented as AXBO.

Major sector is represented as AYBO.

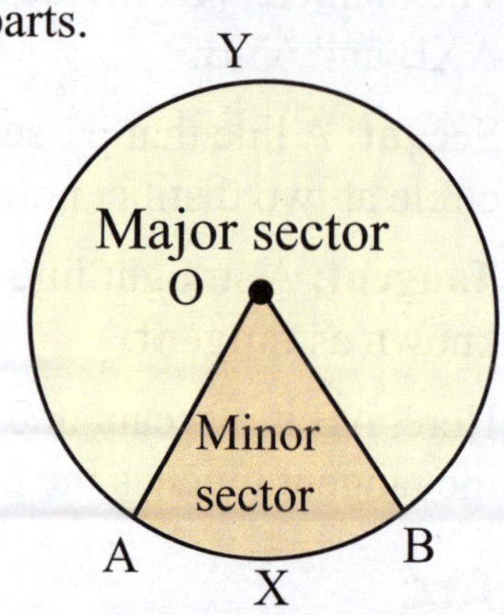

Exercise 11.3

1. **In the given figure, name the following:**

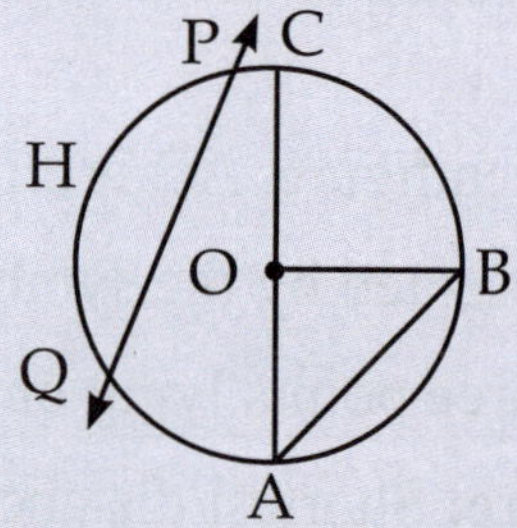

   a. radii
   b. diameter
   c. minor arc
   d. major arc
   e. chord
   f. major segment

2. **Fill in the blanks with appropriate words.**
   a. The line segment whose endpoints lie on a circle is called a ______________ .
   b. Diameter is a line segment whose endpoints lie on a circle and which passes through the ______________ of the circle.
   c. The diameter of a circle divides it into two ______________ parts. Each part is known as a ______________ .
   d. The region bounded by an arc and the two radii drawn from the endpoints of the arc to the centre is called ______________ .
   e. The constant distance from a ______ to any point on the circle is called the radius.

3. **State whether the following statements are true (T) or false (F).**
   a. A circle can have many radii and diameters. ☐
   b. Diameter is the longest chord of a circle. ☐
   c. If a chord passes through the centre of a circle, then the segment formed is called a minor segment. ☐
   d. A diameter divides the circle into two equal halves. ☐
   e. The region inside the boundary of a circle is called circular region. ☐

4. **Write the differences between diameter and chord, sector and segment and arc and semicircle.**

KEY CONCEPTS

Basic Geometrical Concepts

- **Point:** Mark a location in a plane and has no length, breath and thickness.
- Straight path — can be:
  - **Line:** It has neither starting nor end points. For example, $\overleftrightarrow{AB}$
  - **Ray:** It has a starting and end points. For example, $\overrightarrow{AB}$
  - **Line segment:** It has both starting and end points. For example, $\overline{AB}$
- Angle — is: 2 rays starting from a common point.
  - has:
    - 2 rays as side or arms
    - vertex point and vertex angle
- Curve
  - Simple curve — is: Curves that do not cross themselves.
  - Simple curve — are:
    - **Open curves:** Curves that do not start and end at the same point.
    - **Closed curves:** Curves that start and end at the same time.
      - are:
        - **Triangle:** A simple closed figure made up of 3 line segments.
        - **Quadrilateral:** A simple closed figure bounded by four line segments.
        - **Circle:** A collection of all points in a plane that are at a constant distance from a fixed point.
          - parts are:
            - **Semicircle:** Half of a circle obtained by drawing any diameter of the circle.
            - **Arc:** Part of a circle enclosed by any two points on the circle.
            - **Segment:** The region bounded by a chord and its corresponding arc.
            - **Secant:** The region bounded by an arc and the two radii drawn from the endpoints of the arc to the centre.

REVISION EXERCISE

1. Choose the correct option.

a. In the given figure, AB represents a ________.

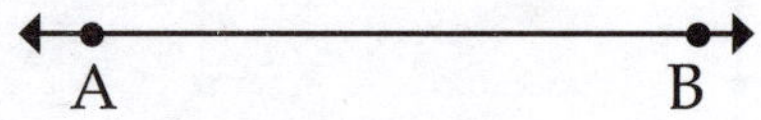

i. line ii. ray
iii. line segment iv. point

b. Which of the following determines an exact location in a plane?

i. Ray ii. Line iii. Line segment iv. Point

c. A line segment that joins a vertex to the midpoint of the opposite side is called _______.

i. median ii. altitude iii. orthocentre iv. centroid

d. Which of the following does not represent a quadrilateral?

A 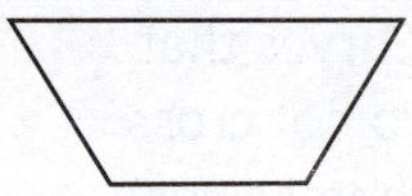 B 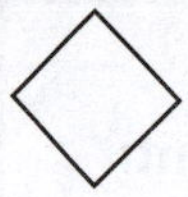 C 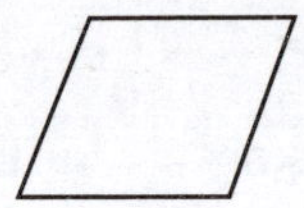 D 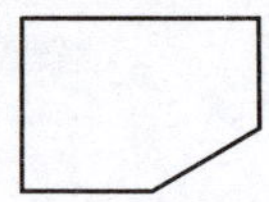

i. A ii. B iii. C iv. D

e. Which of the following figures has both curvilinear and linear boundaries?

A 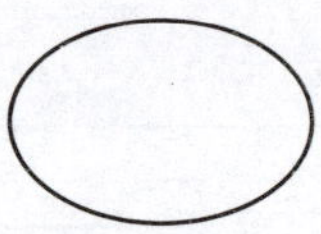 B 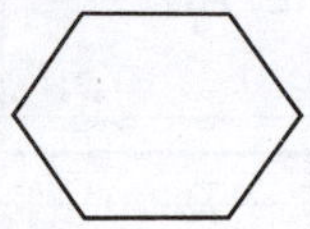 C 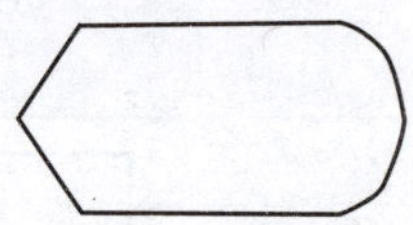 D 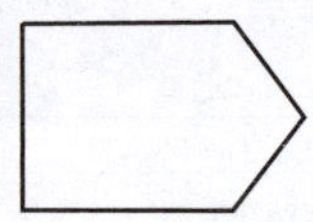

i. A ii. B iii. C iv. D

f. The interior of a circle along with its boundary is called ___________.

i. interior region ii. circular region
iii. exterior region iv. boundary

2. Fill in the blanks.

a. Line segment $\overline{AB}$ is __________ as line $\overline{BA}$.

b. A triangle has __________ sides, whereas a quadrilateral has __________ sides.

c. In ΔPQR, the angles are __________ , __________ and __________ .

d. A diagonal of a quadrilateral joins two __________ vertices.

e. A line that intersects the circle at two distinct points is called a __________ of the circle.

3. State whether the following statements are true (T) or false (F).

a. Rays $\overrightarrow{AB}$ and $\overrightarrow{BA}$ are the same.

b. A triangle has no diagonals.

c. Diameter of a circle is always twice its chord.

d. A quadrilateral has four pairs of opposite angles.

e. There are 3 vertices of a triangle.

4. **Draw the following types of lines and write their proper geometrical notations.**

   a. A line segment RS   b. A ray PQ   c. A line XY

5. **Identify the points that are in the interior, in the exterior and on the boundary of the triangle ABC shown here.**

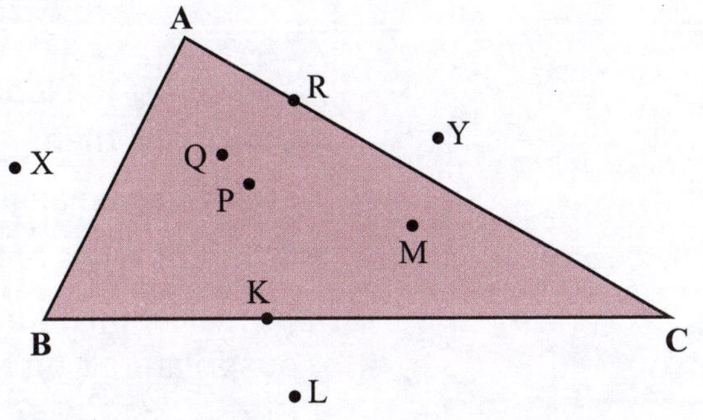

6. **Name the adjacent angles, opposite angles, adjacent sides and opposite sides of the quadrilateral PQRS shown here.**

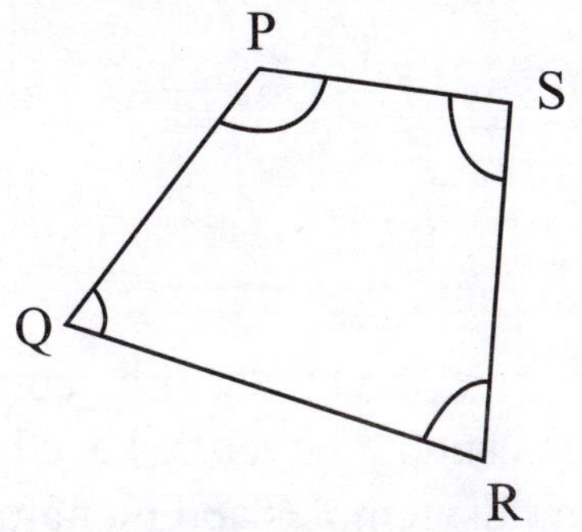

7. **Using the given figure to answer the following questions:**

   a. Name three sets of collinear points.

   b. Name the line segments having one endpoint as C.

   c. Name all line segments.

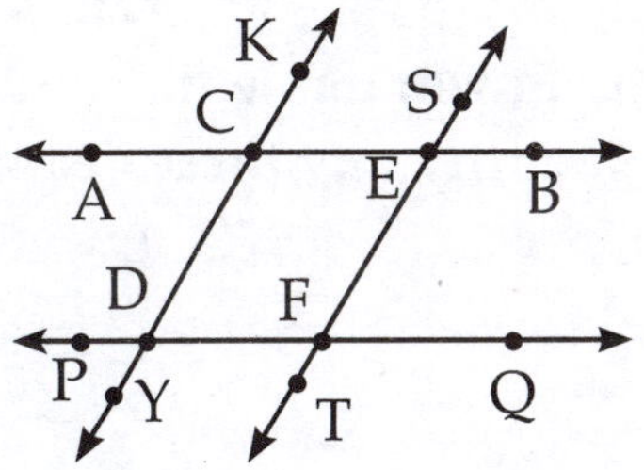

8. **Draw a circle and mark:**

   a. any two points on the boundary of the circle.

   b. any three points in the interior of circle.

   c. any three points in the exterior of the circle.

12 Understanding Elementary Shapes

Prior Knowledge

- Lines
- Rays
- Line segments
- Elements of triangles
- Elements of quadrilaterals
- Elements of circles

Learning Objectives

- Measuring the lengths of line segments and comparing them
- Measuring an angle using a protractor
- Different types of lines and angles
- Classification of angles, triangles and quadrilaterals on the basis of sides and angles
- Different types of regular polygons
- Elements of three-dimensional shapes

Let's Get Started

In architecture, geometry plays a vital role. Architects use geometrical shapes to create a blueprint or to sketch a design. Maths and architecture have been linked to each other since ancient times. The ancient pyramids, temples and monuments were built using many geometrical principles.

Can you name the monument given below? Name it. Where is it situated? Can you identify any three geometrical shapes in it? Mention their names.

We must have the knowledge of geometry for constructing various structures like buildings, bridges, badminton courts, tennis courts and other play areas.

Geometrical shapes form the foundation of many architectural principles.

MEASUREMENT OF LINE SEGMENTS

A line segment is a part of a line and has two distinct end points.
Let us learn how to measure the length of a line segment by using the following:

1. A ruler
2. A divider and a ruler

Using a Ruler

You are already familiar with the ruler present in your geometry box. One of its two edges is marked in centimetres and millimetres. The other edge is marked in inches.

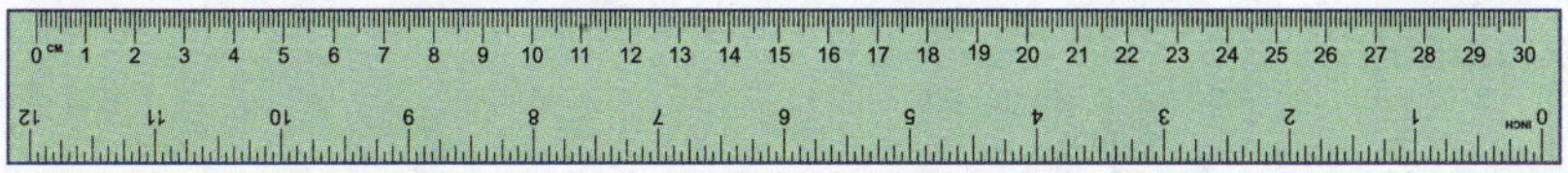

Now, measure the line segment AB by placing the zero of the ruler on the endpoint A and note down the reading on the ruler that coincides with the other endpoint B.

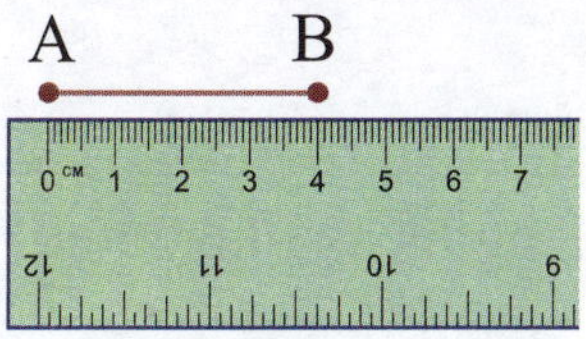

REMEMBER

The zero of the ruler must coincide with one endpoint.

The length of the line segment $\overline{AB}$ is 4 cm.

Using a Ruler and a Divider

A divider has two legs and the ends of each leg represent a point. Open the divider and place one leg of a divider on one end point of the given line segment and open the other leg till the other end point. Without changing the divider's width, place it on the ruler such that one pointer coincides with the zero mark of the ruler. Note down the reading on the ruler with which the other pointer coincides.

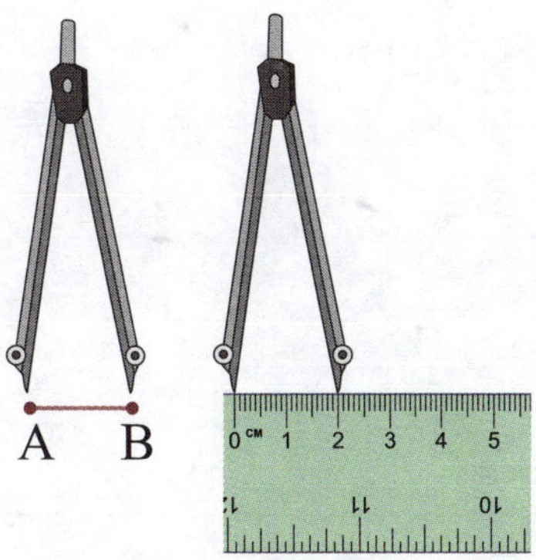

Hence, we find that $\overline{AB}$ = 2 cm as measured using a ruler and divider.

COMPARISON OF LINE SEGMENTS

Two or more line segments can be compared in the following three ways:

- Comparison by observation
- Comparison by tracing
- Comparison using divider

Comparison by Observation

Length of a line segment is the distance between its two endpoints. Observe the line segments $\overline{PQ}$ and $\overline{LM}$. We can easily say that the line segment $\overline{LM}$ is longer than the line segment $\overline{PQ}$. But can you compare AB and CD so easily?

Comparison by Tracing

Trace the line segments $\overline{AB}$ and $\overline{CD}$ on different transparent sheets. Overlap line segment $\overline{AB}$ and $\overline{CD}$ such that point A coincides with point C and then compare their lengths as illustrated in the following figures.

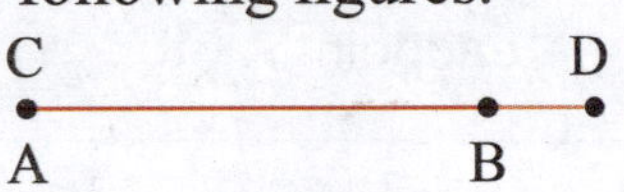

$\overline{AB} < \overline{CD}$

Fig. a.

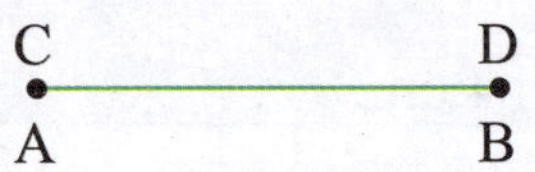

$\overline{AB} = \overline{CD}$

Fig. b.

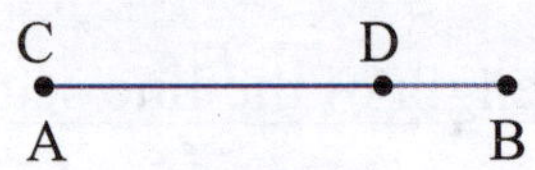

$\overline{AB} > \overline{CD}$

Fig. c.

Comparison Using Divider

Three possibilities arise with one arm at one endpoint:

1. The other arm falls exactly at B. then $\overline{AB} = \overline{CD}$. [See figure b.]

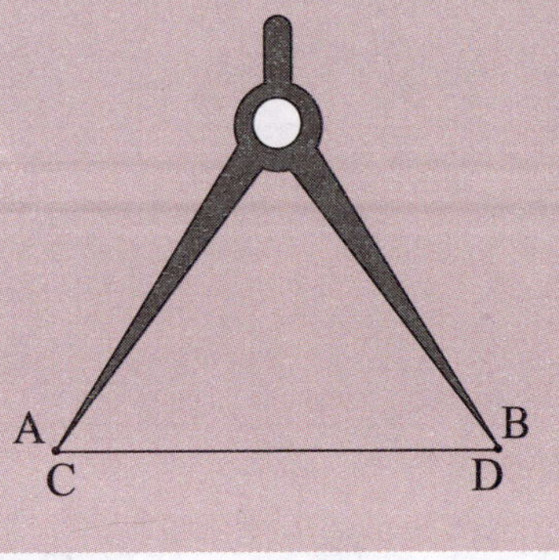

2. The other arm falls between A and B. then $\overline{AB} > \overline{CD}$. [See figure c.]

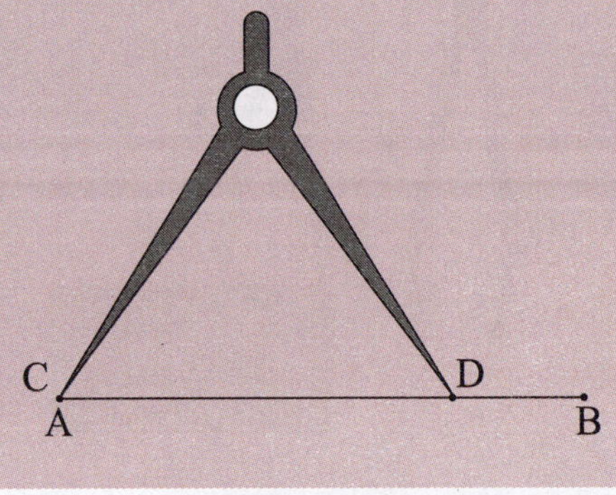

3. The other end falls away from B. then $\overline{AB} < \overline{CD}$. [See figure a.]

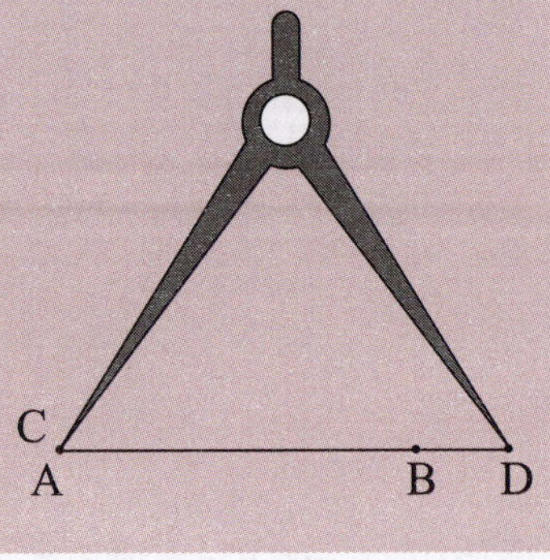

TYPES OF LINES

Parallel Lines

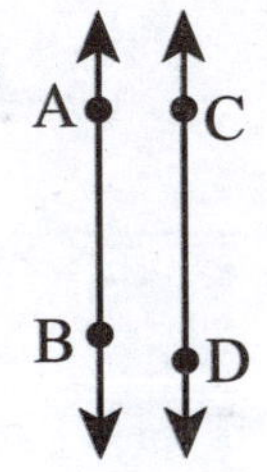

Have you ever noticed the railings of a bridge? Even if they are extended infinitely on both sides, they will never meet and the distance between them remains constant. Such lines are called **parallel lines**.

In the given figure, AB and CD are parallel lines. We write this as AB || CD.

Intersecting Lines

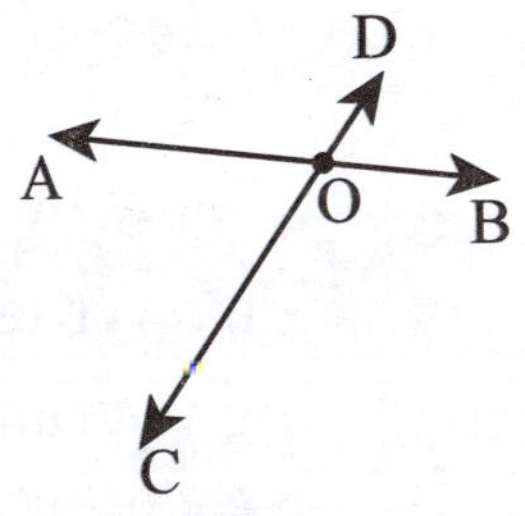

Two lines that are not parallel will meet each other at a particular point. Such lines are called **intersecting lines** and the point where they meet is called the point of intersection.

In the given figure, AB and CD intersect at point O.

REMEMBER

Lines that are not parallel are intersecting lines.

Perpendicular Lines

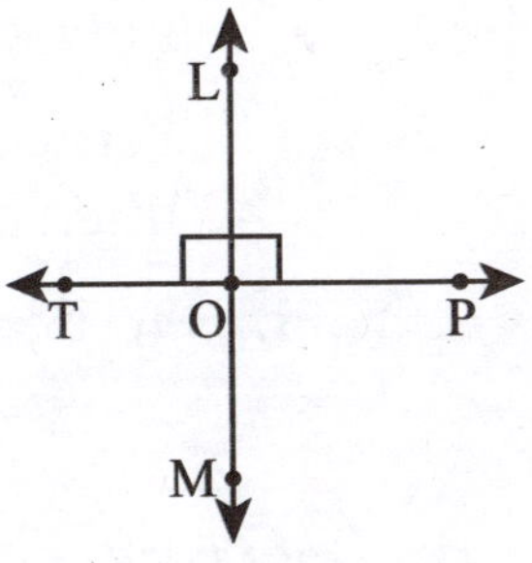

If two lines intersect each other at a right angle, then the lines are said to be **perpendicular lines**. In the given figure, lines TP and LM intersect each other at O making a right angle.

We write this as LM ⊥ TP.

Concurrent Lines

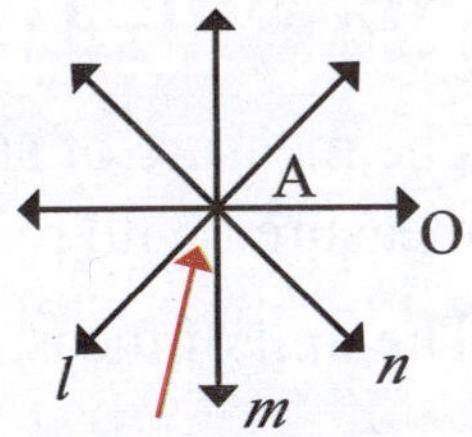

Point of concurrence

Three or more lines are said to be **concurrent** if they pass through a common point. The point through which the lines pass is called their **point of concurrence**.

In the figure, lines *l*, *m*, *n* and *O* pass through the same common point A. These are concurrent lines. A is their point of concurrence.

EXERCISE 12.1

1. **Measure and write the length of the given line segments using a ruler. Verify the lengths using a divider.**

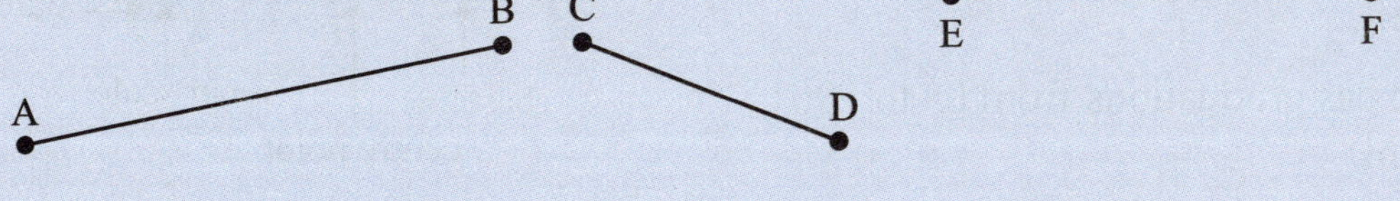

2. **Identify different line segments in the figure. Measure and write their lengths. List the line segments from the longest to the shortest.**

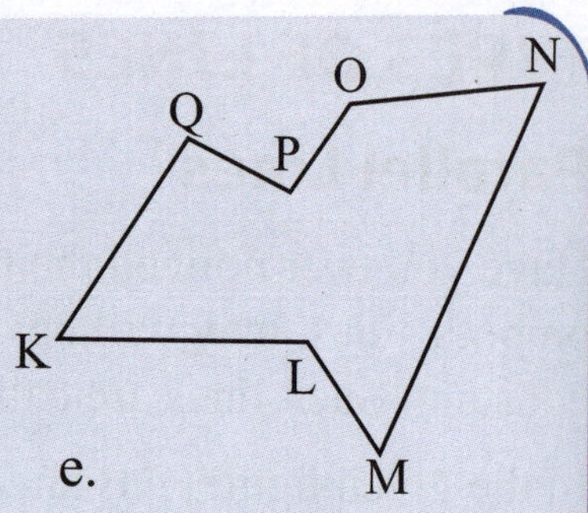

3. **Write the type of lines in each of the following figures.**

a. b. c. d. e.

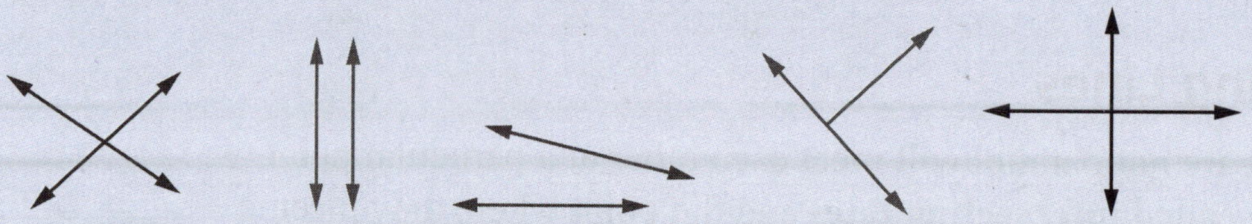

4. **Study the given figure carefully and answer the following questions:**

   a. Write all concurrent lines.
   b. Write all the pairs of lines that intersect at point I.
   c. Write all the pairs of lines that intersect at point D.
   d. Write all the pairs of lines that intersect at point E.
   e. Write all the pairs of lines that intersect at point A.
   f. Write all the pairs of parallel lines.

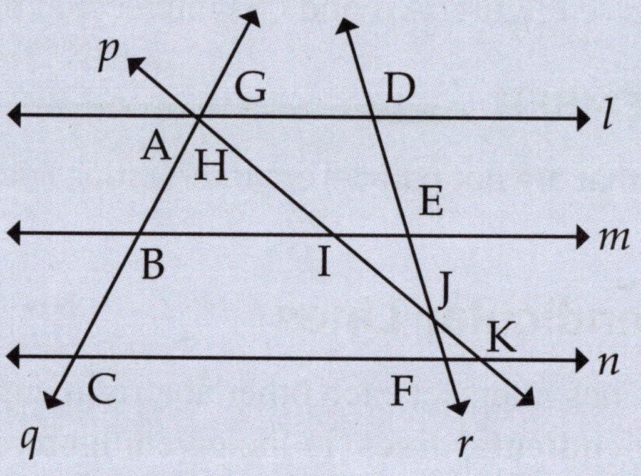

MEASURING ANGLES

The measure of an angle is the total rotation of one arm of that angle (about the vertex) measured with reference to the other arm.

The unit of measurement of an angle is degree, denoted as '°'.

Measuring Angles Using a Protractor

A protractor is used to measure angles.

It has a centre point, a base line, an outer scale and an inner scale.

The inner scale has graduations from 0° to 180° from right to left.

The outer scale has graduations from 0° to 180° from left to right.

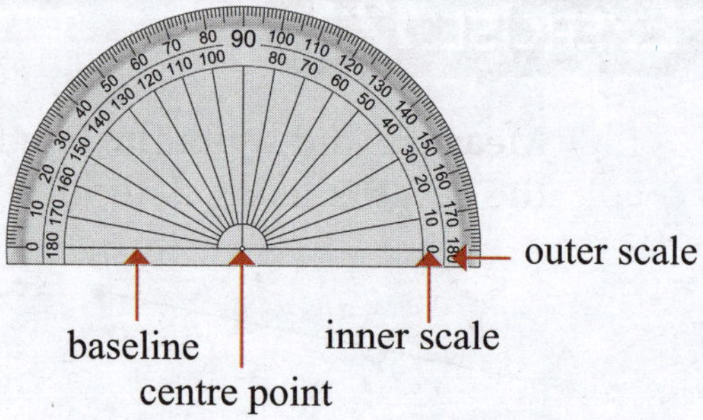

When the angle is opened up towards the right, we use the inner scale and when the angle is opened up towards the left, we use the outer scale.

Types of Angles

The angles are classified as given in the following table.

Angle	Definition	Angles along with Figure
Acute Angle	An angle less than 90° is called an acute angle.	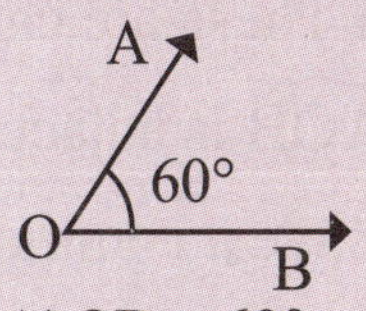 ∠AOB = 60°
Right Angle	An angle equal to 90° is called a right angle.	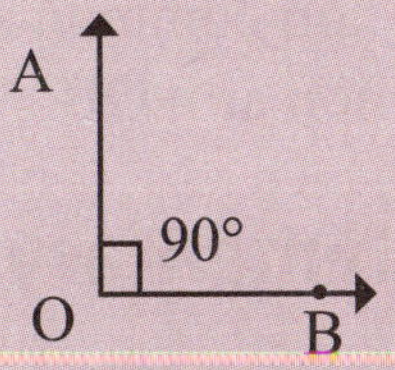 ∠AOB = 90°
Obtuse Angle	An angle greater than 90° but less than 180° is called an obtuse angle.	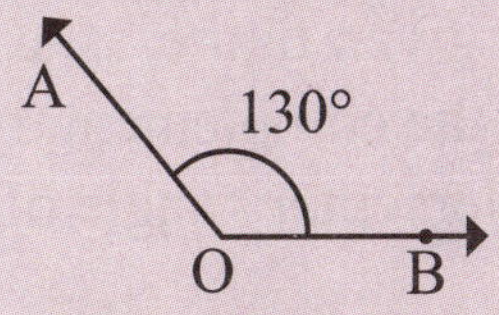 ∠AOB = 130°
Straight Angle	An angle equal to 180° is called a straight angle.	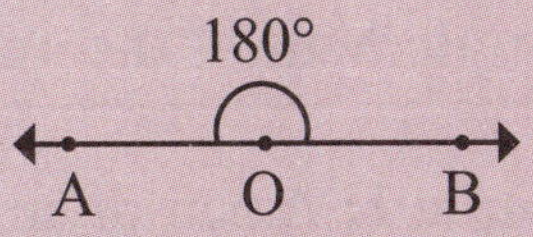 ∠AOB = 180°
Reflex Angle	An angle greater than 180° but less than 360° is called a reflex angle.	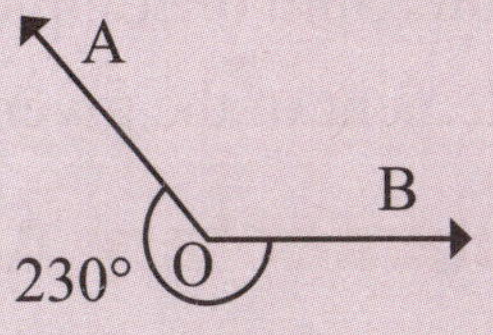 reflex ∠AOB = 230°
Complete Angle	An angle equal to 360° is called a complete angle.	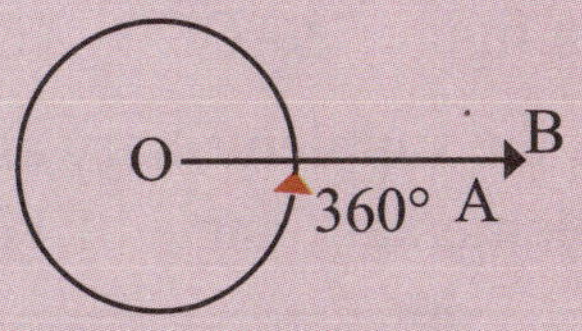 ∠AOB = 360°

When the two rays overlap each other, i.e. none of the ray has moved from its initial position, the magnitude of the angle is **zero degree**.

As started earlier, a complete turn about a point is divided into 360 equal parts.
Thus, 1° × 360° = 360° (one revolution)

Therefore, a 360° angle is called **complete angle**.

SPECIAL PAIRS OF ANGLES

Adjacent Angles

There are two angles in the given figure that share a common arm OB and have a common vertex O. These are called **adjacent angles**.

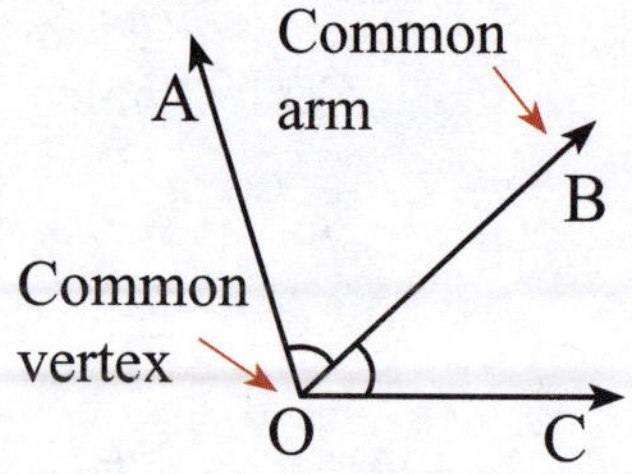

Here, ∠AOB is adjacent to ∠BOC as

- they have a common vertex O.
- they have a common arm OB.
- their non common arms OA and OC lie on the opposite side of common arm OB.

Complementary Angles

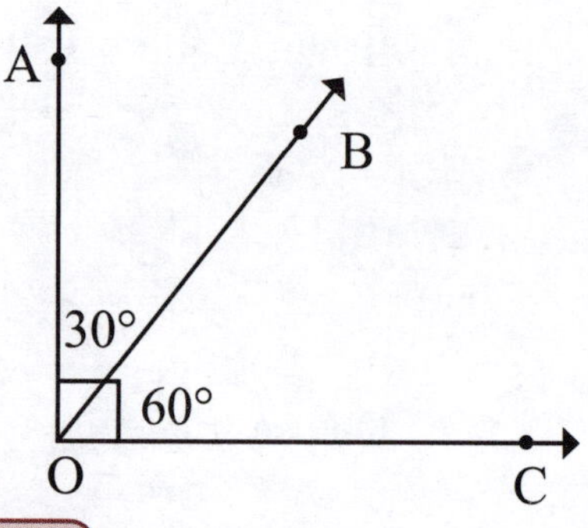

If the measures of two angles add up to 90°, then those angles are said to be **complementary** to each other.
In the given figure, ∠AOB + ∠BOC = 30° + 60° = 90°.
Here, the complementary angle of 30° is 60° and the complementary angle of 60° is 30°.

To find the complement of an angle, we use the following formula:
Complement of the angle = 90° – Measure of the given angle

Example 1: A pair of angles is complementary to each other. If one of them measures 47°, what is the measure of its complement?

Solution: Sum of complementary angles = 90°

Complement of the given angle = 90° – 47° = 43°

Supplementary Angles

If the measures of two angles add up to 180°, then those angles are said to be **supplementary** to each other. In the given figure, ∠AOC + ∠COB = 120° + 60° = 180°.

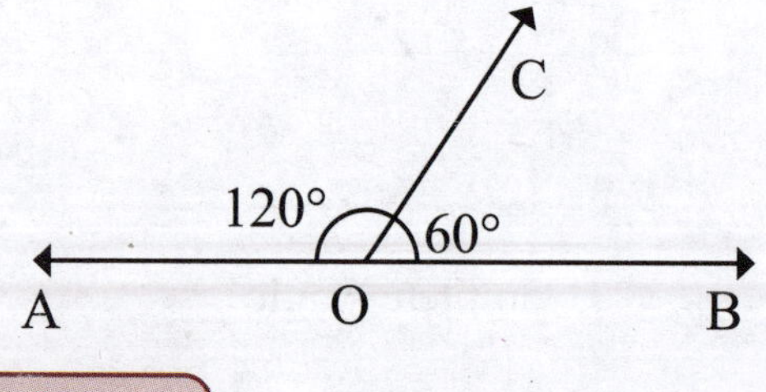

Here the supplementary angle of 60° is 120° and the supplementary angle of 120° is 60°.

To find the supplement of an angle, we use the following formula:
Supplement of the angle = 180° – Measure of the given angle

Example 2: Two angles are supplementary to each other. One of them measures 127°, find its supplement.

Solution: Sum of supplementary angles = 180°

Measure of the given angle = 127°

Supplement of the angle = 180° – 127° = 53°

Linear Pair of Angles

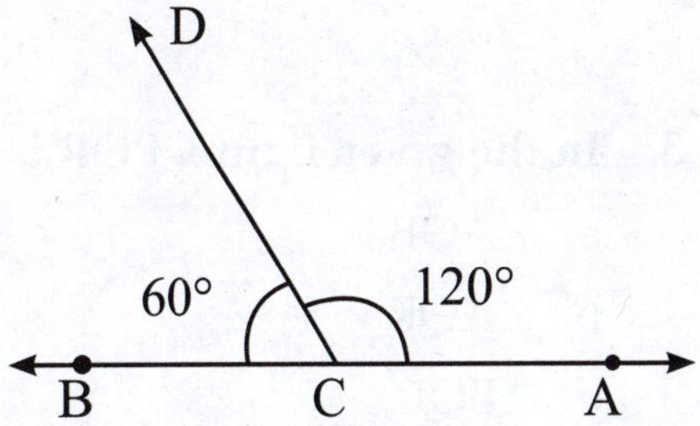

A pair of adjacent angles which are supplementary to each other form a **linear pair**. In the given figure, ∠DCB and ∠DCA = 60° + 120° = 180°.

Hence, they form a linear pair.

Vertically Opposite Angles

Two intersecting lines create four angles around the point of intersection. Among these angles, the pairs of non-adjacent angles are called **vertically opposite angles.**

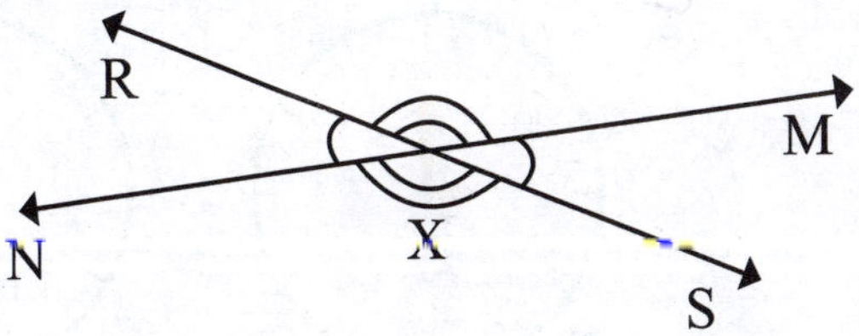

In the given figure, the pairs ∠RXN and ∠MXS; ∠NXS and ∠RXM are vertically opposite angles and they are equal.

Example 3: If ∠RON and ∠NOP form a linear pair, find the value of x.

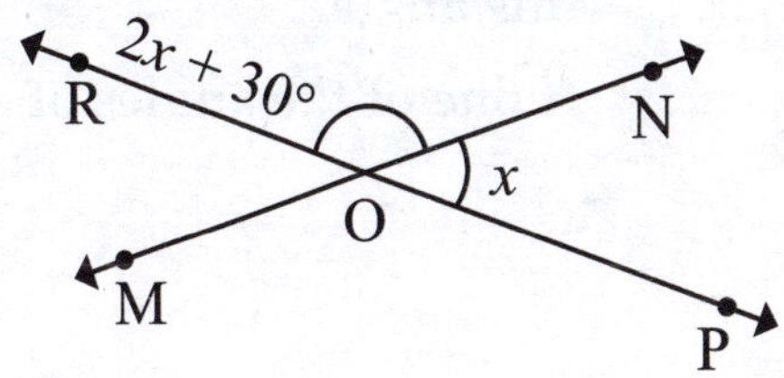

Solution:

$x + 2x + 30 = 180°$ [linear pair]

$\Rightarrow 3x + 30° = 180°$

$\Rightarrow 3x = 180° - 30° = 150°$

$\Rightarrow x = \frac{150°}{3} = 50°$

Exercise 12.2

1. **Compare the following angles and write them in the descending order. Verify your answer by measuring them using a protractor.**

   a. 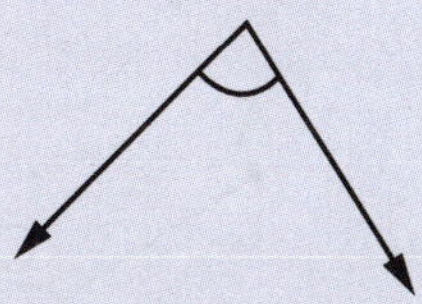 b. 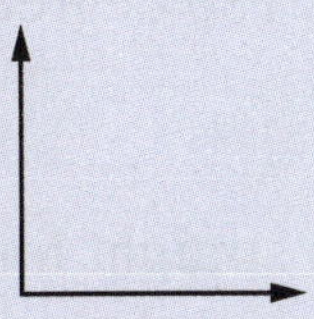 c. 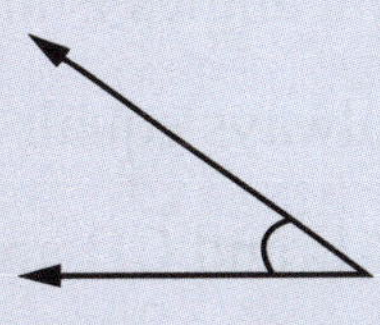 d. 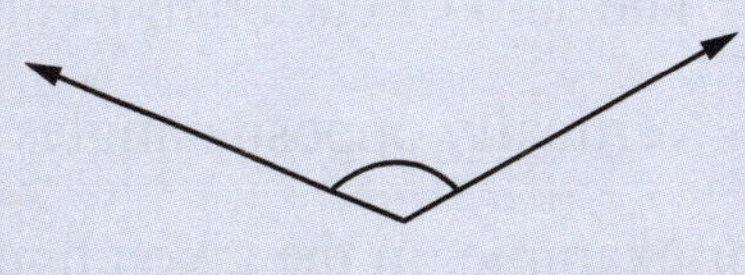

2. **Fill in the blanks with appropriate words.**

   a. An angle that is greater than a right angle and less than a straight angle is __________ angle.

   b The measure of a complete angle is __________ .

   c. An angle whose measure is 265° is called __________ angle.

   d. A straight angle equals __________ right angles.

   e. Four right angles form a __________ angle.

3. **In the given figure, PQR is a straight line. Find the following angles.**

   a. $\angle AQB$

   b. $\angle AQR$

   c. $\angle BQP$

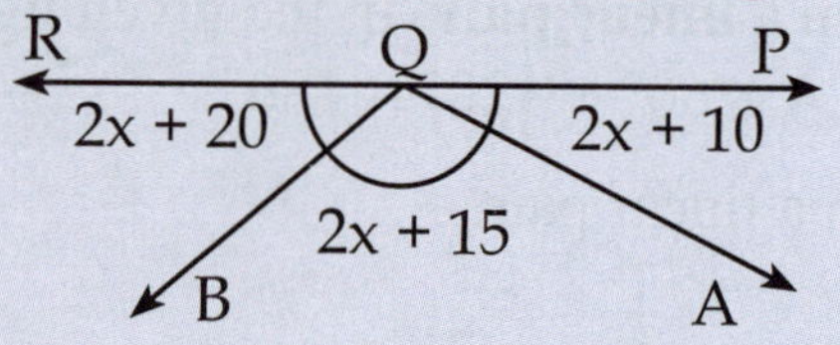

4. **Two complementary angles are in the ratio 5 : 7. Find the angles.**
5. **Measure the angle between the hour hand and the minute hand in each of the following figures.**

   a. 

   b. 

   c. 

   d. 

6. **An angle of 78° is supplement of another angle. What is the measure of this angle?**
7. **If one of the angles of a linear pair is 104°, find the measure of the other angle.**

PROPERTIES OF LINES AND ANGLES

We know that there are different types of lines and angles; each of them has different properties. Let us discuss few important properties of lines and angles.

Property 1: If two straight lines intersect, then

a. The sum of each pair of adjacent angles is always 180 degrees.

b. Vertically opposite angles are always equal.

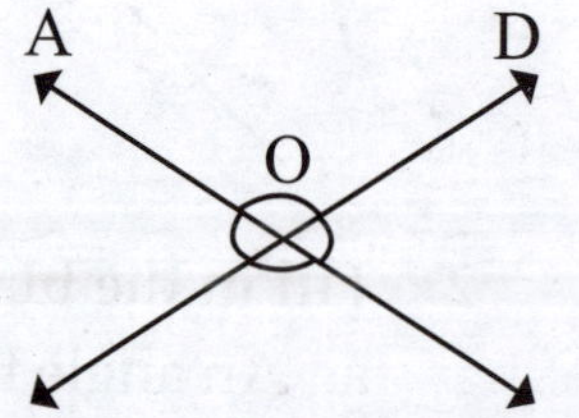

For example, in the given figure, AB and CD are two straight lines that intersect each other.

Here, $\angle AOC + \angle AOD = 180°$

$\angle AOC + \angle COB = 180°$

$\angle AOD + \angle BOD = 180°$

$\angle COB + \angle BOD = 180°$

and $\angle AOC = \angle BOD$ and $\angle BOC = \angle AOD$

Example 4: In the given figure, if ∠AOC = 68°, then find ∠AOD, ∠DOB and ∠BOC.

Solution: We know that if two straight lines intersect, then the vertically opposite angles are equal.

Hence, ∠AOC = ∠DOB = 68°.

Also, we know that if two straight lines intersect, then the sum of each pair of adjacent angles is equal to 180°.

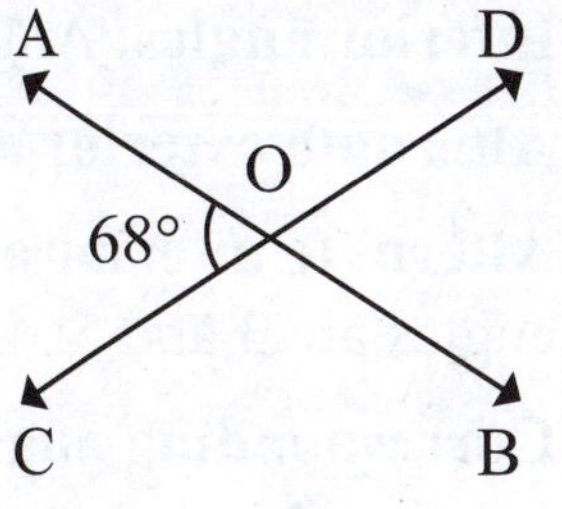

Hence, ∠AOC + ∠AOD = 180° and ∠AOC + ∠BOC = 180°

68° + ∠AOD = 180° and 68° + ∠BOC = 180°

∠AOD = 180° – 68° and ∠BOC = 180° – 68°

∠AOD = 112° and ∠BOC = 112°

Property 2: If the sum of two adjacent angles is 180°, then their exterior arms are always in the same straight line. Or, if the exterior arms of two adjacent angles are in the same straight line, then the sum of two adjacent angles is 180°.

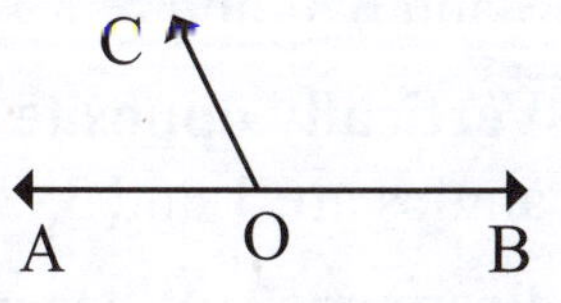

For example, in the given figure, ∠AOC and ∠BOC are two adjacent angles and OA and OB are two exterior arms.

If ∠AOC + ∠BOC = 180°, then OA and OB are in the same straight line.

IF OA and OB are in the same straight line, then ∠AOC + ∠BOC = 180°.

Example 5: In the given figure, if OA and OB are in the same straight line, then find the value of ∠AOC and ∠BOC.

Solution: We know that if the exterior arms of two adjacent angles are in the same straight line, then the sum of two adjacent angles is 180°.

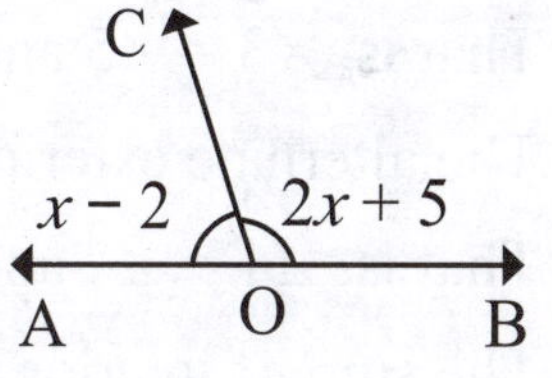

Hence, ∠AOC + ∠BOC = 180°

$$x - 2 + 2x + 5 = 180°$$

$$3x + 3 = 180°$$

$$3x = 177°$$

$$x = 59°$$

∠AOC = $(x - 2)°$ = (59 – 2)° = 57° and ∠BOC = $(2x + 5)°$ = (2 × 59 + 5)° = 123°

Transversal Lines

A transversal is a line which crosses two or more lines.

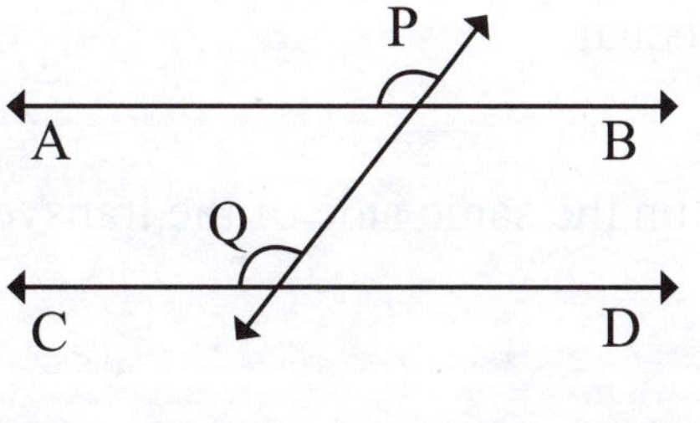

In the above figure, AB and CD are parallel lines and PQ is a transversal.

Angle formed by two lines and their transversal line

When two lines AB and CD are cut by a transversal line PQ, then there are eight angles formed as shown in the figure.

Exterior angles: Angles 1, 2, 7 and 8

Interior angles: Angles 3, 4, 5 and 6

Alternate exterior angles: Two pairs of exterior alternate angles are 1 and 7; 2 and 8

Alternate interior angles: Two pairs of interior alternate angles are 3 and 5; 4 and 6

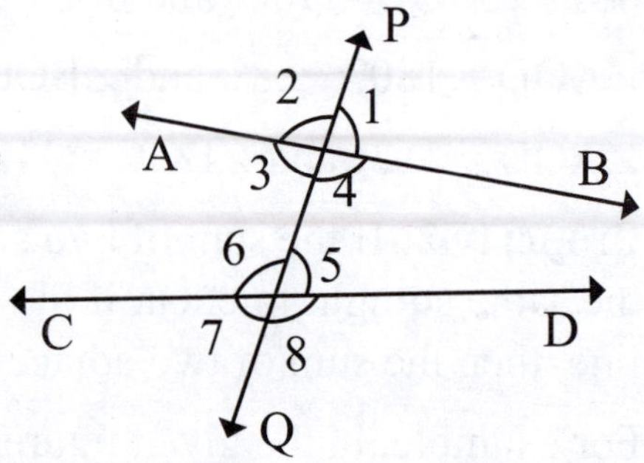

Corresponding angles: The pairs of corresponding angles are 1 and 5; 2 and 6; 3 and 7; 4 and 8

Co-interior angles: The pairs of co-interior angles are 3 and 6; 4 and 5

Vertically opposite angles: The pairs of vertically opposite angles are 1 and 3; 2 and 4; 5 and 7; 6 and 8

Property 3: When a transversal line intersects two parallel lines, then

a. The corresponding angles are equal.
   That is, $\angle 1 = \angle 5$, $\angle 2 = \angle 6$, $\angle 3 = \angle 7$ and $\angle 4 = \angle 8$

b. The vertically opposite angles are equal.
   That is, $\angle 1 = \angle 3$, $\angle 2 = \angle 4$, $\angle 5 = \angle 7$ and $\angle 6 = \angle 8$

c. The alternate interior angles are equal.
   That is, $\angle 3 = \angle 5$ and $\angle 4 = \angle 6$

d. The alternate exterior angles are equal.
   That is, $\angle 1 = \angle 7$ and $\angle 2 = \angle 8$

e. The sum of interior angles on the same side of the transversal line is equal to 180°.
   That is, $\angle 4 + \angle 5 = 180°$ and $\angle 3 + \angle 6 = 180°$

Example 6: In the given figure, find the value of x, y and z.

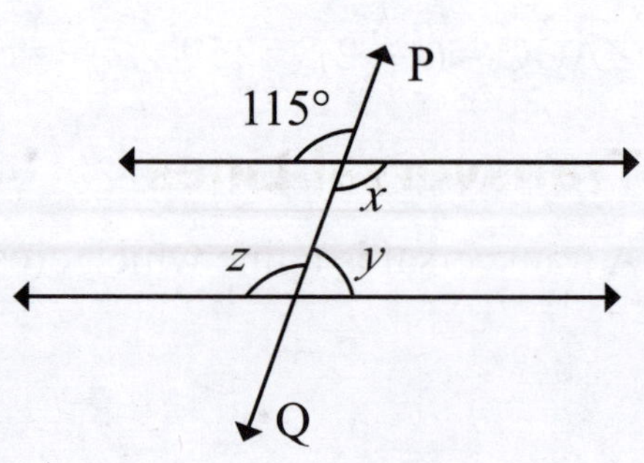

Solution: We know that when a transversal line intersects any two parallel lines, then vertically opposite angles are equal.

Hence, $x = 115°$

Here, corresponding angles are equal.

Hence, $z = 115°$

Also, the sum of interior angles on the same side of the transversal line is equal to 180°.

Hence, $x + y = 180°$

$115° + y = 180°$

$y = 180° - 115° = 65°$

Therefore, the value of $x = 115°$, $y = 65°$ and $z = 115°$.

Example 7: In the given figure, AB and CD are parallel lines intersected by a transversal PQ. and find the value of x.

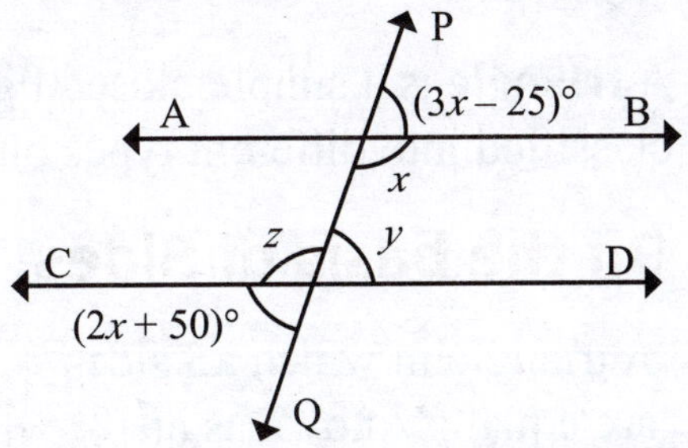

Solution: It is given that AB || CD.

Hence, alternate exterior angles are equal.

That is, $3x - 25° = 2x + 50°$

$3x - 2x = 50° + 25°$

$x = 75°$

EXERCISE 12.3

1. **Observe the figure and find the value of ∠BOD.**

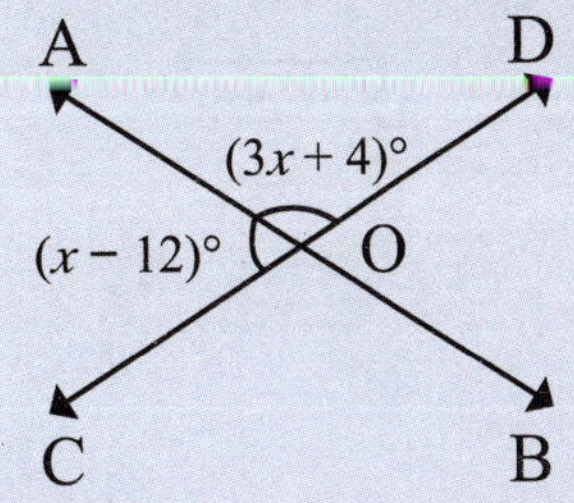

2. **In the given figure, ∠AOD = 112° find the value of ∠AOC, ∠COB and ∠BOD.**

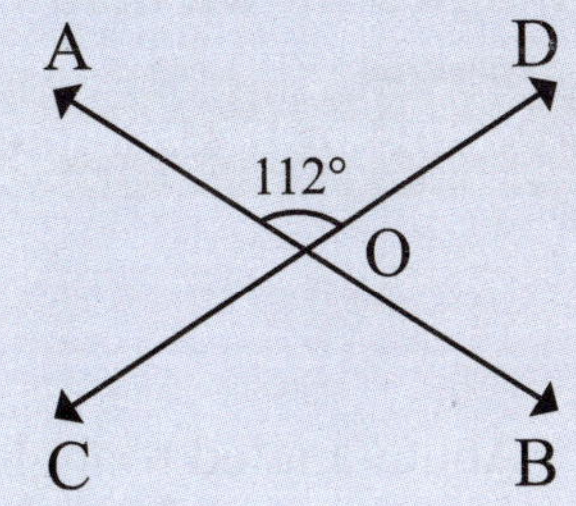

3. **Find the value of x, y, and z, if ∠P = 65°.**

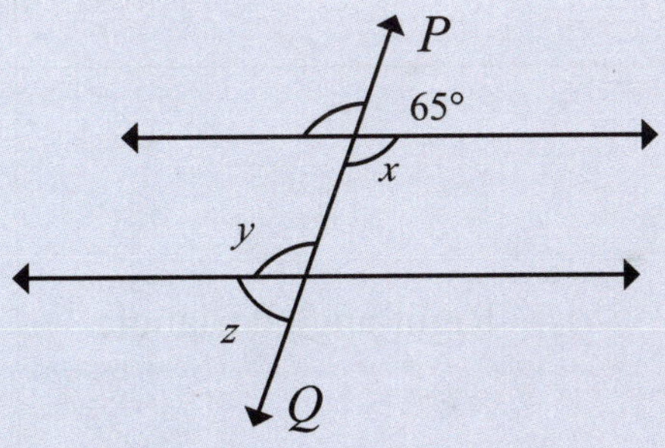

4. **In the given figure, AB and CD are parallel lines intersected by a transversal PQ. Find the value of ∠AMP and ∠DNQ.**

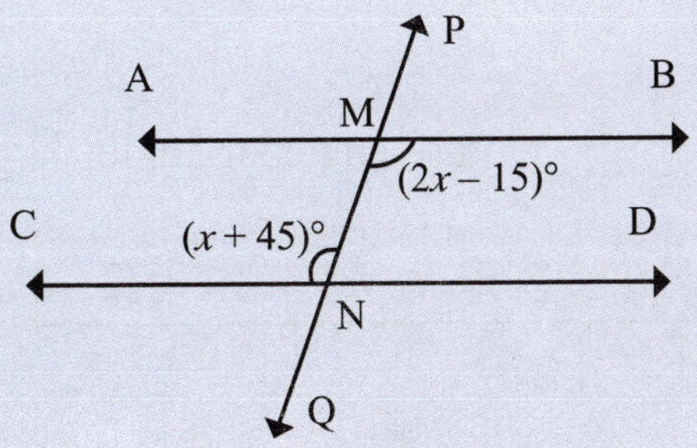

TRIANGLE

A **triangle** is a simple closed figure made up of three line segments. Triangles can be classified into different types on the basis of their sides and angles.

On the basis of Sides

A triangle in which all sides are equal is known as an **equilateral triangle.** 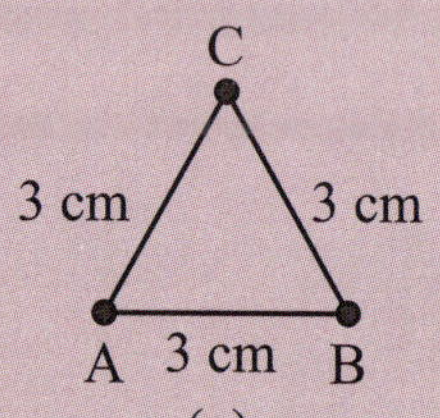 (a)	A triangle in which two sides are equal is known as an **isosceles triangle.** 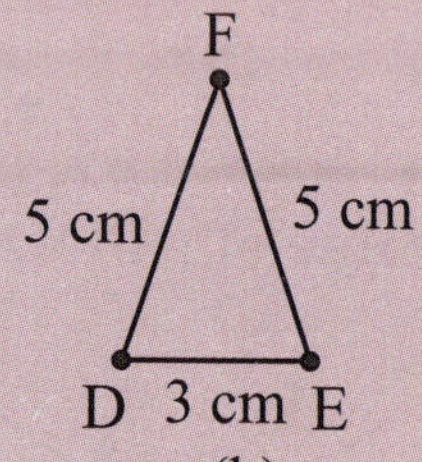 (b)	A triangle in which all sides are different is known as a **scalene triangle.** 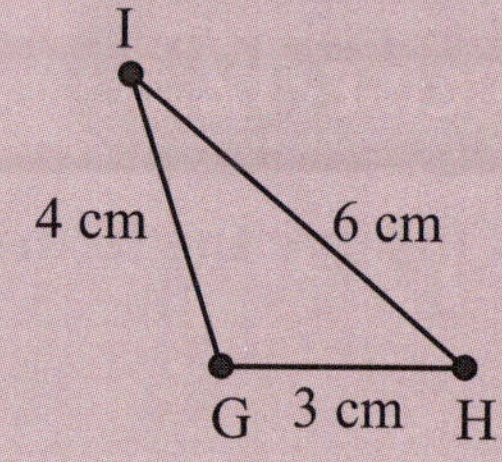 (c)

On the basis of Angles

Observe the angles in each of the triangles shown below.

Angles	Name of the Triangle	Figure
All angles are acute (< 90°).	Acute-angled triangle	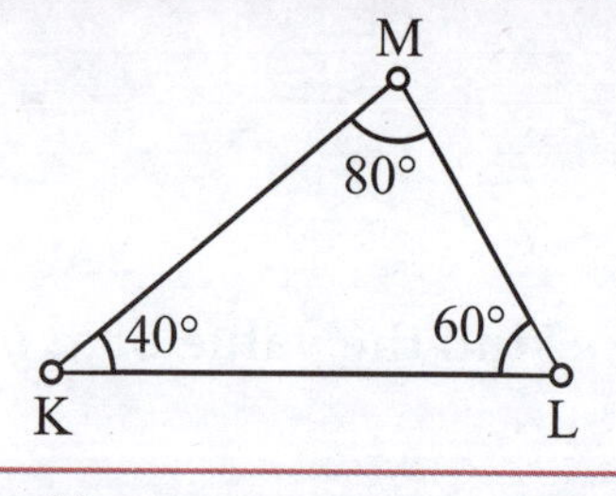
One angle is a right angle (= 90°).	Right-angled triangle	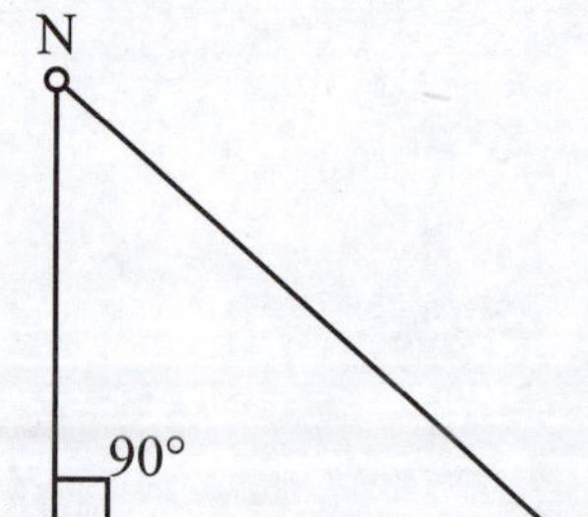
One angle is obtuse (> 90°).	Obtuse-angled triangle	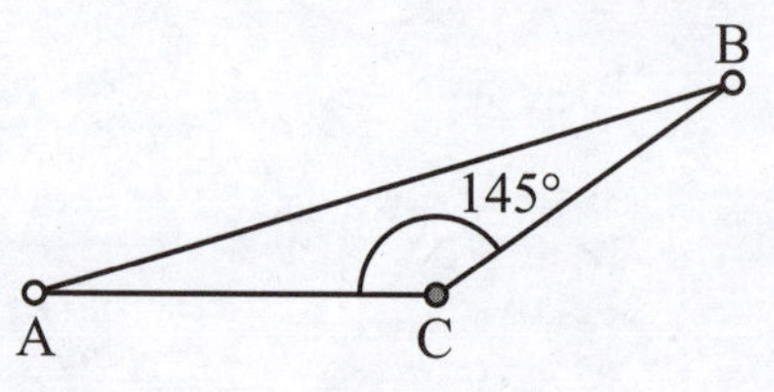

Properties of Triangles

Here are some important propertie of triangles.

1. Sum of all the interior angles of a triangle is always equal to 180°.

   In the given triangle ABC, ∠A + ∠B + ∠C = 180°

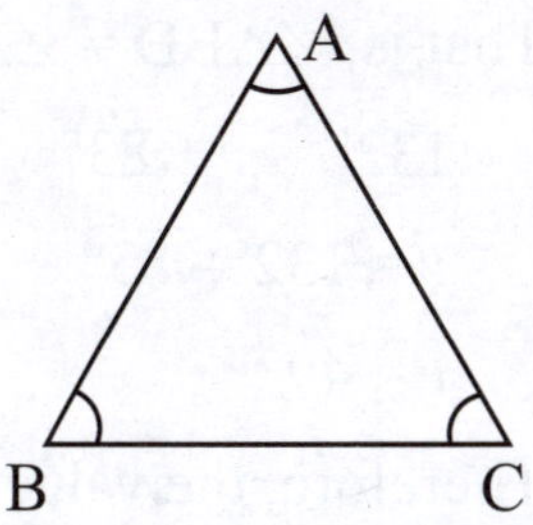

2. When one side of a triangle is extended, then the resulting exterior angle is an adjacent and supplementary angle corresponding to the interior angle of the triangle.

   For example, in the given figure, the base BC is extended to D, then ∠ACD is the exterior angle and ∠ACD is adjacent to ∠ACB. Also, ∠ACD and ∠ACB are supplementary angles.

   That is ∠ACD + ∠ACB = 180°

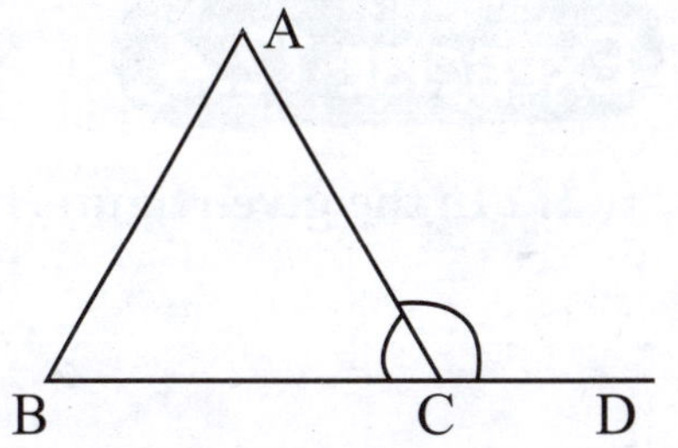

3. When one side of a triangle is extended, then the resulting exterior angle is equal to sum of its two interior opposite angles.

   In the given figure, ∠ACD is an exterior angle.

   Hence, ∠ACD = ∠A + ∠B

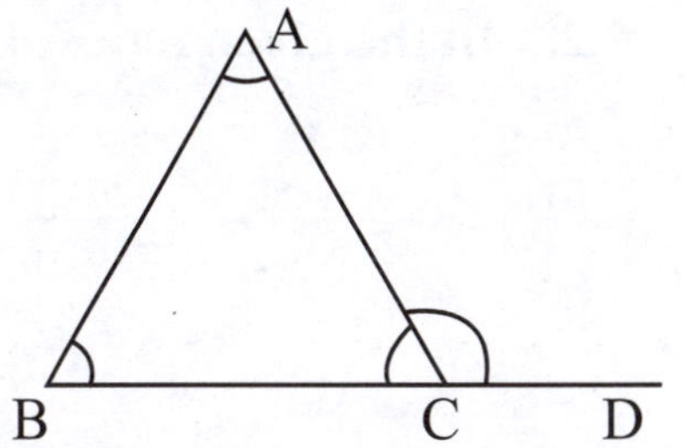

Example 8: Find the value of x in the given figure.

Solution: In triangle ABC, ∠A = 58° and ∠C = 57°.

We know that sum of all the interior angles of a triangle is always equal to 180°.

That is, ∠A + ∠B + ∠C = 180°

$58° + x + 57° = 180°$

$x = 180° - 58° - 57°$

$x = 65°$

Therefore, the value of x is 65°.

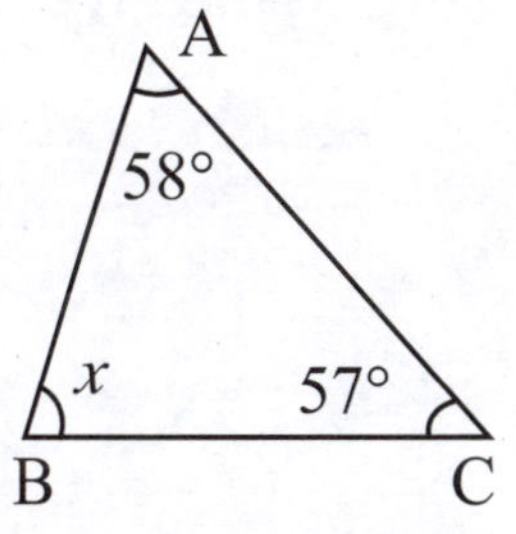

Example 9: Observe the given figure and find the values of x and y.

Solution: In the given triangle ABC,

∠A = y, ∠B = x, ∠C = 83° and ∠ABD = 132°.

We know that in a triangle, the exterior angle is an adjacent and supplementary angle corresponding to the interior angle of the triangle.

That is, ∠ABD + ∠ABC = 180°

$\Rightarrow 132° + x = 180°$

$\Rightarrow x = 180° - 132° = 48°$

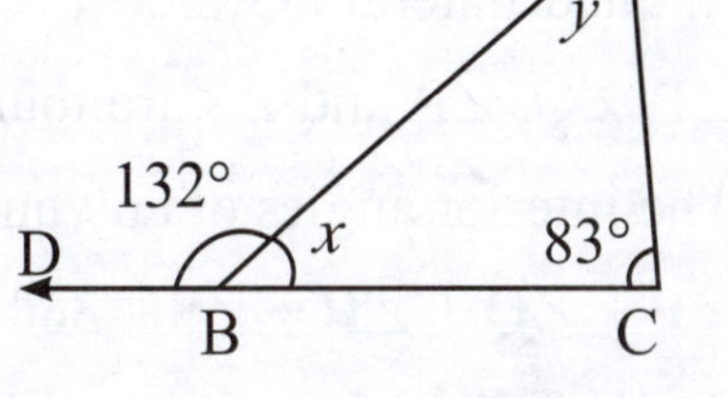

Also, the exterior angle of a triangle is equal to the sum of its two interior opposite angles.

That is, $\angle ABD = \angle A + \angle C$

$132° = y + 83°$

$y = 132° - 83°$

$y = 49°$

Therefore, the value of x is 48° and that of y is 49°.

EXERCISE 12.4

1. **In the given figure, find the value of x.**

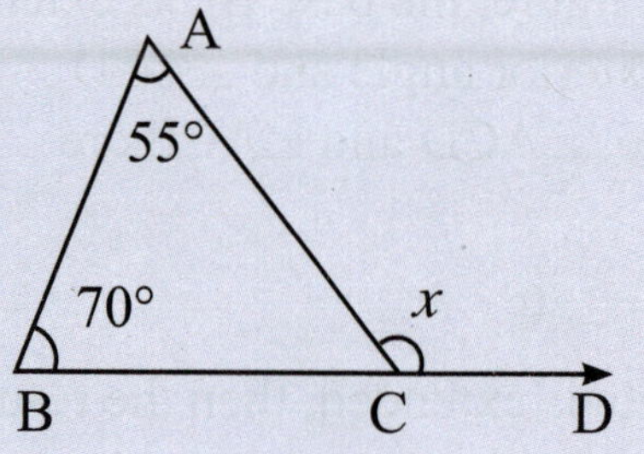

2. **In the given figure, find the values of x and y.**

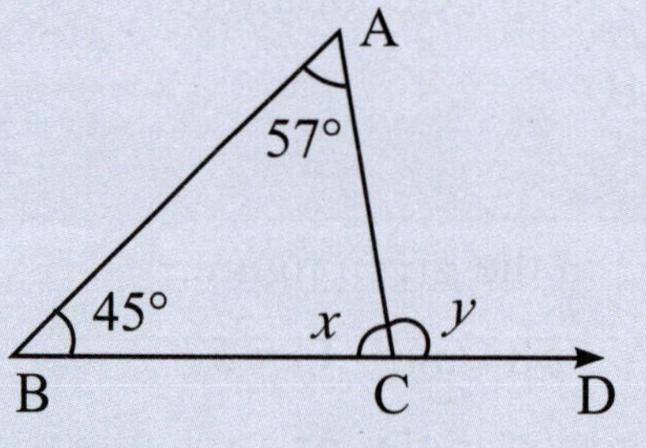

3. **In the given figure, find the values of x and y.**

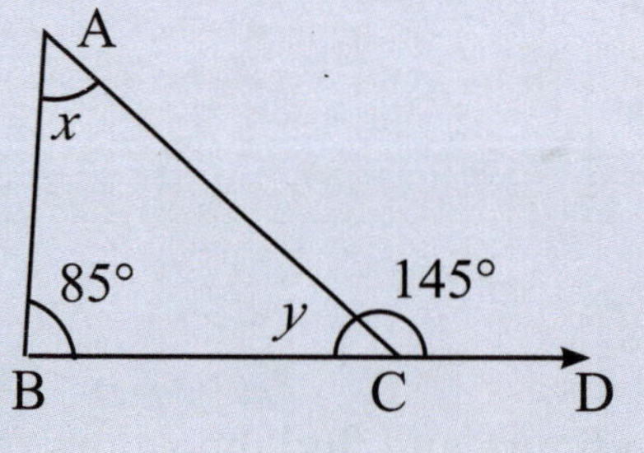

QUADRILATERALS

A **quadrilateral** is a simple closed figure made up of four line segments. There are different types of quadrilaterals with specific properties.

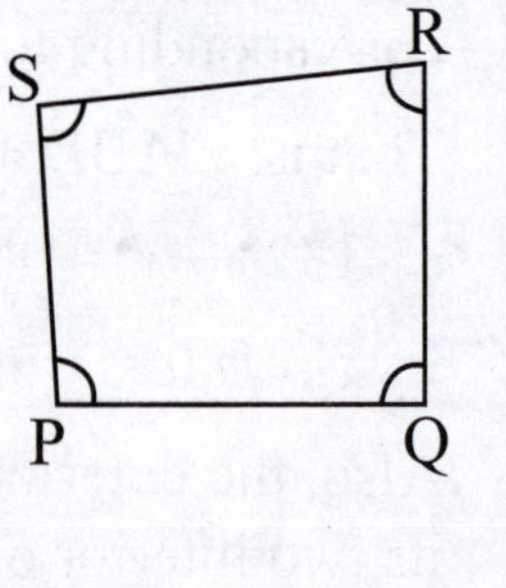

In quadrilateral PQRS,

$\angle P$, $\angle Q$, $\angle R$ and $\angle S$ are four interior angles.

The interior angles of any quadrilateral PQRS add up to 360 degrees, that is

$\angle \mathbf{P} + \angle \mathbf{Q} + \angle \mathbf{R} + \angle \mathbf{S} = \mathbf{360°}$

Sum of all angles of a quadrilateral is 360°.

Types of Quadrilaterals

There are six types of quadrilaterals.

- Rectangle
- Square
- Parallelogram
- Trapezium
- Rhombus
- Kite

Let us see about each type of quadrilateral and its properties.

Rectangle: A rectangle is a quadrilateral in which opposite sides are equal and parallel and each interior angle is a right angle.

The given figure is a rectangle since AB = CD and AD = BC and all interior angles are right angles.

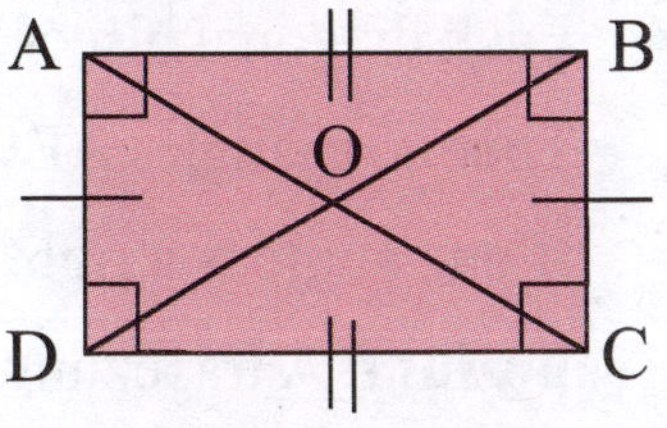

Properties of rectangle

- Opposite sides of a rectangle are equal and parallel.
  That is, AB = CD and AD = BC. Also, AB || CD and AD || BC.
- Each interior angle is equal to right angle.
  That is, $\angle A = \angle B = \angle C = \angle D = 90°$
- The diagonals are equal and bisect each other.
  That is, AC = BD and OA = OB = OC = OD

Square: A square is a quadrilateral in which all sides are equal and all interior angles are right angles.

In the given figure ABCD, AB = BC = CD = DA and all interior angles are right angles. Hence, ABCD is a square.

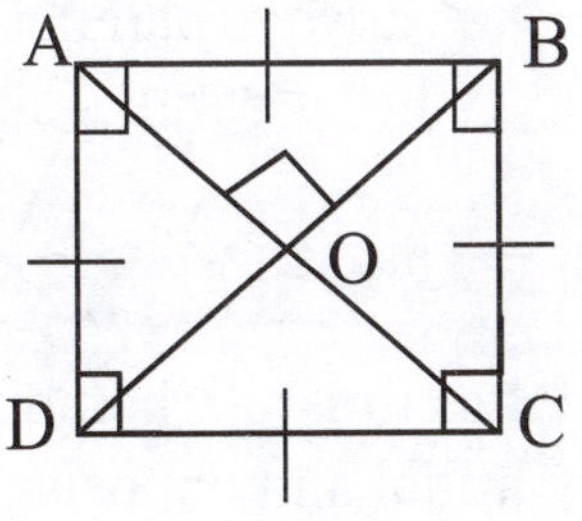

Properties of square

- All four sides are equal and opposite sides are parallel to each other.
  That is, AB = BC = CD = DA. Also, AB || CD and AD || BC.
- Each interior angle is a right angle.
  That is, $\angle A = \angle B = \angle C = \angle D = 90°$
- The diagonals are equal and bisect each other at right angles.
  That is, AC = BD and OA = OB = OC = OD and $\angle AOB = 90°$

Parallelogram: A parallelogram is a quadrilateral in which opposite sides are parallel and equal.

In the given figure, AB || CD and AD || BC. Hence, ABCD is a parallelogram.

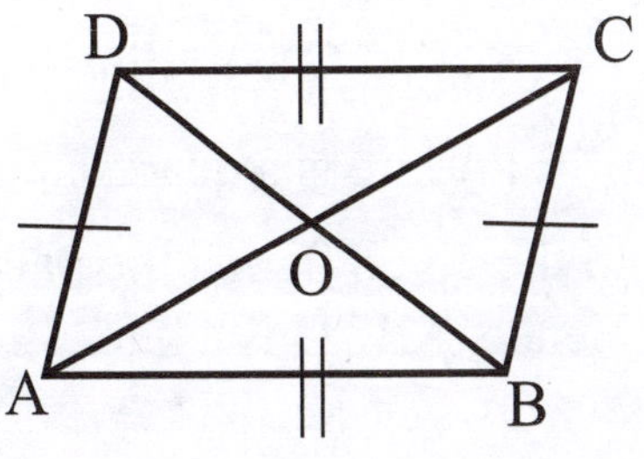

Properties of parallelogram

- The opposite sides are parallel and equal.
  That is, AB = CD and AD = BC. Also, AB || CD and AD || BC.

- The opposite angles are equal.
  That is, $\angle A = \angle C$ and $\angle B = \angle D$
- The sum of two consecutive angles is 180°.
  That is, $\angle A + \angle D = 180°$, $\angle A + \angle B = 180°$, $\angle B + \angle C = 180°$ and $\angle C + \angle D = 180°$.
- Diagonals bisect each other.
  That is, OA = OC and OB = OD
- Each diagonal bisect the parallelogram into two similar triangles.
  That is, triangles ABC and CDA and triangles ABD and CDB are congruent.
- If one angle is a right angle, then all angles are right angles.

Trapezium: A trapezium is a quadrilateral in which one pair of opposite sides is parallel.

In the given figure, AB and CD are opposite sides and also they are parallel to each other. Hence, ABCD is a trapezium.

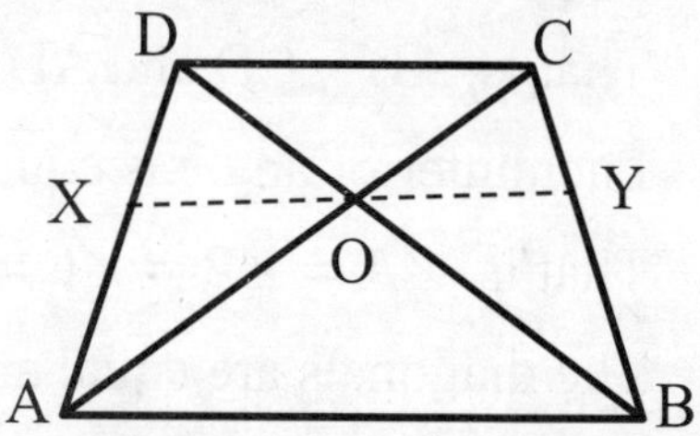

Properties of trapezium

- Only one pair of opposite sides is parallel.
  That is, $AB \parallel CD$
- The line that joins the mid-points of the non-parallel sides is always parallel to the base and is equal to half of the sum of parallel sides.
  That is, $XY = \frac{(AB + CD)}{2}$

Rhombus: A rhombus is a quadrilateral in which all sides are equal, opposite sides are parallel and opposite angles are equal.

In the given figure, AB = BC = CD = DA and $AB \parallel CD$ and $AD \parallel BC$.
Also, $\angle A = \angle C$ and $\angle B = \angle D$.

Hence ABCD is a rhombus.

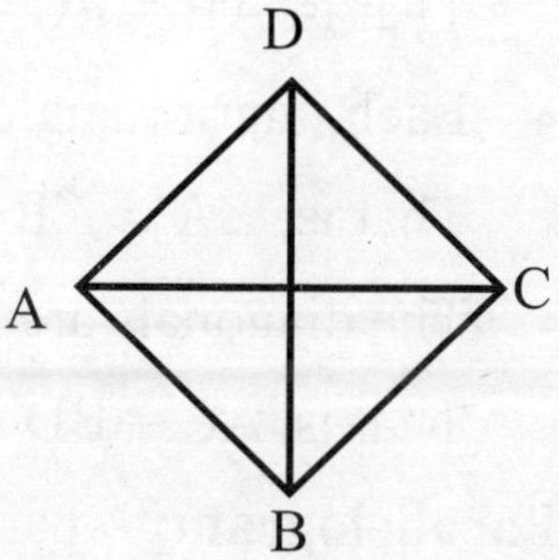

Properties of rhombus

- All sides are equal and opposite sides are parallel.
- Opposite angles are equal.
- Diagonals bisect each other at right angle.
- The sum of two consecutive angles is equal to 180°.
- Diagonals bisect the interior angles.

Kite: A kite is a quadrilateral in which two pairs of adjacent sides are equal.

In the given figure, the pairs of adjacent sides AB and AD and BC and CD are equal. Hence, ABCD is a kite.

Properties of kite

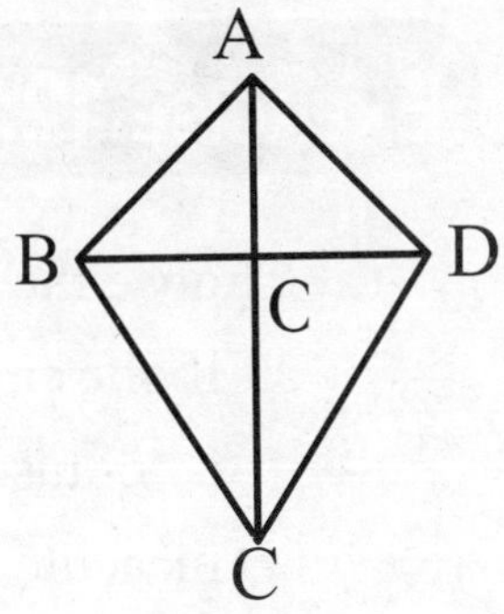

- Two pairs of adjacent sides are equal.
  That is, AB = AD and BC = CD
- Two angles are equal where the unequal sides meet.
  That is, ∠B = ∠D
- Diagonals intersect at right angles.
- One diagonal is bisected by the other.
  That is, OB = OD

Example 10: In the given figure, ABCD is a parallelogram. If ∠A = 80°, then find the other angles.

Solution: Given that ABCD is a parallelogram and ∠A = 80°.

We know that sum of two consecutive angles is equal to 180°.

Hence ∠A + ∠D = 180°

80 + ∠D = 180°

∠D = 100°

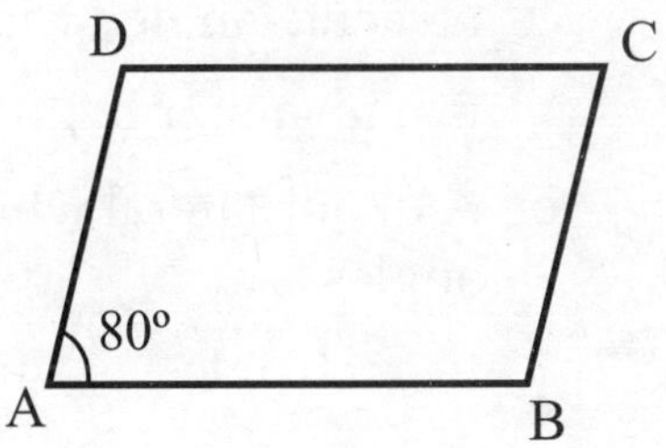

Also, in a parallelogram, opposite angles are equal.

That is, ∠A =∠C and ∠B = ∠D

Hence, ∠C = 80° and ∠B = 100°

Therefore, in a parallelogram ABCD, ∠A = 80°, ∠B = 100°, ∠C = 80° and ∠D = 100°.

Example 11: In the given figure, ABCD is a rhombus and if ∠DAC = 35°, then find the value of ∠ADC and ∠BCD.

Solution: Given that ABCD is a rhombus and ∠DAC = 35°.

In a rhombus, diagonals bisect the angles at vertex.

That is, ∠DAC = ∠CAB

∠CAB = 35°

Hence, ∠DAB =∠DAC + ∠CAB = 35° + 35° = 70°

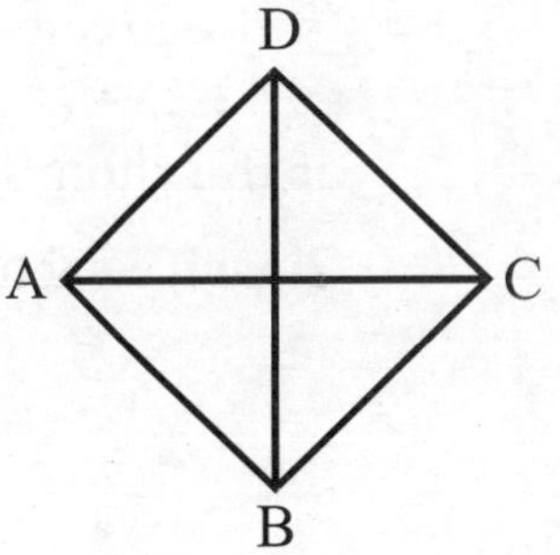

Also, sum of the adjacent angles is 180°.

That is, ∠ADC + ∠DAB = 180°

∠ADC = 180° – 70° = 110°

In a rhombus, opposite angles are equal.

Hence, ∠BCD = ∠DAB = 70°

Therefore, ∠ADC = 110° and ∠BCD = 70°.

EXERCISE 12.5

1. **Choose the correct answer for the following.**
   a. If one angle of a triangle is 90°, then the other two angles are
      i. obtuse angles ii. acute angles
      iii. acute and obtuse angles iv. None of the above
   b. Which of the following measurements forms an isosceles triangle ABC?
      i. AB = 5 cm, BC = 5 cm and CA = 5 cm
      ii. AB = 4 cm, BC = 5 cm and CA = 3 cm
      iii. AB = 4 cm, BC = 4 cm and CA = 5 cm
      iv. AB = 3 cm, BC = 4 cm and CA = 5 cm
   c. If one angle of a triangle is 95°, then the triangle is
      i. acute-angled triangle ii. right-angled triangle
      iii. either a or b iv. obtuse-angled triangle
   d. A quadrilateral whose all four sides are equal and all the four angles are right angles is a
      i. rectangle ii. square iii. rhombus iv. parallelogram
   e. A quadrilateral in which two pairs of adjacent sides are equal is called a ______.
      i. rectangle ii. parallelogram iii. rhombus iv. kite
2. **State whether the following statements are true (T) or false (F).**
   a. All parallelograms are rectangles. b. All squares are rectangles.
   c. All rhombuses are parallelograms. d. All kites are parallelograms.
   e. A rectangle with all sides equal is a parallelogram.
3. **In the given figure, ABCD is a rhombus. If AB = $(2x + 8)$ cm and CD = $(x + 15)$ cm, then find the measurements of all sides of the rhombus.**

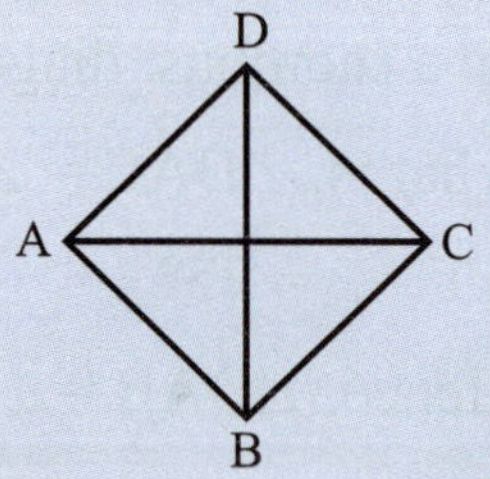

4. **Classify each of these triangles on the basis of their sides.**

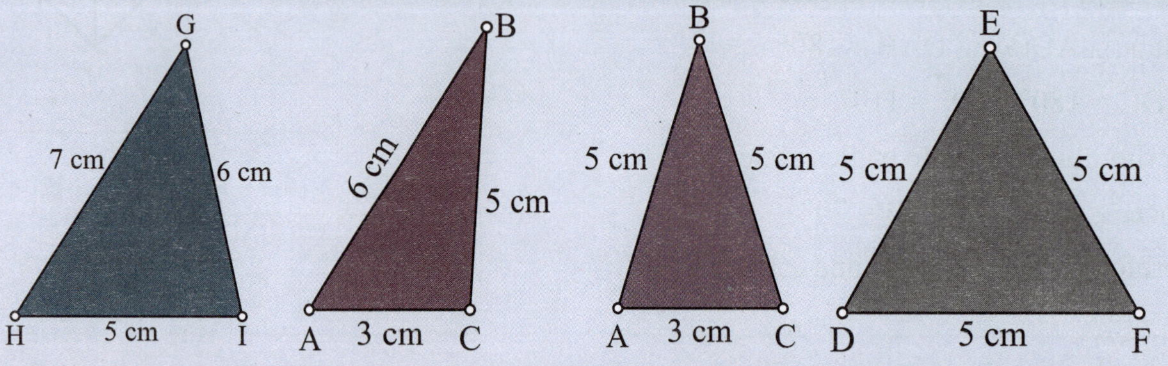

5. In the given figure, ABCD is a kite. If AB = 7 cm, OD = 5 cm and BC = 8 cm, then find the measurement of AD, BD and DC.

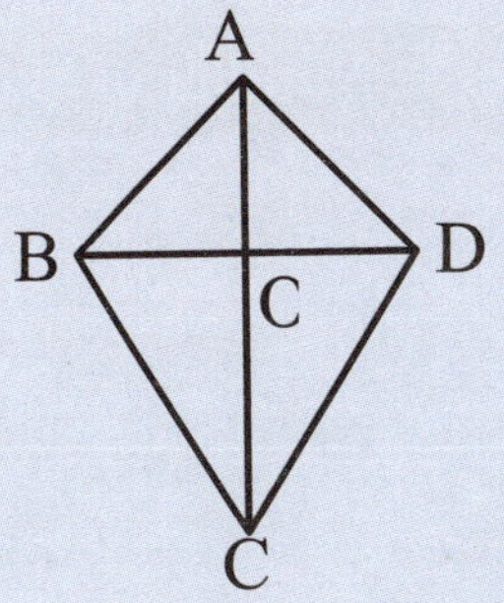

6. ABCD is a square. AC and BD are diagonals that intersect at O. If OA = 3 cm, then find the length of the two diagonals.
7. ABCD is a rectangle. AC and BD are diagonals that intersect at O. If OA = $(x + 3)$ cm and OB = $(2x - 5)$ cm, then find the length of the two diagonals.
8. ABCD is a parallelogram. If ∠A = 67 °, then find the other three angles.
9. Identify the types of triangles given below based on their angles.

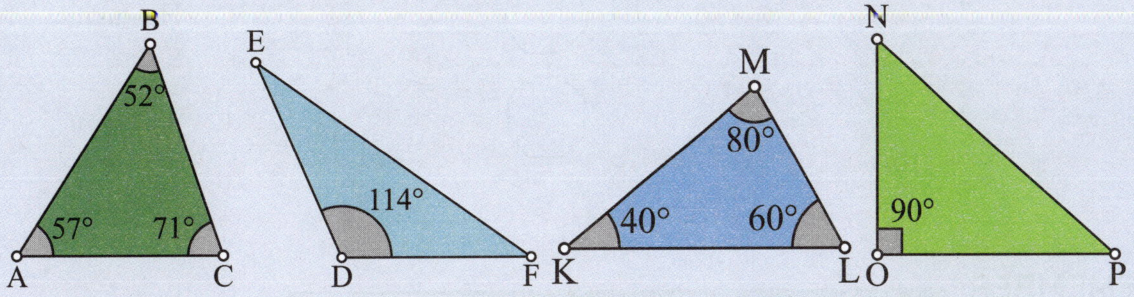

POLYGONS

A polygon is a simple closed figure made up of only line segments.

Polygons	Non-polygons

Regular and Irregular Polygons

Polygons in which all the sides are equal and all the angles are equal are known as **regular polygons** otherwise they are called **irregular polygons**. Some examples of regular and irregular polygons are given below.

Regular Polygons

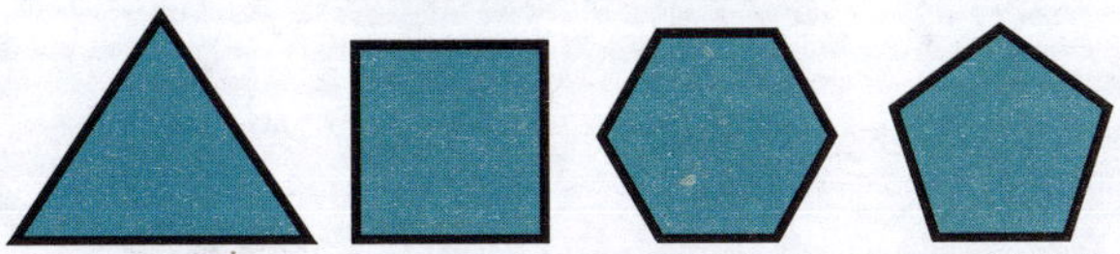

Irregular Polygons

Depending upon the number of sides they contain, polygons have specific names.

Number of Sides	Polygon	Name of Polygon
3	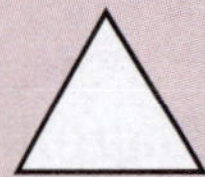	Triangle
4		Quadrilateral
5		Pentagon
6	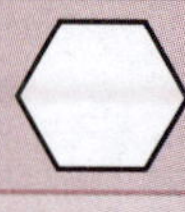	Hexagon
7		Heptagon
8	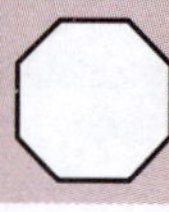	Octagon

REMEMBER

The number of sides of a polygon is equal to the number of angles.

EXERCISE 12.6

1. Name the following polygons.

Illustration				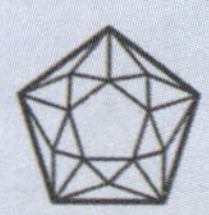	
Name					
Number of Sides					

2. Identify the regular and irregular polygons from the given figures.

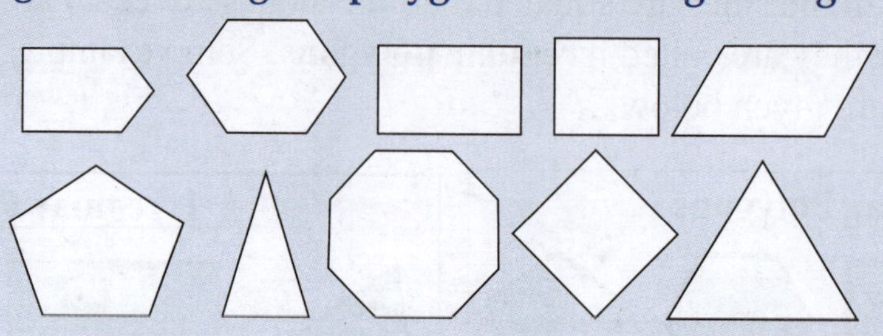

THREE-DIMENSIONAL SHAPES

An object having three dimensions—length, breadth and height is called a **three-dimensional** object or a 3D shape. We also call them **solids**.

Faces, Edges and Vertices

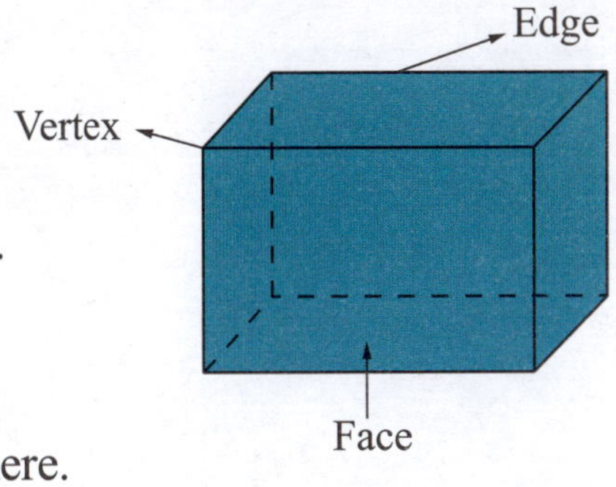

Face: The flat surface of a solid is called its face.

Edge: The line segment where two faces meet is called an edge. It is also referred to as a side.

Vertex: The point where three edges meet is called a vertex.

A **cuboid** has 6 faces, 12 straight edges and 8 vertices as shown here.

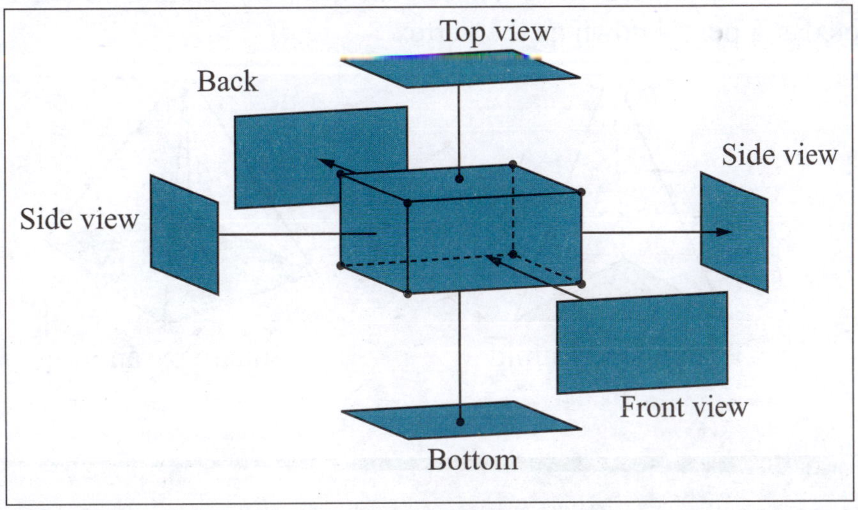

A **cube** also has 6 faces, 12 straight edges and 8 vertices. All 12 edges of a cube are equal.

A **cone** has 1 flat face, 1 curved face and 1 curved edge. It has one vertex.	A **cylinder** has 2 flat faces, 1 curved face and 2 curved edges. It has no vertices.	A **sphere** has 1 curved face. It has no edges and vertices.
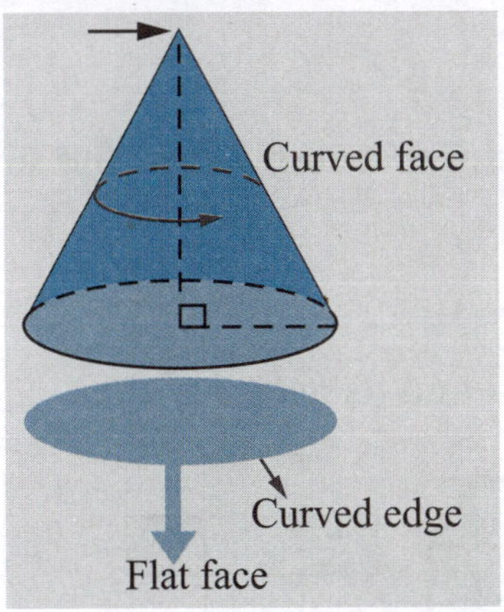	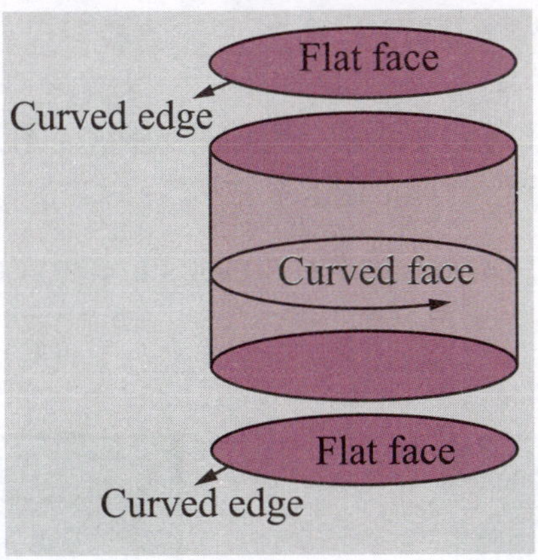	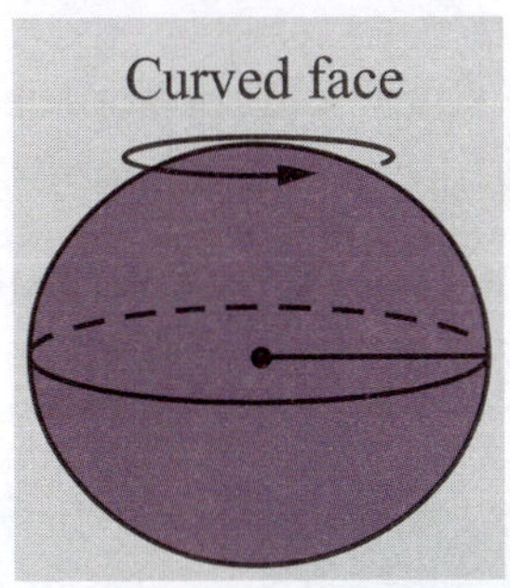

Here, cone, cylinder and sphere are referred to as solids with curved surface.

Prism and Pyramid

A **prism** is a three-dimensional figure whose top and base are polygons and other faces are rectangles.

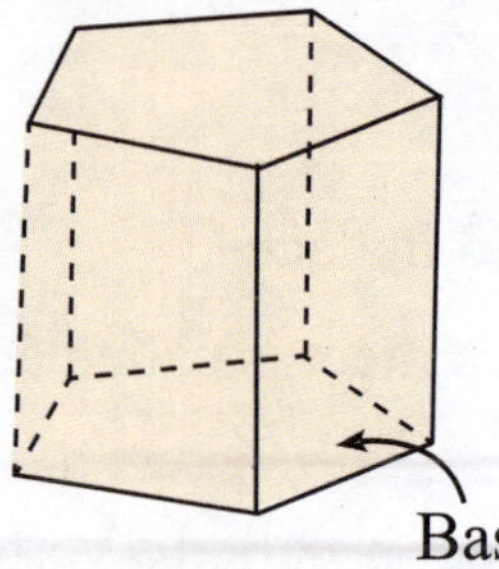

Base

Pentagonal Prism

A **pyramid** is a three-dimensional shape whose base is a polygon and all other faces are triangles connected at a point known as the vertex.

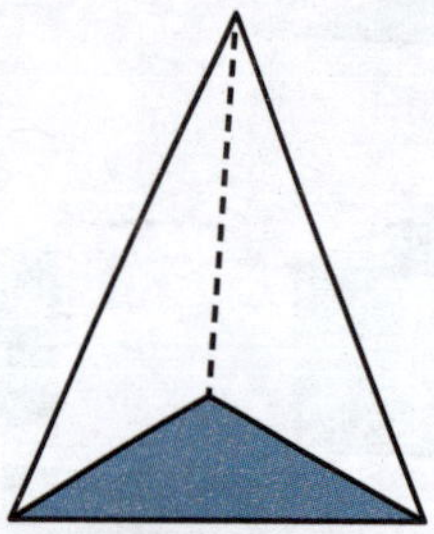

Triangular pyramid

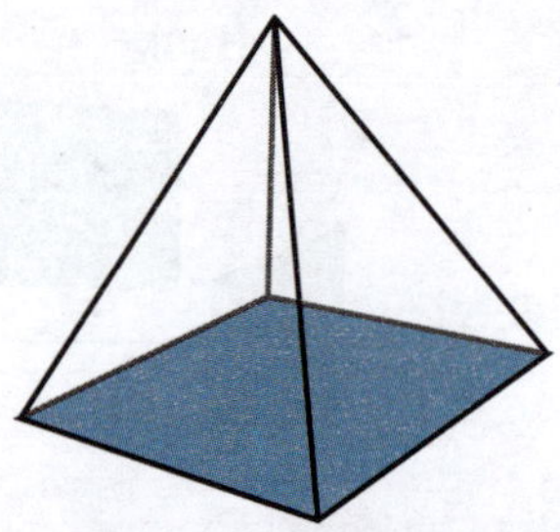

Square pyramid

Remember

- A cuboid is a rectangular prism that has 6 rectangular faces.
- A cube is called a square prism that has 6 square faces.
- A tetrahedron is a triangular pyramid with 4 congruent equilateral triangles having 4 faces, 6 edges and 4 vertices.

NETS OF THREE-DIMENSONAL SHAPES

A 3D shape can be represented in 2D using nets. A net is a 2D figure that shows how the solid looks like when it is opened and laid out flat.

The nets of some common three-dimensional shapes are given below.

Cube and its net

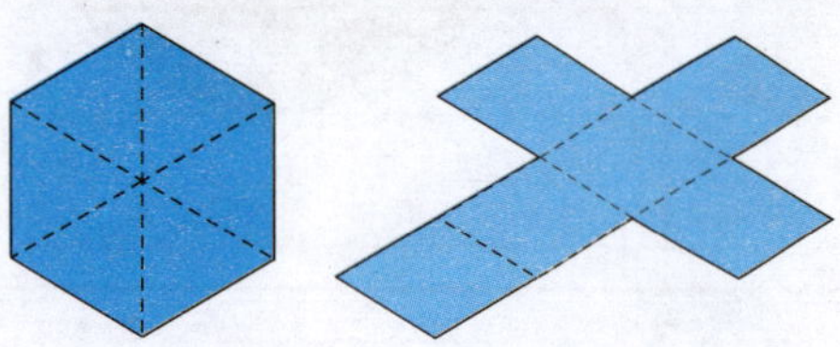

Cuboid and its net

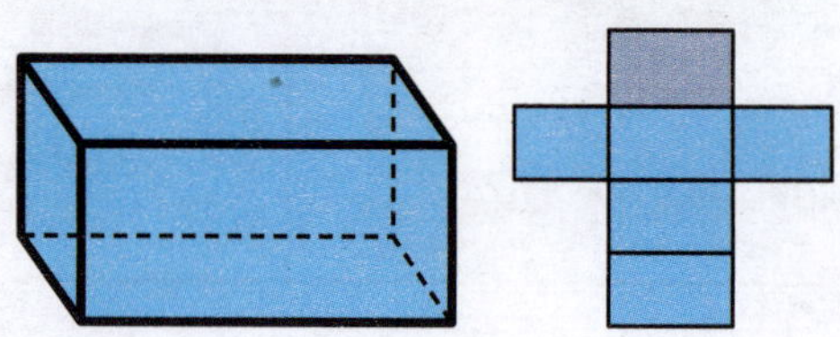

Cylinder and its net

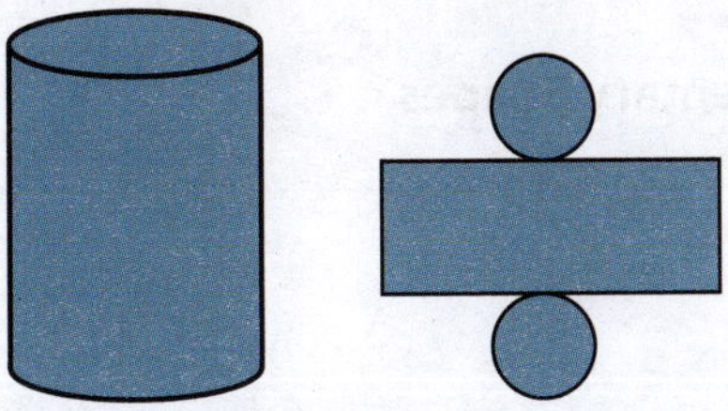

Cone and its net

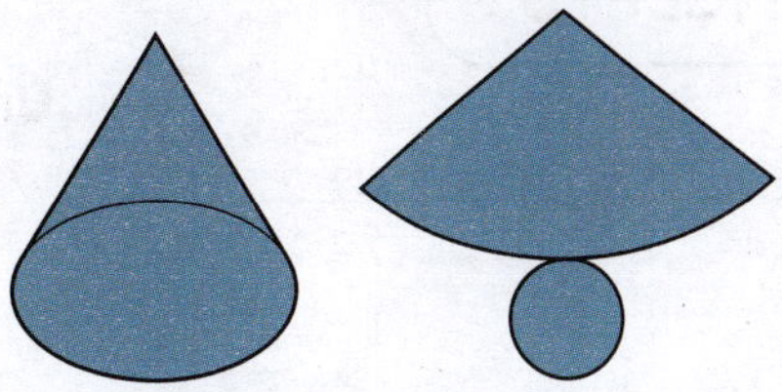

Tetrahedron and its net

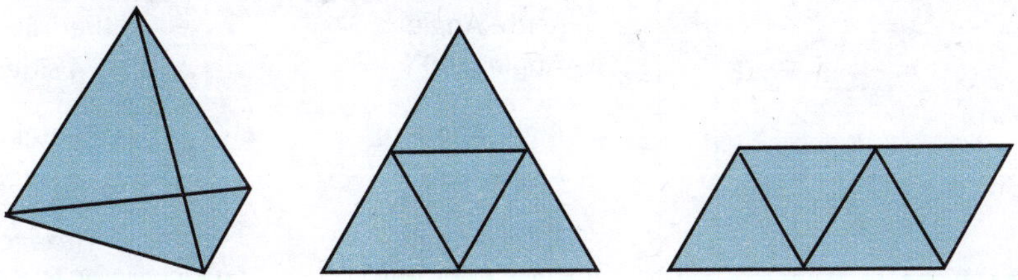

Exercise 12.7

1. **Write the number of vertices, edges and faces of these three-dimensional shapes: cube, cuboid, cylinder, cone and sphere.**
2. **Identify the 3D shape with the given faces, vertices and edges.**

	Number of Faces	Number of Vertices	Number of Edges	Name of the 3D Shape
a.	6	8	12	
b.	5	6	9	
c.	3	0	2	
d.	2	1	1	
e.	5	5	8	

3. **Identify the 3D shape from the following.**

   a. Birthday cap b. Wooden box c. Pipe

   d. Ball e. Dice

4. **Draw a net for the following 3-D shapes.**

   a. Cuboid b. Cone c. Tetrahedron

KEY CONCEPTS

Understanding Elementary Shapes

Lines
- Intersecting lines (meet)
- Parallel lines (do not meet)
- Concurrent lines (coincide)

Types of Triangles

According to the lengths of their sides	According to the measure of their angles
Scalene	Acute-angled
Isosceles	Right-angled
Equilateral	Obtuse-angled

Angles
- Zero Angle: Angle = 0°
- Acute Angle: Angle < 90°
- Right Angle: Angle = 90°
- Obtuse Angle: 90° < Angle < 180°
- Straight Angle: Angle = 180°
- Reflex Angle: 180° < Angle < 360°
- Complete Angle: Angle = 360°

Polygons
- Triangle: 3 sided
- Quadrilateral: 4 sided
- Pentagon: 5 sided
- Hexagon: 6 sided
- Heptagon: 7 sided
- Octagon: 8 sided

3-D Shapes

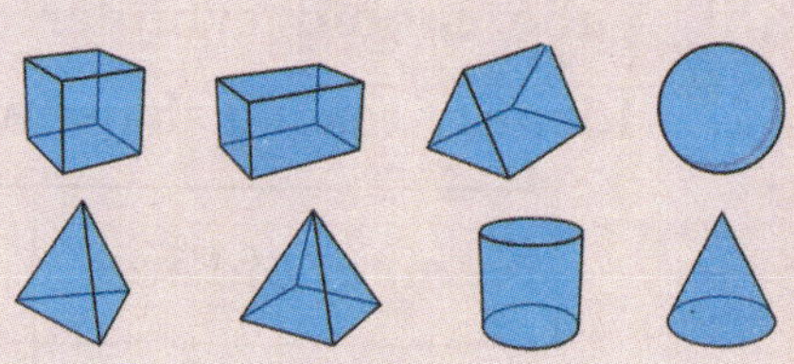

Quadrilateral

- Parallelogram: Two sets of parallel sides
  - With all sides equal → Rhombus
  - All angles are right angles → Rectangle
  - Rhombus + Rectangle (All angles are right angles; All sides are equal) → Square
- Non-parallelogram
  - Trapezium: One pair of parallel sides
  - Kite: Two pairs of adjacent sides are equal in length

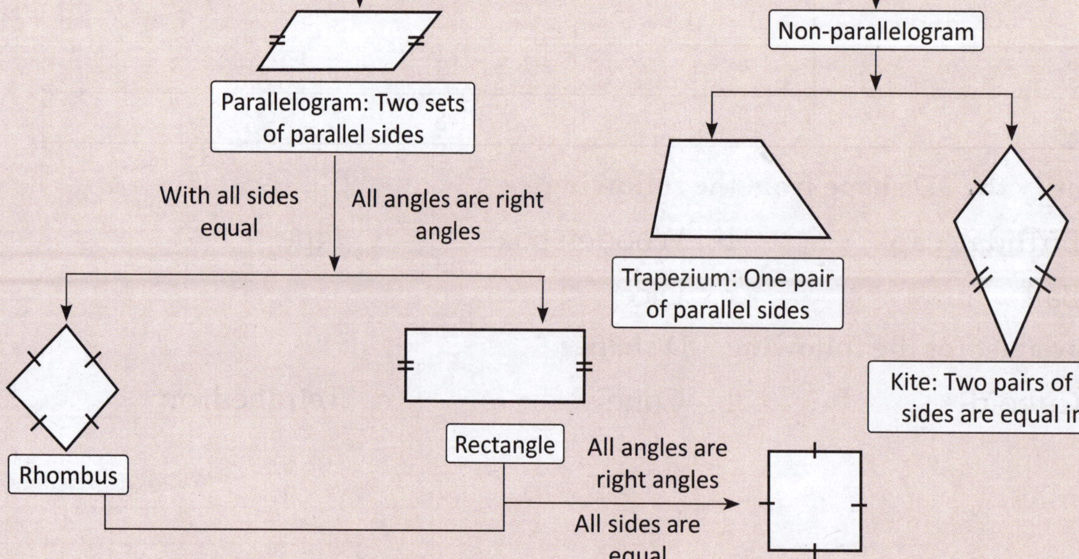

REVISION EXERCISE

1. Choose the correct option for each of the following.

a. A square is __________

i. a parallelogram ii. a rhombus iii. a rectangle iv. All of the above

b. A three-dimensional shape that has only four triangular faces is a __________

i. triangular prism ii. triangular pyramid

iii. rectangular prism iv. rectangular pyramid

c. A triangle with unequal sides is called __________.

i. an equilateral triangle ii. a scalene triangle

iii. an isosceles triangle iv. none of these

d. If the angle formed between two rays is 245°, then the type of angle formed is __________.

i. an acute angle ii. an obtuse angle

iii. a straight angle iv. a reflex angle

e. What is the measure of a complete angle?

i. 360° ii. 270° iii. 180° iv. 90°

2. Fill in the blanks.

a. The measure of the angle between the hands of a clock at 3 o' clock is _____ .

b. Vertically opposite angles are ____ to each other.

c. An exterior angle of a triangle is equal to the sum of its two ____opposite angles.

d. A rhombus with each angle equal to 90° is called a _____ .

e. Each angle of an equilateral triangle measures _______ .

3. State whether the following statements are true (T) or false (F).

a. If the measure of an angle is between 180° and 360°, then that angle is called an obtuse angle.

b. If one angle of a triangle is 80°, then that triangle is called an acute-angled triangle.

c. A parallelogram with all sides equal is called a rhombus.

d. A polygon with 8 sides is called a heptagon.

e. A tetrahedron has 4 faces, 6 edges and 4 vertices.

4. Write the name of the corresponding solids against the given description.

	Description	Name of the Solid
a.	It has four triangular faces and a square base.	
b.	It has only one circular face and no vertex.	
c.	It has square bases and four rectangular faces.	
d.	It has two circular faces and no vertex.	
e.	It has a triangular base and three triangular faces.	

5. Which of the following shapes are three-dimensional?

a. Sphere b. Tetrahedron c. Square d. Triangle

e. Cone f. Quadrilateral g. Square prism h. Cuboid

6. Two complementary angles are in the ratio 4 : 6. Find the angles.

7. The measures of two supplementary angles are (3p + 10)° and (7p + 20)°. Find the value of p.

8. Two of the angles of a quadrilateral measure 88° and 72°, respectively. The other two angles are equal. Find the measure of the equal angles.

9. Look at the figure and write the names of the following:

a. Any two intersecting lines

b. Any two equal angles

c. A right-angled triangle

d. An isosceles triangle

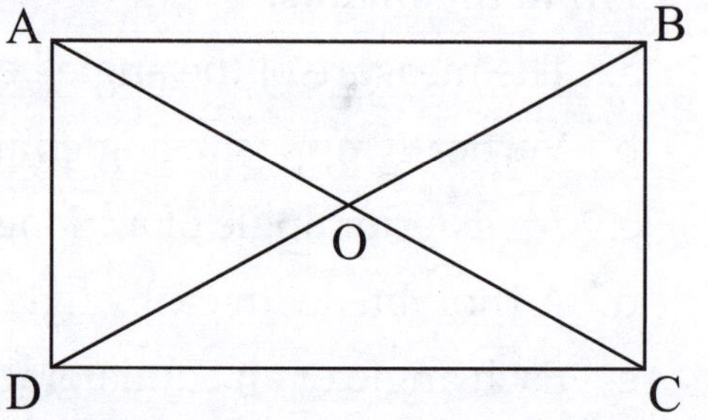

10. Answer the following.

a. Write the similarities and differences between a rhombus and parallelogram.

b. Draw a net for a cuboid and a cylinder.

c. Write the 3 types of triangles based on their angles.

d. Write the names of 3 quadrilaterals that are parallelograms.

e. Draw a tetrahedron and find the number of faces, vertices and edges

13 Symmetry

Prior Knowledge

- Lines
- Angles
- 2D shapes

Learning Objectives

- Lines of symmetry
- Multiple lines of symmetry
- Finding lines of symmetry
- Symmetry in geometrical shapes
- Reflective symmetry
- Mirror symmetry

Let's Get Started

Sachin was interested in collecting pictures from newspapers and journals. From that collection, he found few interesting pictures and took those pictures to the school.

a.

b.

c.

d.

e.

Look at the above pictures. Do you observe anything common in these images?

LINE SYMMETRY

We observe that if the pictures b., d., and e. are folded along the dotted lines shown on them, then both the halves of each picture will coincide.

So, we can say that each picture is divided into two identical parts about the dotted line.

If there is a line about which a figure can be folded so that the two equal parts of the figure coincide, that line is called a **line** or **axis of symmetry** or **mirror line**.

Multiple Lines of Symmetry

The line of symmetry may be vertical, horizontal or both.

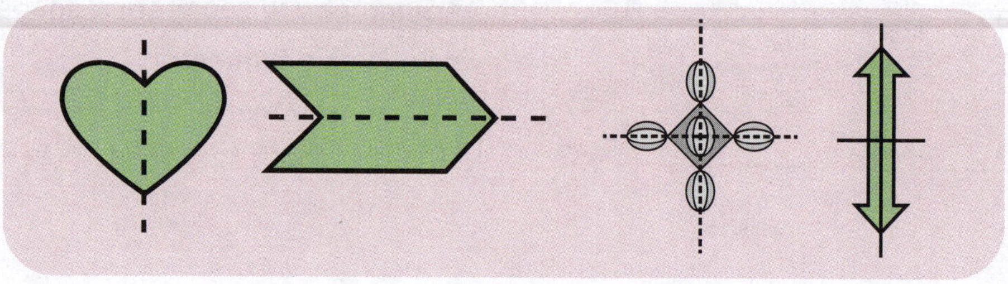

An object can have more than one line of symmetry. Some objects in nature have multiple lines of symmetry.

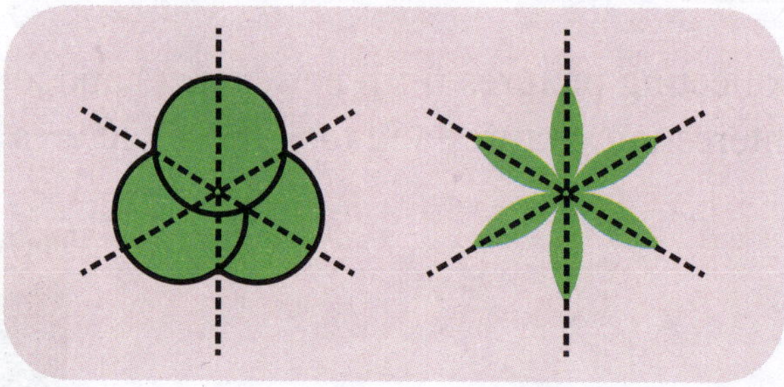

It is not necessary that every figure or shape has a line of symmetry. The figures that have no line of symmetry are called **asymmetrical figures**.

For example, the following figures do not have any line of symmetry.

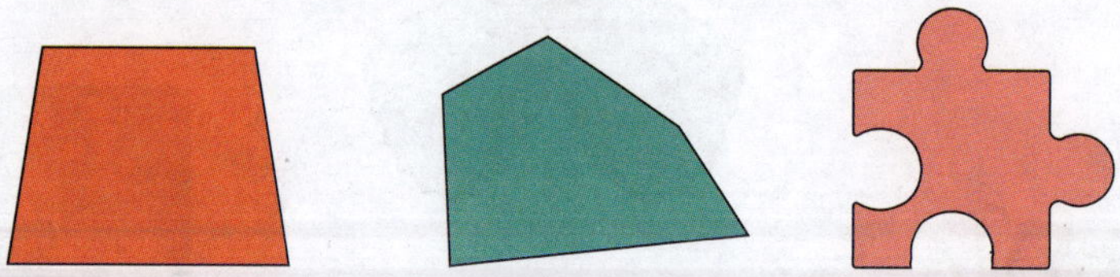

Example 1: Draw the lines of symmetry for each of the following figures.

a. 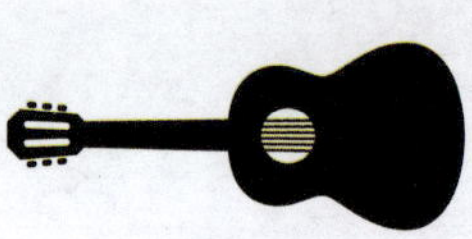

b. 

c. 

d. 

e. 

f. 

Solution: a.

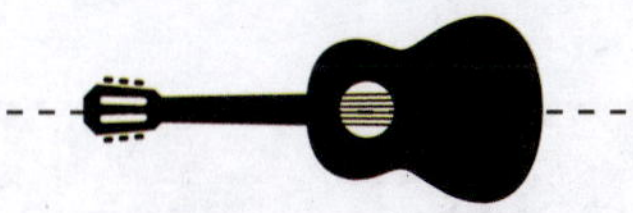

b.

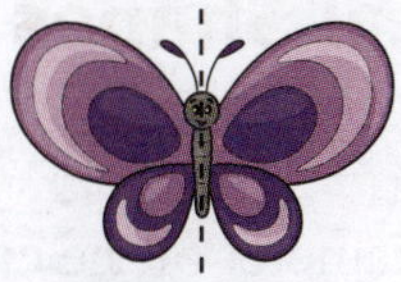

c.

d.

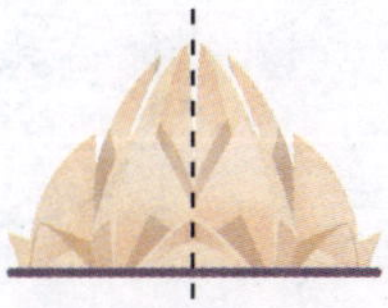

e.

f.

Finding Lines of Symmetry

We can find whether a shape has a line of symmetry or not by folding the shape.

> **REMEMBER**
> The line of symmetry does not have to be up-down or left-right; it can be in any direction.

1. Draw an equilateral triangle on a patty paper.

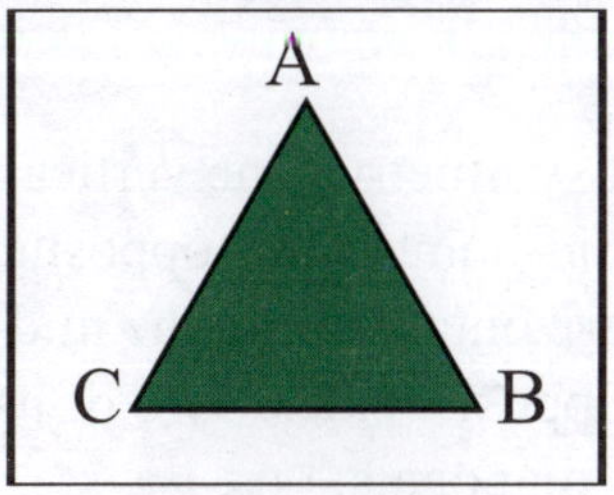

2. Fold it along one of the vertices such that the two parts of the triangle cover each other exactly and crease the fold.

3. Unfold the paper and mark the crease with a dotted line.

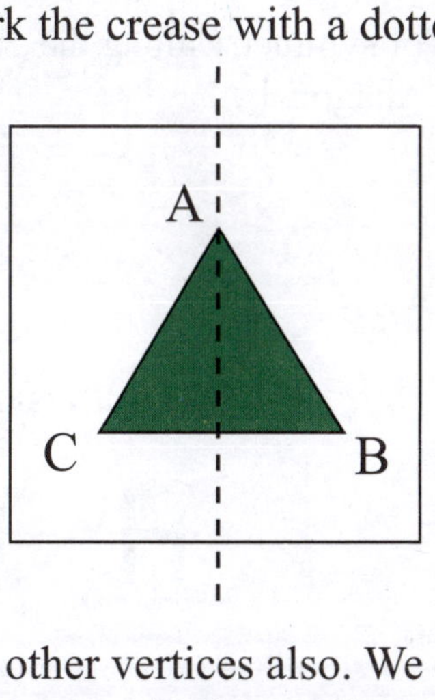

4. Repeat the same with the other vertices also. We observe that there are three lines of symmetry in the equilateral triangle.

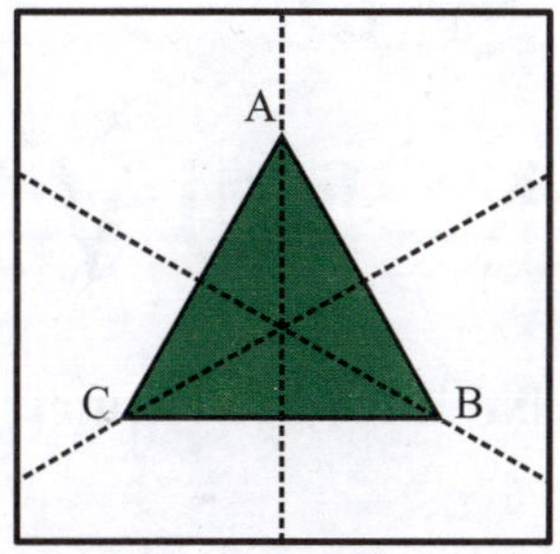

Symmetry in Geometrical Shapes

Geometrical Shapes	Line(s) of Symmetry	Figure
Circle	A diameter of the circle is a line of symmetry of the circle. It means that a circle has infinite lines of symmetry.	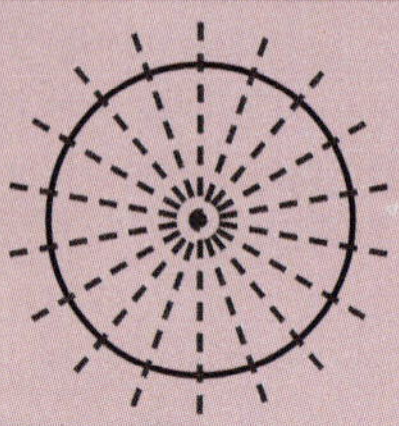
Line	One line of symmetry along its perpendicular bisector.	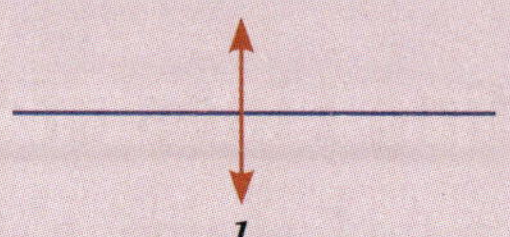
Angle	One line of symmetry along its angle bisector.	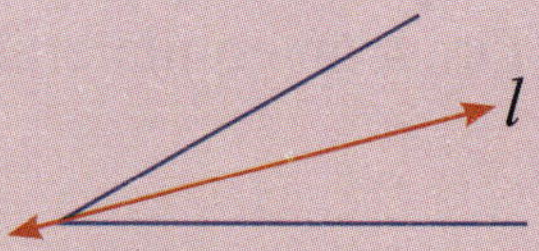
Square	Four lines of symmetry. One vertical joining the mid-points of its opposite sides. One horizontal joining the mid-points of its opposite sides. Two of its diagonals.	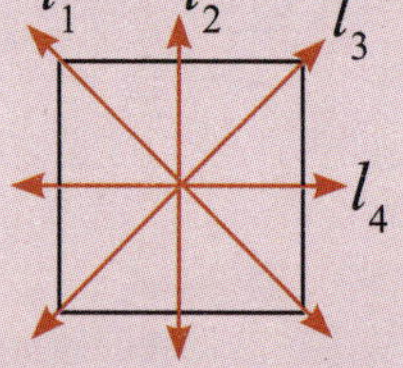
Equilateral triangle	Three lines of symmetry. All are along their its angle bisectors.	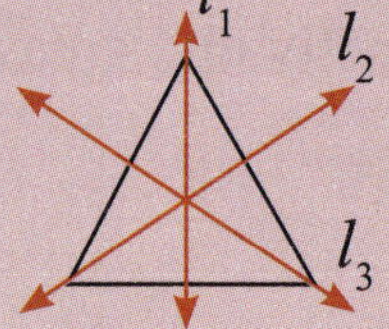
Isosceles triangle	One line of symmetry. The isosceles triangle is symmetric along the bisector of the angle between the two sides of equal length to the midpoint of the opposite side.	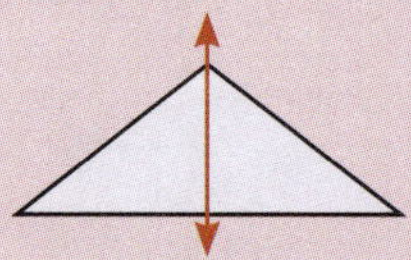
Rhombus	Two lines of symmetry along the diagonals.	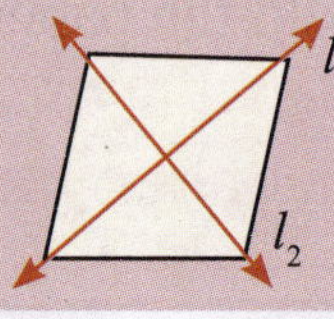

Letters of the English Alphabet

One line of symmetry:

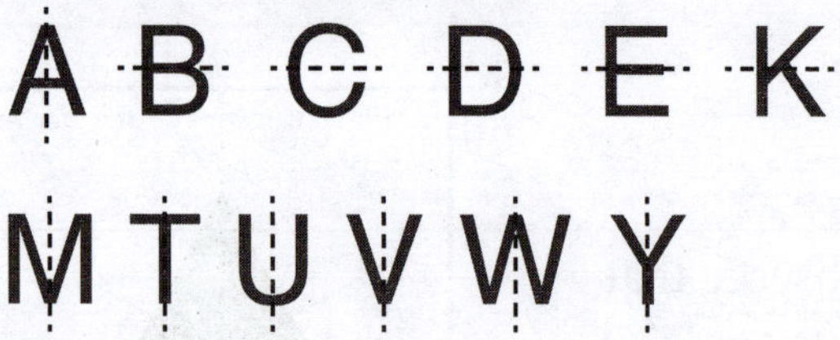

Two lines of symmetry:

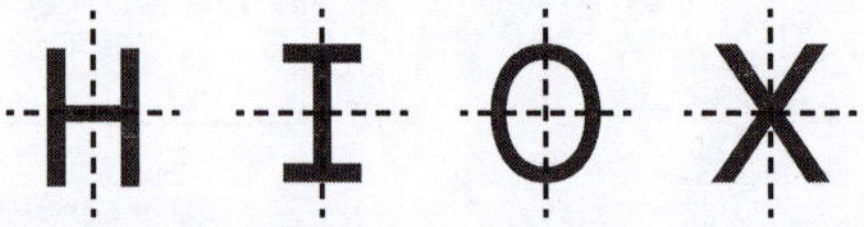

No lines of symmetry: The letters F, G, J, L, N, P, Q, R, S and Z are asymmetric.

Example 2: Find the number of lines of symmetry in each of the following figures:

a. 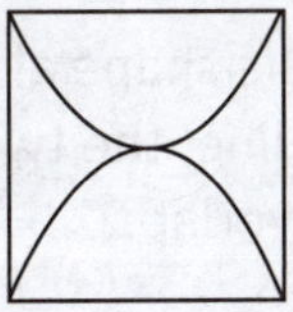 b. 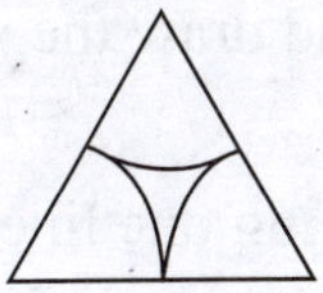 c. 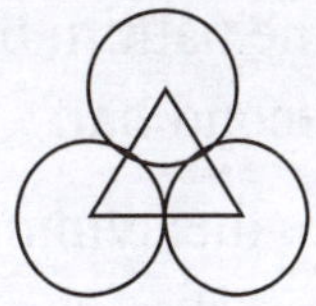

Solution:

a. 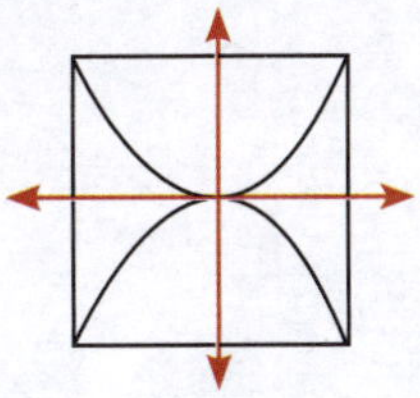

It has two lines of symmetry.

b. 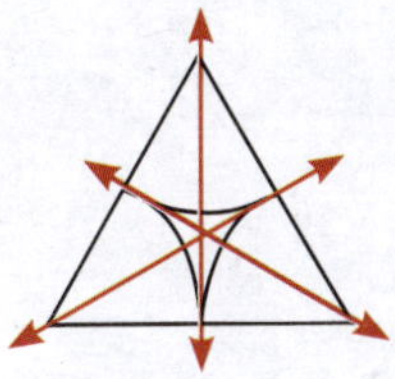

It has three lines of symmetry.

c. 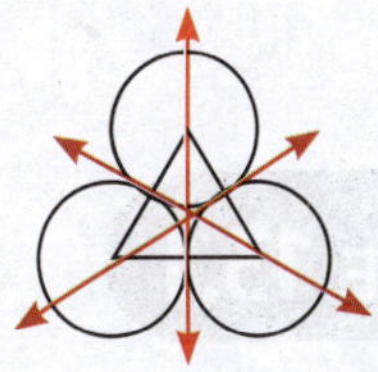

It has three lines of symmetry.

REFLECTION SYMMETRY

Reflection symmetry is symmetry with respect to reflection. An image is said to have **reflection symmetry** if there is at least one line that splits the image into halves so that the portions on the either sides of the line are identical. The mirror line forms the axis of symmetry.

Properties of Reflection

Observe the following images and their reflections.

Mirror Line

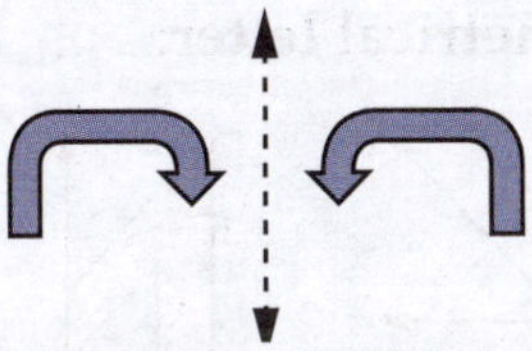

Mirror Line

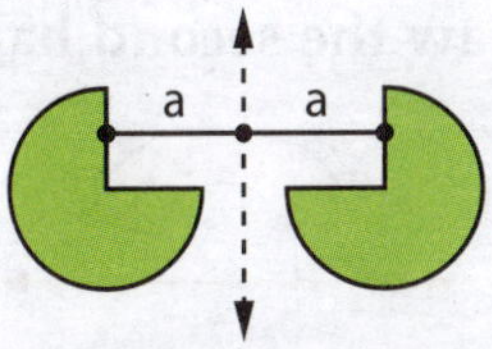

Mirror Line

1. Size of the mirror image is same as that of the object.
2. The direction of the mirror image is opposite to that of the object.
3. The distance between the object and the mirror is same as the distance between the mirror and the image.

CONSTRUCTION OF SYMMETRICAL FIGURES

Consider a shape as shown in the first figure. Let us draw the reflection of the shape given in the figure.

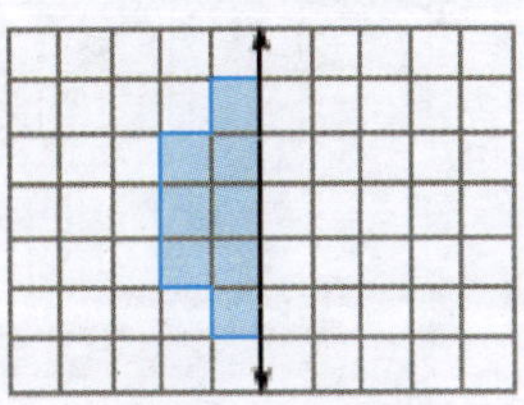

Mirror Line

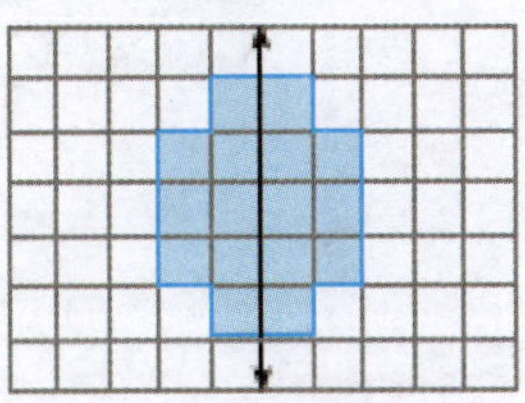

Mirror Line

To construct symmetrical figure, follow the steps given below:

Step 1: Take a sheet of paper and fold it into two halves and draw a line along the crease.

Step 2: Draw any pattern of your choice in one half.

Step 3: Rotate the pattern by 180 degrees and draw the same pattern on the second half.

Now you can see the symmetrical figure having one line of symmetry.

> **REMEMBER**
>
> If we fold the shape along the dotted line, the two sides will overlap.

EXERCISE 13.1

1. **Mark all the lines of symmetry on these shapes. Also, state the total number of lines of symmetry of each shape.**

   a. 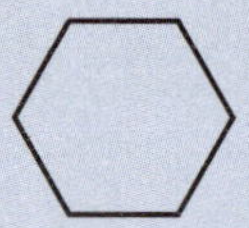 b. 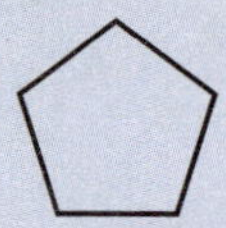 c. 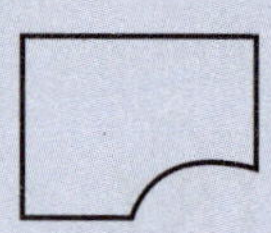

   d. 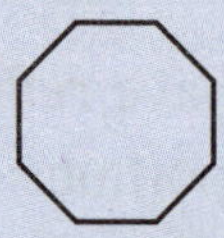 e. 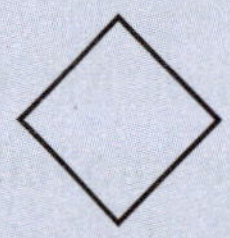 f. 

2. **Draw the line of symmetry of the following geometrical shapes.**

   a. Scalene Triangle b. Irregular Quadrilateral c. Kite

3. **Draw the second half of each symmetrical letter.**

   a. 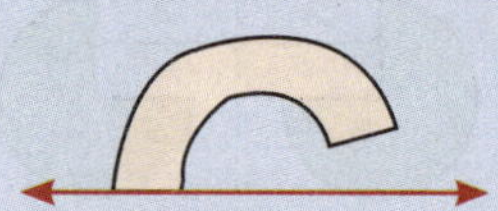 b.  c. 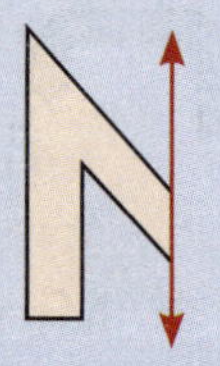 d. 

4. **Draw the mirror images of the following shapes along the dotted lines.**

   a. 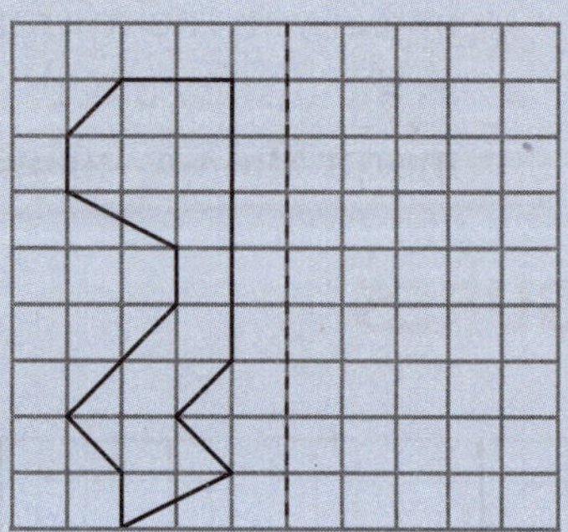 b. 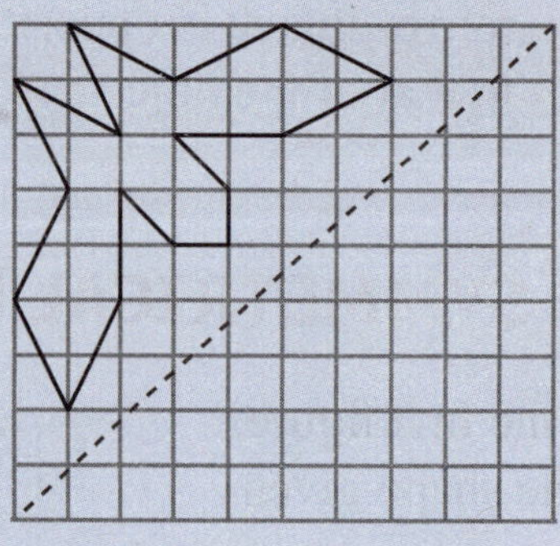 c. 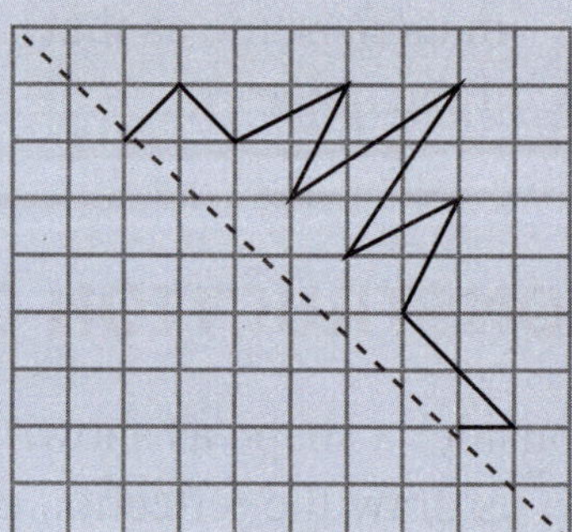

5. **Draw the reflections of following shapes along the dotted lines.**

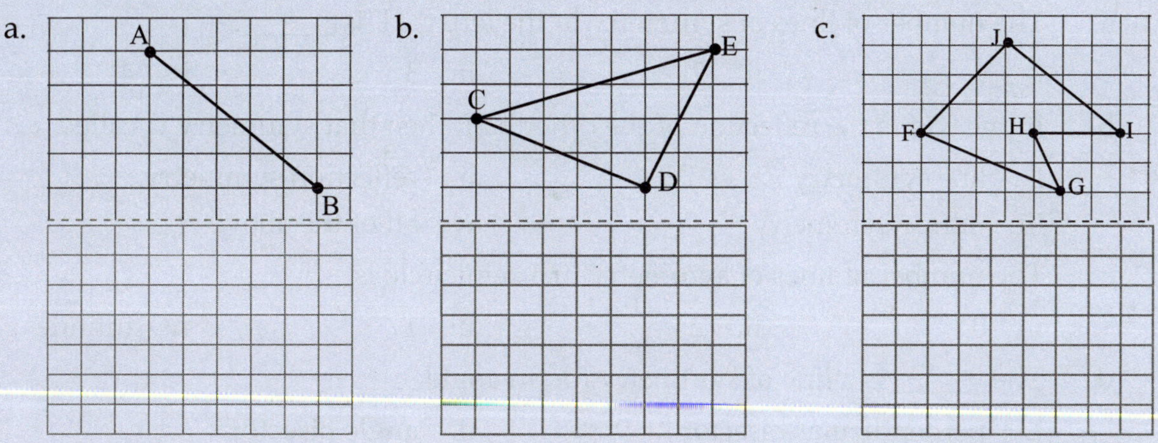

Key Concepts

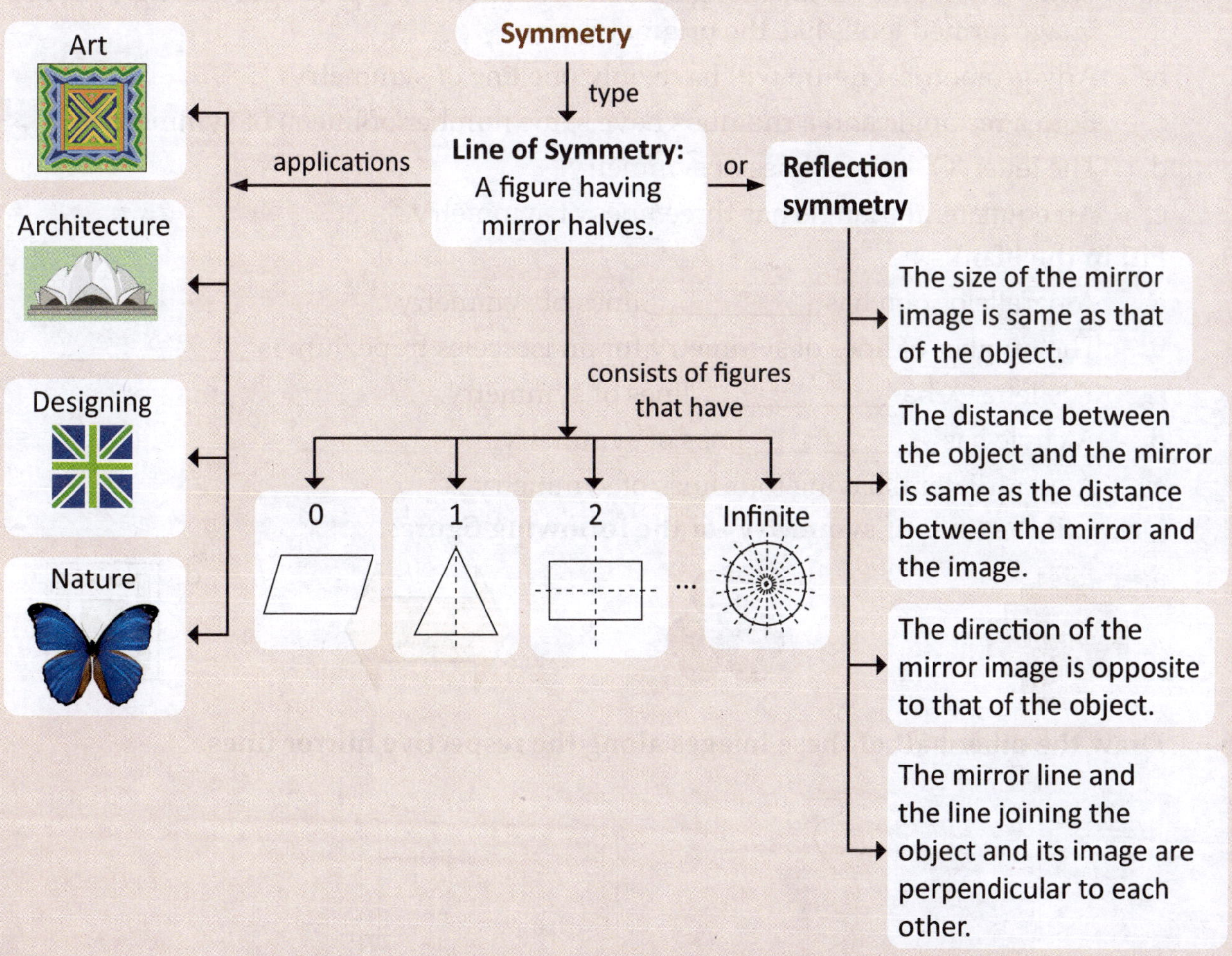

Revision Exercise

1. Choose the correct option.

a. The number of lines of symmetry in the letter 'H' is ______.

i. 1 ii. 2 iii. 3 iv. 4

b. If one half is the reflection of the other half, then that symmetry is called

i. line symmetry ii. reflection symmetry
iii. mirror symmetry iv. all of the above

c. The number of lines of symmetry in a semicircle is ______.

i. 0 ii. 2 iii. 1 iv. infinite

d. The ______ is a line of symmetry for an angle.

i. perpendicular bisector ii. angle bisector
iii. line passing through the point iv. none of these

e. The number of lines of symmetry in a regular heptagon is

i. 5 ii. 7 iii. 9 iv. 14

2. State whether the following statements are true or false.

a. When a mirror is placed along a line of symmetry, the part figure along with the image formed looks like the original figure.

b. Any geometrical figure will have only one line of symmetry.

c. Both a rectangle and a rhombus have same number of line(s) of symmetry.

d. The letter 'O' has ten lines of symmetry.

e. An equilateral triangle has three lines of symmetry.

3. Fill in the blanks.

a. A parallelogram has __________ lines of symmetry.

b. The number of lines of symmetry for an isosceles trapezium is __________.

c. The letter X has __________ lines of symmetry.

d. A circle has __________ lines of symmetry.

e. A quadrilateral having four lines of symmetry is __________.

4. Draw all the lines of symmetry for the following figures.

a. 

b. 

c. 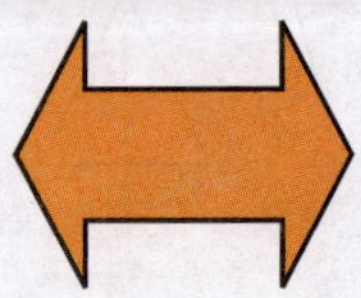

d. 

5. Draw the other half of these images along the respective mirror lines.

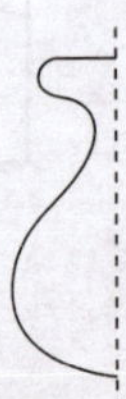

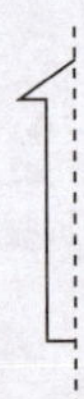

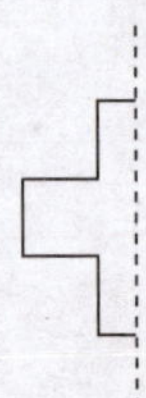

14 Constructions

Prior Knowledge

- Drawing tools
- Understanding of elementary shapes

Learning Objectives

- Constructing perpendicular bisectors and angle bisectors
- Constructing angles using a protractor
- Constructing special angles using a compass
- Constructing perpendicular to a line at a point on it or from a point outside it
- Constructing triangles and circles

Let's Get Started

Tilak was an architect. He got a contract to make a house construction plan using different measurements like length of the line segment, angle between two line segments, length of three sides of a triangle, etc. Using these measurements, he prepared a sketch as shown below.

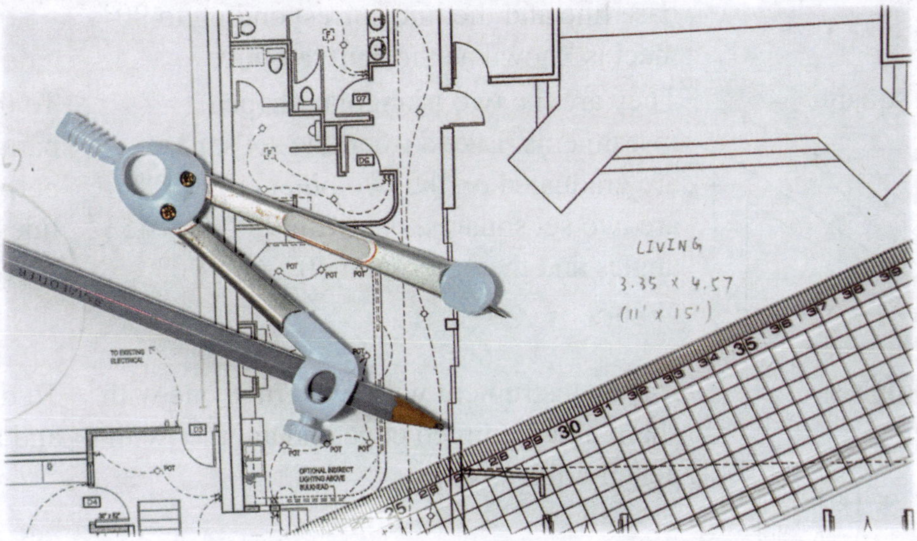

He prepared a sketch of the house using the measurements given by the client.

Which instrument is being used by the architect for construction?

In this chapter, we are going to learn about construction of line segments, angles between two line segments, angle bisectors, perpendicular bisectors and some special angles.

INSTRUMENTS IN A GEOMETRY BOX

In this chapter, we will use the instruments given in the table to construct circles, line segments, angles, perpendiculars and angle bisectors.

Instrument	Description	Purpose
Divider 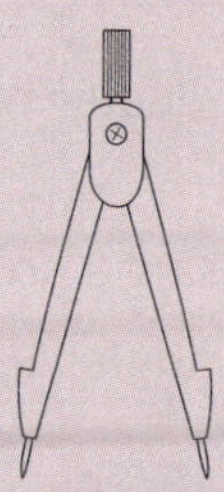	It is an instrument consisting of two straight, adjustable legs hinged together and sharp endpoints. It has two pointers.	To compare line segments
Ruler 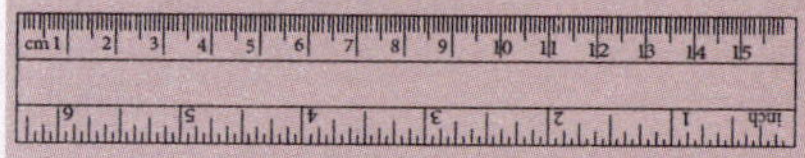	It is a straight-edged tool which is calibrated in centimetres along the top and inches along the bottom.	To draw straight lines and measure distances
Protractor 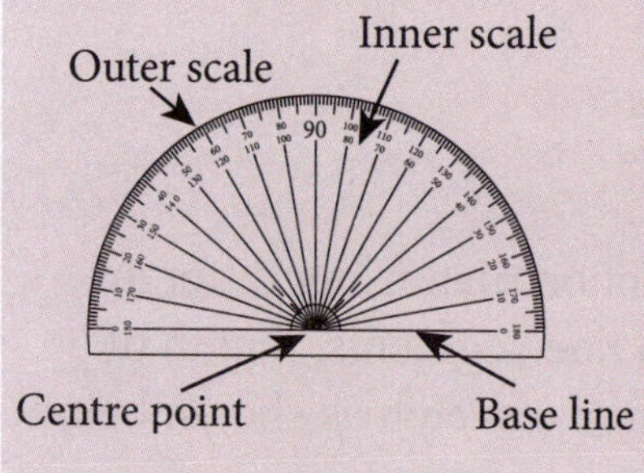	It is a D-shaped instrument. There are two rows of measurements from 0° to 180° going in opposite directions. They are called **scales**. One is the inner scale and the other is the outer scale. There are 180 divisions between 0 and 180. Each division represents **one degree**. The bottom line is known as the **base line**. The point where the base line and the line corresponding to 90° meet is known as the **centre point**.	To measure and draw angles
Set square 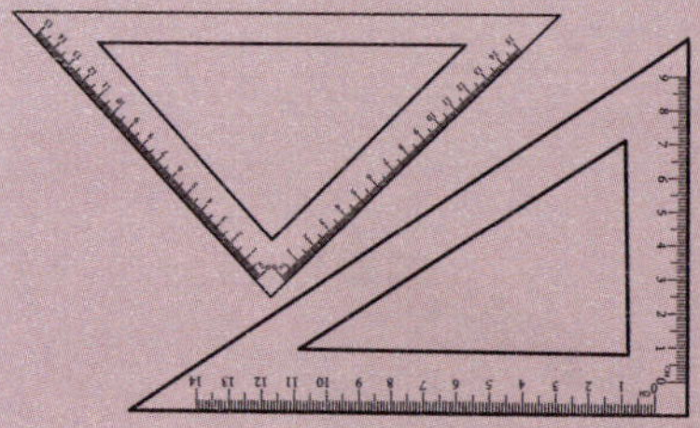	They are the two triangular-shaped instruments. Like a ruler, the set squares are graduated on the two outer edges. There are two set squares, one with 90°–45°–45° angles and the other with 30°–60°–90° angles.	To draw parallel lines, perpendicular lines and some specific angles
Compass 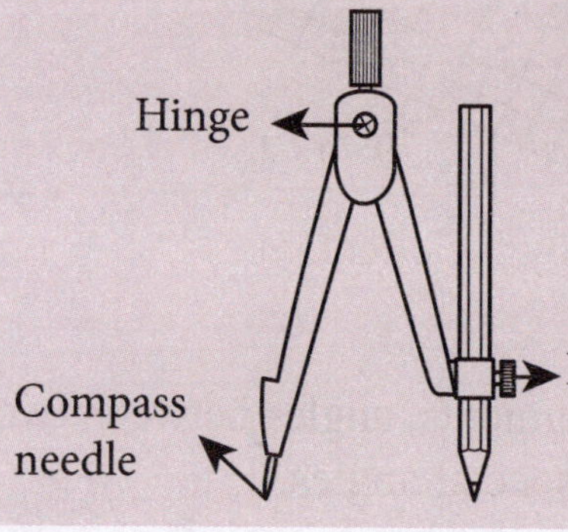	It is an instrument with two arms, one with sharp metal pointed edge and another with a pencil holder.	To draw circles and arcs

CONSTRUCTION OF LINE SEGMENT OF A GIVEN LENGTH

Construct a line segment of length 5 cm.

Step 1: Draw a line of any length and mark a point on it and label the point as A.

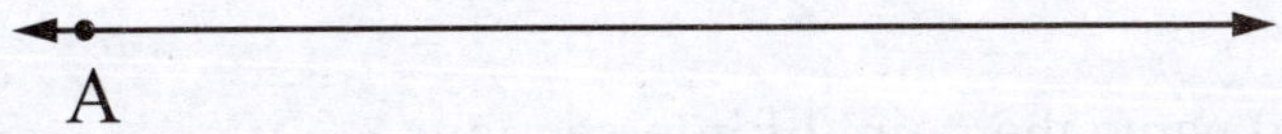

Step 2: Place the pointer of the compass on the zero mark of the ruler and open it so that the pencil points at 5 cm mark.

Step 3: Without changing the radius of the compass, place the needle of compass at point A on line ℓ and draw an arc, which cuts the line at a point.

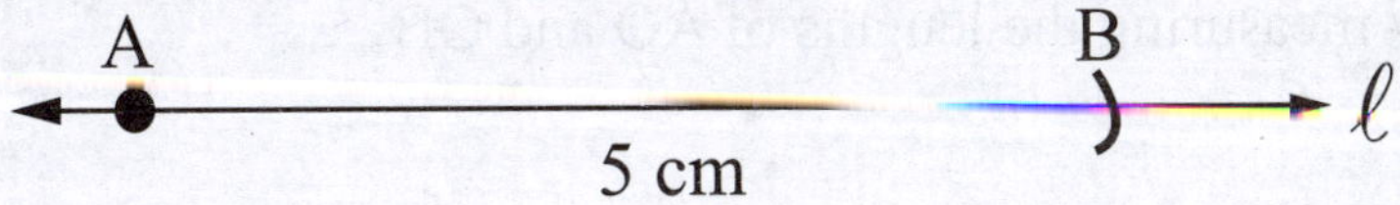

Name this point as B.

AB is the required line segment for the given measurement.

CONSTRUCTION OF PERPENDICULAR BISECTORS OF LINE SEGMENTS

To bisect means to divide anything into halves. A perpendicular bisector divides a line segment exactly into two halves, making an angle of 90° at the point of intersection.

Example 1: With the help of a compass, draw a perpendicular bisector to line segment AB of length 6 cm.

Solution: Step 1: Draw a line segment AB of length 6 cm.

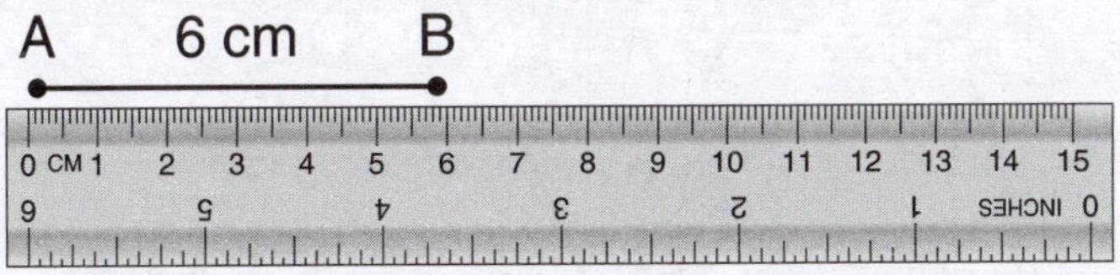

Step 2: With A as centre and more than half of AB as radius, draw a long arc.

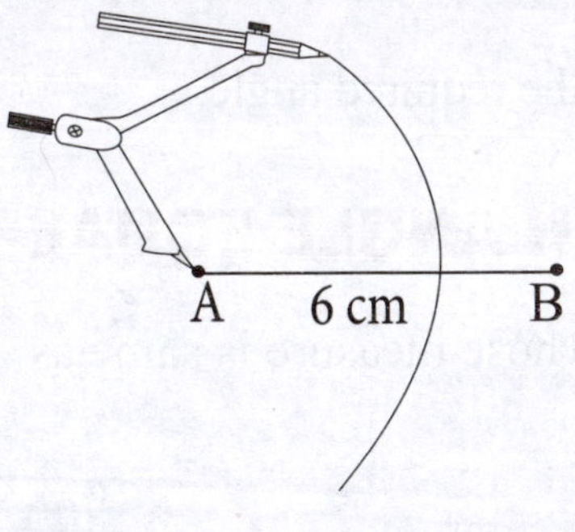

Step 3: With B as centre and without changing the radius, draw another arc that intersects the previously drawn arc at points E and F.

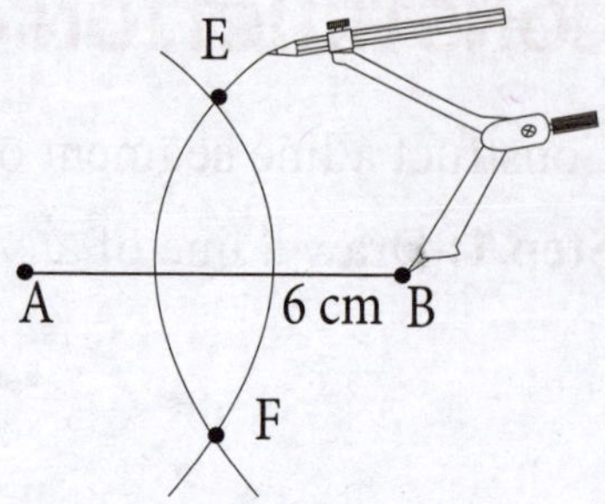

Step 4: Join E and F and name the point of intersection of EF and AB as O.

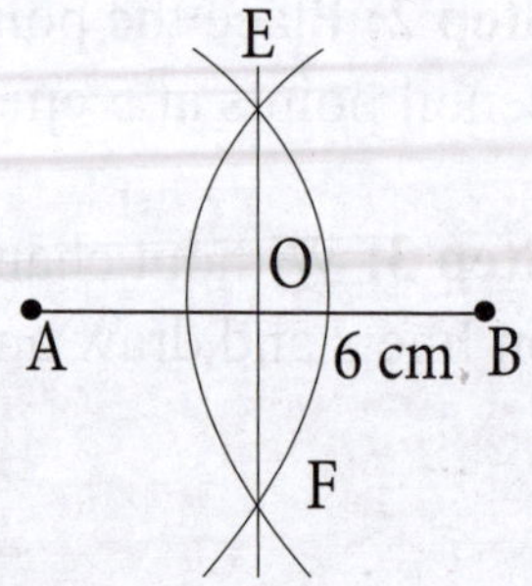

Step 5: We get the required bisector EF ⊥ AB and AO = OB = 3 cm.

We can verify this by measuring the lengths of AO and OB using the ruler.

CONSTRUCTION OF ANGLES USING A PROTRACTOR

Example 2: Construct a 65° angle using a protractor.

Step 1: Draw a ray AB. Place the centre of the protractor at point A and adjust it in such a way that its base line coincides with ray AB.

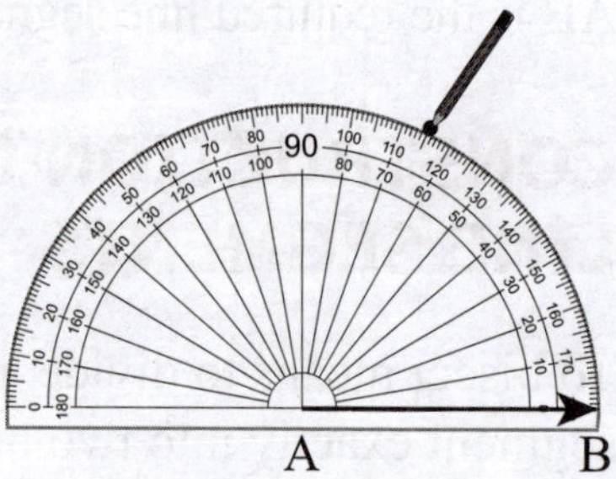

Step 2: Starting from the right, read the inner scale till the desired angle, that is, 65° is reached. Mark a point C at that reading.

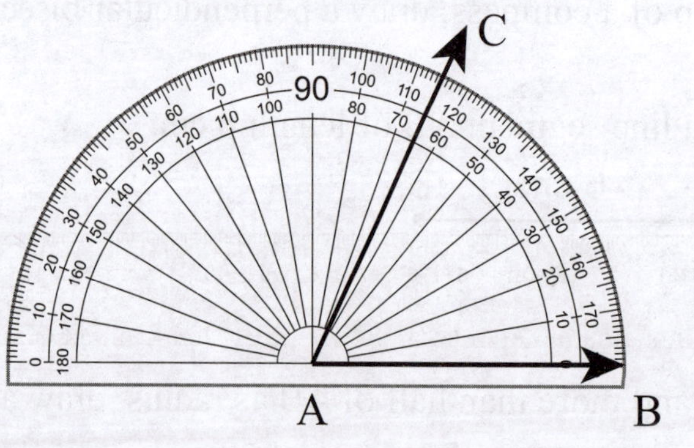

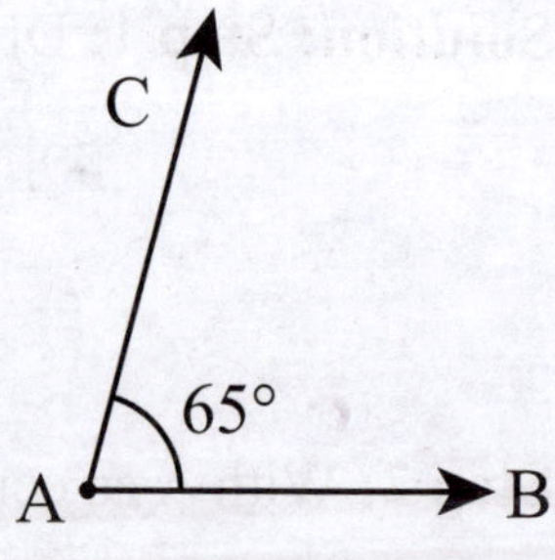

Step 3: Draw a ray AC. ∠CAB is the required angle.

CONSTRUCTION OF AN ANGLE EQUAL TO A GIVEN ANGLE

Example 3: Construct an angle whose measure is same as ∠ABC.

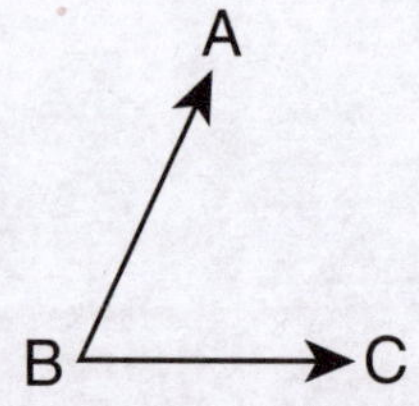

Step 1: Draw a line ℓ and choose a point P on it.

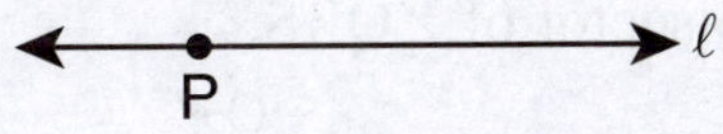

Step 2: With B as the centre, draw any convenient arc, cutting the arms of the given $\angle ABC$ at K and L.

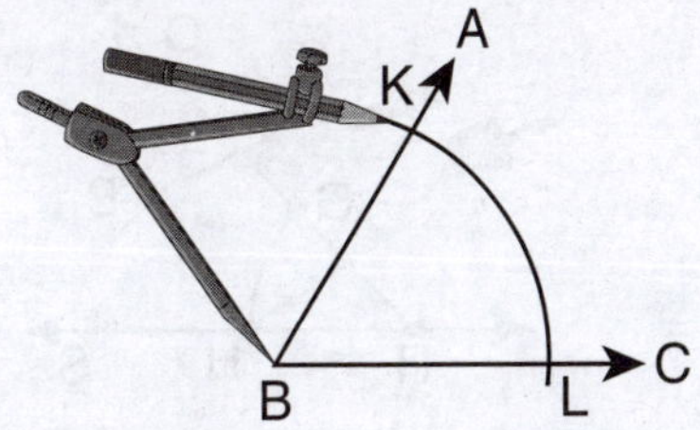

Step 3: Without changing the radius, keep the pointer at P and draw an arc cutting line ℓ at Q.

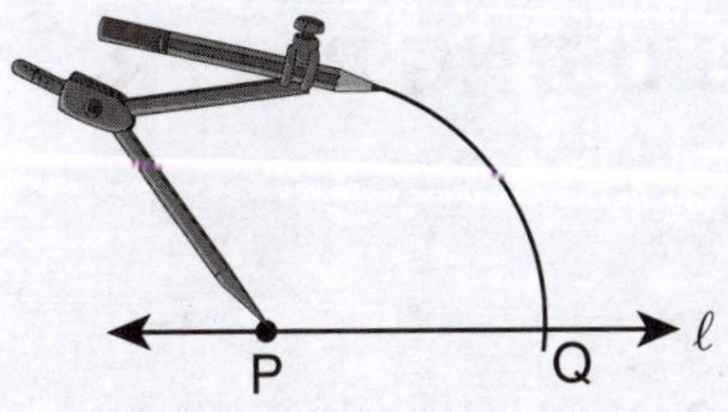

Step 4: Stretch the arms of the compass to the same length as KL.

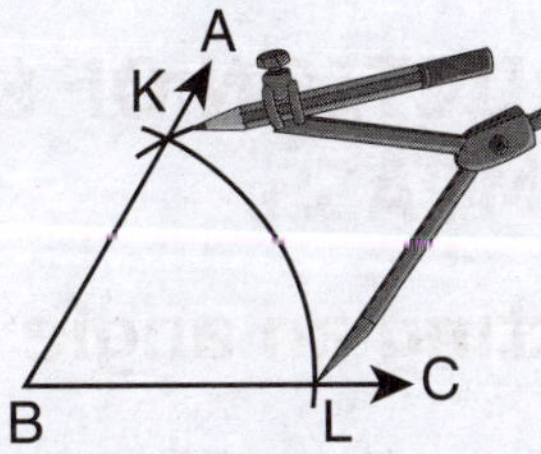

Step 5: With the same radius and point Q as the centre, draw an arc to cut the previous arc at R.

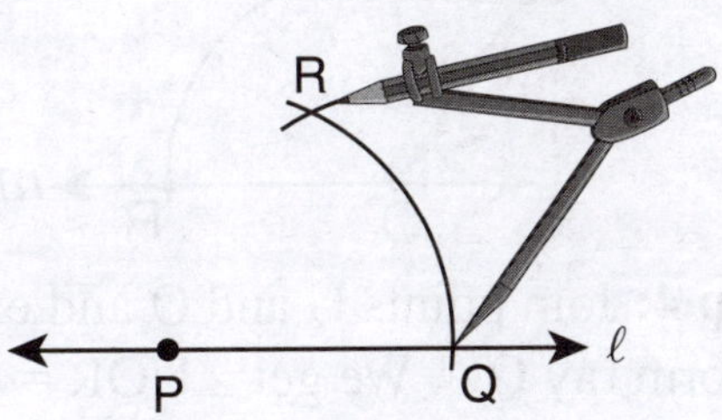

Step 6: Join the points P and R and extend it further to make $\overrightarrow{PR}$. $\angle RPQ$ is the required angle whose measure is equal to $\angle ABC$.

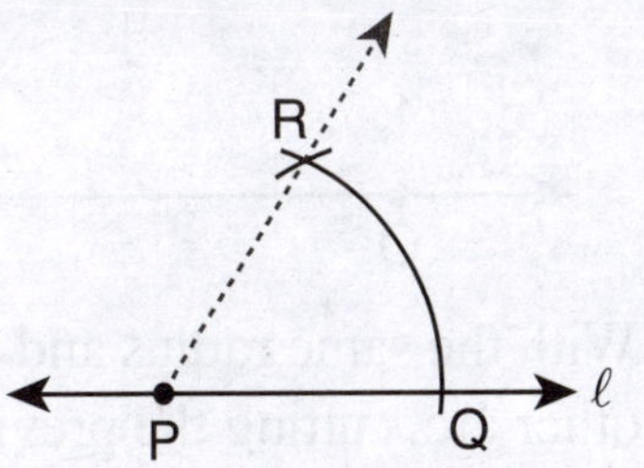

We can verify that $\angle ABC = \angle RPQ$ by copying both the angles on a patty paper and then placing them one over the other or by measuring the angles using a protractor.

CONSTRUCTION OF THE ANGLE BISECTOR OF A GIVEN ANGLE

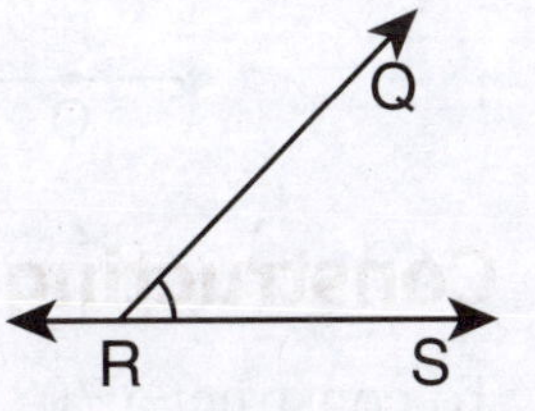

Example 4: Construct the angle bisector of $\angle QRS$.

Step 1: Draw an arc with R as the centre and any convenient radius to cut the two arms of the angle at points G and H.

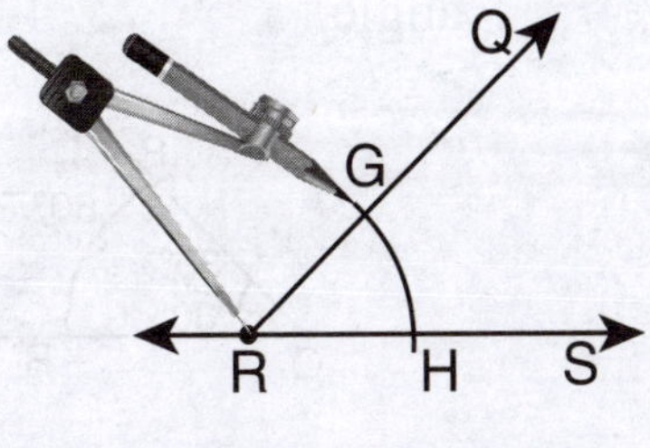

Step 2: With G as the centre and radius more than half the length of GH, draw an arc as shown.

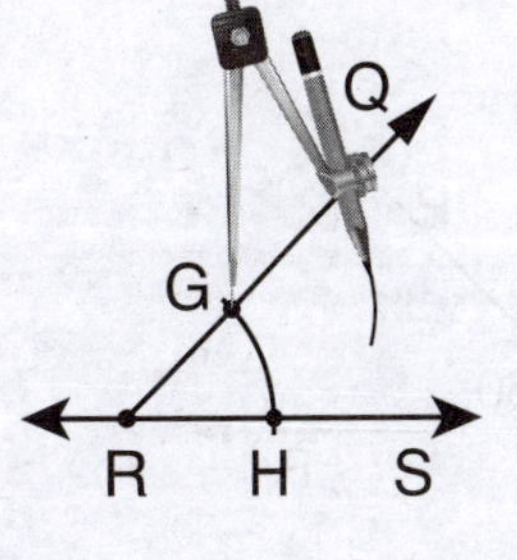

Step 3: With the same radius and H as the centre, draw another arc cutting the previous arc at B.

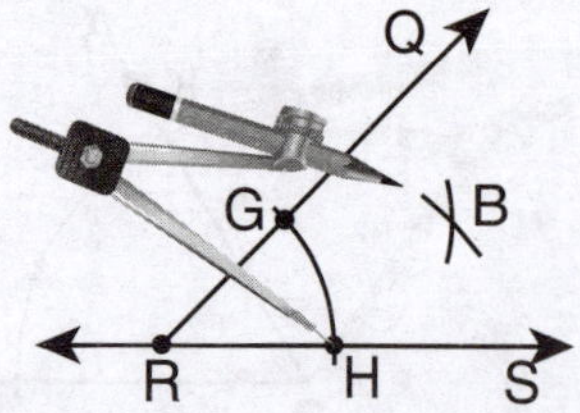

Step 4: Join points R and B to form ray RB. Rays RB and RS form the required angle bisector of ∠QRS.

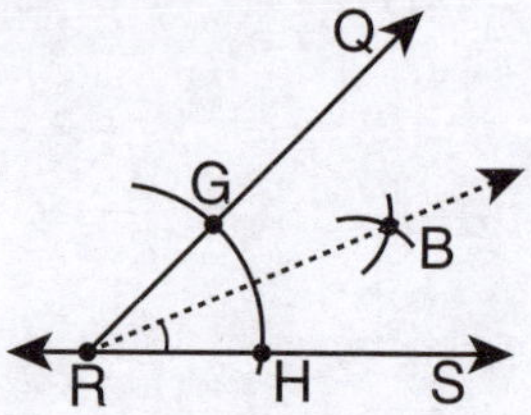

We can verify the above construction by measuring the bisected angles using a protractor or by copying ∠QRS on a patty paper and then folding the angle along RB.

CONSTRUCTION OF SPECIAL ANGLES USING RULER AND COMPASS

Constructing an angle of measure 60°

Step 1: Draw a line *m* and mark a point O on it.

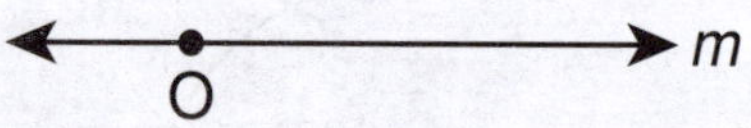

Step 2: With O as the centre and a convenient radius, draw an arc, cutting line *m* at R.

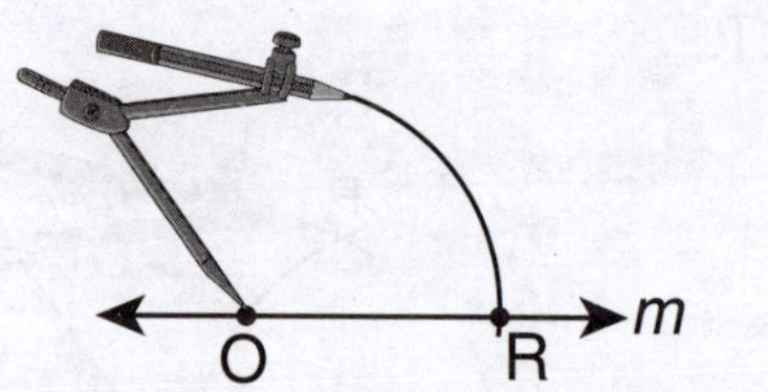

Step 3: With the same radius and R as the centre, draw another arc, cutting the previous arc at U.

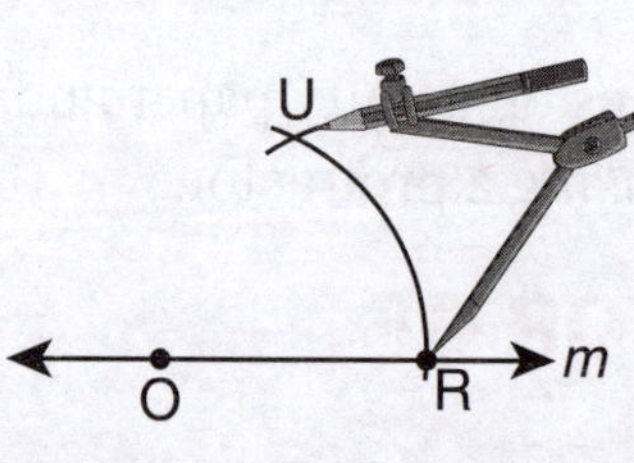

Step 4: Join points U and O and extend it to form ray OU. We get ∠UOR = 60°.

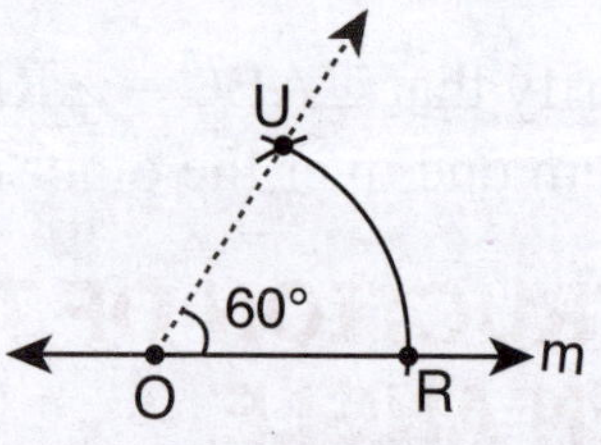

Constructing an angle of measure 30°

To construct a 30° angle, first construct an angle of 60° and then bisect the constructed angle to get two angles measuring 30° each.

Step 1: Construct an angle ∠PQR = 60°.

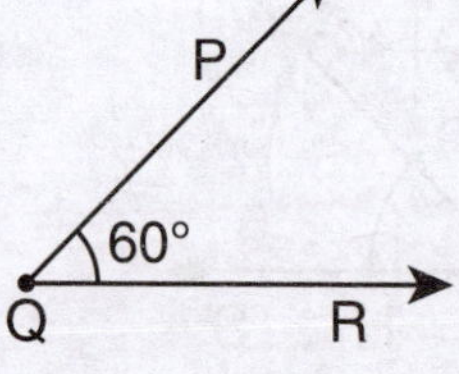

Step 2: Construct the angle bisector of ∠PQR.

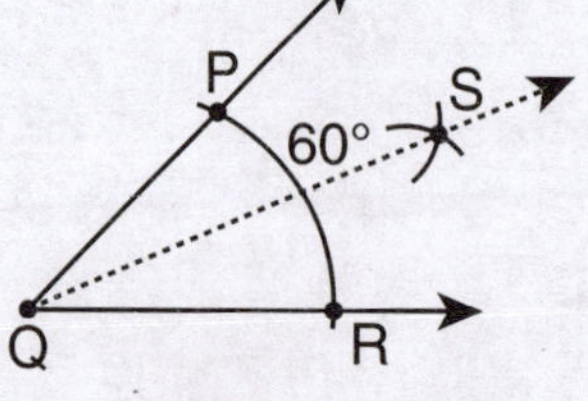

Step 3: ∠PQS = ∠SQR = 30°, which is the required angle.

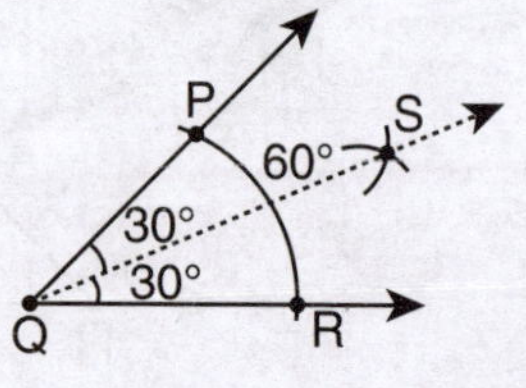

Constructing an angle of measure 120°

Step 1: Draw a line *m* and mark a point O on it.

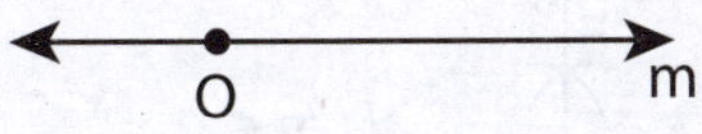

Step 2: With O as the centre and any convenient radius, draw an arc (nearly a semicircle) that cuts the line *m* at X.

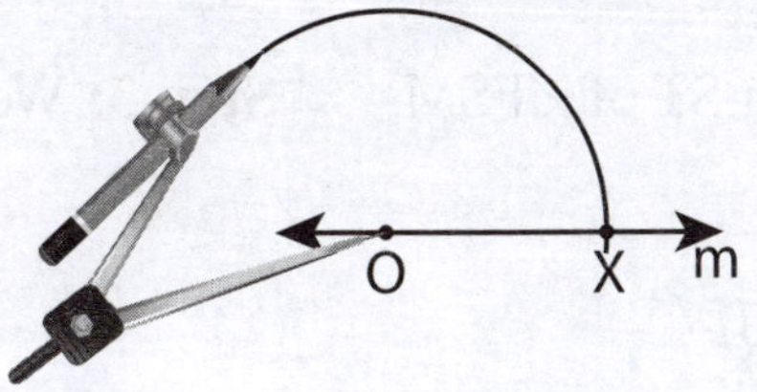

Step 3: With the same radius and X as the centre, draw an arc cutting the previous arc at Y.

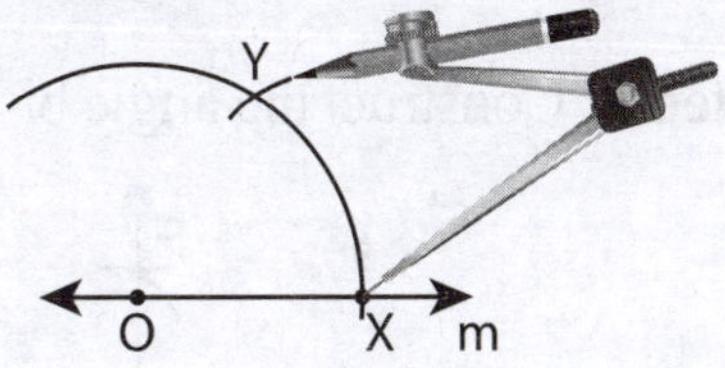

Step 4: With the same radius and Y as the centre, draw another arc cutting the first arc at Z.

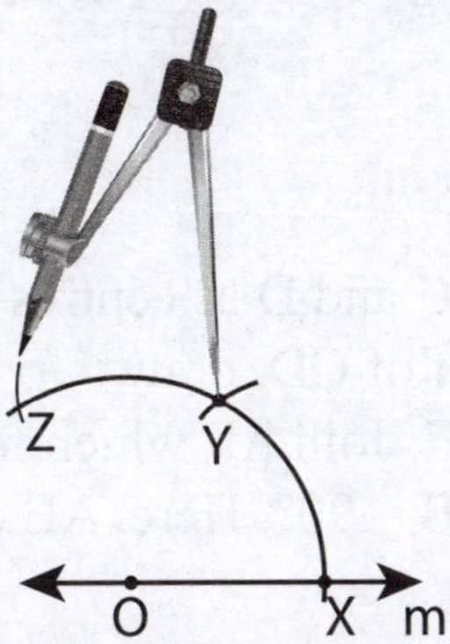

Step 5: Join O and Z and extend it to form ray OZ. ∠ZOX = 120° is the required angle.

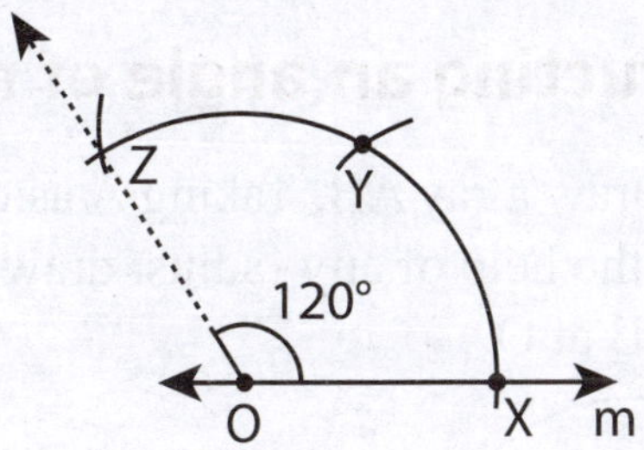

Constructing an angle of measure 90°

Step 1: Draw a line *m* and mark a point S on it.

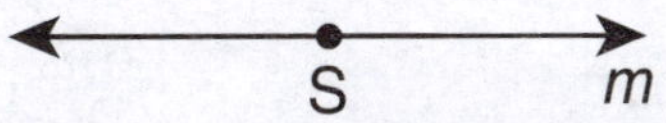

Step 2: With S as the centre and any convenient radius, draw an arc intersecting line *m* at U and T.

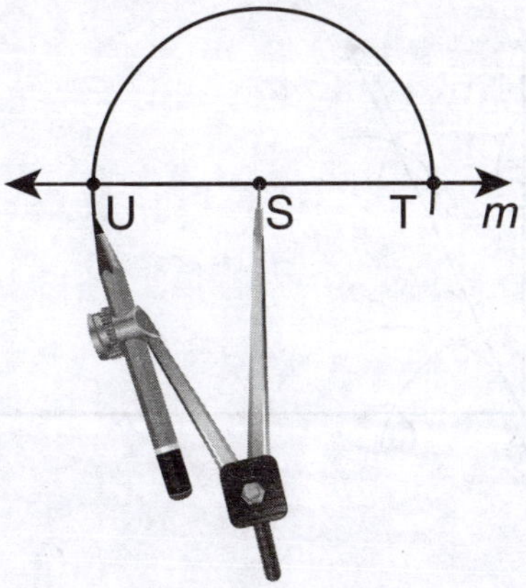

Step 3: With T as the centre and the same radius, draw an arc that cuts the previous arc at Y. With same radius and Y as the centre, draw another arc cutting the first arc at Z. Now with Y and Z as centres and radius equal to more than half of YZ, draw two arcs cutting each other and name the point of intersection as R. Join R and S.

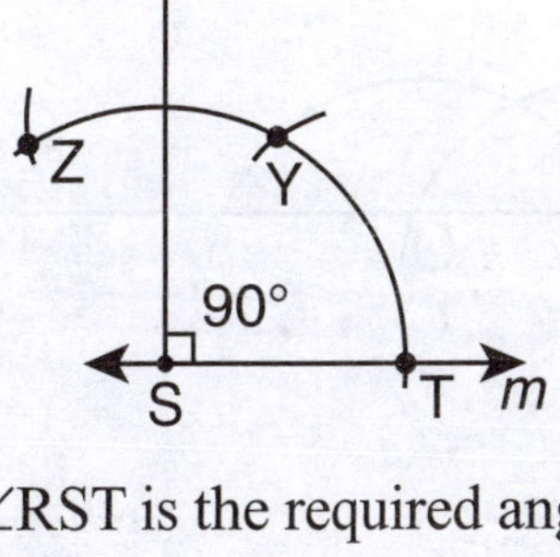

∴ ∠RST is the required angle.

Constructing an angle of measure 45°

45° is exactly between 0° and 90°.

We bisect 90°. That is, divide it into two equal halves.

Step 1: Construct an angle ∠FSM = 90°.

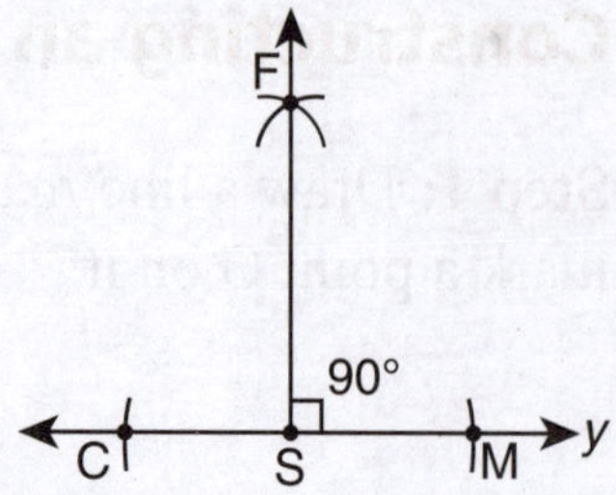

Step 2: Construct the angle bisector ST of ∠FSM.

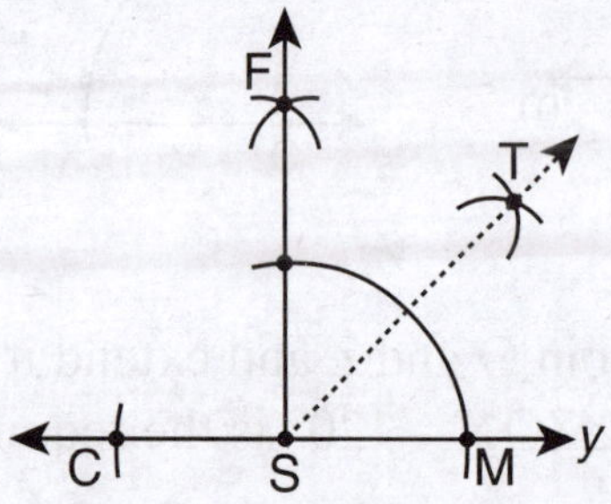

Step 3: We get ∠FST= ∠TSM = 45°

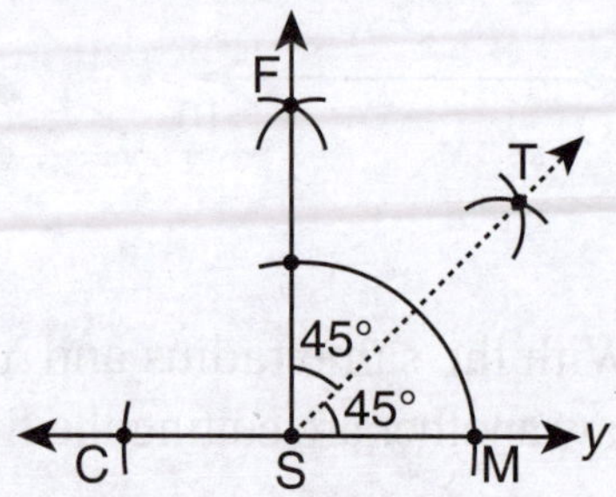

Constructing an angle of measure 75°

Step 1: Draw a ray AB. Taking A as centre and with the help of any radius, draw an arc cutting AB at O.

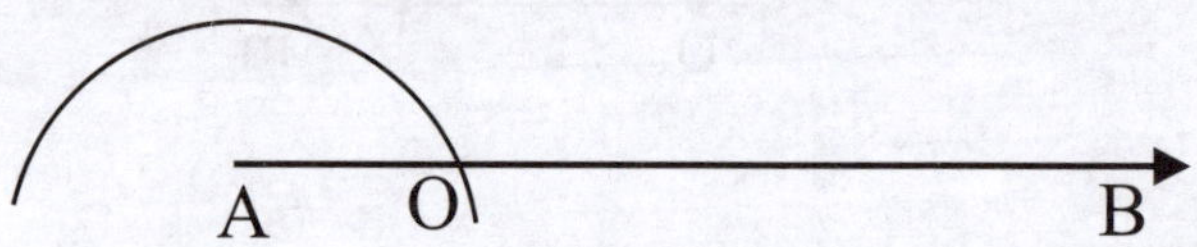

Step 2: Now, taking O as centre and with the same radius as taken in step 1, draw an arc intersecting the previous arc at C.

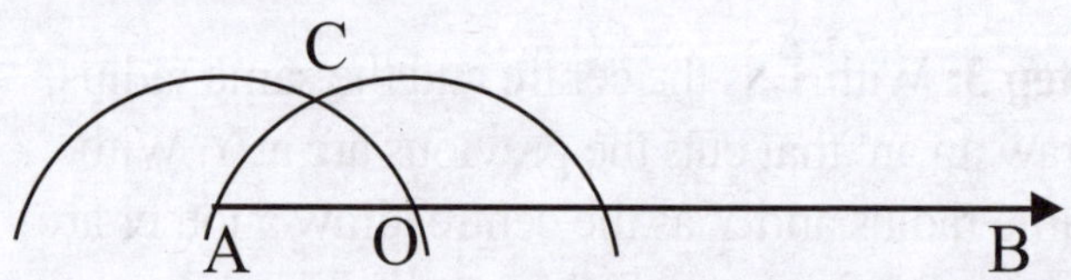

Step 3: With C as centre and using the same radius, cut off an arc cutting again the first arc at D.

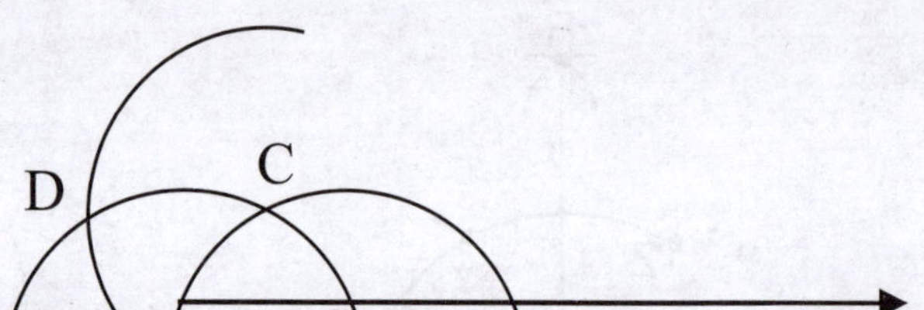

Step 4: With C and D as centres and radius of more than half of CD, draw two arcs cutting each other at E. Join AE which forms 90°. That is, ∠EAB = 90°. Here, AE cuts the first arc at F.

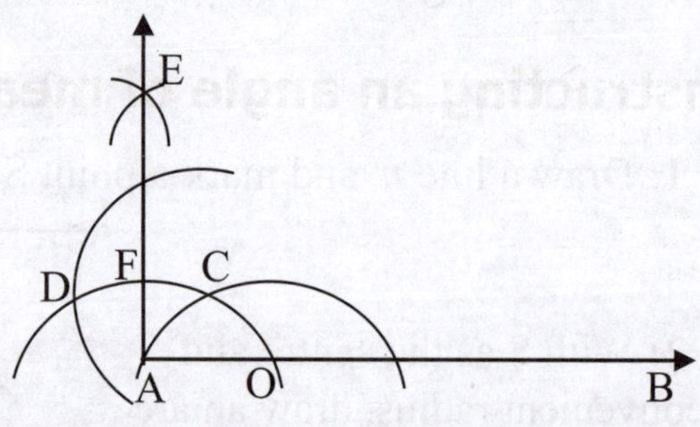

Step 5: Now with C and F as centres, draw two arcs intersecting at G and then join AG. Then, ∠GAB = 75°.

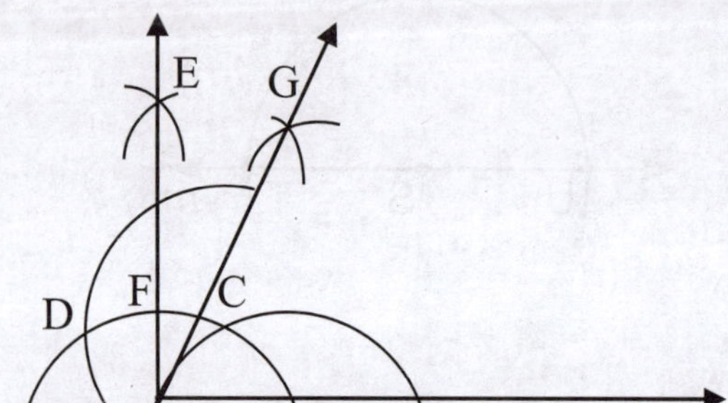

CONSTRUCTION OF TRIANGLES

To construct a triangle, a minimum of three measurements are required. A triangle can be constructed using a ruler, a compass and a protractor.

Triangles can be constructed using the following measurements:

- Measurements of three sides of a triangle
- Measurement of two sides and an angle between the two sides
- Measurements of any two angles and the included side

When the lengths of three sides are given:

Example 5: Construct a triangle ABC such that AB = 6 cm, BC = 5 cm and CA = 4 cm.

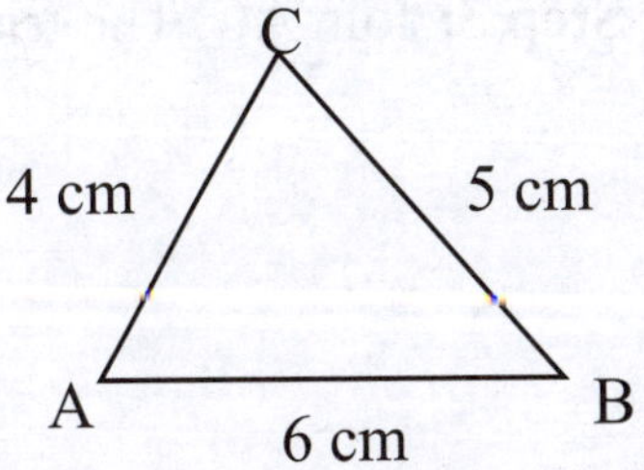

Solution:

Step 1: Draw a rough sketch of the triangle using the given measurements.

Step 2: Draw the longest side of the triangle, that is draw AB = 6 cm.

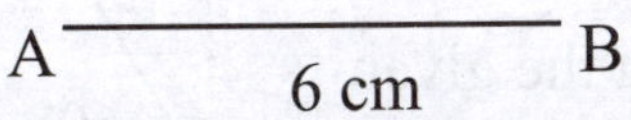

Step 3: Using a compass and taking A as centre, draw an arc of length 4 cm.

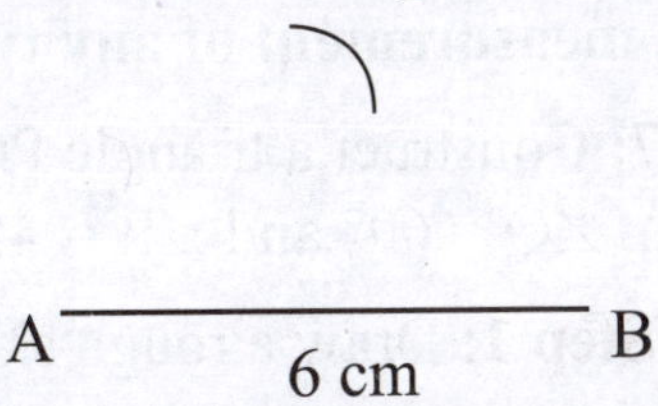

Step 4: With B as centre, draw an arc of length 5 cm, which cuts the first arc at point C.

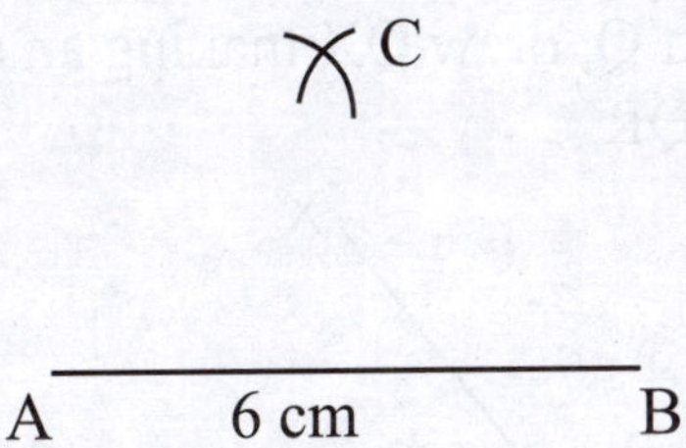

Step 5: Join AC and BC, the triangle obtained is the required triangle ABC.

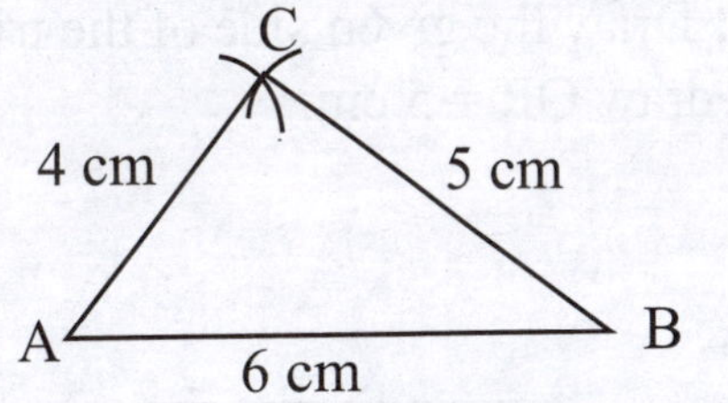

When the measurements of any two sides and an included angle are given:

Example 6: Construct a triangle ABC using AB = 5 cm, BC = 7 cm and ∠B = 70°.

Solution:

Step 1: Draw a rough sketch of the triangle using the given measurements.

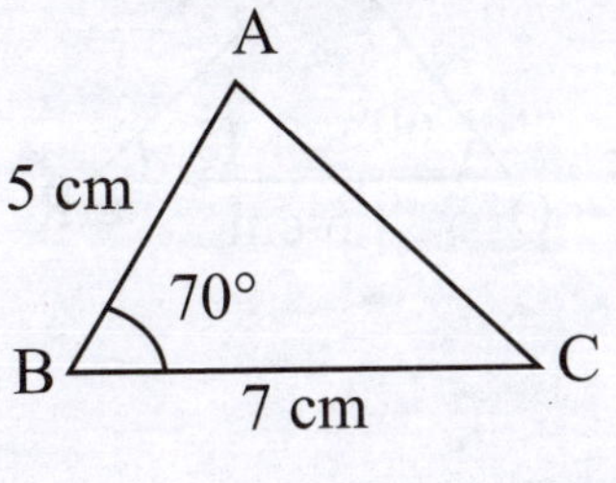

Step 2: Draw the longest side of the triangle, that is, draw BC = 7 cm.

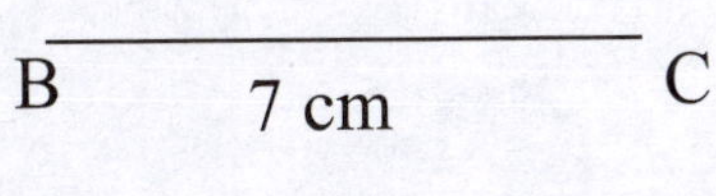

Step 3: Using a protractor, at the point B, mark a 70° angle by drawing a ray BX.

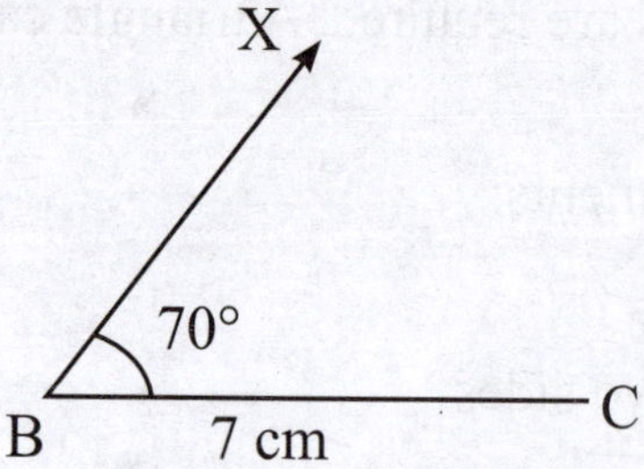

Step 4: With B as centre, draw an arc of length 5 cm, which cuts the line BX at A.

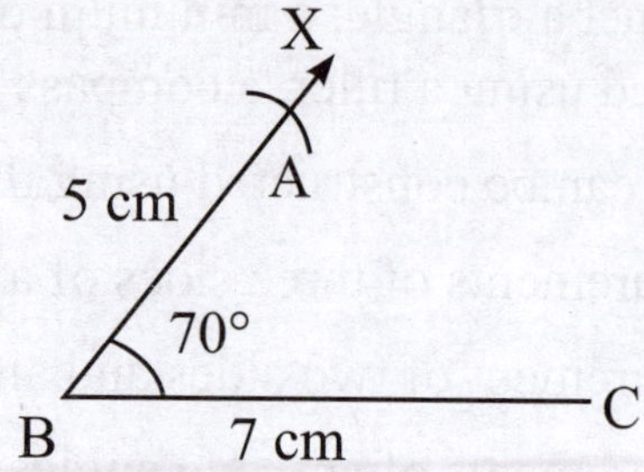

Step 5: Join AC. The triangle obtained is the required triangle ABC.

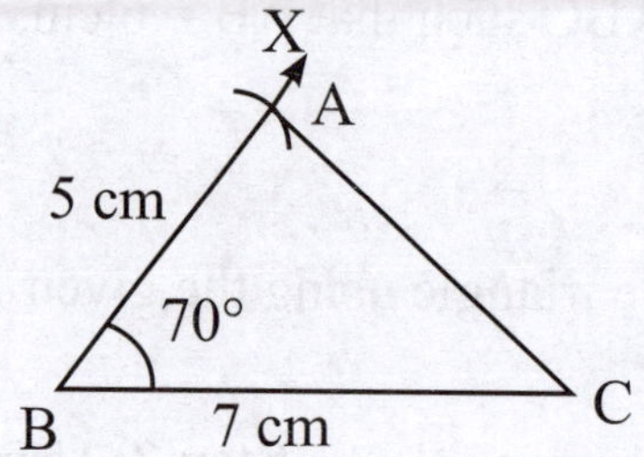

When the measurement of any two angles and an included side are given:

Example 7: Construct a triangle PQR using the measurements QR = 5 cm, $\angle Q = 60°$ and $\angle R = 45°$.

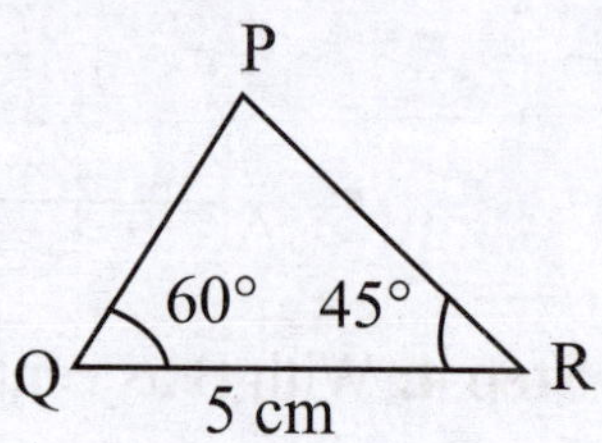

Solution: Step 1: Draw a rough sketch of the triangle using the given measurements.

Step 2: Draw the given side of the triangle, that is, draw QR = 5 cm.

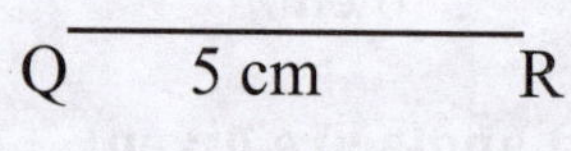

Step 3: At Q, draw QX making an angle of 60° with QR.

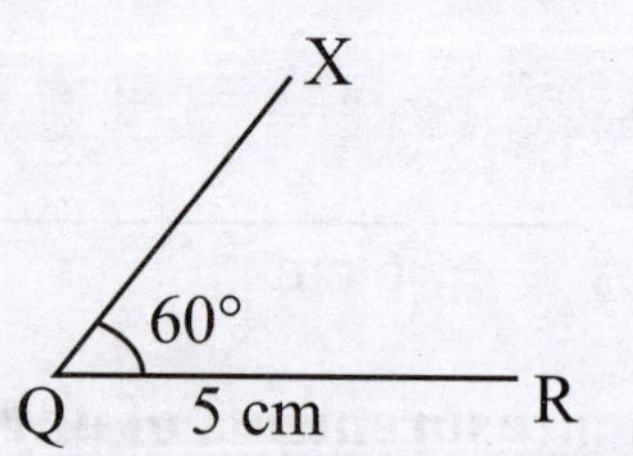

Step 4: At R, draw RY making an angle of 45° with QR.

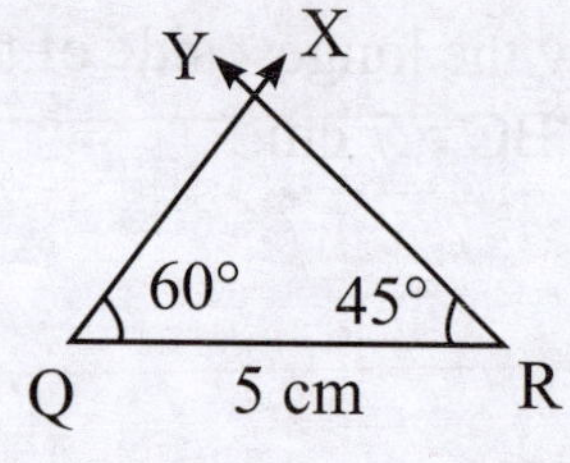

Step 5: QX and RY intersect each other at point P. The triangle obtained is the required triangle PQR.

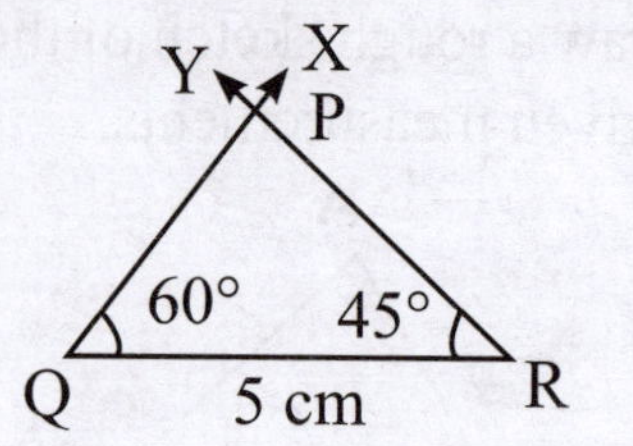

CONSTRUCTION OF A PERPENDICULAR TO A LINE THROUGH A POINT ON IT

Method 1 Using Ruler and Set Squares

Step 1: A line ℓ and a point P on it are given.

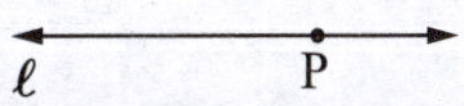

Step 2: Place a ruler with one of its edges along line ℓ.

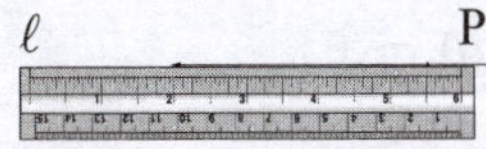

Step 3: Holding the ruler firmly, place a set square with one of its edges along the ruler as shown here.

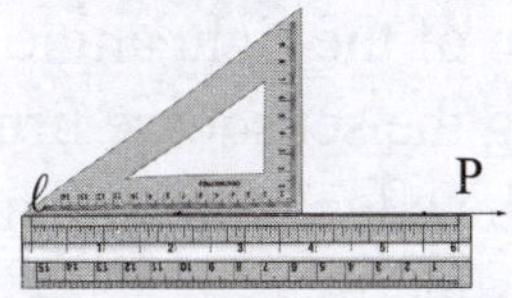

Step 4: Slide the set square along the edge of the ruler until its right-angled corner coincides with the point P.

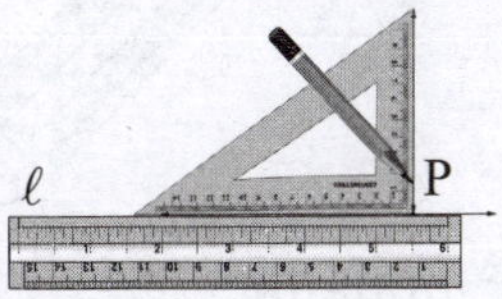

Step 5: Holding the ruler and the set square firmly, draw a line *m* along the edge of the set square.

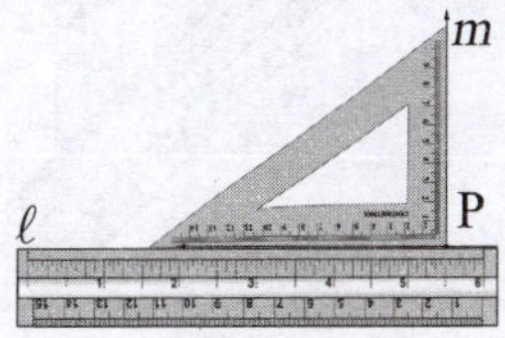

The line *m* is the required perpendicular line.

Method 2 Using Ruler and Compass

Step 1: A line ℓ and a point P on it are given.

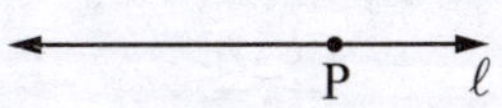

Step 2: With point P as the centre and a convenient and suitable radius, make an arc to intersect line ℓ at C and D.

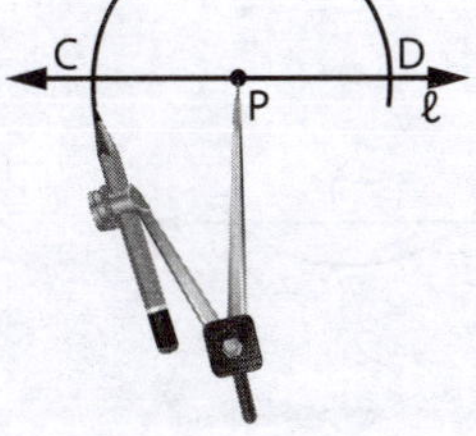

Step 3: With C as the centre and a radius greater than CP, draw an arc.

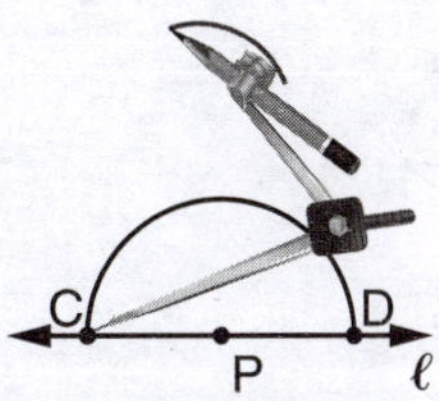

Step 4: With D as the centre and the same radius, draw an arc intersecting the arc drawn in Step 3. Mark the point of intersection as A.

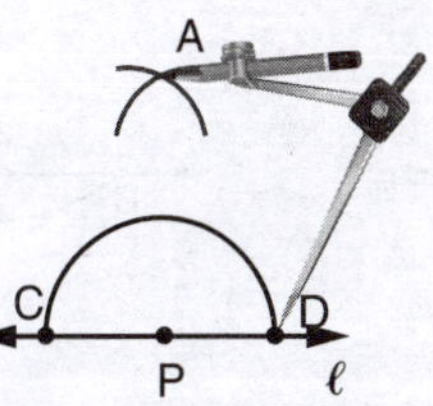

Step 5: Join points A and P. AP is the perpendicular to the given line.

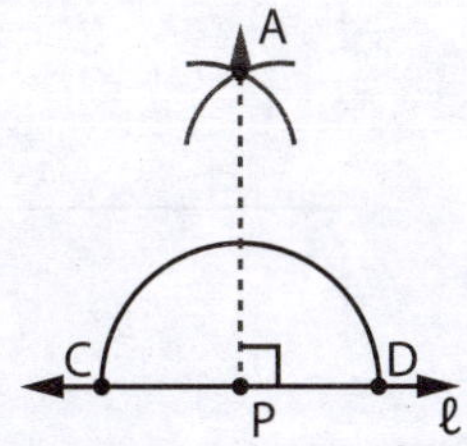

CONSTRUCTION OF A PERPENDICULAR TO A LINE THROUGH A POINT NOT ON IT

Method 1 Using Ruler and Set Squares

Step 1: A line ℓ and a point P not on it are given.

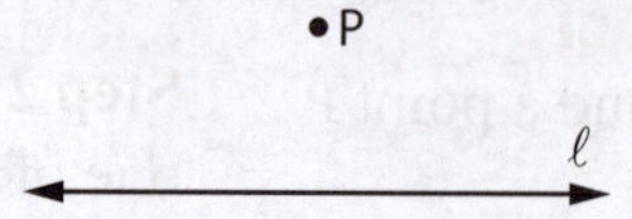

Step 2: Place a set square on line ℓ such that one arm of the right angle is along line ℓ. Holding the set square firmly, place a ruler along the edge, opposite to the right angle of the set square.

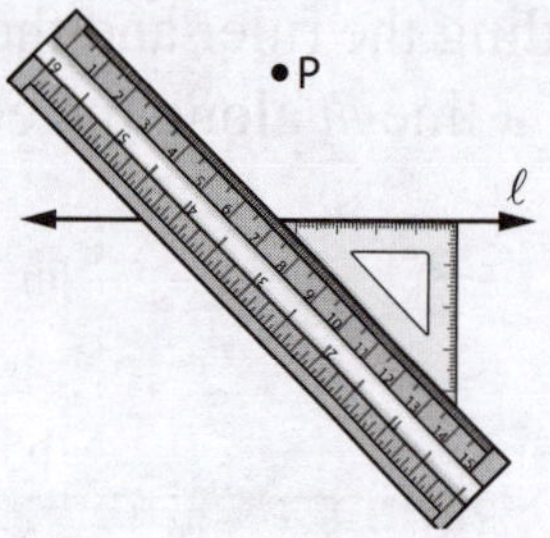

Step 3: Slide the set square along the ruler until the point P touches the other arm of the set square.

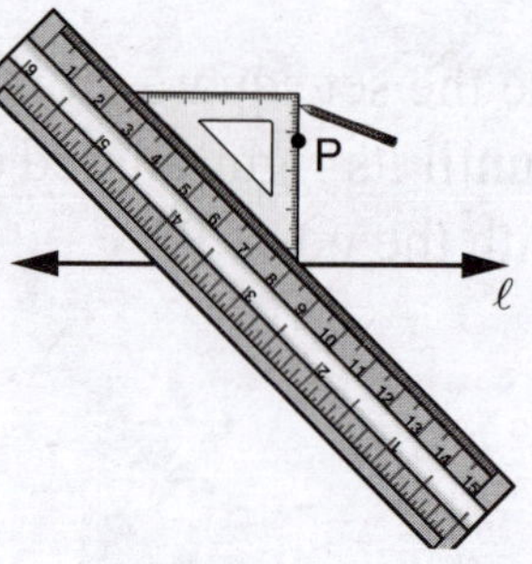

Step 4: Holding the ruler and the set square firmly, draw a line along the edge of the set square.

Therefore, PQ is the required perpendicular to the line *l*.

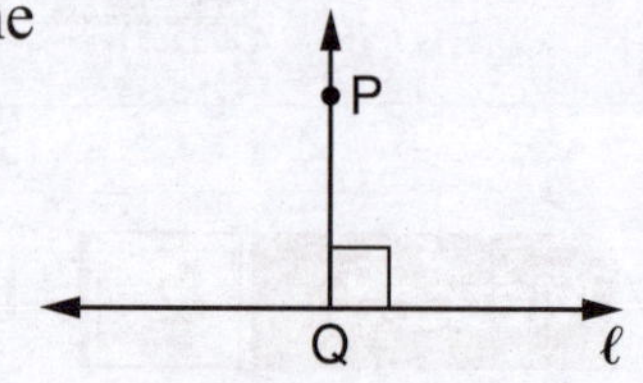

Method 2 Using Ruler and Compass

Step 1: A line ℓ and a point P not on it are given.

Step 2: With point P as the centre and a suitable radius, make an arc to intersect the line ℓ at C and D.

Step 3: With points C and D as centres and taking a convenient radius, draw arcs that intersect at a point E on the other side of ℓ.

Step 4: Join points P and E to get PE, which is perpendicular to the given line.

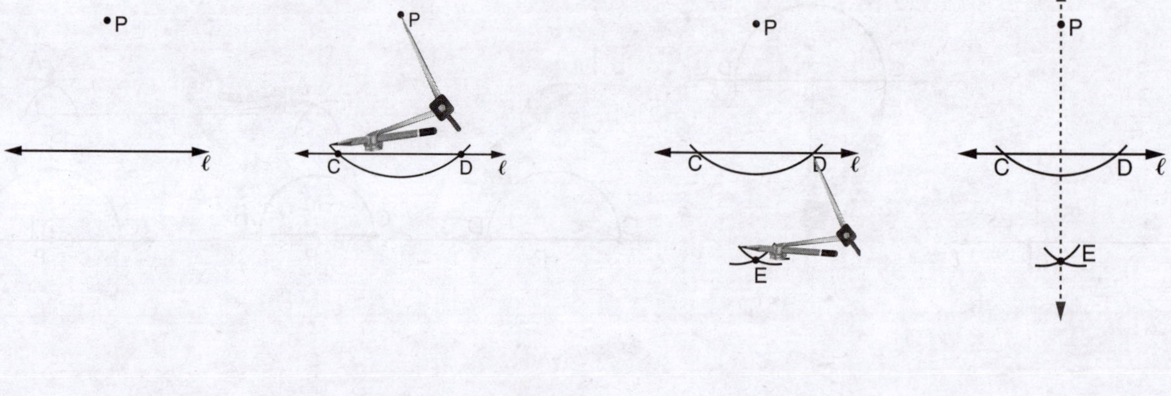

CONSTRUCTION OF A CIRCLE

Step 1: Mark a point O on paper. •O

Step 2: Take the compass and measure 5 cm using a ruler.

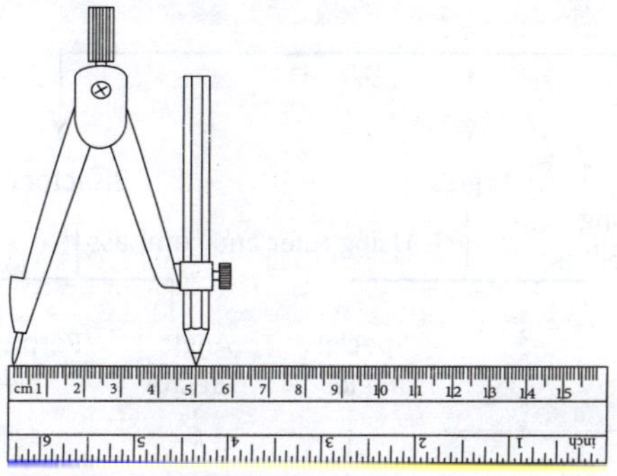

Step 3: Without disturbing the compass, place its tip on the point O. Move the pencil around to get a circle of radius 5 cm.

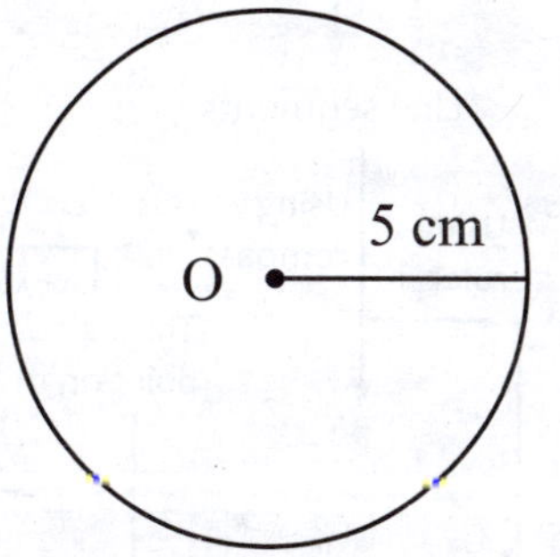

REMEMBER

1. Make sure that the pencil tip and the metal pointer are at the same level.
2. Once the metal pointer is placed at a point, it should not be moved while drawing the circle.
3. Ruler and protractor are measuring tools; they are not construction tools.

EXERCISE 14.1

1. **Construct line segments using a ruler.**

   a. 1.2 cm b. 3.5 cm c. 4.8 cm d. 5.5 cm

2. **Draw a line segment AB = 11 cm. Draw PQ perpendicular to AB such that PB = BQ = 5.5 cm.**
3. **Construct a triangle ABC, such that BC = 6.5 cm, AC = 4 cm and $\angle C = 30°$.**
4. **Draw a line segment AB = 12 cm. Take a point S on AB such that AS = 6.5 cm. Draw a ray perpendicular to AB at S by**

   a. using a ruler and a compass and

   b. using a ruler and set squares.

5. **With the help of a compass and ruler, construct the following angles:**

   a. 60° b. 120° c. 75°

6. **Construct a triangle PQR, such that PQ = 8 cm, PR = 5 cm and QR = 7.5 cm.**
7. **A line segment has a length of 6.4 cm. Taking this as diameter, construct a circle.**
8. **Construct a triangle ABC, such that $\angle A = 120°$, $\angle B = 30°$ and AB = 6.5 cm.**

Key Concepts

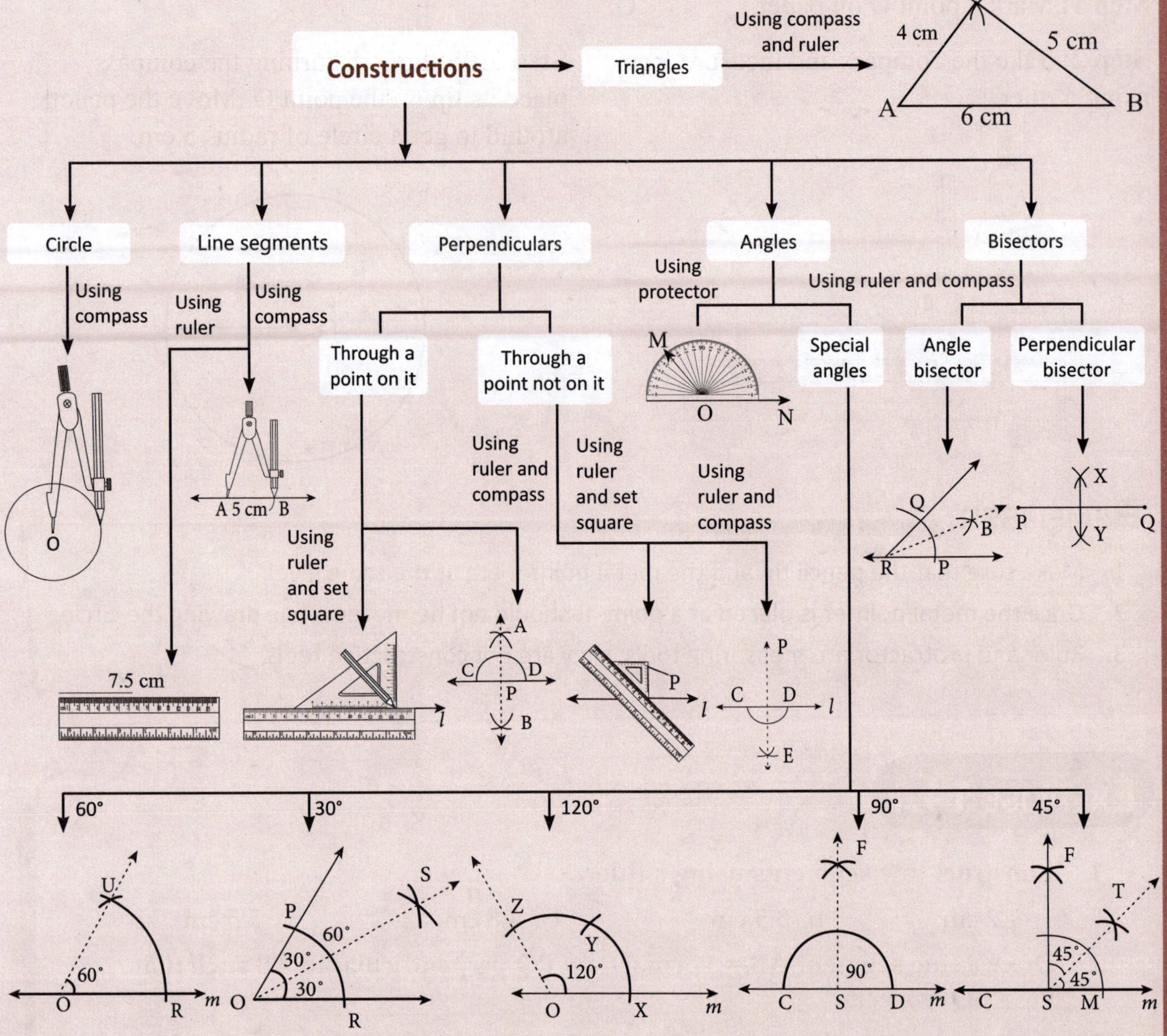

Revision Exercise

1. **Choose the correct option.**

   a. A rectangular geometrical instrument having graduated edges is called a

   i. divider ii. ruler iii. compass iv. set square

   b. How many scales does a protractor have?

   i. 1 ii. No scale iii. 2 iv. 3

   c. Which of the following is used to draw arcs and circles?

   i. Ruler ii. Protractor iii. Compass iv. Divider

   d. Arrange the following steps in the correct order to construct a erpendicular bisector EF for a line segment AB.

   P: With B as centre and without changing the radius, draw another arc that intersects the previously drawn arc at the points E and F.

   Q: With A as centre and more than half of AB as radius, draw a long arc.

   R: Join E and F and name the point of intersection of EF and AB as O.

   S: Draw a line segment AB of the given length.

   i. P, Q, R and S ii. Q, S, P and R

   iii. S, P, Q and R iv. S, Q, P and R

   e. By which of the following combination of instruments, can we construct a 120° angle?

   i. Ruler and Set square ii. Divider and compass

   iii. Ruler and Compass iv. Compass and set square

2. **Construct a line segment of length 7.8 cm and then construct a perpendicular bisector of it.**
3. **Draw the following angles using a protractor and then bisect the angles.**

   a. 45° b. 80° c. 150° d. 125°

4. **Construct a triangle XYZ, such that XY = 9 cm, YZ = 7.5 cm and XZ = 8 cm.**
5. **Construct angles measuring 105° and 135° using a compass and a ruler. Write the steps of construction.**
6. **Draw $\angle XYZ$ of your choice and then draw $\angle XYZ = \angle ABC$ using a ruler and a compass.**
7. **Construct angles measuring 60°, 90° and 120° using a ruler and compass and bisect the constructed angles.**
8. **Construct a line perpendicular to the the line segment AB of length 13 cm at a point on it which is 5 cm from A.**
9. **Construct a circle with centre O and diameter 9 cm.**
10. **Construct angles measuring 85° and 130° using a protractor and then bisect the angles.**

15 Perimeter and Area

Prior Knowledge

- Plane shapes
- Measuring length
- Unit conversions of length and area

Learning Objectives

- Perimeter of regular figures (triangle, rectangle and square)
- Different shapes with same perimeter
- Area of rectangle and square
- Misconception on perimeter and area

Let's Get Started

Perimeter and area are two important mathematical concepts. Understanding how much space you have and knowing the measure of a plot or its boundary will help you when you paint a building, buy a plot, etc.

The map of a badminton court and its dimensions are given in the below figure.

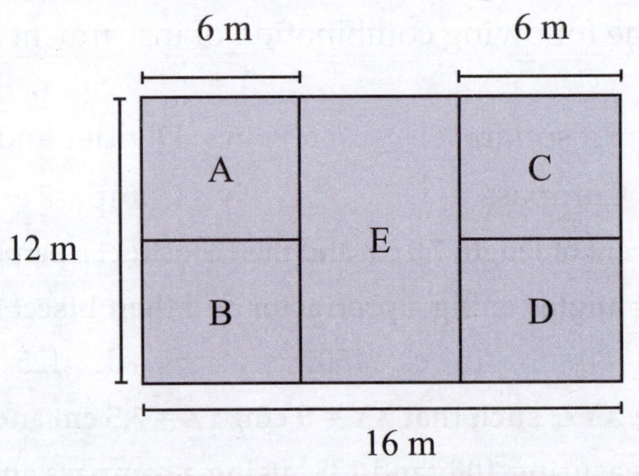

A, B, C, D are squares and E is a rectangle. Answer the following questions.

a. Which one has greater area, rectangle E or square B?

b. If square A is removed from the figure, find the perimeter of the remaining figure.

c. Which of the following plots will give the greatest area when added?

i. Square A and square D

ii Square B and rectangle E

iii. Squares B, C and D

PERIMETER

Look at the figures shown:

These are known as closed figures. The region shaded in green is the area of the corresponding figure. The line along the shaded region that separates the shaded region from the outer region is known as its **boundary**.

The length of the boundary of a closed figure is also known as its **perimeter**.

For example, in the figure given alongside, ABCDEF is a polygon.

Perimeter of ABCDEF = AB + BC + CD + DE + EF + FA

In general, perimeter of a closed figure = sum of the lengths of all its sides.

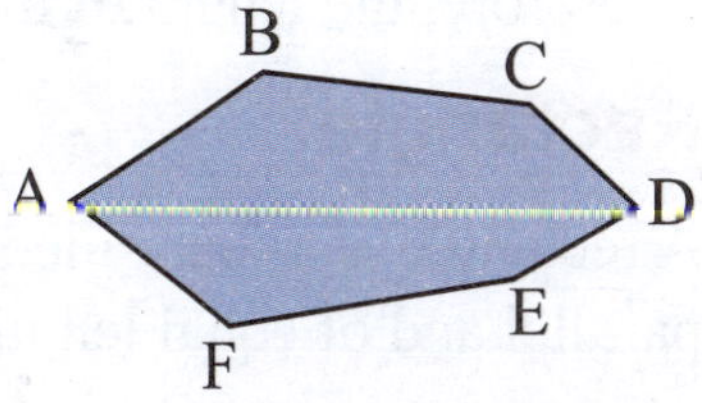

It is measured using the units of length such as m, cm and inches.

PERIMETER OF REGULAR FIGURES

Triangle

A triangle is a closed figure made up of three line segments.

Let ABC be a triangle with sides AB = a cm, BC = b cm and AC = c cm, then:

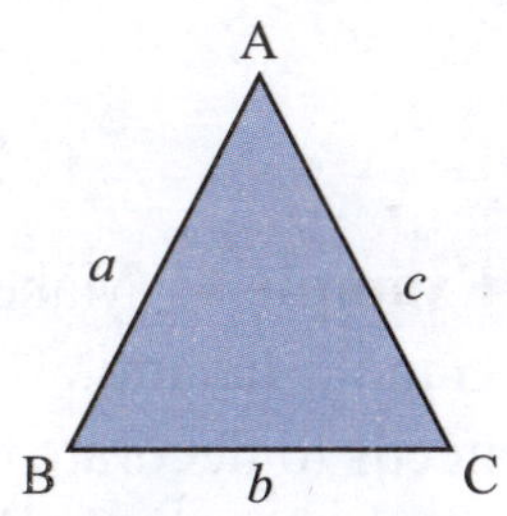

Perimeter of a triangle = Sum of the lengths of its sides

Perimeter of $\Delta ABC = (a + b + c)$ cm

Example 1: Find the perimeter of the following triangles.

a.

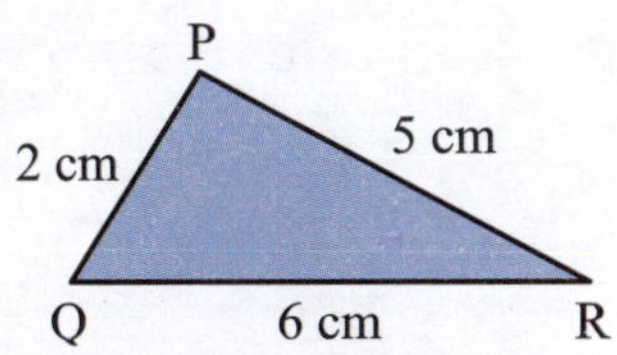

b.

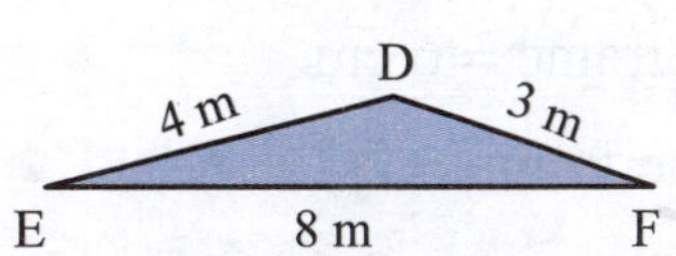

Solution: a. Perimeter of triangle PQR
= 2 cm + 5 cm + 6 cm = 13 cm

b. Perimeter of triangle DEF
= 4 m + 3 m + 8 m = 15 m

Example 2: The perimeter of an equilateral triangle is 6 cm. What is the length of each side?

Solution: Since an equilateral triangle has three equal sides, let each side of the triangle be x cm.

Perimeter of a triangle = $3x$

The given perimeter is 6 cm.

$\therefore\ 3x = 6 \text{ cm} \Rightarrow x = 2 \text{ cm}$

Example 3: The perimeter of a triangle is 42 cm. If the lengths of two sides are 13 cm and 14 cm, then find the length of the third side.

Solution: The perimeter of a triangle = 42 cm

Let us take the length of the third side as x cm

Hence, dimensions of the triangle are 13 cm, 14 cm and x cm.

Perimeter of the triangle = $13 + 14 + x$

$$42 = 27 + x$$

$$x = 42 - 27$$

$$x = 15$$

Therefore, the length of the third side of the triangle is 15 cm.

Rectangle

A rectangle is a four-sided flat shape where all angles are of 90° and opposite sides are parallel and of equal length.

Let ABCD be a rectangle with the length l unit and breadth b unit, then AD = BC = b units and AB = CD = l units

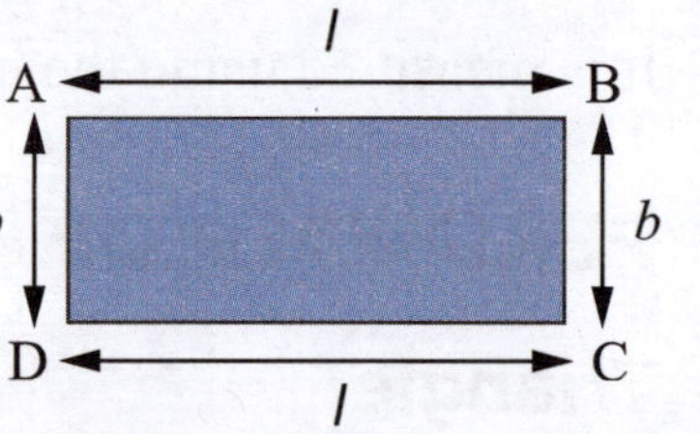

Perimeter of a rectangle = Sum of the length of its sides

$= (l + b + l + b)$ units

$= 2 \times (l + b)$ units

Perimeter of rectangle ABCD = 2 × (Length + Breadth)

Example 4: Mahesh is decorating a photo frame of Mahatma Gandhi on the occasion of Gandhi Jayanti. The length and breadth of the frame are 10 cm and 6 cm, respectively. He needs to decorate the borders of the photo frame with a ribbon. What is the length of the ribbon required to do so?

Solution: Length of the ribbon would be the perimeter of the photo frame.

Length of the frame = 10 cm

Breadth of the frame = 6 cm

Perimeter of the frame = $2(l + b)$

$= 2(10 + 6) = 2 \times 16 = 32$ cm

Therefore, Mahesh needs 32 cm of ribbon to decorate the borders of the photo frame.

Example 5: If the length of a rectangle is 3 m and its breadth is 1.5 m, then find the perimeter of the rectangle.

Solution: Length of the rectangle = 3 m

Breadth of the rectangle = 1.5 m

Perimeter of the rectangle = $2(l + b)$

$= 2(3 + 1.5) = 2 \times 4.5 = 9$ m

Square

A square is a flat shape with four equal sides.

Let ABCD be a square with the length of s unit, then perimeter of a square = sum of the length of all its sides

$= (s + s + s + s)$ units

$= (4 \times s)$ units $= 4 \times s$ units

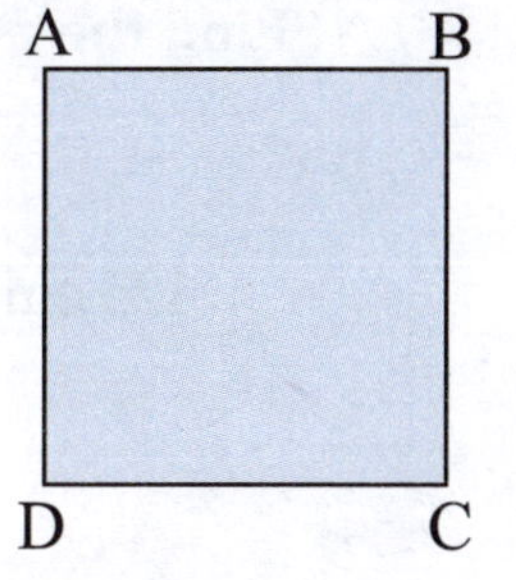

Example 6: If the perimeter of a square is 72 cm, then find the length of the square.

Solution: The perimeter of the square = 72 cm

Perimeter of square ABCD
= 4 × length of the side

Let us take the length of the square to be s.

We know that perimeter of the square $= 4s$

That is $4s = 72$ cm $\Rightarrow s = 72 \div 4 = 18$

Hence, the length of the square is 18 cm.

Example 7: A farmer has a square field of side 300 m. He wants to fence it with 4 rounds of barbed wire. What is the total length of wire he requires?

Solution: The farmer has to cover the field four times at its boundary. Therefore, the total length of barbed wire required is four times of its perimeter.

Perimeter of the field = 4 × Length of a side

= 4 × 300 m

= 1200 m

Total length of wire required = 4 × 1200 m = 4800 m.

Regular Pentagon

A regular pentagon has five sides. If the length of each side of a regular pentagon ABCDE is a units, then

Perimeter of pentagon ABCDE

= AB + BC + CD + DE + EA

$= a$ units $+ a$ units $+ a$ units $+ a$ units $+ a$ units

$= 5a$ units

= 5 × length of each side

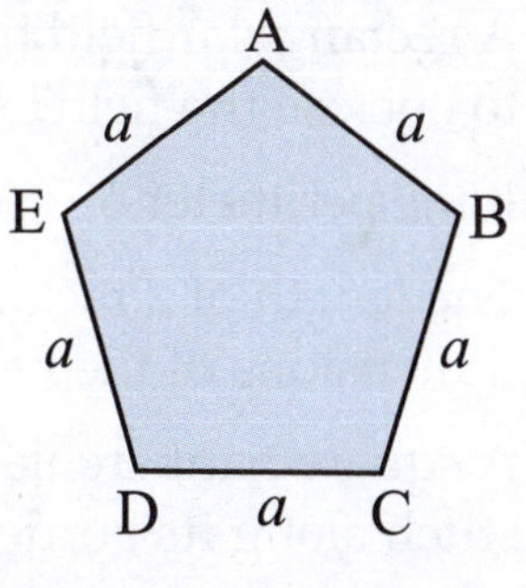

In general,

Perimeter of a regular polygon = number of sides of the polygon × length of each side

EXERCISE 15.1

1. Find the perimeter of the following objects using the correct formulae.

a. 125 cm

125 cm

b. 15 cm

15 cm

c. 52 in

30 in

d. 10 in

10 in

e. 15 cm 15 cm

15 cm

f. 20 cm

45 cm

2. Find the perimeter of the following:

a. An equilateral triangle of side 10 cm

b. An isosceles triangle with equal sides of length 8 cm each and the third side of length 5 cm

c. A square of side 17 cm

d. A rectangle of length 11 cm and breadth 10 cm

e. A regular hexagon of side 11 cm

f. A regular pentagon of side 9 cm

3. Answer the following questions.

a. What is the length of the third side of a triangle if one side measures 10 cm, the second measures 15 cm and the perimeter is 45 cm?

b. A rectangular field has dimensions 30 m by 40 m. How much fencing is needed to enclose the field?

c. If the perimeter of a square is 60 cm, what is the length of each side of the square?

d. The length of a rectangle is twice its breadth. If its perimeter is 144 feet, find the dimensions of the rectangle.

e. A square hankerchief cloth is 6 inches long. Find the cost of the lace required to stitch along its border if the lace is charged at ₹5 per inch.

f. A 60 cm long wire is used to make the following shapes. What will be the length of the side in each case?

i. A square ii. A regular pentagon iii. A regular hexagon

DIFFERENT SHAPES WITH SAME PERIMETER

Ranjana wants to build a fence and grow a garden. She has bought 16 metres of fence. She arranges the fence in different shapes as given below.

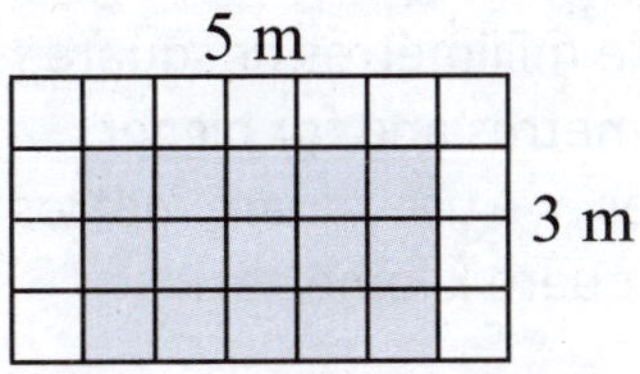

$P = 2(5\text{ m} + 3\text{ m}) = 16\text{ m}$

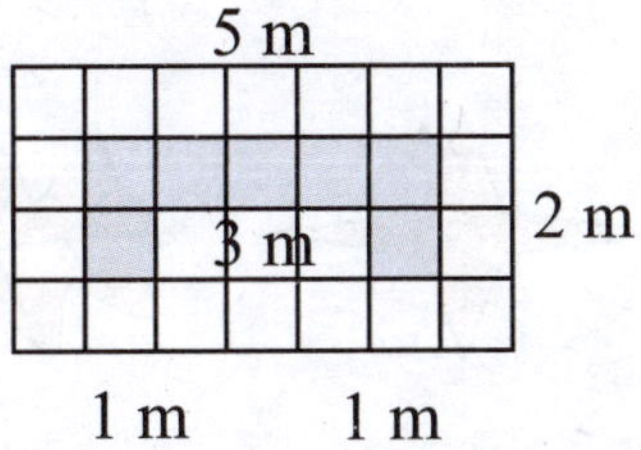

$P = 5\text{ m} + 2\text{ m} + 1\text{ m} + 1\text{ m}$
$+ 3\text{ m} + 1\text{ m} + 1\text{ m} + 2\text{ m} = 16\text{ m}$

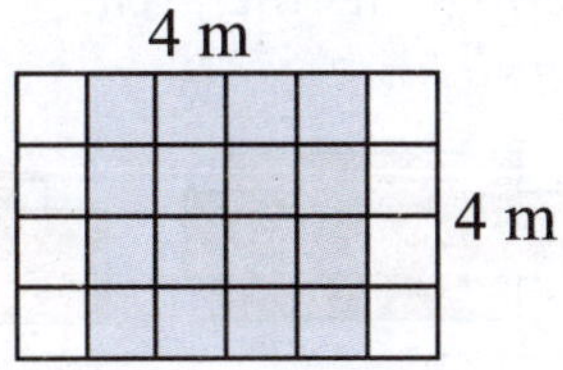

$P = 4 \times 4\text{ m} = 16\text{ m}$

We can observe that they all are of different shape but have the same perimeter, i.e., P = 16 metres.

EXERCISE 15.2

1. **Which of the following figures has the same perimeter as that of the figure shown alongside?**

a. 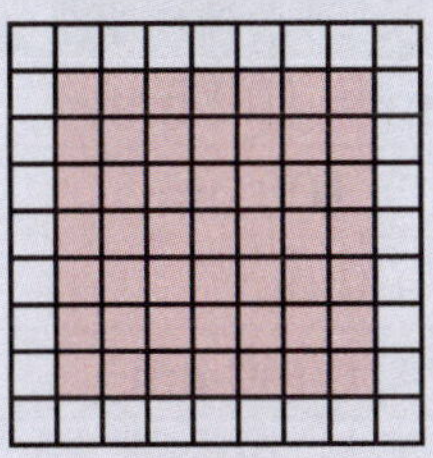

b. 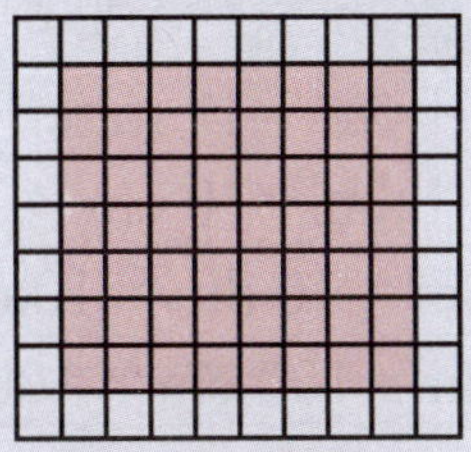

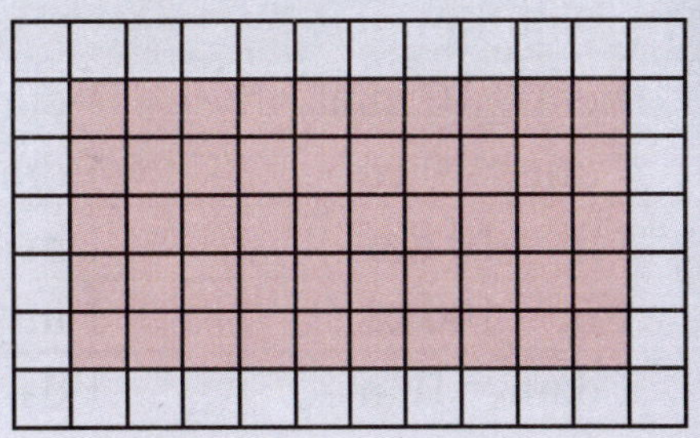

c. 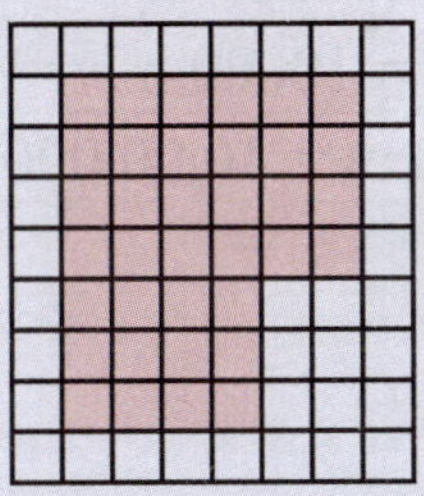

d. 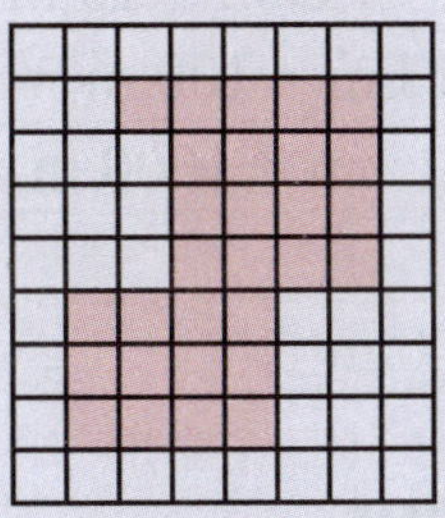

2. **Draw any three different shapes with a perimeter of 24 cm.**

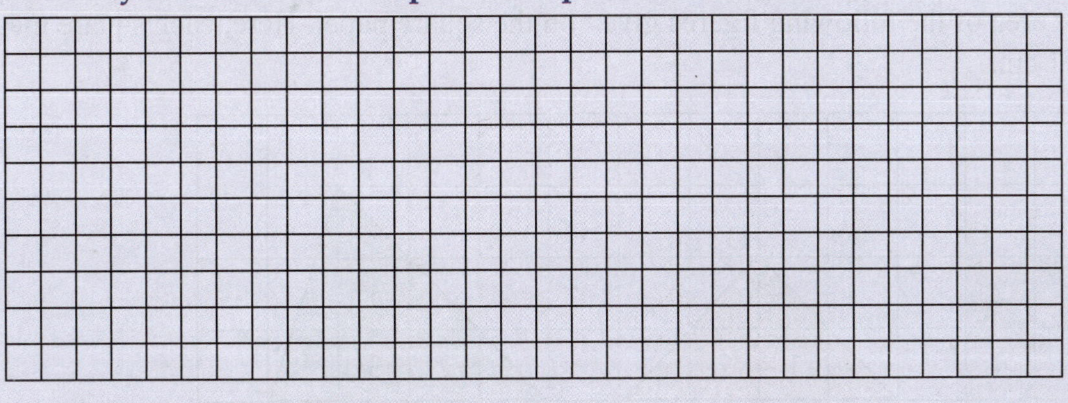

AREA

The amount of surface enclosed by a closed figure is called its **area**. The shaded portion in each of the following figures represents the area.

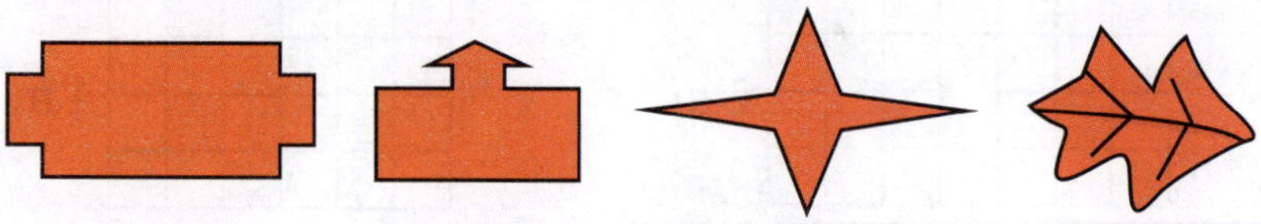

> **REMEMBER**
>
> For smaller figures, we use square millimetres or square centimetres and for bigger figures, we use square metres and square kilometres.

The standard unit of area is **square units**.

Conversion of Units

The area of a square of side 1 unit is 1 sq. unit.

So, the area of a square of side 1 cm is 1 sq. cm, or 1 cm^2.

The standard unit of area is 1 sq. cm.

The conversion relations are given in the following table.

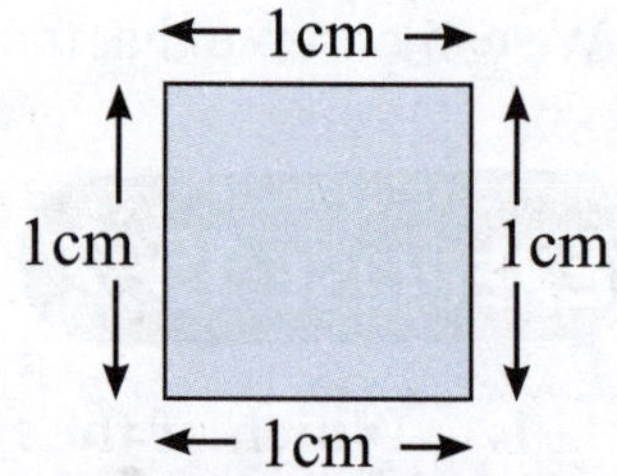

Length units	Area units
1 cm = 10 mm	1 cm^2 = 1 cm × 1 cm = 10 mm × 10 mm = 100 mm^2
1 dm = 10 cm	1 dm^2 = 1 dm × I dm = 10 cm × 10 cm = 100 cm^2
1 m = 10 dm	1 m^2 = 1 m × 1 m = 10 dm × 10 dm = 100 dm^2
1 m = 100 cm	1 m^2 = 1 m × 1 m = 100 cm × 100 cm = 10000 cm^2
1 dam = 10 m	1 dam^2 = 1 dam × 1 dam = 10 m × 10 m = 100 m^2 = 1 are
1 hm = 100 m	1 hm = 1 hm × 1 hm = 100 m × 100 m = 10000 m^2 = 1 hectare
1 km = 1000 m	1 km^2 = 1 km × 1 km = 1000 m × 1000 m = 10,00,000 m^2
	1 are = 100 m^2
	1 hectare = 10000 m^2

Finding Area using Squared Paper

Find the area of the following figures given on the square paper. Here, each square measures 1 cm × 1 cm.

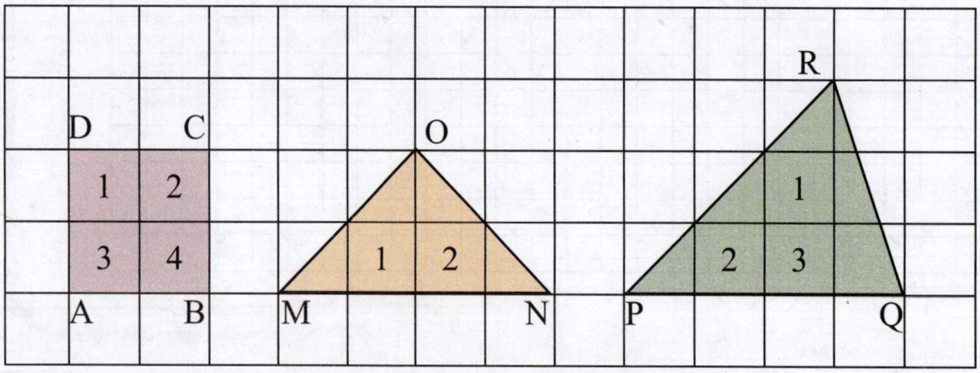

To find the area of figures drawn on the squared paper, we have to follow the following steps:

Step 1: Count the number of complete squares of unit length enclosed by the figure.

Step 2: Count the number of those squares which are shaded more than half.

Step 3: Count the number of those squares which are shaded exactly half and divide the number by 2.

Step 4: Leave those squares which are shaded less than half.

Step 5: The steps 1, 2 and 3 is used to obtain the area of the complete figure.

Area of the figure = Number of complete squares + Number of squares having more than half parts enclosed + $\frac{1}{2}$ (Number of squares having half parts enclosed)

So, the area of the above figures are:

a. Area of the figure ABCD = 4 × area of one square = $4 \times 1\ cm^2 = 4\ cm^2$

b. Area of the figure MNO = Number of complete squares + $\frac{1}{2}$ × Number of half squares

$$= 2 \times 1\ cm^2 + \frac{1}{2} \times 4 \times 1\ cm^2$$
$$= 2\ cm^2 + 2\ cm^2$$
$$= 4\ cm^2$$

c. Area of the figure PQR = Number of complete squares + Number of squares having more than half parts enclosed + $\frac{1}{2}$ × Number of half squares

$$= 3 \times 1\ cm^2 + 2 \times 1\ cm^2 + \frac{1}{2} \times 3 \times 1\ cm^2$$
$$= 3\ cm^2 + 2\ cm^2 + \frac{3}{2}\ cm^2$$
$$= 5\ cm^2 + \frac{3}{2}\ cm^2 = 5\ cm^2 + 1.5\ cm^2$$
$$= 6.5\ cm^2$$

Areas of Rectangle and Square

Consider a rectangular hall of dimensions 11 feet by 10 feet. The floor of this hall is to be covered with tiles of size 1 ft × 1 ft.

To find the number of tiles required to cover the floor, we have to find the area of the hall.

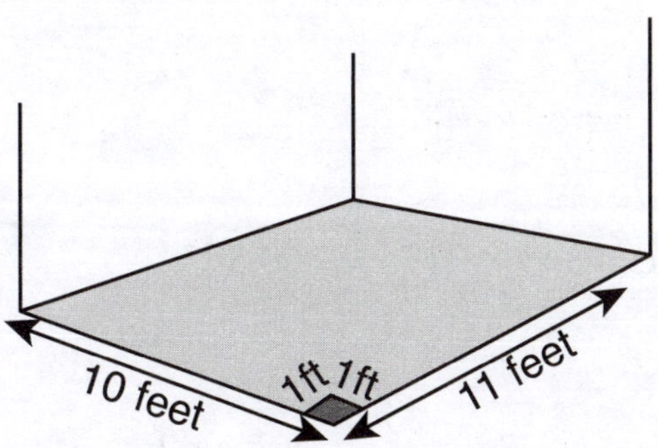

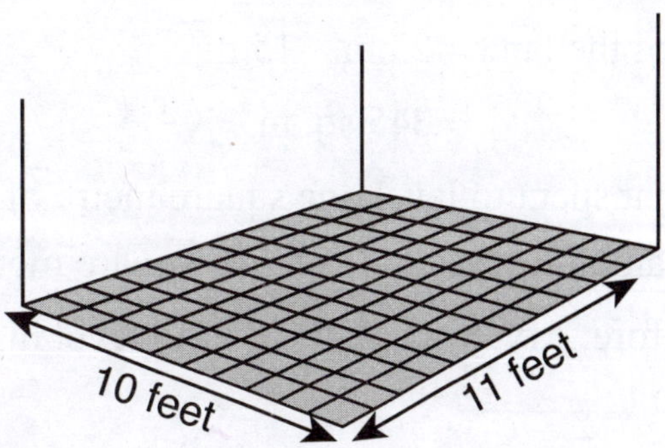

After paving the floor, we find that 110 tiles were required to cover the whole floor. Therefore, the area of the rectangular hall is 110 sq. ft.

What do you observe? We observe that length × breadth is always equal to the number of 1 × 1 tiles required to fill a shape.

∴ Area of rectangle = length × breadth

Length, $l = \frac{A}{b}$ and breadth, $b = \frac{A}{l}$

As the square is a special case of a rectangle whose length and breadth are equal, its area is given by $A = s \times s = s^2$, where s is its side length, That is, its side, $s = \sqrt{A}$.

Example 8: A classroom has a length of 10 feet and a width of 18 feet. The school decides to cover the floor of the entire class with tiles. If each tile has a length of 3 feet and a width of 2 feet, how many tiles are needed to cover the classroom floor?

Solution: Area of the classroom = Length × Width = 10 ft × 18 ft = 180 ft^2

Area of each tile = Length × Width = 3 feet × 2 feet

= 6 square feet

Number of tiles required to cover 180 ft^2 = $\frac{180}{6} = 30$

Therefore, 30 tiles are required to cover the classroom floor.

REMEMBER

Among all rectangles having equal perimeter, a rectangle whose all sides are equal (i.e. a square) has the greatest area.

For example, if the perimeter of a rectangle is 18 cm, so there can be a rectangle with length 6 cm and breadth 3 cm and area of that rectangle is 18 cm^2.

If we have a square with perimeter 18 cm.

Each side = 18÷4 = 4.5 cm

And the area of a square is 20.25 cm^2.

(20.25 > 18)

Example 9: A square garden with side 100 m has a square swimming pool at the very centre of it with side 20 m. Calculate the area of the garden.

Solution: Since the swimming pool is at the centre of the garden,

Area of the garden = Area of the total space – Area of the swimming pool

= (100 × 100) – (20 × 20)

= 10000 – 400

= 9600 sq. m

Therefore, the area of the garden is 9600 sq. m.

Example 10: Aryan levelled his rectangular piece of land of dimensions 23 m and 15 m. If he spent ₹175 per square metre on doing so, then find the total amount spent by him to level his land.

Solution: Length and breadth of the rectangular piece of land are 23 m and 15 m, respectively.

Area of the land = 23 m × 15 m

= 345 sq. m

Amount spent to level one square metre of land = ₹175

Total amount spent to level 345 square metres of land = 345 × ₹175 = ₹60,375

Therefore, Aryan spent ₹60,375 to level his land.

Example 11: Sanyam has one square-shaped field and one rectangular field. The area of the rectangular field is double the area of the square field. The side of the square field measures 36 m, and the width of the rectangular field is 48 m. Find the length of the wire required to fence the rectangular field.

Solution: Area of the square field = $s \times s = (36 \times 36)\ m^2 = 1{,}296\ m^2$

Area of the rectangular field = $(2 \times 1{,}296)\ m^2 = 2{,}592\ m^2$

Width of the rectangular field = 48 m

Length of the rectangular field = $\frac{\text{Area}}{\text{Width}} = \frac{2{,}592}{48}$ m = 54 m

Length of the wire required

= Perimeter of the rectangle

= $2(l + b) = 2(54 + 48)$ m

= 2×102 m = 204 m

Area of Right Isosceles Triangle

Right isosceles triangle is a right triangle with two equal sides.

In the given triangle, AB and BC are equal sides. BC is the base and AB is the height.

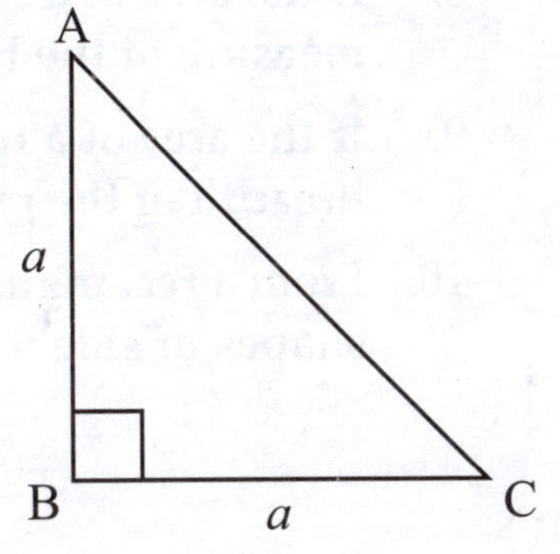

Let BC = AB = a cm

Area of triangle ABC = $\frac{1}{2}(BC \times AB) = \frac{1}{2}(a \times a)$

$= \frac{1}{2}a^2$, where a is the length of one of the equal sides

Example 12: An engineer surveyed a plot of land that is in the shape of a right triangle. The area of the land is 25,000 sq. m. If the base of the triangular plot is 100 m long, what is the height of the plot?

Solution: Area of the plot = 25,000 sq. m

Base of the plot = 100 m

Let the height of the plot be h.

Area of the triangle = $\frac{1}{2}(\text{Base} \times \text{Height})$

$25{,}000 = \frac{1}{2}(100 \times h)$

$25{,}000 = 50h$

$h = \frac{25{,}000}{50} = 500$

Hence, the height of the plot is 500 m.

Exercise 15.3

1. Find the area of a rectangle whose length and breadth are 30 cm and 16 cm, respectively. Also, find the perimeter of the rectangle.
2. Find the cost of cultivating a square field of side 42 m at ₹15 per sq. m.
3. A room is 15 m long and 8 m wide. A square carpet of side 6 m is laid on its floor. Find the area of the floor that is not carpeted.
4. What will happen to the area of a square if the lengths of its sides are halved?
5. The floor of a room is 90 cm by 120 cm. Find the number of tiles needed to cover the floor if the length and breadth of one tile are 9 cm and 4 cm, respectively.
6. If the area of a right isosceles triangle is 128 sq. m, what will be the length of the identical sides of the triangle?
7. If the base and height of a triangle are 12 cm and 9 cm, respectively, then find the area of the triangle.
8. If the area of a triangle is 432 sq. cm and its height is 16 cm, then find the measure of the base of the triangle.
9. If the area of a rectangle is 864 sq. cm and its length is 32 cm, then find the breadth of the rectangle.
10. From a rectangular sheet of dimension 45 cm and 35 cm, Reena cut two square shapes of side 9 cm. Find the remaining area of the rectangular sheet.

MISCONCEPTIONS ON PERIMETER AND AREA

The following are few misconceptions on 'perimeter and area and their relationship'.

1. Different shapes cannot have the same perimeter. Similarly, different shapes cannot have the same area.

Counter examples:

i. The given figures (fig. a and b) have the same perimeter of 20 units even though they are of different shapes.

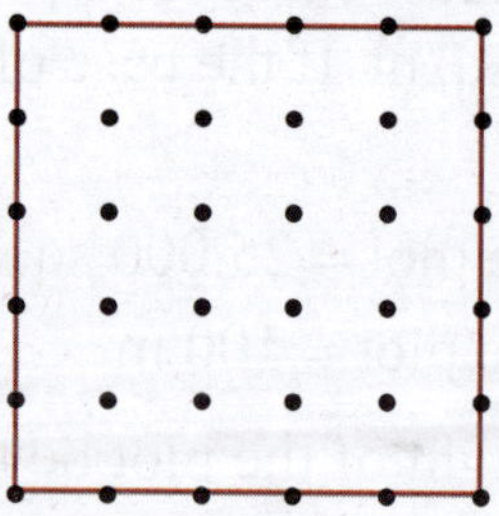

Fig a.

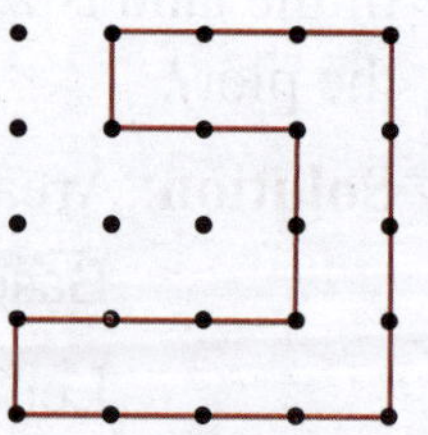

Fig b.

ii. The given figures (fig c and d) have the same area of 16 sq. units, even though they are of different shapes.

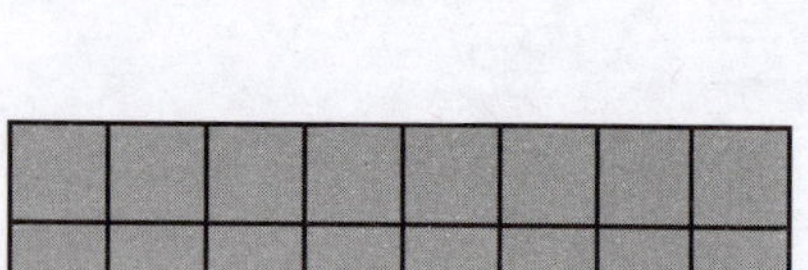

Fig c.

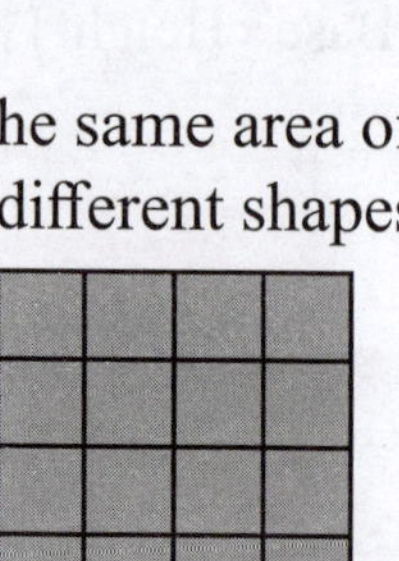

Fig d.

2. If the perimeters of two figures are the same, then their areas are also the same.

Counter example:

The figures e. and f. have same perimeter as 16 units, but they have different areas.

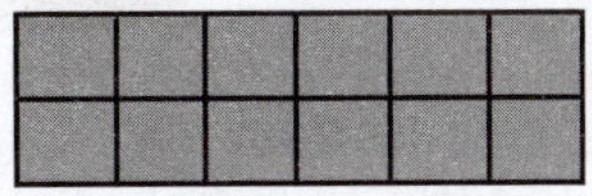

Fig e.

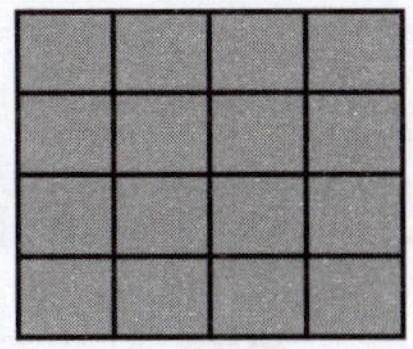

Fig f.

The area of Fig e. is 12 sq. units, and that of Fig f. is 16 sq. units.

3. If the areas of two figures are the same, then their perimeters are also the same.

Counter example:

The figures c. and d. have same area, that is, 16 sq. units but they have different perimeters. The perimeter of Fig c. is 20 units and that of Fig d. is 16 units.

4. The area of the figure changes when it is converted into another figure.

Counter example:

Figure g is made up of 10 unit squares and hence, its area is 10 sq. units. The unit squares are rearranged and the 2nd figure is formed. The figure h also consists of 10 units squares and hence, its area is also 10 sq. units.

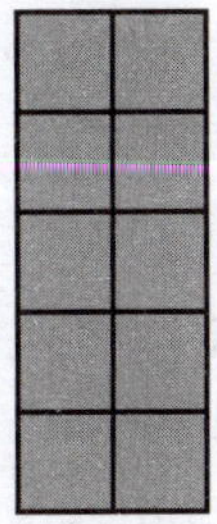

Fig g.

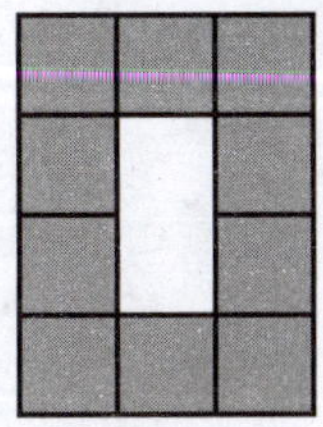

Fig h.

KEY CONCEPTS

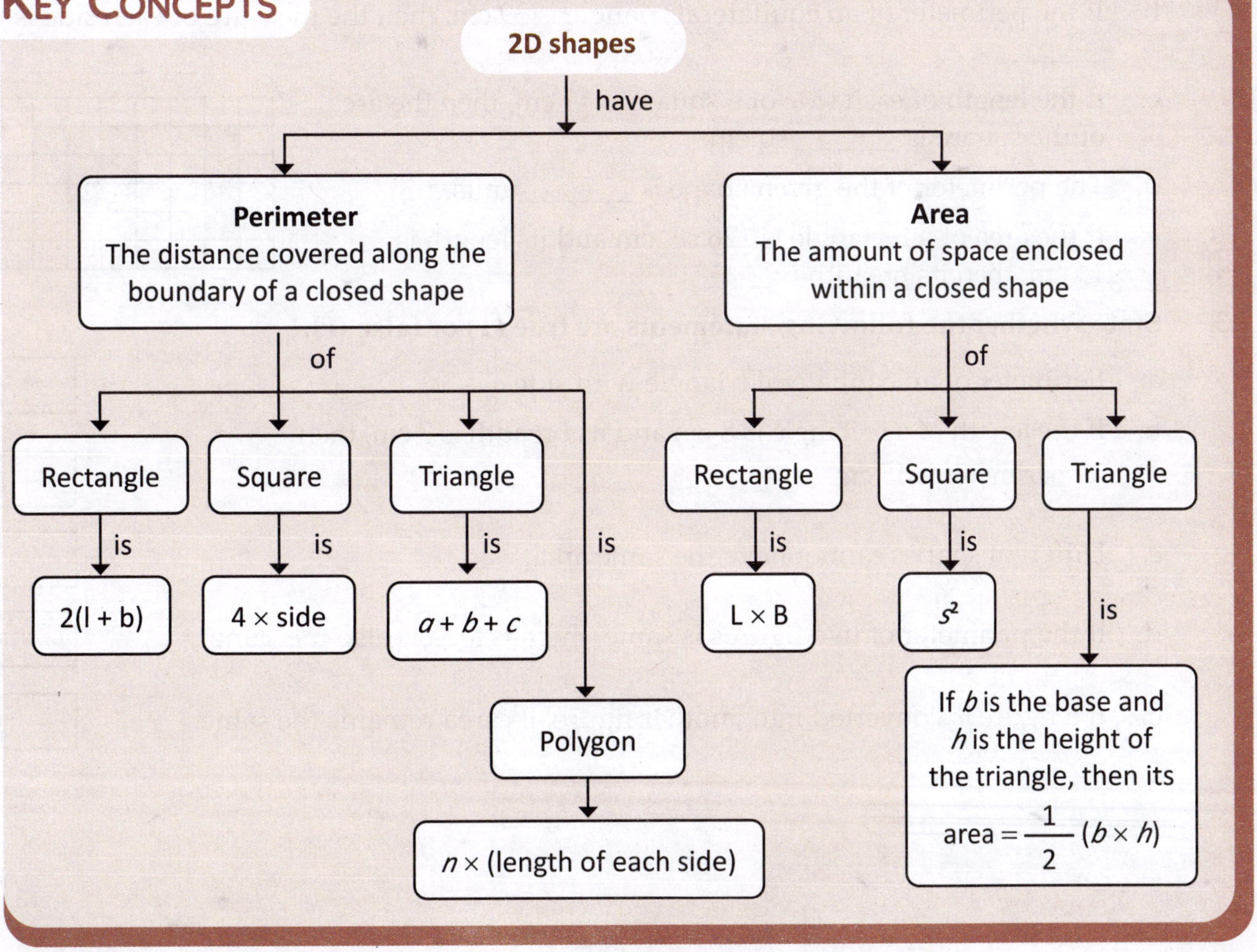

REVISION EXERCISE

1. Choose the correct option.

a. If 'a' is the length of a side of a square, then what is the perimeter of the square?

i. a^2 ii. $2a$ iii. $4a$ iv. a^4

b. If l is the length and b is the breadth of a rectangle, then the area of the rectangle is _____.

i. $4(l + b)$ ii. $l + b$ iii. $2(l + b)$ iv. $l \times b$

c. If the area of a square is 49 cm, then the perimeter of the square is _____.

i. 7 cm ii. 28 cm iii. 14 cm iv. 49 cm

d. If the sides of a triangle are 9 cm, 11 cm and 7 cm, then find the perimeter of the triangle.

i. 27 cm ii. 54 cm iii. 21 cm iv. 29 cm

e. If the area of a rectangle is 221 m and its breadth is 13 m, then find the length of the rectangle.

i. 15 m ii. 17 m iii. 11 m iv. 19 m

2. Fill in the blanks.

a. ________ is the distance covered along the boundary of a closed shape.

b. If the perimeter of an equilateral triangle is 39 cm, then the measure of each side is ________.

c. If the length of each side of a square is 11 cm, then the area of the square is ________ sq.cm.

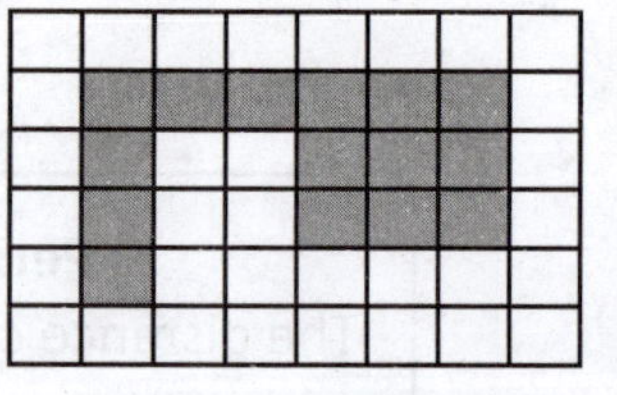

d. The perimeter of the given shape is ________ units.

e. If the area of a rectangle is 126 sq. cm and its length is 14 cm, then its breadth is ________.

3. State whether the following statements are true (T) or false (F).

a. Perimeter of an equilateral triangle with side a is $3a$. ☐

b. If the length of a rectangle is 8 cm and its breadth is 7 cm, then its perimeter is 15 cm. ☐

c. Different shapes cannot have the same area. ☐

d. If the perimeter of two figures is same, then its area is also the same. ☐

e. If a figure is converted into another figure, its area remains the same. ☐

4. **Answer the following.**

a. If the perimeter of an equilateral triangle is 36 cm, find the measure of each side of the triangle.

b. Find the cost of fencing a triangular park with each side equal to 235 m at the rate of ₹15 per metre.

c. Which of the following has greater area: a square with side 95 cm or a rectangle with length 150 cm and breadth 60 cm?

d. Find the cost of dyeing a square piece of cloth at the rate of ₹120 per sq. m if the length of one side is 30 m.

e. Ravi wants to fence his backyard for his dog. He plans to make one side 8 feet wide and another side 17 feet long. How much fencing will he need? How much space is obtained by fencing?

f. I am thinking of a rectangle with an area of 24 cm^2. What could be its maximum perimeter?

g. The dimension of a rectangular sheet is 4 inches in length and 11 inches in width. What is the perimeter of the sheet?

h. What happens to the area of a rectangle if its length is doubled and the breadth is reduced to half?

i. The perimeter of square A is four times the perimeter of another square B. What is the ratio of the area of square B to the area of square A?

j. Three similar rectangles are used to form a figure. Each rectangle has a length of 4 cm and a breadth of 2 cm. Find the area and perimeter of the figure.

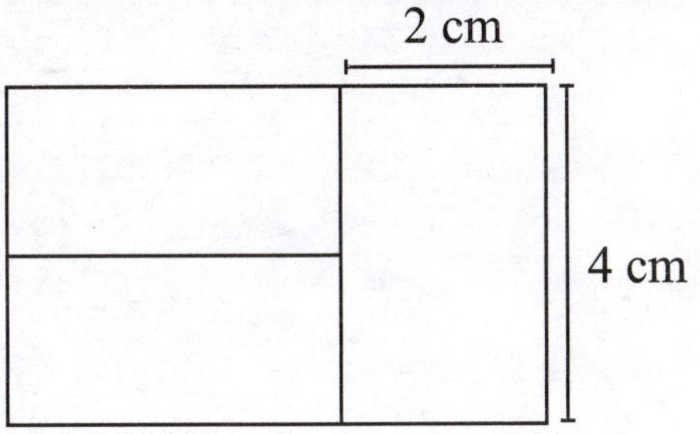

16 Data Handling

Prior Knowledge

- Basic terms of statistics
- Basic operations on numbers
- Ascending and descending order

Learning Objectives

- Collecting and organizing data using tally marks
- Making frequency distribution tables
- Reading and drawing pictographs and bar graphs
- Mean and median of ungrouped data

Let's Get Started

Collect the information about the blood group of your classmates and fill the details in the table given below.

Blood Group	Number of Students	Tally Marks
A^+		
A^-		
B^+		
B^-		
O^+		
O^-		
AB^+		

Draw the pictograph for the above collected data by taking  = 2 students.

Blood Group	Number of Students
A^+	
A^-	
B^+	
B^-	
O^+	
O^-	
AB^+	

Let us learn more about data handling in this chapter.

COLLECTION AND ORGANISATION OF DATA

A collection of raw information in the form of numbers, figures or names is called **data**.

There are two types of data—primary data and secondary data.

1. **Primary data**: The data that is collected by a person or an organisation from the original source for a purpose is called primary data.

   Some common ways of collecting primary data are conducting surveys and interviewing people.

2. **Secondary data**: Data that is not collected from the original source, or not originally collected by the people who are using it, is called secondary data.

   Some common sources of secondary data are research articles, newspapers and magazines as well as reports published by government agencies.

Raw data

Data collected in its original or unorganised form is called **raw data**. For example, consider the given data: Raju, Manoj, Javed, Arvind, Swati, 86%, 95%, 65%, 46%, 43%, 80%. This is raw data.

Organisation of Data

When the raw data is arranged in a tabular form, the process is called **organisation of data**.

Tally Marks

Tally marks are always represented in bunches of five. First to fourth are drawn like |, ||, |||, ||||
and fifth tally mark is drawn diagonally across the first four like ~~||||~~ to make a group of five.

Frequency

When collecting data, the number of times a particular item occurs is called its **frequency**.

Frequency Distribution Table

The distribution of frequency of various observations in the form of a table is called a **frequency distribution table**.

Range

Range is the difference between the highest and the lowest observations in the data.

Example 1: The shoe size of 38 people is given below:

8, 5, 8, 7, 6, 8, 9, 8, 6, 7, 5, 7, 7, 8, 8, 5, 8, 6, 6, 6, 7, 5, 8, 7, 6, 9, 7, 7, 5, 6, 6, 6, 9, 7, 7, 7, 6, 5

Represent the data in tabular form with tally marks.

Solution: The tabular form representing the tally marks is as shown:

Size of Shoes	Tally Marks	Number of People
5	~~||||~~ |	6
6	~~||||~~ ~~||||~~	10
7	~~||||~~ ~~||||~~ |	11
8	~~||||~~ |||	8
9	|||	3

From the frequency table, we observe that most common shoes size is 7 (since 11 people have this size) and least common shoes size is 9 (since 3 people have it).

Arrayed Data

When raw data is arranged in ascending or descending order, it is called **arrayed data**.

Example 2: Happy Children's Club has children from different age groups. The raw data showing ages of 30 children in years is given below.

8, 8, 6, 12, 11, 7, 8, 6, 7, 8, 8, 10, 11, 9, 7, 7, 9, 7, 7, 9, 10, 8, 9, 8, 10, 11, 11, 12, 12, 8

Make a frequency distribution table for this data.

Solution: By arranging the data in ascending order, we get the following array of numbers.

6, 6, 7, 7, 7, 7, 7, 7, 8, 8, 8, 8, 8, 8, 8, 8, 9, 9, 9, 9, 10, 10, 10, 11, 11, 11, 11, 12, 12, 12

Now, make the frequency distribution table using tally marks.

REMEMBER

It is not necessary to always make an array of numbers. When the data is large, it is easier to use the data as given and use tally marks to tabulate it.

Age (in Years)	Tally Marks	Number of Children
6	||	2
7	~~||||~~ |	6
8	~~||||~~ |||	8
9	||||	4
10	|||	3
11	||||	4
12	|||	3

Exercise 16.1

1. **The weekly wages (in ₹) of 25 workers in a factory are given below.**

   2332, 2315, 2216, 2347, 2332, 2315, 2217, 2216, 2347, 2332, 2332, 2315, 2217, 2315, 2217, 2216, 2347, 2332, 2347, 2332, 2315, 2217, 2216, 2347, 2347

   Represent the above data in a frequency distribution table.

2. **Construct a frequency distribution table for the data on heights (in feet) of some of the tallest monuments in the world.**

   203, 240, 157, 159, 164, 260, 135, 138, 148, 157, 164, 184, 187, 200, 203, 325, 330, 420, 381, 132, 360, 354,132, 200, 203, 289,132, 132, 148, 153, 157, 132, 135, 132, 289

3. **Construct a frequency distribution table for the data on the number of items sold in a grocery store over a month.**

   30, 34, 30, 30, 33, 35, 50, 45, 50, 35, 45, 30, 34, 30, 30, 42, 50, 30, 33, 35, 50, 45, 50, 45, 30, 34, 30, 30, 42, 50

4. **Given below is the data on the number of storybooks read by students of Class 6 in a year. Make the frequency distribution table for the data.**

   30, 12, 10, 10, 12, 30, 20, 25, 15, 16, 24, 10, 20, 30, 12, 15, 30, 30, 12, 10, 10, 12, 15, 10, 10, 20, 10, 20, 30, 10

5. **Construct a frequency distribution table for the data on number of visitors visited the maths and science exhibition in 20 days.**

   654, 735, 870, 654, 565, 870, 925, 735, 675, 870, 925, 735, 654, 675, 735, 870, 735, 925, 675, 770

Pictograph

Numerical information can also be represented by using pictures.

A **pictograph** is a pictorial representation of numerical data in the form of pictures or symbols.

Example 3: The following pictograph shows the number of visitors to a museum on weekdays.

Observe the adjoining pictograph and answer the following questions.

a. How many visitors visited the museum on Monday?

b. How many more visitors visited the museum on Wednesday than on Tuesday?

c. How many less visitors visited the museum on Friday than on Thursday?

Visitors who visited the museum on different weekdays

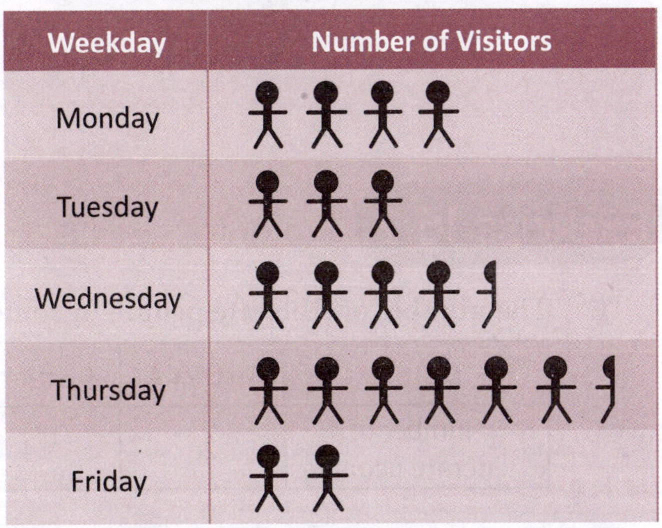

Scale: = 100 visitors and = 50 visitors

d. On which day did the maximum number of visitors visit the museum?

e. What is the total number of visitors who visited the museum on these five days?

Solution: a. Number of visitors on Monday = 4 × 100 = 400

b. Number of visitors on Wednesday = (4 × 100) + (1 × 50) = 450

Number of visitors on Tuesday = 3 × 100 = 300

450 – 300 = 150

So, 150 more visitors visited on Wednesday than on Tuesday.

c. Number of visitors on Thursday = (6 × 100) + (1 × 50) = 650

Number of visitors on Friday = 2 × 100 = 200

650 – 200 = 450

So, 450 less visitors visited on Friday than on Thursday.

d. Maximum number of visitors visited the museum on Thursday.

e. Total number of visitors on all days = 400 + 300 + 450 + 650 + 200 = 2000

Example 4: The number of people who voted in the election of a city is given in the table below:

Party Name	X	Y	Z	W	U
Number of People	300	275	400	125	75

Solution: Scale for the pictograph: ☺ = 50 people; ☾ = 25 people

Party Name	Number of People
X	☺ ☺ ☺ ☺ ☺ ☺
Y	☺ ☺ ☺ ☺ ☺ ☾
Z	☺ ☺ ☺ ☺ ☺ ☺ ☺ ☺
W	☺ ☺ ☾
U	☺ ☾

EXERCISE 16.2

1. **The number of illiterate people in some districts is given below.**

District	District A	District B	District C	District D	District E
Number of illiterate people	28	14	35	35	56

Taking the scale 🯅 = 7 people, draw a pictograph for this data.

2. **The number of chocolates sold in a shop on different days of a week is given below.**

Days	Monday	Tuesday	Wednesday	Thursday	Friday	Saturday
No. of chocolates	35	55	40	65	50	45

Taking the scale ▯ = 5 chocolates, draw a pictograph for this data.

3. **Swati collected some information about the colours of scooties riding on a street on a particular day. The information is given below:**

Colour of Scooty	Black	White	Red	Pink	Green
Number of Scooties	32	24	12	36	16

Draw a pictograph for the given data. Form any four questions based on the pictograph.

4. **The pictograph given below shows the number of chapatis prepared on different days by a chapati-making unit.**

Each 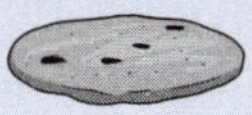 = 70 chapatis;  = 35 chapatis

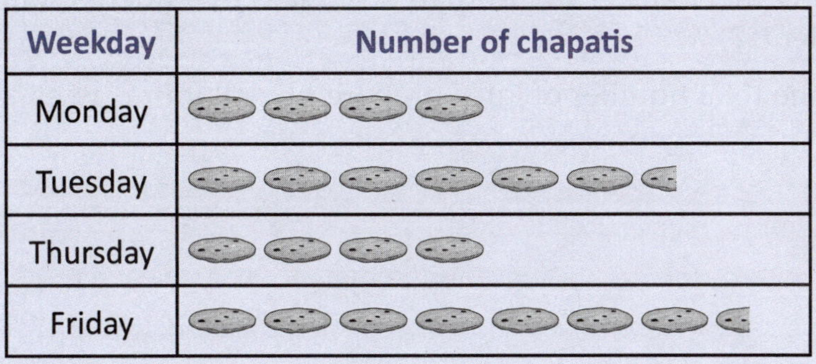

Answer the following questions based on this pictograph.

a. How many chapatis were prepared on Monday?

b. How many fewer chapatis were prepared on Thursday than on Tuesday?

c. How many chapatis were prepared on Thursday and Friday altogether?

d. On which day was the maximum number of chapatis prepared? How many chapatis were made on this day?

e. How many more chapatis were made on Friday than on Monday?

5. **The data given below shows the number of kites prepared by students of class VI to IX.**

Class	Number of Kites
VI	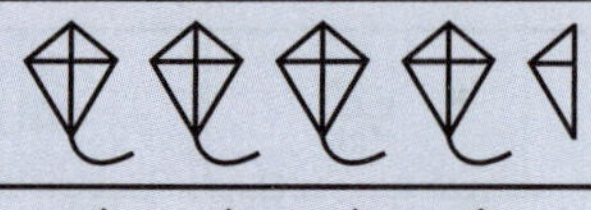
VII	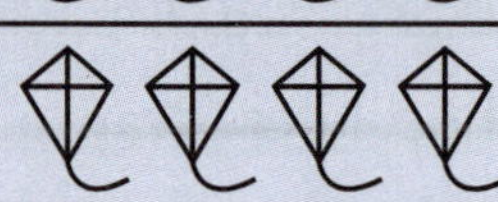
VIII	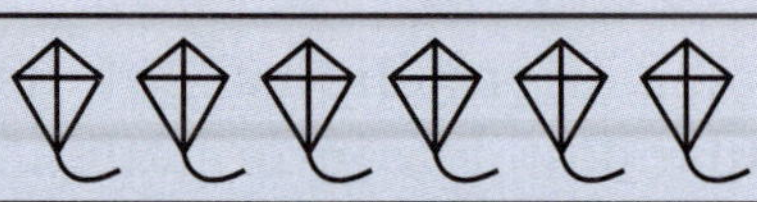
IX	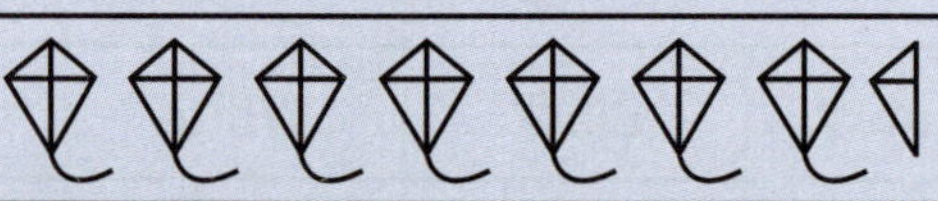

Scale:  represents 6 kites.

Observe the pictograph and answer the questions:

a. Students of which class prepared the most number of kites and how many?

b. How many less kites were prepared by class VII students compared to class IX students?

c. What is the total number of kites prepared by class VI and VIII students?

d. How many more kites were prepared by class IX students compared to class VIII students?

e. What is the total number of kites prepared by all four classes?

Bar Graph

A **bar graph** is a pictorial representation of numerical data in the form of rectangles having equal width but different heights depending upon the values they represent.

Every bar graph should have a title, labelled x-axis and y-axis, and scale.

- The title depicts the information that is presented in the bar graph.
- On x-axis, we usually represent different categories mostly non-numerical data like days of the week, colour, states, etc.
- On y-axis, we represent the numerical data like number of students, temperature, etc.
- The scale gives the information on what each unit on x-axis or y-axis represents.

Construction of Bar Graph

The time taken by students of class VI to complete a unit test is as follows.

Time (in minutes)	20	23	17	21
Number of Students	8	11	5	14

Construct a bar graph representing the above data.

Step 1: Choose the title 'Time taken by class VI students to complete a unit test'.

Step 2: Label 'Time' along x-axis and 'Number of students' along y-axis.

Step 3: Choose the scale on y-axis as 1 unit = 2 students.

Step 4: The heights of the rectangles are calculated as follows:

Time (in minutes)	Number of students	Height of the rectangle
20	8	$8 \div 2 = 4$
23	11	$11 \div 2 = 5.5$
17	5	$5 \div 2 = 2.5$
21	14	$14 \div 2 = 7$

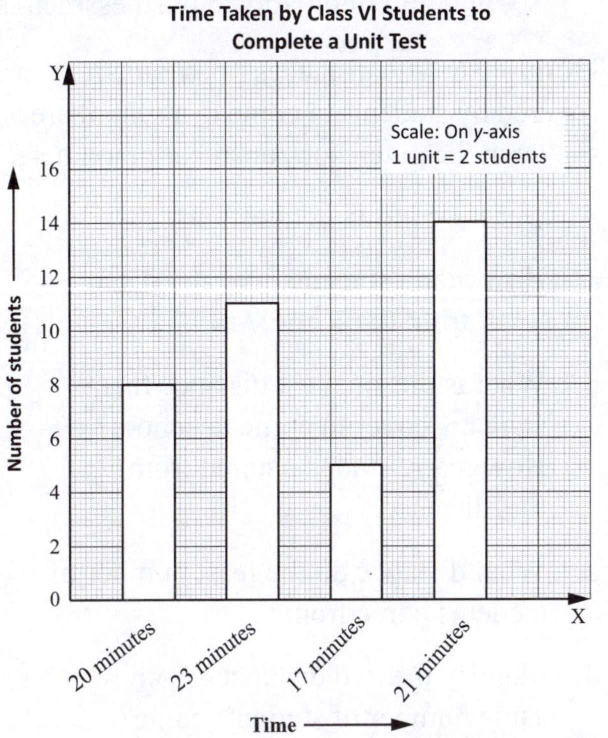

Example 5: In a survey of 500 people of a town, their occupations were recorded. The data is represented by using a bar graph given alongside. Answer the following questions.

a. How many engineers are there in the town?

b. How many people are either doctors or teachers?

c. Name the most popular occupation in the town.

d. Find the ratio of doctors to businessmen.

Solution: a. There are 125 engineers in the town.

b. Number of doctors = 75

Number of teachers = 127

$75 + 127 = 202$

So, 202 people are either doctors or teachers.

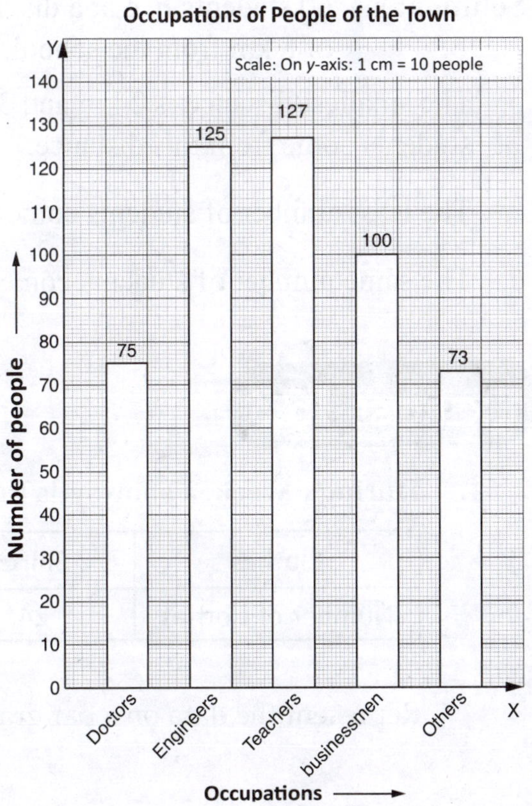

c. Teaching is the most popular occupation in the town.

d. Number of doctors = 75

Number of businessmen = 100

Ratio = 75 : 100 = 3 : 4

So, the ratio of doctors to businessmen is 3 : 4.

Example 6: The distances (in kilometres) covered by students to come to a school are shown in the given horizontal bar graph here.

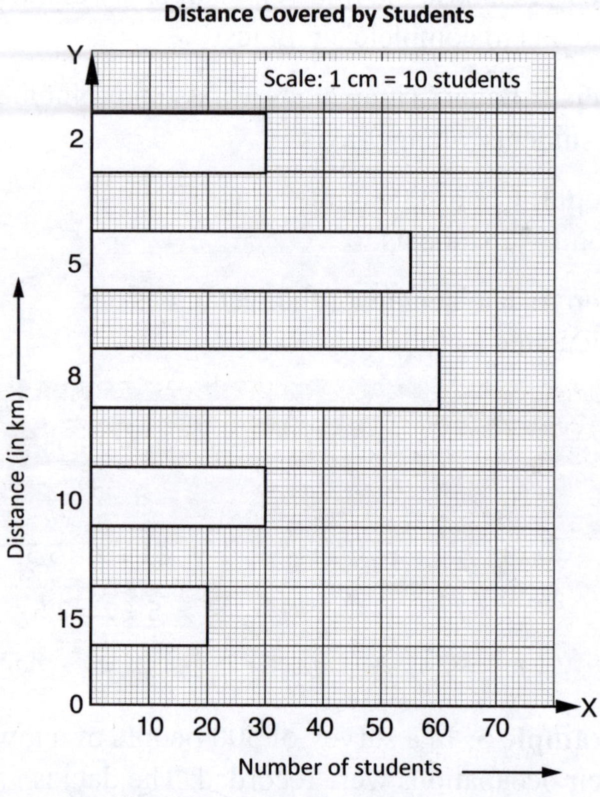

Answer the following questions.

a. How many students live at a distance of 8 km from the school?

b. What is the smallest distance that students cover to come to school? How many students come from this distance?

c. What distance do the least number of students come from?

d. Identify the two distances from which same number of students come?

Solution: a. 60 students live at a distance of 8 km from the school.

b. The smallest distance is 2 km and 30 students come from this distance.

c. The least number of students come from a distance of 15 km.

d. The same number of students come from a distance of 2 km and 10 km.

Exercise 16.3

1. **During a week, a shop sells the following types of clothes.**

Clothes	Shirts	Jackets	Sweaters	Trousers
Number of clothes	24	10	16	13

Represent the data on a bar graph.

2. **The given graph shows the names of the favourite wild animals of the students. Observe the bar graph and answer the following questions.**

    a. What is the information shown in the bar graph?

    b. How many students like lions?

    c. Name the animal that is liked by most of the students.

    d. What is the ratio of the number of students who like zebra to the number of students who like giraffe?

    e. How many more students like tigers than lions?

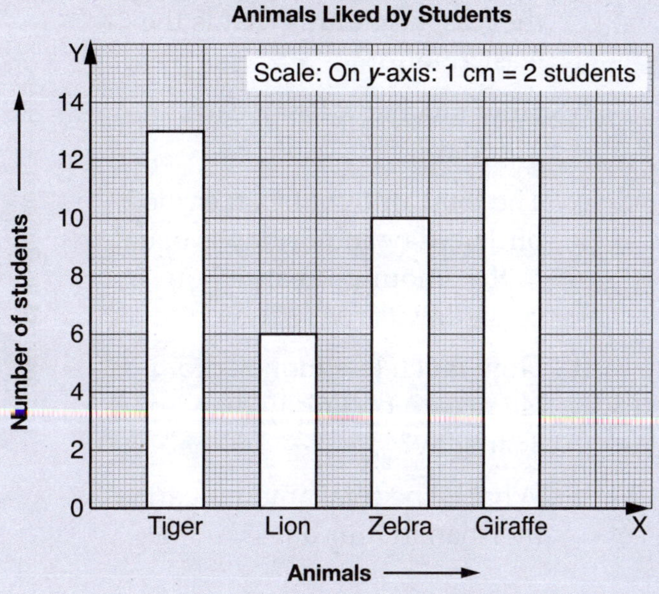

3. **The given bar graph shows the heights of some mountain peaks (in metres). Read the bar graph and answer the following questions.**

    a. Name the tallest mountain peak. What is its height?

    b. Which mountain peak is 7500 m tall?

    c. How much taller is Mt. Everest than Himadri?

    d. Arrange these mountain peaks in the decreasing order of their heights.

    e. How much shorter is Nanga Parbat than Mt. Everest?

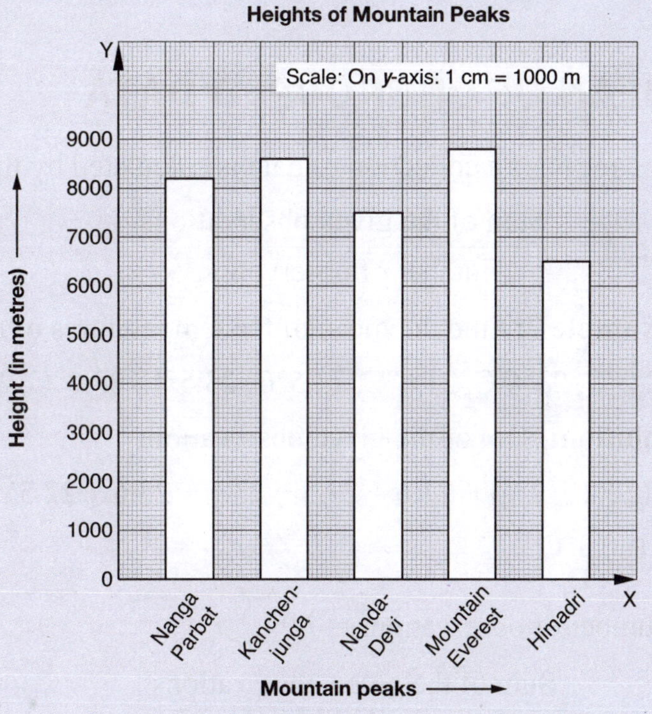

4. **The following data gives information of the number of children involved in different activities.**

Activities	Dance	Music	Art	Cricket	Football
Number of children	35	20	15	30	45

Construct a bar graph.

5. **Complete the given bar graph and answer the questions that follow.**

a. On which day did Ishan earn the least amount? What is the least amount?

b. How much did Ishan earn on Monday?

c. The total amount Ishan earned on Tuesday and Friday is equal to the amount he earned on Thursday. (True/False)

d. How much less money did Ishan earn on Friday than on Thursday?

e. What is the total amount earned by Ishan in four days?

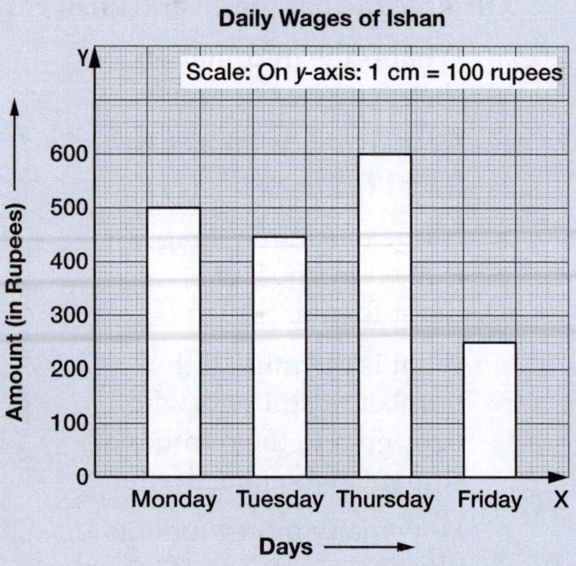

MEAN OF UNGROUPED DATA

The mean of a collection of data is calculated by the following formula:

$$\text{Mean} = \frac{\text{Sum of the given observations}}{\text{Number of observations}}$$

Example 7: Find the mean of the temperatures of a city during one week.

22.2°C, 23.4°C, 21.6°C, 23.5°C, 23.5°C, 23.6°C, 22.5°C

Solution: Sum of the given observations

= (22.2 + 23.4 + 21.6 + 23.5 + 23.5 + 23.6 + 22.5)°C

= 160.3°C

Number of observations = 7

$$\text{Mean} = \frac{\text{Sum of the given observations}}{\text{Number of observations}}$$

$$= \frac{160.3}{7} = 22.9°\text{C}$$

So, the mean temperature of the city for that week is 22.9°C.

MEDIAN OF UNGROUPED DATA

The **median** of data is the value of the middle observation when the given data is arranged in ascending or descending order.

Steps for finding the median of ungrouped data

Let the number of observations of any data be n.

Step 1: Arrange the data in ascending or descending order.

Step 2: Check if the number of observations is odd or even.

- If n is odd, then

  Median = value of $\left[\frac{1}{2}(n+1)\right]^{th}$ observation

- If n is even, then

  Median $= \frac{1}{2}\left[\left(\frac{n}{2}\right)^{th} \text{observation} + \left(\frac{n}{2}+1\right)^{th} \text{observation}\right]$

REMEMBER

When the number of observations is odd, then add 1 to n and divide the result by 2 to find the middle term.

Example 8: The heights of 9 students (in cm) are given below. Find the median height (in cm).

162, 151, 150, 159, 154, 160, 149, 155, 157

Solution: Arranging the heights in ascending order, we get

149, 150, 151, 154, 155, 157, 159, 160, 162

Here $n = 9$, so n is odd.

$\therefore$ Median height = value of $\left[\frac{1}{2}(n+1)\right]^{th}$ term = value of $\left[\frac{1}{2}(9+1)\right]^{th}$ term

= value of 5th term = 155

Therefore, the median height is 155 cm.

Example 9: The weights of 10 students (in kg) are given below. Find the median weight (in kg).

45, 50, 52, 46, 48, 55, 49, 54, 57, 43

Solution: Arranging the weights in the ascending order, we get

43, 45, 46, 48, 49, 50, 52, 54, 55, 57

Here $n = 10$, so n is even.

$$\therefore \text{Median weight} = \frac{1}{2}\left[\left(\frac{10}{2}\right)^{th} \text{term} + \left(\frac{10}{2}+1\right)^{th} \text{term}\right] = \frac{1}{2}\left(\text{5th term} + \text{6th term}\right)$$

$$= \frac{1}{2}\left(49 + 50\right) = \frac{99}{2} = 49.5$$

Therefore, the median weight is 49.5 kg.

EXERCISE 16.4

1. **Find the mean of the following numbers.**

   a. 24, 35, 20, 18, 28
   b. 3, 8, 13, 18, 23, 28, 33
   c. 16, 18, 21, 25, 20, 17, 22, 24, 23, 14
   d. 101, 103, 107, 109, 113
   e. 21, 28, 35, 42, 49, 56, 70, 77
   f. 14, 32, 59, 67, 89, 105, 200, 350
   g. 4, 6, 8, 9, 10, 12, 14, 15, 16, 18, 20

2. **Find the median of the following.**

   a. 3, 6, 7, 4, 5
   b. 20, 22, 30, 32, 40, 42, 50, 62, 70
   c. 75, 35, 48, 47, 50, 55, 58, 60
   d. 80, 82, 84, 86, 88, 90, 92

3. **The wages (in ₹) of a worker from Monday to Saturday are given below.**

   750, 600, 550, 1000, 850, 900

   Find the mean wage of the worker per day.

4. **The cost of different tickets (in ₹) bought by different passengers travelling in a train is given below. Find the median cost.**

   54, 51, 55, 45, 40, 45, 38, 50, 35, 42

5. **Rohan played outdoor a for 30 min, 1 h, 45 min, 50 min and 40 min respectively on consecutive days. Find out his mean play time per day.**

6. **The heights (in cm) of 6 students of class VI are given below. Find the mean height of the 6 students.**

   142, 148, 145, 135, 144, 138

7. **Find the median cost of the books for the following data.**

Cost (in ₹)	55	45	40	60	58	48

8. **Find the mean of the first 10 odd numbers.**

9. **The weight of 12 students are given below. Find the median weight of the students.**

   32 kg, 35 kg, 33 kg, 42 kg, 37 kg, 35 kg, 39 kg, 32 kg, 40 kg, 36 kg, 37 kg, 44 kg

10. **The temperature of a city in 15 days is given below. Find the median temperature of the city.**

    31.6°C, 33°C, 34.1°C, 29.7°C, 39.3°C, 35.8°C, 36°C, 34.6°C, 31.6°C, 29.1°C, 34.1°C, 31.6°C, 35.8°C, 39.3°C, 35.8°C

KEY CONCEPTS

DATA HANDLING

DATA HANDLING is → The study of collection, organisation, presentation, analysis and interpretation of numerical data.

- **Data** → The collection of numerical facts relating to a particular information.
  - **Primary Data**: The data collected by an individual for some specific purpose.
  - **Secondary Data**: The data collected by someone else other than the individual.
  - **Raw Data**: The data collected in its original form.
  - **Tabulation of Data**: Arrangement of data in a systematic form in a table.
- **Frequency:** Number of times a value occurs in a data.
- **Range:** Difference between highest and lowest value in the data.
- **Central Tendency**
  - **Median:** The value of the middle observation when the given data is arranged in the ascending or the descending order.
    - Median $= \frac{1}{2}(n+1)^{th}$ term; when n is odd.
    - Median $= \frac{1}{2}[\frac{n}{2}^{th}$ term $+ (\frac{n}{2}+1)^{th}$ term]; when n is even
  - Mean $= \frac{\text{Sum of the given observations}}{\text{Number of observations}}$
- **Pictograph:** Pictorial representation of numerical data in the form of pictures or symbols.
- **Bar graph:** Pictorial representation of numerical data in the form of rectangles having equal width but different heights depending upon the values they represent.

REVISION EXERCISE

1. Choose the correct option.

a. The data collected in its original form is called ___________.

i. Primary data ii. Secondary data iii. Raw data iv. None of these

b. The frequency of 15 in the data 18, 15, 22, 25, 15, 18, 25, 20, 15, 22, 25, 15 is ___________.

i. 5 ii. 3 iii. 2 iv. 4

c. The pictograph given below shows the number of students in each class of a school. If there are 124 students in that school, then (symbol) represents how many students?

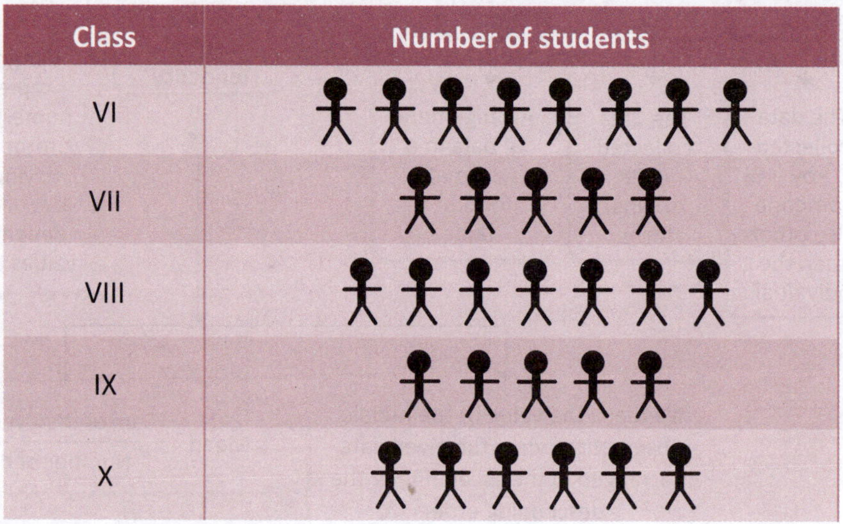

i. 4 ii. 5 iii. 6 iv. 8

d. Find the mean of the following data.

34, 29, 31, 35, 27, 33, 28

i. 29 ii. 30 iii. 30.5 iv. 31

e. Find the median of the following values.

125, 134, 142, 118, 120, 132, 135, 129, 127, 123

i. 124 ii. 125 iii. 126 iv. 128

2. Fill in the blanks.

a. The pictorial representation of numerical data in the form of rectangles with equal width but different height is known as _______.

b. The number of times a value occurs in a collection of data is called ______.

c. The mean of the data: 12, 10, 15, 20, 22, 16 and 17 is ______.

d. The median weight of the data: 45 kg, 38 kg, 37 kg, 43 kg, 49 kg, 34 kg, 40 kg, 38 kg and 45 kg is ______.

e. Pictograph is the representation of data through ______.

3. **State whether the following statements are true (T) or false (F).**

a. The data collected by an individual for some specific purpose is called secondary data.

b. Range is the difference between first and last value of a set of data.

c. Mean is the value of the middle observation of the data, when arranged in either ascending or descending order.

d. The median of the data 15, 17, 12, 16, 10, 14, 19 and 20 is 15.5.

e. The mean of the data 25, 35, 40. 30, 20, 45 and 50 is 35.

4. Classes 3 to 8 in a school made different number of kites for a carnival. Draw a pictograph for the data.

Class	Class 3	Class 4	Class 5	Class 6	Class 7	Class 8
Number of kites	25	20	35	40	20	25

Take the scale 1  = 5 kites.

5. The number of children who enrolled for different summer coaching camps is shown in the bar graph given alongside. Answer the following questions.

a. Name the most popular and the least popular camps.

b. How many children have enrolled for the art & craft camp?

c. How many more children have joined the sports camp than the yoga camp?

d. What could be the reasons for fewer children opting for music classes?

Enrollment in Summer Coaching Camps

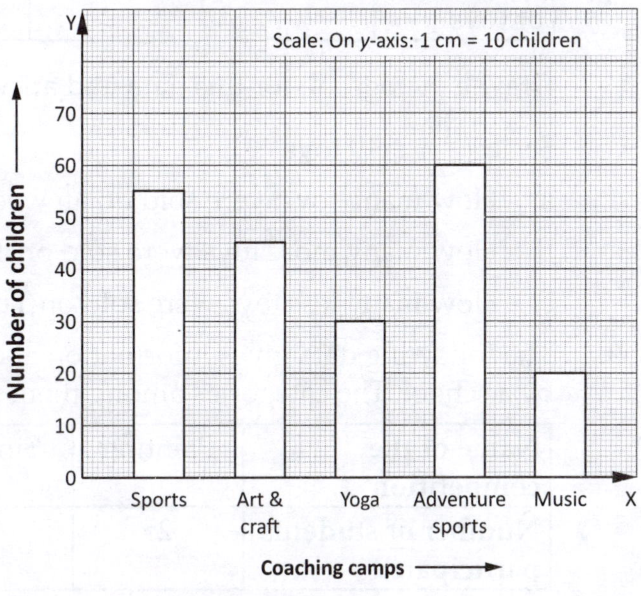

6. The following pictograph shows the number of cars serviced on some weekdays by Darshan Service Centre.

Scale: Each  = 5 cars

Weekday	Number of Cars
Monday	
Tuesday	
Thursday	
Friday	

Answer the following questions based on the above pictograph.

a. On which day was the maximum number of cars serviced? How many cars were serviced on that day?

b. On which day was the minimum number of cars serviced? How many cars were serviced on that day?

c. On which day were 25 cars serviced?

d. How many more cars will have to be serviced on Thursday to make the number equal to the number on Tuesday?

7. The below given data is the daily wages (in rupees) of 12 employees in a locality. Find the mean and median wages of 12 employees.

575, 625, 445, 580, 720, 525, 485, 615, 475, 550, 650 and 535

8. The following pictograph represents the total number of toys sold on different weekdays.

Weekdays	Monday	Tuesday	Wednesday	Thursday	Friday
Number of toys	50	30	40	20	10

Draw a pictograph for this data and answer the following questions:

Scale:  = 10 toys

a. How many toys were sold on all weekdays?

b. How many more toys were sold on Tuesday compared to Friday?

c. How many less toys were sold on Tuesday compared to Monday?

9. The following data gives information about the inter-school arts competition organized by a school. The categories among them were painting, singing, drama and solo dance.

Name of the competition	Painting	Singing	Drama	Solo dance
Number of students participated	25	15	50	10

Construct a bar graph and fill in the blanks.

a. The total number of students who participated in the competition is _______.

b. The difference between the number of students who participated in drama and those who participated in dance is _______.

c. The difference between the number of students who participated in singing and those who participated in painting is _______.

10. The temperature recorded on Monday in Kodagu at different times of the day is as follows. Find the mean and median temperature.

21.2°C, 21.3°C, 21.4°C, 21.5°C, 21.1°C, 21.3°C, 22.3°C, 21.9°C

Test Paper 1

1. Choose the correct option.

a. The natural numbers along with 0 are called ______.

i. whole number ii. integers

iii. prime numbers iv. factors

b. The method(s) in which we list the elements of a given set is (are) called _______.

i. Roster form ii. Listing method

iii. Set-builder form iv. All of the above

c. What should be added to (−26) to get 17?

i. 53 ii. 63 iii. 43 iv. 9

d. The difference in the place values of the two fives in 1,57,850 is ______.

i. 4,950 ii. 49,950 iii. 49,500 iv. 500

e. The LCM of 48 and 72 is ______.

i. 144 ii. 154 iii. 164 iv. 72

f. Which of the following is a set?

i. Collection of birds in India

ii. Collection of students in a university

iii. Collection of first ten even numbers

iv. Both i. and ii.

g. Which of the following shaded figures represents the fraction $\frac{3}{4}$?

i. 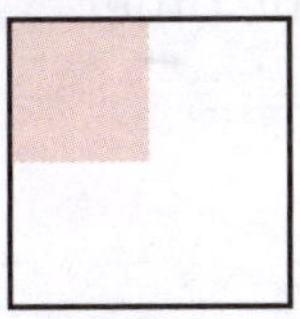
ii. 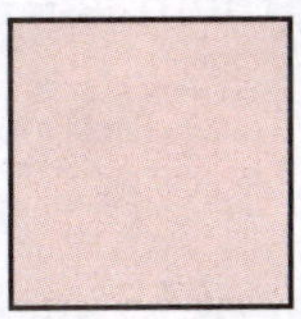
iii. 
iv 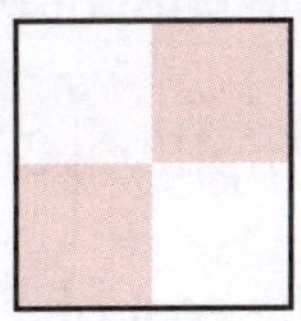

h. Which of the following pairs of fractions is not equivalent?

i. $\frac{5}{9}, \frac{30}{54}$ ii. $\frac{3}{10}, \frac{12}{40}$

iii. $\frac{7}{13}, \frac{21}{25}$ iv. $\frac{8}{7}, \frac{72}{63}$

i. What is the place value of 4 in the decimal number 18.543?

i. $\frac{4}{1000}$ ii. $\frac{4}{100}$ iii. $\frac{4}{10}$ iv. 4

j. The HCF of two numbers is 3 and their LCM is 90, if one of the numbers is 15, find the other.

i. 18 ii. 31 iii. 41 iv. 11

2. **Fill in the blanks.**

a. The product of an integer and zero is ____________.

b. A number that is one more than another number is called its ______________.

c. Two natural numbers which do not have a common prime factor are called __________.

d. (−64) + (+49) = ____________

e. The number corresponding to thirty-two lakh six thousand five hundred sixtyeight is ________________.

f. Fractions with different denominators are called ______________.

g. The fractions in which the denominators are 10, 100, 1000, etc. are called __________.

h. The cardinal numbers of the set B = {a, b, c, d, e, a, b, f, g, d} is ______________.

i. Numbers that have more than two factors are called ________ numbers.

j. $21\frac{3}{5} \div 3\frac{11}{15}$ = _______________.

3. **Write T for True and F for False.**

a. 35672109 > 35672209

b. The product of two negative integers is always a positive integer.

c. Every whole number is an integer.

d. 24 is a multiple of 7.

e. The HCF of 36 and 60 is 12.

4. **Answer the following questions briefly.**

a. How many four-digit numbers are there?

b. The sum of two integers is −32. If one of them is −12, find the other.

c. Simplify: $\left(3\frac{3}{5}+1\frac{3}{8}\right) \div \left(2\frac{3}{4}-2\frac{1}{2}\right)$.

d. The cost of a book is ₹19.85. Find the cost of 55 such books.

e. Write the greatest 8-digit number using the digits 0, 1, 5, 4, 3, 9, 8 and 7 only once. Also, write the number in both Indian and International place value systems.

f. Find the highest common factor of 184, 230 and 276 using the long division method.

g. Simplify: (229 + 233) ÷ (505 – 484)

h. Mahesh gave $\frac{7}{12}$ of his money to a friend, $\frac{3}{5}$ of remaining amount to his son and the remaining to his wife. If his wife got Rs.3500, what was the total amount?

TEST PAPER 2

1. Choose the correct option.

a. If $p : q :: r : s$, then ___________.

i. $ps = qr$ ii. $pr = qs$ iii. $pq = rs$ iv. $pqr = s$

b. A ratio $a : b$ is in simplest form if HCF of a and b is ___________.

i. 0 ii. 1 iii. 2 iv. 3

c. 35% as a fraction is ___________.

i. $\frac{35}{100}$ ii. $\frac{35}{10}$ iii. $\frac{35}{50}$ iv. $\frac{35}{25}$

d. $\frac{15}{50}$ expressed as percentage is ___________.

i. 15% ii. 30% iii. 50% iv. 45%

e. Monthly salary of Amar is ₹17,500, if his salary is increased by 25%, then what is his present salary?

i. ₹21,875 ii. ₹19,725 iii. ₹22,575 iv. ₹20,185

2. Fill in the blanks.

a. The value of x in $3 : 4 :: x : 20$ is ___________.

b. In a proportion, the first and the last terms are called ___________.

c. The grid with 100 squares, of which 12 squares are shaded represents ___________ percentage.

d. If an athlete covers 100 m in 10 s, then the speed of the athlete is ___________.

e. If the cost of 25 kg of rice is ₹1,025, then the cost of 1.5 kg of rice is ___________.

3. Write T for True and F for False.

a. If a bike travels 200 km with 5 litres of petrol, then the mileage per litre is 40 km per litre.

b. If the first and third terms are equal in a proportion, then the proportion is called **continued proportion**.

c. 8% as a fraction is $\frac{2}{25}$.

d. Distance travelled = Speed ÷ Time taken

e. The ratio of ₹5.75 to 50 p in its simplest form is 23 : 2.

4. Fill in the blanks.

a. 4.8 km = ___________ m.

b. 3.2 hours = ___________ min.

c. 15 m/s = ___________ km/h.

d. 198 km/h = ___________ m/s.

e. 50 hm = ______ km.

5. **Check whether the following ratios are in proportion. Write Yes or No in the last column.**

Ratio 1	**Ratio 2**	**Is Ratio 1 to Ratio 2 a proportion?**
Ratio of 6 kg to 3000g	Ratio of ₹5 to 250 paise	
Ratio of 400 mℓ to 600 mℓ	Ratio of 10 to 15	
Ratio of 500 g to 1 kg	Ratio of 40 m to 800 cm	
Ratio of 16 to 32	Ratio of 1 : 2	
Ratio of ₹6 to 500 paise	Ratio of 3 hrs to 150 min	

6. **Answer the following questions.**

a. The cost of a 15 m cloth is ₹1,537.50. Find the cost of 10 m cloth.

b. If the speed of a car is 32.4 km/h, find its speed in terms of metres per second.

c. The ratio of the number of apples to that of oranges in a fruit basket is 9 : 5. If the total number of oranges in the basket is 1,560, find the number of apples and the total number of fruits in the basket.

d. The cost of 1 pack of candles is ₹75. Find the price of 3 candles if there are 5 candles in each pack.

e. In a test match, Anuj completed his double century with 12 sixes and 16 boundaries. What percentage of runs did he make by running between the wickets to the double century?

f. Divide ₹7350 among three friends Naresh, Mahesh and Rajesh in the ratio of 2 : 5 : 7.

g. A rope of length 112 m is divided in the ratio 3 : 4. Find the length of each piece.

h. 12 men can complete a piece of work in 15 days. How many days are required to complete the same work by 28 men?

i. A car covers 104 km with 13 litres of petrol. How many kilometres will it cover with 8 litres of petrol?

j. A train covers 14 km in 12 min. Find the time taken to cover the same distance if the speed of the train is reduced by 3 km/h.

k. What is the distance covered by a bike racer in 6 min if he rides at a speed of 96 km/h?

TEST PAPER 3

1. Choose the correct option.

a. In $7xy$, the numerical factor (part) is __________.

i. x ii. y iii. xy iv. 7

b. In the expression $3x - 6y + 5$, the constant term is __________.

i. 3 ii. 6 iii. 5 iv. y

c. The degree of the polynomial $5x^3 + 3x^2 - 6$ is __________.

i. 3 ii. 2 iii. 1 iv. 0

d. The algebraic equation for 'If 8 is added to four times a number, the result is 9' is ?

i. $8 + x^4 = 9$ ii. $8 + 4x = 9$

iii. $4x - 8 = 9$ iv. $8 + x = 9$

e. Gopal's age is 5 more than twice the age of Anup. If the sum of ages of Gopal and Anup is 51 years, then find Gopal's age.

i. 25 ii. 21 iii. 28 iv. 23

2. Fill in the blanks.

a. The literal coefficient of the term $12pq^2$ is __________.

b. An algebraic expression having two terms is called a __________.

c. The degree of the polynomial $a^3b^3 + a^2b^2 + ab + 5$ is __________.

d. The value of $7a^2 + 12ab$ when $a = 4$ and $b = 5$ is __________.

e. The algebraic expression for 'the square of a number multiplied to the sum of three times the number and 12' is __________.

f. The area of a rectangle whose length is a units and breadth is b units is __________.

g. The generalization of the pattern 4, 9, 14, 19..... is __________.

h. The perimeter of a square whose side is ℓ units is __________.

i. $3 + m$ is an example of a __________.

j. The number of sides of a quadrilateral is an example of a __________.

3. Write T for True and F for False.

a. The expression $5x$ has 2 terms.

b. $6xy$, $-4yx$, $5xy$ are unlike terms.

c. $5x^2 + 5 = 2x - 4$ is an example for linear equation.

d. The nth term of an odd number pattern is given by the formula $2n + 1$.

e. $4x^2 - 3x + \frac{5}{x} + 8$ is a polynomial.

4. Write how each of the following algebraic expressions is formed.

a. $6m - 2$ b. $\frac{27}{n}$ c. $4n + 5$ d. $\frac{10}{3b} - b$ e. $y + 2$

5. Match the follwing.

a.	$-\frac{2}{xy}$	i.	Trinomial
b.	$3 + \frac{x}{y}$	ii.	Polynomial
c.	$\frac{1}{p^2} + 2q - 3r^3$	iii.	Algebraic equation
d.	$2xy^2 - 3xy + 5$	iv.	Monomial
e.	$u + 5 = -3$	v.	Binomial

6. Answer the following questions.

a. Write the following in mathematical form using symbols and signs.

i. Five-sixth of p multiplied by the sum of q and 15

ii. Quotient of x by 5 multiplied by y decreased by 12

b. Write the formula for the following to find the number.

i. A number reduced by 25 divided by the number reduced by 10 gives 15.

ii. The sum of the square of a number and 8 multiplied by 5 gives 21.

c. Write the rule for the number of petals in the nth flower in the following flower pattern.

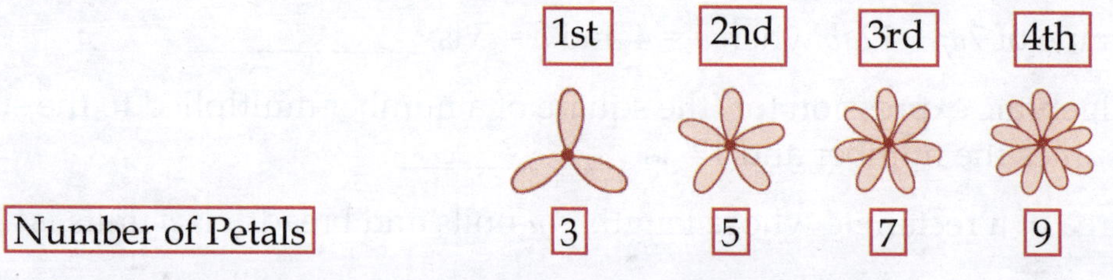

d. Find the sum of the following algebraic expressions: $4a + 4c - 2ab$, $3ca - 4b + 3c$ and $4bc + a - 3b$

e. Find the product of the following.

i. $2xy$ and $3x - 5y$

ii. $3ab - a + 2b$ and ab

iii. $5p + 3q - 2r$ and $2pqr$

f. Find the value of $\frac{a^2 + b^3 - c^2}{ab - bc + ac}$ when $a = 4$, $b = 5$ and $c = 3$.

g. The base fare in a cab is ₹25 for a minimum of 2 km. Then for each additional kilometre, the cost is ₹6. Write an algebraic expression to calculate the cab bill.

h. Sukanya's grandmother is 4 years less than eight times the age of Sukanya. If Sukanya's grandmother is 76 years old, write an equation to find Sukanya's age.

TEST PAPER 4

1. Choose the correct options.

a. A simple closed curve divides the plane into ________ regions.

i. 1   ii. 3
iii. 0   iv. infinite

b. An angle whose measure is more than 180° but less than 360° is called ______.

i. acute angle   ii. reflex angle
iii. obtuse angle   iv. complete angle

c. The largest chord of the circle is the __________ of the circle.

i. Diameter   ii. Radius
iii. Tangent   iv. Secant

d. Which of the following net consists of one rectangle and two circles?

i. Cube   ii. Cuboid
iii. Cylinder   iv. Cone

e. Which of the following letters does not have a vertical line of symmetry?

i. H   ii. Y
iii. E   iv. M

f. A scalene triangle has ______ line(s) of symmetry.

i. 1   ii. 2
iii. 3   iv. 0

g. Which of the following is used to construct a circle?

i. Compass only
ii. Ruler only
iii. Ruler and divider
iv. Ruler and compass

2. Fill in the blanks.

a. A line segment has ____________ endpoints.

b. If an angle measures exactly 180°, then it is known as a ____________.

c. If two lines intersect each other at a common point, they are known as __________.

d. _____ and _____ together form a quadrilateral region.

e. ______ is a three dimensional figure whose top and base are polygons and all other faces are rectangles.

f. A circle has ______________ line(s) of symmetry.

g. A rhombus has _____________ lines(s) of symmetry.

h. If the radius of a circle is 198 m, then its diameter is _____________.

3. **Write T for True and F for False.**

a. The vertex of the angle lies in the interior of an angle.

b. A ray AB is represented as $\overline{AB}$.

c. Parallel lines meet each other at a definite point.

d. A triangular pyramid has four triangular faces.

e. When one side of a triangle is extended, then the resulting exterior angle is equal to sum of its two opposite interior angles.

f. The line of symmetry of a line segment is its perpendicular bisector.

g. Divider is used to compare lengths.

4. **Answer the following questions briefly.**

a. Draw two simple closed figures:

i. By using straight lines only

ii. By using both straight and curved lines

b. Construct 120° using protractor. Bisect the constructed angle.

c. Complete the following figures such that they are symmetrical along the black line.

i. ii.

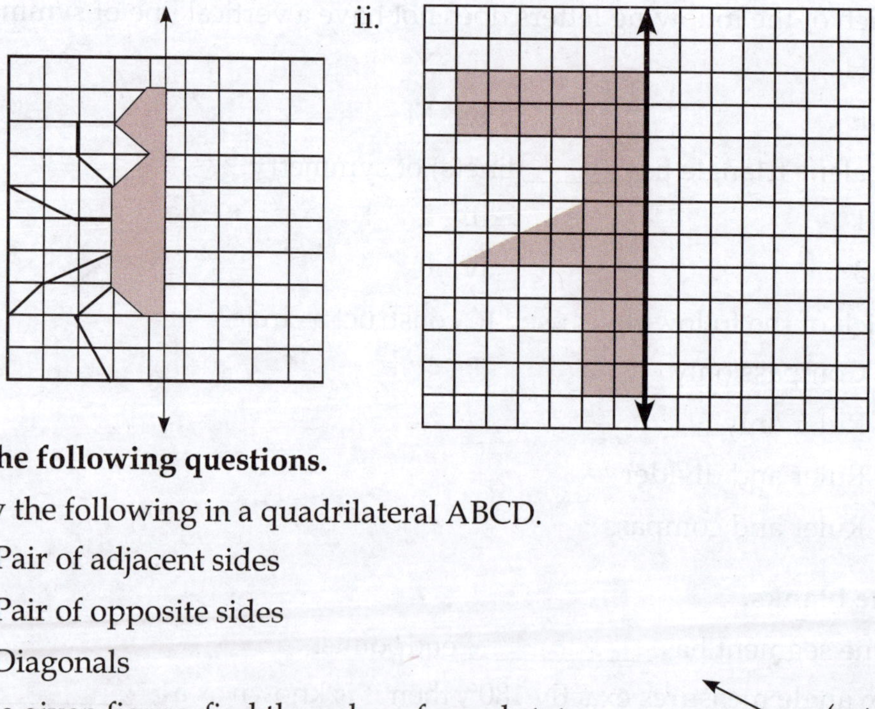

5. **Answer the following questions.**

a. Identify the following in a quadrilateral ABCD.

i. Pair of adjacent sides

ii. Pair of opposite sides

iii. Diagonals

b. In the given figure, find the value of x and state whether it is acute angle or obtuse angle.

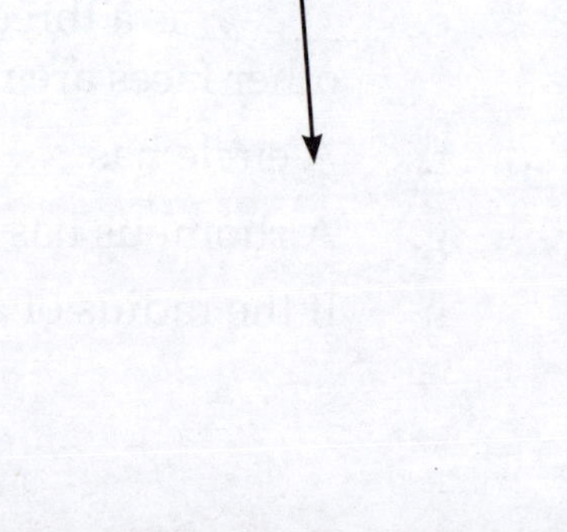

c. Draw a line segment of length 12 cm using a ruler and construct a perpendicular bisector using compass. Write the steps of construction.

d. Write the English alphabets having

i. one line of symmetry

ii. no line of symmetry

iii. more than one line of symmetry

TEST PAPER 5

1. Choose the correct option.

a. The dimension of a rectangle is 14 cm × 9 cm The area of the rectangle is __________.

i. 23 sq. cm　　ii. 46 sq. cm

iii. 126 sq. cm　　iv. 106 sq. cm

b. The area of a square of side 6 mm is __________.

i. 36 mm^2　　ii. 360 mm^2

iii. 3600 mm^2　　iv. 3.6 mm^2

c. The area of a right isosceles triangle whose equal sides are 34 cm each is __________.

i. 578 cm^2　　ii. 1156 cm^2

iii. 68 cm^2　　iv. 408 cm^2

d. If the dimension of a farm is 2.6 units, 2.6 units, 4.1 units and 3.7 units respectively, then the perimeter of the farm is __________.

i. 9.3 units　　ii. 8.9 units

iii. 13 units　　iv. 10.4 units

e. A wire which is in the shape of a square of side 15 cm is re-bent into a rectangle of breadth 10 cm. What is the length of the rectangle formed?

i. 20 cm　　ii. 30 cm

iii. 40 cm　　iv. 50 cm

2. Fill in the blanks.

a. Area of a rectangle whose length and breadth are l and b respectively is __________.

b. The total cost of flooring a room at ₹15 per sq. m is ₹1,335. If the breadth of the room is 5 m, then the length of the room is __________.

c. Area of a square whose side is a unit = __________

d. The area of a square increases by __________ times if all the sides are doubled.

e. Area of a triangle = __________ area of rectangle.

3. Write T for True and F for False.

a. Different figures can have same perimeter.

b. Area of a square having 4 units as its side = Area of a rectangle with the dimension of 8 units × 2 units.

c. Different figures having same area will have same perimeter.

d. The area and perimeter of an equilateral triangle is always same.

e. If the area of a square is 36 units, then its each side is 6 units.

4. **Complete the follwing table.**

Length	Breadth	Perimeter	Area
12 cm	10 cm		
9 cm	16 cm	50 cm	
12 cm		48 cm	144 cm^2
	8 m	46 m	120 m^2
36 m	4 m		

5. **Solve the following questions.**

a. The ratio of the perimeter of Square A to the perimeter of Square B is 4 : 6. If the perimeter of Square B is 60 cm, then what is the difference between the perimeters of the two squares?

b. Area of a rectangle is 120 square units. Find the length, if its breadth is 8 units.

c. The length of each side of an octagonal garden is 24 m 70 cm. If it costs ₹50 per metre to fence it once, then how much does it cost to fence four rounds?

d. Find the area and perimeter of the square whose side is 4 units. Are they same? Is the area and perimeter of a square always same?

e. The length of one side of Raman's square plot is 20 m. He used half of his plot for keeping hens. What area of his plot is vacant?

f. The perimeter of a rectangle is 360 cm and breadth is 54 cm. Find the length and area of the rectangle.

g. A hall is 23 m long and has a floor area of 414 sq. cm. Find its perimeter.

h. The ratio of the perimeter of square A to the perimeter of square B is 4 : 6. If the perimeter of square B is 60 cm, then what is the difference between the perimeters of the two squares?

i. What will happen to the area of a rectangle, if its length is doubled and breadth is tripled?

j. The area of a right isosceles triangle is 242 cm^2. Find the length of the identical sides of the triangle.

TEST PAPER 6

1. Study the bar graph and fill in the blanks.

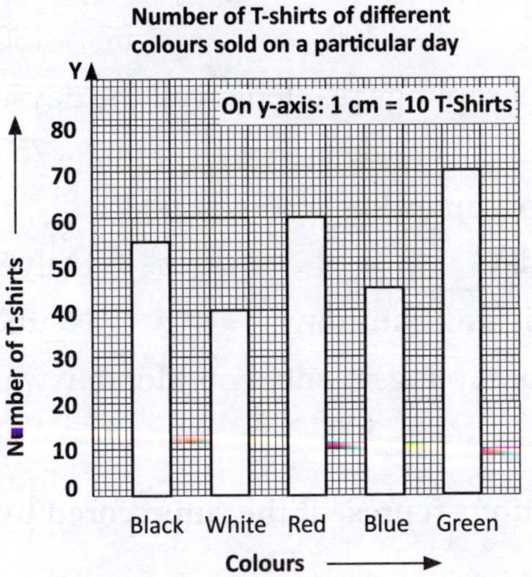

a. The number of green T-shirts sold is ________ more than the number of blue T-shirts.

b. __________ T-shirts are sold in least number.

c. The total number of T-shirts sold on that day is __________.

d. The highest demand was for _________ T-shirts.

e. The number of blue T-shirts sold is ________ more than the number of white T-shirts

2. The pictograph given below shows different saplings planted on different days of the week. Each  = 50 saplings.

Weekdays	Number of saplings
Monday	
Tuesday	
Wednesday	
Thursday	
Friday	
Saturday	
Sunday	

Study the pictograph and choose the correct option.

a. The maximum number of saplings is planted on ___________.

i. Monday ii. Tuesday iii. Wednesday iv. Thursday

b. The total number of saplings planted on Sunday was ___________.

i. 50 ii. 100 iii. 150 iv. 200

c. The total number of saplings planted on all the days is ___________.

i. 700 ii. 800 iii. 750 iv. 650

d. The least number of saplings is planted on ___________.

i. Only Wednesday ii. Only Saturday

iii. Both Wednesday and Saturday iv. Neither Wednesday nor Saturday

e. The total number of saplings planted on Monday was __________.

i. 50 ii. 100 iii. 150 iv. 200

3. The following observations represent the runs scored by 5 students in a school cricket match.

20, 30, 25, 45, 50

Look at the scores and state whether the following statements are true or false.

a. The total number of runs scored in the match is 160.

b. The number of observations is 5.

c. The mean of the following data is 34.

d. The median of the observations is calculated by the formula: $\left(\frac{n+2}{2}\right)^{th}$ term.

e. The median of the data is 25.

4. Answer the following questions.

a. Number of students who like different types of music is given in the following table.

Construct the bar graph for the data.

Type of Music	Folk	Rock	Pop	Jazz	Melody
Number of Students	14	13	10	8	15

Using the graph, answer the following.

i. Which is the favourite type of music among the students?

ii. How many fewer students like jazz than folk music?

b. Construct a frequency distribution table for the data of marks scored by 10 students of a class using tally marks.

99, 95, 96, 99, 95, 96, 97, 98, 96, 94

c. In a cricket match, scores of eleven players are listed below.

8, 16, 123, 52, 107, 82, 1, 16, 19, 11, 16

Find the mean and median of this data.

Answers

Chapter – 1

Exercise 1.1

1. **Indian place value system**
   a. One lakh thirty-five thousand two hundred four
   b. Ninety lakh fifty-two thousand twenty
   c. Five crore twenty-one lakh forty-seven thousand six hundred eighty-three
   d. Five crore four lakh twelve thousand five hundred sixty-five
   e. Two crore fifty-three lakh eighty-six thousand one hundred twenty-five
   f. Five crore two lakh sixty-three thousand fifty
   g. Five crore twenty lakh ten thousand five hundred nine
   h. Two crore forty-five lakh two thousand twelve

   International place value system
   a. One hundred thirty-five thousand two hundred four
   b. Nine million fifty-two thousand twenty
   c. Fifty-two million one hundred forty-seven thousand six-hundred eighty three
   d. Fifty million four hundred twelve thousand five hundred sixty-five
   e. Twenty-five million three hundred eighty-six thousand one hundred twenty-five
   f. Fifty million two hundred sixty-three thousand fifty
   g. Fifty-two million ten thousand five hundred nine
   h. Twenty-four million five hundred two thousand twelve

2.

	Number	Digit	Face Value	Place Value
a.	57,495,702	7	7	7,000,000
		9	9	9,000
b.	75,50,293	7	7	70,00,000
		5	5	50,000
c.	140,849,021	1	1	10,00,00,000
		4	4	40,000
d.	75,95,008	5	5	5,00,000
		9	9	90,000
e.	17,003,004	7	7	7,000,000
		3	3	3,000
f.	23,45,892	2	2	20,00,000
		8	8	800
g.	6,80,36,203	8	8	80,00,000
		3	3	30,000
h.	2,35,67,890	3	3	30,00,000
		8	8	800

3. a. 3,70,40,205 b. 9,01,33,807 c. 99,41,590
   d. 67,00,004 e. 2,00,00,000

4. a. 37,050,205 b. 34,700,006 c. 5,000,004
   d. 7,000,060 e. 4,000,004
5. a. 80,73,401 b. 9,05,280 c. 40,05,06,789

Exercise 1.2

1. a. > b. > c. < d. < e. <
   f. > g. < h. >
2. a. 3052608, 3350720, 4345608, 21007891, 72456218
   b. 1112222, 2000123, 9999901, 10200123, 20450012, 20607812
   c. 1243015, 10206789, 12010214, 12043015, 23015670
   d. 1000245, 10024005, 70050236, 70522369, 78045123, 79050510
   e. 2344889, 2344898, 2344988, 2345888
3. a. 7856824, 5067891, 5026078, 1262187, 1205679
   b. 81110203, 28902823, 22102183, 20801503, 20450023, 20104712
   c. 70130600, 70130350, 70130114, 70130112, 70130110
   d. 43551012, 31278451, 31251236, 31250202, 31010230, 25020245
   e. 90174442, 60376990, 60131485, 50890600, 10130123
4. Greatest number: 98,752, Ninety-eight thousand seven hundred fifty-two
   Smallest number: 25,789, Twenty-five thousand seven hundred eighty-nine
5. Difference: 77,77,083

Exercise 1.3

1. 59,63,000 m
2. 3,26,01,625 g sweets; 4,65,73,750 g savouries
3. 5,56,87,500 mL 4. ₹9,39,65,176 5. 28,450 g
6. 4,56,35,910 7. 92,250 8. ₹1,13,142
9. ₹4,35,000 10. 1,563

Exercise 1.4

1. 7240; 7200; 7000
   50420; 50400; 50000; 50000
   21900; 21900; 22000; 20000
   1205390; 1205400; 1205000; 1210000
2. a. 400 b. 600 c. 1200 d. 10 e. 8000 f. 40000
   g. 40000 h. 40000
3. Estimated sum = 1,38,60,000
   Actual sum = 1,38,66,619
   Estimated sum is nearest to the actual sum.
4. ₹73,400
5. 4000 km

Revision Exercise

1. a. iii b. iv c. ii
   d. iii e. i
2. a. 9,92,04,206 b. 19,071,938 c. 7,13,24,909
   d. 2,004,211 e. 8,75,40,150 f. 4,014,905

Ascending order: 2004211 < 4014905 < 19071938 < 71324909 < 87540150 < 99204206

3.

	Number	Indian place value system	International place value system	Number name in Indian place value system	Number name in International place value system
a.	6045896	60,45,896	6,045,896	Sixty lakh forty-five thousand eight hundred ninety-six	Six million forty-five thousand eight hundred ninety-six
b.	20456087	2,04,56,087	20,456,087	Two crore four lakh fifty-six thousand eighty-seven	Twenty million four hundred fifty-six thousand eighty-seven
c.	20850135	2,08,50,135	20,850,135	Two crore eight lakh fifty thousand one hundred thirty-five	Twenty million eight hundred fifty thousand one hundred thirty-five
d.	5021369	50,21,369	5,021,369	Fifty lakh twenty-one thousand three hundred sixty-nine	Five million twenty-one thousand three hundred sixty-nine
e.	90001009	9,00,01,009	90,001,009	Nine lakh one thousand nine	Niinety million one thousand nine
f.	10302410	1,03,02,410	10,302,410	One crore three lakh two thousand four hundred ten	Ten million three hundred two thousand four hundred ten

g.	10238001	1,02,38,001	10,238,001	One crore two lakh thirty-eight thousand one	Ten million two hundred thirty-eight thousand one
h.	68759087	6,87,59,087	68,759,087	Six crore eighty seven lakh fifty nine thousand eighty-seven	Sixty-eight million seven hundred fifty nine thousand eighty-seven

The smallest number is 50,21,369 and the largest number is 9,00,01,009.

4. a. 1825970, 1825901, 1825790, 1089201, 185297
   b. 78596541, 78543012, 9985214, 7852016, 7852015
   c. 98568025, 98562875, 98562140, 98562104, 98562001
   d. 98752149, 90086001, 90085637, 90085609, 90085602
   e. 8434550, 8434422, 8345600, 8344450, 8343450
5. a. < b. > c. < d. > e. <
6. Largest number: 99,99,987
   Smallest number: 11,11,123
7. a. 6000 b. 30,000 c. 8,00,000
   d. 20,00,000 e. 3,00,00,000
8. a. 2,50,00,000 b. 60,00,000 c. 10,00,000
   d. 33333.33... e. 900 f. 4000
   g. 5400 h. 125
9. 1899
10. a. 9,00,00,000 b. 67,980 – 67,809 = 171
    c. 18,113 feet d. ₹10,82,739 e. 1,08,700 kg
    f. 13 boxes

Chapter – 2

Exercise 2.1

1. a. 5,84,346 b. 7,87,602 c. 47,89,237
   d. 99,81,350
2. a. 8,44,359 b. 42,57,332 c. 87,40,022
   d. 46,02,285
3. 54,39,259; 54,39,260
4. 97
5. 2,715

Exercise 2.2

1. a. 3049 b. 90,333 c. 0 d. 6031

Exercise 2.3

1. a. 604 b. 0 c. 1 d. 806
   e. (205 + 705)
2. a. Commutative property under multiplication
   b. Associative property under multiplication
   c. Multiplicative property of zero
   d. Multiplicative identity
3. a. 2,03,70,000 b. 4,30,50,000 c. 1,00,42,000
   d. 20,09,00,000 e. 1,20,50,000 f. 2,05,00,000
4. a. 37 b. 102 c. 502
   d. 111 e. 41,722
5. a. Q = 32, R = 6 b. Q = 9, R = 96
   c. Q = 25, R = 23 d. Q = 223, R = 3
   e. Q = 111, R = 2 f. Q = 3843, R = 15
6. The other number is 201.
7. a. 12 b. 6728 c. 3 d. 10102
8. a. 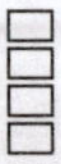 b. 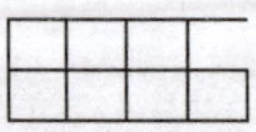
   c.  d. 
9. a.

2	7	6
9	5	1
4	3	8

b.

9	2	7
4	6	8
5	10	3

c.

24	9	12
3	15	27
18	21	6

d.

21	16	23
22	20	18
17	24	19

Revision Exercise

1. a. iii b. ii c. i d. iv e. i
2. a. 0 b. 0 c. 1 d. 5
   e. 2335
3. a. 39,133 b. 54,570 c. 40,59,000
   d. 1,10,24,000
4. a. 5,57,220 b. 5,90,254 c. 67,81,536
   d. 8,87,65,000
5. a. 3360 b. 4356
6. a. 11 b. 1 c. 129 d. 230
7. a. 16, 36 b. 48, 384 c. 88, 113 d. 107, 83
   e. 130, 163
8. a. 7073 d. 2 + (3 × 4) is not equal to (2 + 3) × (2 + 4)
   e. 2000

Chapter – 3

Exercise 3.1

1. a. +25 metres b. –36°C c. –2 kg
   d. 0°C e. –10 metres f. +₹1000
2. 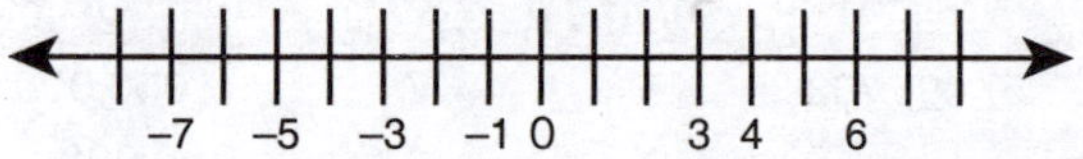

3. a. < b. > c. > d. > e. < f. >
4. a. –10, –4, –2, 0, 1, 4, 5 b. –24, –11, –9, –5, –2, 3, 8
   c. –13, –8, –1, 0, 6, 11,13 d. –40, –6, –5, –2, 1, 2, 5, 9
   e. –9, –3, –2, 0, 1, 4, 7
5. a. 10, 7, 4, –3, –5, –10, –13 b. 8, 3, 0, –2, –9, –11, –24
   c. 19, 11, 5, –2, –3, –8, –36 d. 16, 12, 11, –2, –3, –6, –9
   e. 11, 7, 4, 0, –2, –5, –7, –11
6. a. –4, –3, –2, –1, 0, 1, 2 b. –10, –9, –8, –7, –6, –5, –4
   c. –3, –2, –1 d. –2, –1, 0
   e. –1, 0, 1
7. a. 3 b. 232 c. 0 d. –3
   e. –3 f. 0
8. a. 9 b. 8 c. 22 d. 5
   e. 29 f. 58 g. 67

Exercise 3.2

1. a. 11 b. –3 c. 3 d. –11 e. 0
2. a. 144 b. –10 c. 5 d. –5 e. 1
3. a. –4 b. 47 c. –100 d. 5 e. –5
4. a. –40 b. 53 c. –32 d. –120 e. –97
5. a. < b. = c. < d. = e. <
6. a. 0 b. +20 c. 14 d. –5 e. 7
7. –54 8. 136 9. 16°C 10. 322 km

Revision Exercise

1. a. Negative sign b. Positive sign c. Positive sign
   d. Negative sign e. Negative sign
2. a. –5 b. –3 c. +3 d. +5 e. +7
3. a. True b. False c. True d. False e. False
4. a. < b. > c. > d. < e. < f. >
5. Four integers smaller than –2: –3, –4, –5, –6
   Four integers greater than –23: –22, –21, –20, –19
6. a. –5, –4, –3, –2, –1, 0 b. –3, –2, –1, 0, 1, 2, 3
   c. 3, 4, 5, 6, d. –8, –7, –6, –5, –4, –3
   e. –4, –3, –2, –1, 0, 1, 2, 3, 4
7. 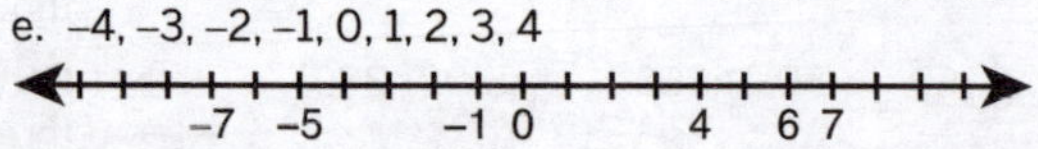

8. a. –7 b. –142 c. –65 d. –29
   e. 45 f. 45 g. 72 h. 50
   i. –43 j. –3 k. 0 l. 5
   m. 7 n. 7 o. 10

Chapter – 4

Exercise 4.1

1. a. It is not a set as it is not well defined. b. It is a set
   c. It is a set d. It is a set e. It is a set f. It is a set
2. a. False b. True c. False d. True

Exercise 4.2

1. a. {–19, –18, –17, –16, –15, –14, –13, –12, –11, –10, –9, –8, –7, –6}
   b. {80, 81, 82, 83, 84, 85, 86, 87, 88, 89, 90, 91, 92, 93, 94, 95, 96, 97, 98, 99}
   c. {8, 16, 24, 32, 40, 48, 56, 64, 72}
   d. {7, 21, 35, 49, 63}
   e. {K, R, N, T}
2. a. D = {x: x is an even number, $50 < x < 68$}
   b. P = {x: x is prime number, $100 < x < 150$}
   c. M = {x: x is a month after August in a year}
   d. F = {x: x is a prime number, $1 < x < 12$}
   e. S = {x: x is first four inner planets close to sun}
3. Description Method:
   a. Set of all prime numbers less than 24
   b. Set of all multiples of 5 that are less than 40
   c. Set of all whole numbers less than 11
   d. Set of all multiples of 4 between –20 and 16

   Set-builder form:
   a. {x: x is a prime number, $1 < x < 24$}
   b. {x: x is a mulitple of 5 that are less than 40}
   c. {x: x is a whole number less than 11}
   d. {x: $x = 4n$, $-5 < n < 4$, n is an integer}
4. a. $n(A) = 5$ b. $n(B) = 6$ c. $n(C) = 1$
   d. $n(D) = 2$ e. $n(E) = 4$ f. $n(F) = 5$

Exercise 4.3

1. e 2. a
3. a. Empty set b. Singleton set c. Singleton set
   d. Empty set e. Empty set
4. a. Finite set b. Infinite set c. Finite set
   d. Infinite set e. Finite set
5. a. Overlapping set b. Overlapping set c. Disjoint set
   d. Overlapping set e. Disjoint set

Revision Exercise

1. a. ii b. i c. iii d. iii e. iii
2. a. iii b. vi c. ii d. i e. iv
3. a. T b. F c. F d. T e. T
4. a. It is set as it contains well defined objects.
   b. It is a set as it contains well defined objects.
   c. It is not a set as we can not exactly find the beautiful flowers in the garden.
   d. It is not a set as the word 'fast' is not well defined.
   e. It is a set as it contains well defined objects.
5. a. A = {2, 3} and n (A) = 2
   b. B = {C, O, U, R, A, G, E} and n (B) = 7
   c. C = {6, 12, 18, 24, 30, 36} and n (C) = 6
   d. D = { } and n (D) = 0
   e. E = {3, 5, 7, 11, 13, 17, 19} and n (E) = 7
6. a. A = {x : x is a prime number less than 14}
   b. B = {x : x is a month having 31 days}
   c. C = {x : x is a multiple of 5 less than 32}
   d. D = {x : x is a letter in the word "mathematics"}
   e. E = {x : x is an even natural number}
7. a. Infinite set b. Finite set c. Empty set
   d. Infinite set e. Empty set f. Finite set

Chapter – 5

Exercise 5.1

1. b. $\frac{2}{6}$ c. $\frac{3}{8}$ d. $\frac{1}{8}$
2. a. 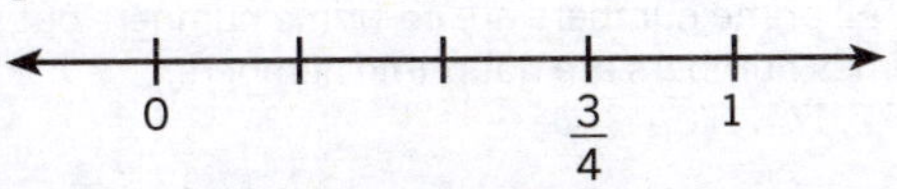

   b. 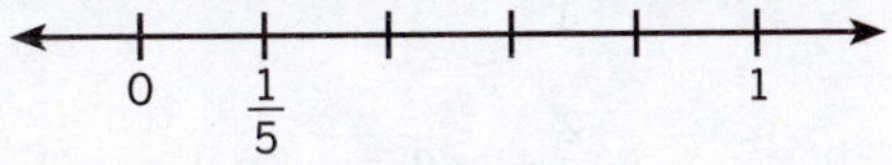

   c. 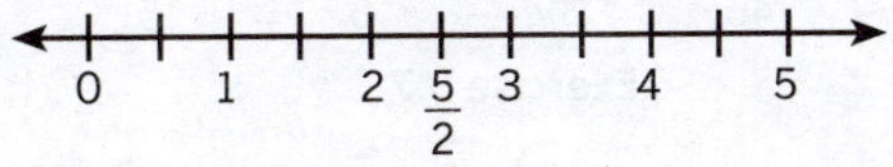

   d. 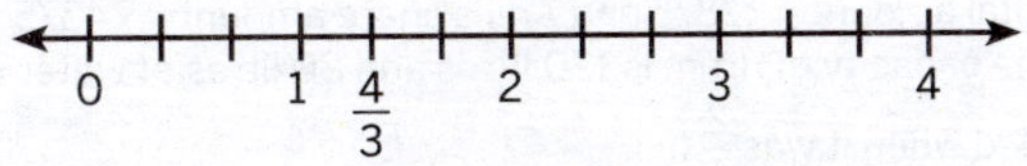

Exercise 5.2

1.

Proper fractions	Improper fractions	Mixed fractions
$\frac{1}{4}, \frac{9}{11}, \frac{7}{10}, \frac{1}{8}$	$\frac{7}{3}, \frac{13}{7}, \frac{14}{5}, \frac{12}{11}$	$1\frac{8}{9}, 2\frac{3}{5}, 2\frac{4}{7}, 5\frac{1}{7}$

2.

Like fractions	Unlike fractions
$\frac{1}{2}$ and $\frac{5}{2}$	$\frac{7}{8}$ and $\frac{8}{7}$
$\frac{5}{6}$ and $\frac{1}{6}$	$\frac{4}{9}$ and $\frac{4}{7}$
$\frac{6}{10}$ and $\frac{7}{10}$	

3. a. $1\frac{5}{6}$ b. $4\frac{1}{2}$ c. $1\frac{7}{10}$ d. $2\frac{2}{3}$ e. $1\frac{10}{11}$
4. a. $\frac{12}{5}$ b. $\frac{14}{3}$ c. $\frac{12}{7}$ d. $\frac{11}{4}$ e. $\frac{18}{5}$

Exercise 5.3

1. a. $\frac{4}{5} = \frac{8}{10} = \frac{12}{15} = \frac{16}{20} = \frac{20}{25}$ b. $\frac{6}{7} = \frac{12}{14} = \frac{18}{21} = \frac{24}{28} = \frac{30}{35}$
   c. $\frac{3}{4} = \frac{6}{8} = \frac{9}{12} = \frac{12}{16} = \frac{15}{20}$ d. $\frac{5}{8} = \frac{10}{16} = \frac{15}{24} = \frac{20}{32} = \frac{25}{40}$
2. a. $\frac{5}{8} \neq \frac{8}{12}$ b. $\frac{1}{8} \neq \frac{6}{10}$ c. $\frac{4}{9} = \frac{12}{27}$ d. $\frac{5}{13} \neq \frac{6}{14}$
3. a. $\frac{2}{3}$ b. $\frac{1}{5}$ c. $\frac{1}{4}$ d. $\frac{2}{3}$

Exercise 5.4

1. a. < b. > c. < d. > e. > f. <
2. a. $\frac{3}{11} < \frac{3}{10} < \frac{3}{7} < \frac{3}{5} < \frac{3}{4}$ b. $\frac{3}{14} < \frac{3}{7} < \frac{4}{7} < \frac{9}{14} < \frac{6}{7}$
   c. $\frac{1}{5} < \frac{2}{5} < \frac{3}{5} < \frac{4}{5} < \frac{5}{5}$ d. $\frac{1}{6} < \frac{1}{3} < \frac{1}{2} < \frac{2}{3} < \frac{5}{6}$
3. a. $\frac{4}{5} > \frac{4}{7} > \frac{4}{8} > \frac{4}{9} > \frac{4}{10}$ b. $\frac{4}{5} > \frac{2}{3} > \frac{2}{5} > \frac{1}{3} > \frac{1}{5}$
   c. $\frac{9}{10} > \frac{8}{10} > \frac{7}{10} > \frac{4}{10} > \frac{3}{10}$ d. $\frac{3}{4} > \frac{5}{8} > \frac{1}{2} > \frac{1}{4} > \frac{1}{8}$

Exercise 5.5

1. a. $\frac{5}{9}$ b. $\frac{5}{6}$ c. $1\frac{2}{15}$ d. $6\frac{11}{14}$
2. a. $\frac{1}{3}$ b. $\frac{1}{2}$ c. $\frac{1}{12}$ d. $\frac{7}{12}$
3. $3\frac{7}{15}$ 4. $4\frac{9}{28}$

Exercise 5.6

1. a. 9 b. $\frac{35}{66}$ c. $8\frac{2}{5}$ d. $3\frac{1}{5}$ e. $37\frac{1}{2}$ f. $\frac{5}{32}$

2. a. $13\frac{1}{2}$ b. $\frac{2}{45}$ c. $\frac{2}{3}$ d. $\frac{4}{5}$ e. $1\frac{11}{16}$ f. $3\frac{2}{3}$

Exercise 5.7

1. 510 boys
2. Total amount = ₹7875 and Anil's share amount = ₹4375
3. The capacity of drum is 120 litres and 80 litres of water was filled when it was $\frac{2}{3}$ full.
4. Sketch pen costs ₹$4\frac{1}{4}$ more than pen. 5. 11 m

Exercise 5.8

1. 0.21 2. 0.111 3. 4.8
4. 5.5 5. 1.23 6. 0.19

Exercise 5.9

1. a. 5.5 b. 83.17 c. 267.003 d. 14.203
   e. 10.087
2. a. $\frac{7}{10}$ b. 7 c. 70 d. $\frac{7}{1000}$ e. $\frac{7}{100}$ f. 700
3. a. 400 + 90 + 5 + 0.6 b. 20 + 3 + 0.1 + 0.08
   c. 10 + 4 + 0.08 + 0.007
   d. 3000 + 500 + 20 + 7 + 0.1 + 0.07
   e. 500 + 5 + 0.5 + 0.005
   f. 7000 + 600 + 50 + 4 + 0.3 + 0.02 + 0.001
4. a. Like decimals b. Unlike decimals
   c. Unlike decimals d. Unlike decimals
   e. Like decimals f. Unlike decimals
5. a. < b. < c. > d. > e. = f. >
6. a. 0.003, 0.03, 0.3, 0.33, 3.03, 3.3
   b. 1.463, 4.346, 4.364, 4.436, 4.643
   c. –4.25, –3.05, –1, 0, 0.13, 2.05, 2.45, 3.92
   d. 1.4576, 1.5467, 1.7564, 1.8927
7. a. 55.5, 50.5, 5.5, 5.05, 0.55, 0.505
   b. 3.999, 3.712, 3.617, 3.434, 3.279
   c. 6.75, 1.78, 0.404, –1.75, –2, –3.45
   d. 0.9366, 0.63121, 0.6312, –0.936, –0.93661
8. a. 0.07 b. 0.4 c. 6.18
   d. 1.3 e. 65.076 f. 0.128
9. a. $\frac{29}{50}$ b. $\frac{7}{10}$ c. $\frac{327}{250}$ d. $\frac{1}{50}$ e. $\frac{6021}{500}$ f. $\frac{5}{8}$

10. a.

b.

c.

d.

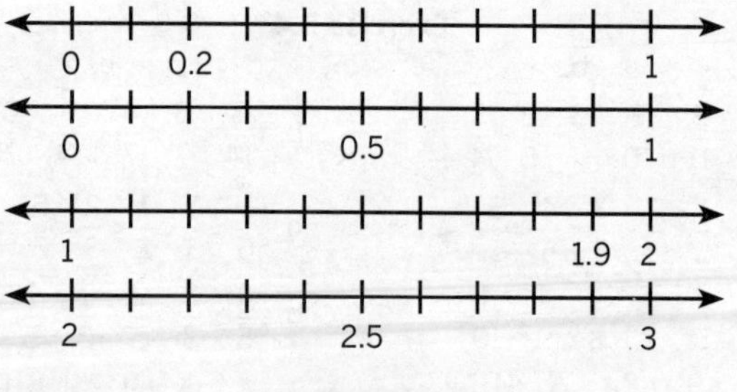

Exercise 5.10

1. a. 99.01 b. 72.05 c. 149.115
   d. 116.767 e. 131.383 f. 688.509
2. a. 36.73 b. 69.31 c. 21.577
   d. 99.999 e. 308.093 f. 42.173
3. a. 24.08 b. 6.62 c. 1.973
   d. 34.79 e. 12.77 f. 65.415
4. 3.751 5. 8.534 6. ₹356 7. 16.1 km

Exercise 5.11

1. ₹33.50 2. 14.25 kg 3. 1.9 m
4. 9 L 950 mL

Exercise 5.12

1. a. 1.35 b. 4.9 c. 2.46 d. 0.72
   e. 1.25 f. 14.2 g. 0.013 h. 5
2. 217.2 cm 3. 42.4 kg 4. ₹181.4
5. 18.75 km 6. 3 hours 7. ₹23.15

Revision Exercise

1. a. iii. b. iii. c. i. d. iii
2. a. 0.513
   b. tenths; tens c. $1\frac{4}{25}$
   d. decimal point e. decreases; ten
3. a. $1\frac{1}{5}$ b. $11\frac{3}{20}$ c. $1\frac{5}{18}$ d. $\frac{2}{9}$ e. $\frac{1}{12}$
   f. $\frac{11}{12}$ g. 12 h. $\frac{5}{24}$ i. $1\frac{1}{3}$ j. $6\frac{3}{4}$
   k. $\frac{1}{40}$ l. $1\frac{2}{25}$ m. $\frac{2}{3}$
4. a. 0.6 b. 0.5 c. 3 d. 0.64
5. a. $\frac{1}{2}$ b. $1\frac{1}{2}$ c. $\frac{123}{1000}$ d. $12\frac{23}{100}$
6. a. 10 + 2 + 0.2; 30 + 2 + 0.4 + 0.04; 600 + 40 + 4 + 0.3 + 0.06 + 0.008
   b. i. 4.3 ii. 32.78 iii. 121.104
   c. i. $\frac{4}{100}$ ii. $\frac{5}{10}$ iii. $\frac{7}{1000}$
7. a. 152.6 b. 76.04 c. 2.4 d. 221.691
   e. 55.26 f. 1.51 g. 5 h. 1.949
8. a. $3\frac{4}{7}$ b. $\frac{9}{14}$ c. $3\frac{3}{20}$ d. $1\frac{3}{4}$
9. a. > b. > c. < d. <
10. a. Megha bought $3\frac{19}{20}$ kg fruits.
    b. $4\frac{1}{8}$ litres of petrol is left in the bike.
    c. 72 members are absent.
    d. ₹512.5
    e. 28 days

Chapter – 6

Exercise 6.1

1. a. T b. T c. F d. F e. T
2. a. 1, 2, 4, 5, 8, 10, 20, 40 b. 1, 5, 13, 65
   c. 1, 2, 3, 5, 6, 9, 10, 15, 18, 30, 45, 90
   d. 1, 2, 3, 5, 6, 10, 15, 25, 30, 50, 75, 150
   e. 1, 2, 4, 5, 8, 10, 20, 25, 40, 50, 100, 200
3. a. 3, 6, 9, 12, 15, 18 b. 11, 22, 33, 44, 55, 66
   c. 8, 16, 24, 32, 40, 48 d. 4, 8, 12, 16, 20, 24
   e. 7,14, 21, 28, 35, 42
4. a. 5 b. 10 c. 45
   d. 1, 2, 3, 4, 6, 8, 12, 24 e. 1, 2, 3, 6
5. Yes, 351 is a multiple of 13.

Exercise 6.2

1. b, d
2. a. 5, 7, 11, 13, 17, 19
   b. 17, 19, 23, 29, 31,37, 41, 43, 47
   c. 67, 71, 73, 79, 83
   d. 23, 29, 31, 37, 41, 43, 47, 53, 59, 61, 67, 71, 73
   e. 113 and 127
3. a. False, For example: 15 is an odd number but not prime.
   b. False, For example: 2 is an even prime number.
   c. True
   d. True
   e. False, All prime numbers are co-prime numbers but all co-primes numbers are not prime numbers.
4. 170, 172, 174, 176,...240

5. 1,389, 1,391, 1,393,1,395,... 1,491

Exercise 6.3

1.

Number	Divisible by									
	2	3	4	5	6	7	8	9	10	11
7,020	Yes	Yes	Yes	Yes	Yes	No	No	Yes	Yes	No
11,456	Yes	No	Yes	No	No	No	Yes	No	No	No
7,31,541	No	Yes	No	No	No	No	No	No	No	No
97,240	Yes	No	Yes	Yes	No	No	Yes	No	Yes	Yes

2. a. F, Every number divisible by 9 is always divisible by 3.
   b. T
   c. F
   d. F, That number will be divisible by the product of 2 and 5.
   e. F, 84 is not divisible by 8 which is a multiple of 4.
3. a. 782964 b. 752 c. 21345

Exercise 6.4

1. a. 2 × 2 × 2 × 17 b. 2 × 2 × 3 × 3 × 7
   c. 7 × 11 × 11 × 11 d. 3 × 3 × 5 × 23
   e. 5 × 11 × 11 × 23
2. 210
3. 1000 = 2 × 2 × 2 × 5 × 5 × 5
   9999 = 3 × 3 × 11 × 101

Exercise 6.5

1. a. 4 b. 6 c. 24 d. 9 e. 5
2. a. 4 b. 8 c. 12 d. 8 e. 18
3. a. 13 b. 40 c. 6 d. 14 e. 60
4. 24 m 5. 96 students 6. 115
7. 6 students 8. 22 pieces

Exercise 6.6

1. a. 6 b. 28 c. 15 d. 50 e. 75
2. a. 72 b. 240 c. 2250 d. 1120 e. 1800
3. a. 720 b. 540 c. 4200 d. 4900 e. 240
4. 180 days 5. 261 6. 180 7. 200 minutes
8. 12 days 9. 9,93,300 10. 48 11. 2 12. 48

Exercise 6.7

1. a. –18 b. 16 c. 22 d. 2 e. –12
   f. 25 g. 0 h. 5
2. a. 1050 b. 198 c. 15 d. 1

Revision Exercise

1.

Number	Divisible by									
	2	3	4	5	6	7	8	9	10	11
12,453	No	Yes	No	No	No	Yes	No	No	No	No
34,512	Yes	Yes	Yes	No	Yes	No	Yes	No	No	No
78,145	No	No	No	Yes	No	No	No	No	No	No
8,45,746	Yes	No	No	No	No	No	No	No	No	Yes

2. a. F b. T c. F d. F e. T
3. a. 1, 2, 3, 6, 59, 118, 177, 354 b. 1, 2, 89, 178
   c. 1, 2, 3, 4, 6, 8, 12, 24 d. 1, 5, 29, 145
4. a. 13 b. 29 c. 26 d. 77 e. 120
5. a. 126 b. 300 c. 468 d. 432 e. 420
6. The largest square tile is 40 cm. 9 tiles along width and 49 tiles along length can be tiled.
7. 24 8. 24 9. 15 10. 10,080

Chapter - 7

Exercise 7.1

1. a. 1:3 b. 5:7 c. 13:16 d. 17:11 e. 37:29
2. a. 4:1 b. 10:3 c. 36:11 d. 48:5 e. 23:80
3. a. 1:6 b. 7:24 c. 9:10 d. 3:2 e. 4:5
4. a. yes b. no c. no d. yes e. no
5. a. (6:7) > (5:6) b. (19:25) > (37:50)
   c. (24:13) > (12:7) d. (43:100) > (21:50)
   e. (9:11) > (5:7)

Exercise 7.2

1. a. yes b. yes c. yes d. no e. yes
2. a. 12 b. 12 c. 40 d. $5\frac{1}{4}$ e. $\frac{185}{63}$
3. a. 3 b. 20 c. 30 d. 9 e. 8
4. 2
5. a. 8 : 1 b. 54 cm, 60 cm c. 2.52 litres
   d. 30°, 60° and 90° e. i. 7 : 8 ii. 7 : 15
   f. i. 3 : 2 ii. 3 : 5

Exercise 7.3

1. 300; 12 kg flour; 56 rupees; 5 dozen eggs; 9 litres of apple juice
2. a. 50 students b. 12 km/h c. 10 kg
   d. 1645 bricks e. 225 pages f. 4:3

Exercise 7.4

1. a. 4.5 m/s, 12.5 m/s, 87.5 m/s
   b. 4.32 km/h, 126 km/h, 2250 km/hr
2. 50 km/hr 3. 1.35 minutes 4. 450 m
5. 7.5 km 6. 10.5 min 7. 21.6 km/hr
8. 12 km/hr 9. 5.5 hr 10. 388.5 km
11. 37.5 km/hr 12. 385 km 13. 55 km/hr
14. 36.25 km/h

Revision Exercise

1. a. iii b. ii c. i d. iii e. i
2. a. F b. T c. T d. F e. F
3. a. 1 : 2 b. 37 : 47 c. 5 : 6 d. 17 : 30
   e. 31 : 29
4. a, c
5. 15 km/hr; 60 km; 90 minutes; 5.4 km/hr; 1080 m; 1200 seconds
6. a. 8.89 m/s b. 25 m/s c. 45 m/s d. 200 m/s e. 65m/s
7. a ₹40,000; ₹64,000 b. 15kg c. ₹750
   d. 40.5 km e. 67.5 km/hr f. 1 m/s
   g. In Mr. Sharma's shop onions are cheaper and they are cheaper by ₹0.5
   h. yes, they are in proportion. i. No j. 4 kg

Chapter – 8

Exercise 8.1

1. a. 25% b. 70% c. 62.5% d. 88%
   e. 1.85%
2. a. $\frac{9}{20}$ b. $\frac{33}{25}$ c. $\frac{9}{5}$ d. $\frac{19}{20}$ e. $\frac{19}{25}$
3. a. 6% b. 16.5% c. 235% d. 0.8% e. 60%
4. a. 1.05 b. 0.04 c. 0.001 d. 0.18 e. 0.6
5. a. 40% b. 30% c. 65% d. 50% e. 25%

Exercise 8.2

1. $12\frac{1}{2}$ % 2. 30% 3. 81.25 cm
4. 54% 5. ₹5,415 6. 60
7. 12% 8. 16%
9. Percentage of boys = 44.4% and Percentage of girls = 55.56%

Revision Exercise

1. a. ii b. iv c. I d. iii e. ii
2. a. T b. T c. T d. F e. T
3. a. 9% b. $\frac{1}{20}$ c. 378 e. 16% e. $\frac{13}{20}$
4. a. i. $\frac{9}{20}$; 0.45 ii. $\frac{3}{5}$; 0.60 iii. $\frac{2}{25}$; 0.08
   iv. $\frac{23}{20}$; 1.15 v. $\frac{21}{25}$; 0.84
   b. i. 4% ii. 28% iii. 73% iv. 230% v. 105%
   c. i. 37.5% ii. 70% c. 52% d. 95% e. 80%

d. 24%   e. 20%

f. Expenditure = ₹23,343; Savings = ₹14,307

g. 25%   h. 8%   i. 1575   j. 3:5   k. 20%

Chapter - 9

Exercise 9.1

1. a. The next term is 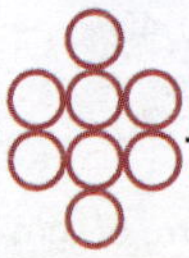. The nth term is $2n$.

   b. The next term is . The nth term is $2n + 1$.

2. a. The distance covered by cheetah in t seconds = $29t$

   b. ₹$12n$ c. $7t$ d. $42l$

3. a. Variable: x, Constant: 5, 6

   b. Variable: m; Constant: 2

   c. Constant: 100

   d. Variable: l; Constant: 56

   e. Variable: b; Constant: 39

4. Rule is $2n$, 15th term is 30.

5. $10p$ 6. $6x$ 7. $(y - 2)$ hours

Exercise 9.2

1. a. $5x + 7$ b. $4x + 13$ c. $7 - 10x$ d. $\frac{1}{2}(2x + 2y)$

   e. $t - 3$ f. $\frac{4}{a}$

2. a. 10 added to the product of 25 and p gives 60.

   b. When 16 times of m is divided by 2, the quotient becomes 24.

   c. 15 subtracted from the sum of $10x$ and $7y$

   d. The product of 15 and y taken away from 100.

   e. 5 is added to the product of 11 and x gives 27.

3. a. $7l$ b. $2(l + b)$ c. $3s$ d. $6m$

4. a. ₹$500p$ b. $\frac{₹10,000}{k}$ c. $6x + 6$

   d. ₹$(100p + 60q)$ e. ₹$(25x + 50y)$ f. $10x$ km

Exercise 9.3

1.

Algebraic Expression	Terms	Numeri Coefficient	Power of the variable
a. $-25x^3 + 2x^2 + x$	$-25x^3$	-25	3
	$2x^2$	2	2
	x	1	1
b. $4a^3b^2 - 2b^2 + 3a - 4$	$4a^3b^2$	4	3, 2
	$-2b^2$	-2	2
	$3a$	3	1
	-4	Constant term	
c. $52z^2 + 19zx$	$52z^2$	52	2
	$19zx$	19	1, 1
d. $6x^4 + 4x^5 + 20x^3 - 6x^2 + 2$	$6x^4$	6	4
	$4x^5$	4	5
	$20x^3$	20	3
	$-6x^2$	-6	2
	2	Constant term	
e. $2l^3 + 24$	$2l^3$	2	3
	24	Constant term	
f. $(a + 4b + 5) \div 2$	$\frac{a}{2}$	$\frac{1}{2}$	1
	$2b$	2	1
	$\frac{5}{2}$	Constant term	

2. a. $10p^2q, -6qp^2; -4pq^2, 12q^2p$ b. $12a^2, -10a^2$; $5a, -8a, 9a$

   c. $2x^2y^3, -3x^2y^3; 5x^3y^2, -10x^3y^2$

   d. $24y^{10}, -4y^{10}; y^6, -26y^6; 4y^2, 7y^2$ e. $4yx, 5xy; 7z, -3z$

3. a. The powers of the variables are different.

   b. The variables are different.

   c. Variables and the powers of the variables are different.

   d. The powers of the variables are different.

   e. The variables are different.

4. Monomials – a, b and f ; Binomials –c and g; Trinomials – d; Polynomial – e

5. a. 1   b. 0   c. 0   d. 2   e. 2

Exercise 9.4

1. a. –37   b. 87   c. –28   d. 0

2. a. –1002   b. 582   c. 2294   d. 15

3.

x	2	4	8	11
Value of the expression	38	38	59	76.53

4. 27

Exercise 9.5

1. a. $-a^2 + 3b^2 - 3a + 7b + 2ab$ b. $7a^2 - 4b^2 - 3ab - 9$

   c. $8x^2 + 8y^2 - xy$

2. a. $x - 9y + 7z$ b. $-2ab + 2cd + 6ac + 6bd$

   c. $4b^3 + 3a^4 - 6b - 6a$

3. a. $-12x^4y^5z^5$ b. $12x^2y^3 - 8x^3y^2$

   c. $9a^2b - 15ab^2$ d. $-15x^2y + 18x^3y + 21x^2y^2$

   e. $24a^2 - 30a^2b - 18ac$

4. a. $7a^2$ b. $-5x^3$ c. $6a + 8 - 11a^2$

   d. $-3m + m^2 - 7m^3$ e. $7p - 3p^3 - 13$

Revision Exercise

1. a. ii   b. iii   c. iii   d. iv   e. ii   f. iii

2. a. –4   b. 0   c. $2n - 1$ d. $80p$ e. like terms

3. a. False   b. True   c. True   d. True

4. a. Variable: x, Constants: 5, 10

   b. Variable: y, Constants: 12, 10

   c. Variables: y, z, Constants: 1, 16, –7

   d. Variable: a, Constant: 26, –5

5. Rule is that every time given object is increasing by 1.

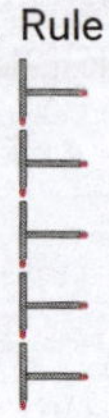

The rule for nth term is $n + 1$.

6. a. $(x + 110)$ metres   b. $z + 3$ c. $4k$ d. $30x$

7. a. $3x + 3$ b. $\frac{4}{x} - 2$ c. $d - 3$ d. $\frac{(3x)}{2}$ e. $5x + 7$

8. Like terms: $14x^3, -11x^3; -26y^2, 49y^2; 100x^2y, 30x^2y;$
   $36a^3, 23a^3; 42x^2, -12x^2; -19a^2b^2, 13a^2b^2$

9. a. –1   b. 42   c. 7

10. Monomials: $-2xy$ with degree 2, $4y^2$ with degree 2,
    Binomials: $5x - 1$ with degree 1, $x^2 - 4x$ with degree 2,
    $2a^2 + 3a^2b^2$ with degree 4

Trinomials: $3x^3 + x^2 + 6$ with degree 3, $3x^2 - 4x + 10$ with degree 2, $2x + 3y + 2$ with degree 1

11. Number of dahlias are x, number of roses are $x + 8$.
12. $(3x + 4)$ years

Chapter – 10

Exercise 10.1

1. a, b, e
2. a. 22 b. 3 c. 6 d. 15 e. 15 f. 5 g. 14 h. 21 i. 8 j. 6
3. a. 1 b. 4 c. 5 d. 14 e. 5
4. a. 27, 41 b. Length = 48 cm; Breadth = 24 cm
   c. 6 years, 1 year d. 18
   e. Cost of a table = ₹348; Cost of a chair = ₹268
   f. 45

Revision Exercise

1. a. iii b. ii c. i d. iii e. iv
2. a. 1 b. 40 c. 12 d. 23 years e. 16
3. a, b, c, e
4. a. i. $\frac{27}{2}$ ii. –2
   b. Mother's age = 32 years; Son's age = 9 years
   c. 80 d. 84
   e. 20 years, 17 years f. 53

Chapter – 11

Exercise 11.1

1. a. AC, CA b. BE, EB
   c. CD, DE, CE d. ray BA, ray AB
   e. Ray DC, ray CE, ray EC, ray DE
2.

Points	H, I, J, O
Lines	DE, CF
Line Segments	IJ, IO, JO, JH
Rays	OA, OB, OC, OD, OE, OF, JG

3. (a), (c), (e)
4. a. Interior: A, F and D; Exterior: B, C and E
   b. Interior: A, C and E; Exterior: B, D and F
5. a. T b. T c. F d. F e. T
6. Linear: b, f Curvilinear: c, d
   Both linear and curvilinear: a, e

Exercise 11.2

1. a. 3
   b. Interior points: A,H; Exterior points: F, C, D; Boundary points: B, G, O, E;
   c. ∠QOP and ∠ROP
2. ΔABE, ΔBCE, ΔECD, ΔEAC
   Sides and angles of ΔABE: AB, BE, AE, ∠ABE, ∠BAE, ∠AEB
   Sides and angles of ΔBCE: BC, BE, CE, ∠CBE, ∠BCE, ∠CEB
   Sides and angles of ΔECD: EC, CD, ED, ∠CDE, ∠DCE, ∠CED
   Sides and angles of ΔEAC: EA, AC, EC, ∠AEC, ∠EAC, ∠ACE
3.

Points on the Triangle	Points in the Interior of the Triangle	Points in the Exterior of the Triangle
R U V	P S	T Q X

4.

Interior Points	Exterior Points	Boundary Points
X Y Z	K L M N	A B C D

5. Adjacent angles—∠W and ∠X, ∠X and ∠Y, ∠Y and ∠Z, ∠Z and ∠W. Opposite angles—∠W and ∠Y, ∠X and ∠Z

Exercise 11.3

1. a. OC, OB and OA b. AC c. AB, PHQ
   d. QBP, AHB e. AB, PQ and AC f. AQHPB, QABP
2. a. chord b. centre c. equal, semicircle
   d. sector e. centre
3. a. F b. T c. F d. T e. T
4. **Diameter and Chord:**
   A line segment whose endpoints lie on the circle and that passes through the centre of the circle is called diameter.
   A line segment whose endpoints lie on the circle is called a chord. Diameter is the longest chord of a circle.
   Sector and segment:
   The area enclosed by two radii of the circle and their connecting arc is called a sector, while the region enclosed by the chord and the arc of a circle is called a segment.
   Arc and Semicircle:
   An arc refers to the set of points on a circle that lie on the boundary of the circle.
   The end points of a diameter of a circle divide the circle into two equal parts; each part is called a semi-circle.

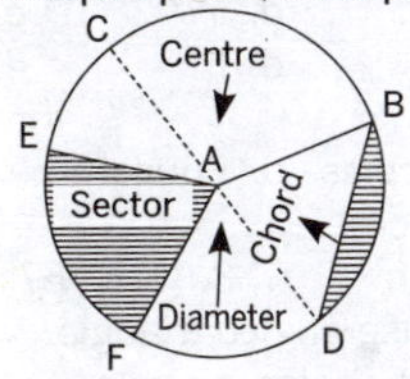

Revision Exercise

1. a. i b. iv c. i d. iv e. iii f. ii
2. a. same b. three, four c. ∠P, ∠Q and ∠R
   d. non-adjacent e. secant
3. a. F b. T c. F d. F e. T
4. a.

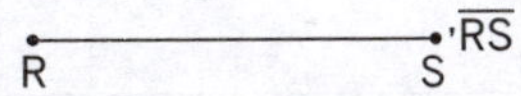

b.

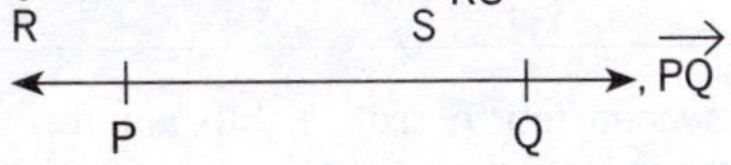

c.

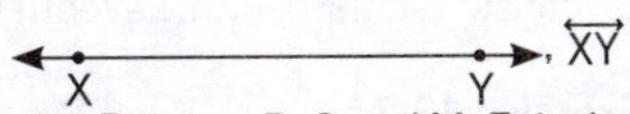

5. Interior Points – P, Q and M; Exterior points – X, L and Y; Boundary Points – R and K
6. Adjacent angles – ∠P and ∠Q; ∠Q and ∠R; ∠R and ∠S; ∠S and ∠P
   Opposite angles – ∠P and ∠R; ∠Q and ∠S
   Adjacent sides – PQ and QR; QR and RS; RS and SP; SP and PQ
   Opposite sides – PQ and SR; PS and QR
7. a. A, C, E, B; P, D, F, Q; S, E, F, T
   b. CE and CD c. CE, CD, DF, EF
8.

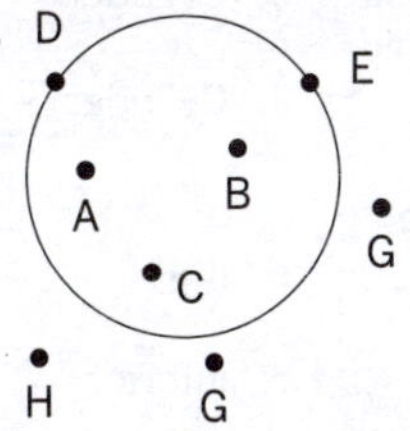

Chapter – 12

Exercise 12.1

1. AB = 4.8 cm, CD = 3.7 cm, EF = 4.2 cm
2. LM, MN, NO, OP, PQ, QK and KL are all line segments.
   LM = 1.5 cm, MN = 4.2 cm, NO = 2 cm, OP = 1 cm, PQ = 1.2 cm, QK = 2.5 cm, KL = 2.6 cm
   MN > KL > QK > NO > LM > PQ > OP

3. a. Intersecting lines b. Parallel lines
   c. Non parallel lines d. Perpendicular lines
   e. Perpendicular lines
4. a. Concurrent lines = *p*, *q*, *l* b. Line *p* and *m*
   c. Line *l* and *r* d. Line *m* and *r*
   e. Lines *p*, *q* and *l*
   f. *l* and *m*, *m* and *n*, *l* and *n* ($l \parallel m$, $m \parallel n$, $n \parallel l$)

Exercise 12.2

1. d > b > a > c
2. a. obtuse angle b. 360° c. Reflex angle
   d. two e. complete
3. a. 60° b. 125° c. 115°
4. 37.5° and 52.5°
5. a. 90° b. 0° c. 30° d. 150°
6. 102° 7. 76°

Exercise 12.3

1. 35° 2. ∠AOC = 68°, ∠COB = 112° and ∠BOD = 68°
3. x = 115°, y = 115° and z = 65° 4. ∠AMP = 105° and ∠DNQ = 75°

Exercise 12.4

1. 125° 2. 78° and 102° 3. 60° and 35°

Exercise 12.5

1. a. ii b. iii c. iv d. ii e. iv
2. a. F b. T c. T d. F e. F
3. All sides are 22 cm each.
4. a. Scalene b. Scalene c. Isosceles d. Equilateral
5. AD = 7 cm, BD = 10 cm and DC = 8 cm
6. 6 cm each 7. 22 cm each 8. 113°, 67°, 113°
9. a. Acute-angled triangle b. Obtuse-angled triangle
   c. Acute-angled triangle d. Right-angled triangle

Exercise 12.6

1.

Name	Triangle	Trapezium	Heptagon	Pentagon	Octagon
Number of sides	3	4	7	5	8

2. Regular polygons: second, fourth, sixth, eighth, nineth, tenth figure; Irregular polygons: first, third, fifth, seventh figure

Exercise 12.7

1.

Shapes	Vertices	Edges	Faces
Cube	8	12	6
Cuboid	8	12	6
Cylinder	0	2	3
Cone	1	1	2
Sphere	0	0	1

2. a. Cube or Cuboid b. Triangular prism c. Cylinder
   d. Cone e. Square pyramid
3. a. Cone b. Cuboid c. Cylinder
   d. Sphere e. Cube

Revision Exercise

1. a. iv b. ii c. ii
   d. iv e. i
2. a. 90° b. equal c. interior
   d. square e. 60°
3. a. F b. T c. T
   d. F e. T
4. a. square pyramid b. sphere c. square prism
   d. cylinder e. triangular pyramid
5. a, b, e, g, h 6. 36°, 54° 7. 15
8. 100°, 100°
9. a. AC and BD
   b. ∠AOD and ∠BOC; ∠AOB and ∠COD
   c. ΔADC, ΔBCD, ΔABC, ΔDAB
   d. ΔAOD, ΔBOC, ΔAOB, ΔCOD
10. c. Acute-angled triangle, Obtuse-angled Triangle, Right-angled triangle
    d. Square, rectangle, and rhombus

Chapter – 13

Exercise 13.1

1. a. 6 b. 5 c. 0 d. 8 e. 4 f. 6
2. a. 0 b. 0 c. 1
3. a. 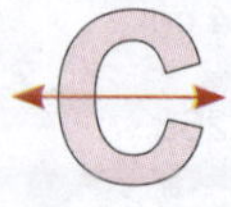 b. 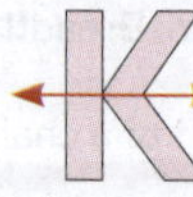 c. 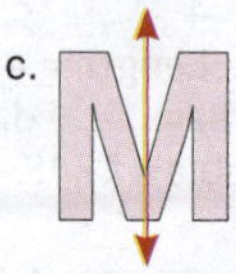 d. 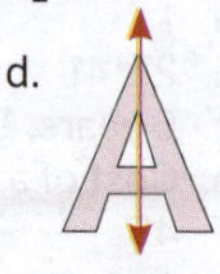
4. a. 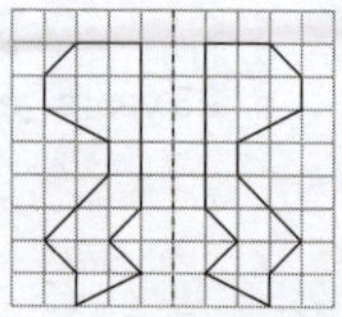 b. 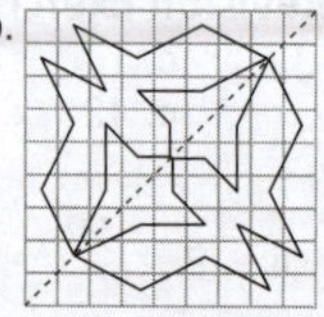 c. 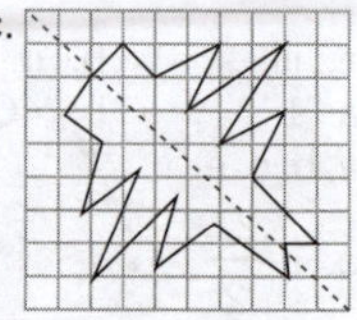
5. a. 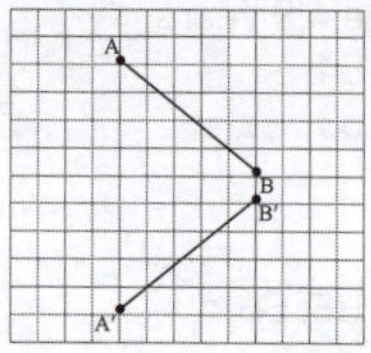

b. 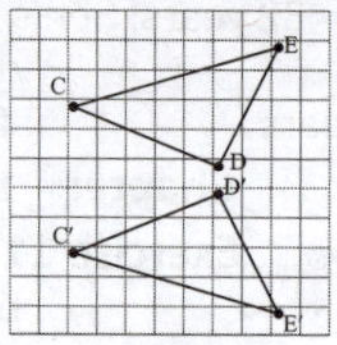

c. 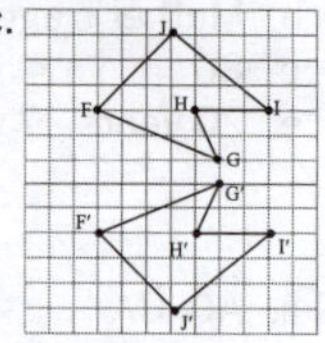

Revision Exercise

1. a. ii b. iv c. iii
   d. ii e. ii
2. a. True b. False c. True
   d. False e. True
3. a. No b. one c. two
   d. infinite e. square
4. a. 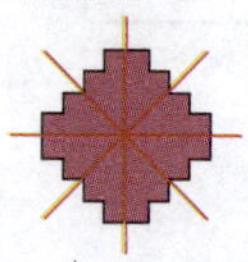 b. 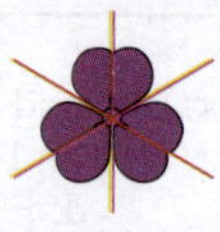 c. 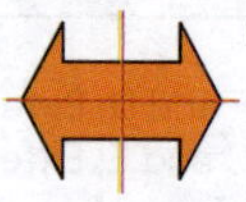 d. 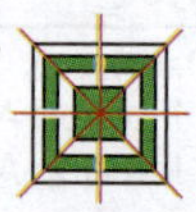
5. a.  b.  c. 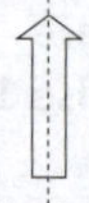 d. 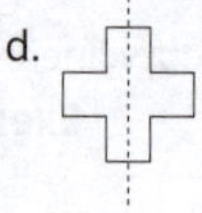

Chapter – 14

Revision Exercise

1. a. ii b. iii c. iii
   d. iv e. iii

Chapter – 15

Exercise 15.1

1. a. 500 cm b. 60 cm c. 164 in d. 40 in
   e. 45 cm f. 130 cm
2. a. 30 cm b. 21 cm c. 68 cm d. 42 cm
   e. 66 cm f. 45 cm
3. a. 20 cm b. 140 m c. 15 cm
   d. Length = 48 feet, breadth = 24 feet e. ₹120
   f. i. 15 cm ii. 12 cm iii 10 cm

Exercise 15.2

1. b.
2. 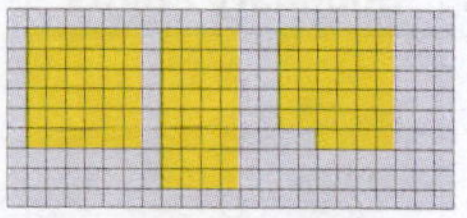

Exercise 15.3

1. Area = 480 sq. cm , perimeter = 92 cm   2. ₹26,460
3. 84 sq. m   4. Area will be reduced by $\frac{1}{4}$th of original area.
5. 300 tiles   6. Length of identical sides = 16 m
7. 54 sq. cm   8. 54 cm   9. 27 cm
10. 1413 sq. cm

Revision Exercise

1. a. iii   b. iv   c. ii
   d. i   e. ii
2. a. Perimeter   b. 13 cm   c. 121 sq. cm
   d. 24   e. 9 cm
3. a. T   b. F   c. F
   d. F   e. F
4. a. 12 cm   b. ₹10,575
   c. A square of side 95 cm   d. ₹1,08,000
   e. 50 feet; 136 sq. feet   f. 50 cm
   g. 30 inches   h. No change in area
   i. 1:16
   j. Area of the figure = 24 sq. cm
   Perimeter of the figure = 20 cm

Chapter – 16

Exercise 16.1

1.

Wages (₹)	2216	2217	2315	2332	2347
Tally marks	||||	||||	卌	卌|	卌|
No. of workers	4	4	5	6	6

2.

Height (feet)	132	135	138	148	153	200	203	240	260	289	157	159	164	184	187	325	330	354	360	381	420
Tally marks	卌|	||	|	||	|	||	|||	|	|	||	|||	|	||	|	|	|	|	|	|	|	|
No. of Mountains	6	2	1	2	1	2	3	1	1	2	3	1	2	1	1	1	1	1	1	1	1

3.

No. of items sold	30	33	34	35	42	45	50
Tally marks	卌卌	||	|||	|||	||	||||	卌|
No. of Days	10	2	3	3	2	4	6

4.

No. of storybooks	10	12	15	16	20	24	25	30
Tally marks	卌||||	卌	|||	|	||||	|	|	卌|
No. of students	9	5	3	1	4	1	1	6

5.

No. of visitors	565	654	675	735	770	870	925
Tally marks	|	|||	|||	卌	|	||||	|||
No. of days	1	3	3	5	1	4	3

Exercise 16.2

1.

District	A	B	C	D	E
Number of illiterate people	☺☺☺☺	☺☺	☺☺☺☺☺	☺☺☺☺☺	☺☺☺☺☺☺☺☺☺

2.

Days	Monday	Tuesday	Wednesday	Thursday	Friday	Saturday
No. of Chocolates	▯▯▯▯▯▯▯	▯▯▯▯▯▯▯▯▯▯▯	▯▯▯▯▯▯▯▯	▯▯▯▯▯▯▯▯▯▯▯▯▯	▯▯▯▯▯▯▯▯▯▯	▯▯▯▯▯▯▯▯▯

3. ○ = 4 Scooties

Colour of scooty	Black	White	Red	Pink	Green
No. of Scooties	○○○○ ○○○○	○○○○ ○○	○○○	○○○○ ○○○○ ○	○○○○

Four questions based on pictograph:
Q1. Find the number of black coloured scooties.
Q2. Which colour of scooty is mostly seen in the street?
Q3. Find the difference between the number of white and red colour scooties.
Q4. Find the total number of scooties riding in the street.

4. a. 280   b. 175   c. 805
   d. Friday, 525   e. 245
5. a. Class IX, 45   b. 21   c. 63
   d. 9   e. 132

Exercise 16.3

1.
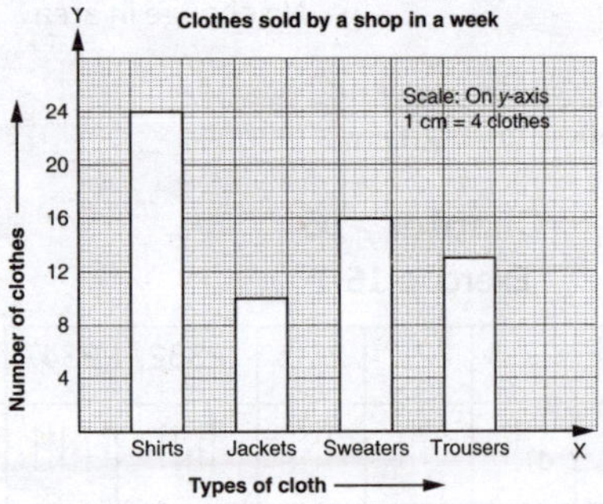

2. a. The bar graph gives information about the animals liked by the students of Class 6
   b. 6 students like lion.
   c. Tiger is liked by most of the students.
   d. Ratio = $\frac{10}{12}$ = 5 : 6
   e. 7 students
3. a. Mt. Everest – 8800 metres
   b. Nanda Devi
   c. 8800 – 6500 = 2300 metres.
   d. Mt. Everest > Kanchenjunga > Nanga Parbat > Nanda Devi > Himadri
   e. 600 meters
4.
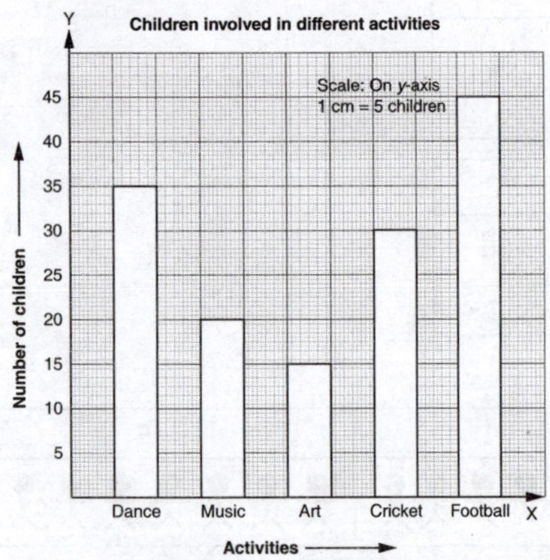

5. a. Friday; ₹250   b. ₹500   c. False
   d. 600 – 250 = ₹350   e. ₹1800

Exercise 16.4

1. a. 25   b. 18   c. 20   d. 106.6
   e. 47.25   f. 114.5   g. 12
2. a. 5   b. 40   c. 52.5   d. 86
3. ₹775   4. ₹45   5. 45 min   6. 142 cm
7. ₹51.5   8. 10   9. 36.5 kg   10. 34.1 °C

Revision Exercise

1. a. iii   b. iv   c. i
   d. iv   e. iv
2. a. bar graph   b. frequency   c. 16
   d. 40 kg   e. pictures
3. a. F   b. F   c. F
   d. T   e. T

4.
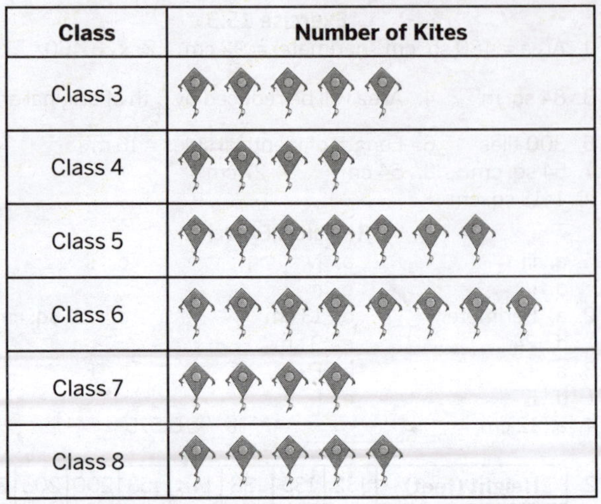

Scale: 1 = 5 kites

5. a. Adventure sports and yoga
   b. 45   c. 25 students
6. a. Tuesday, 40 cars   b. Monday, 20 cars
   c. Friday   d. 10 cars
7. Mean = ₹565
   Median = ₹562.5
8.

   a. 150 toys   b. 20 toys   c. 20 toys
9.
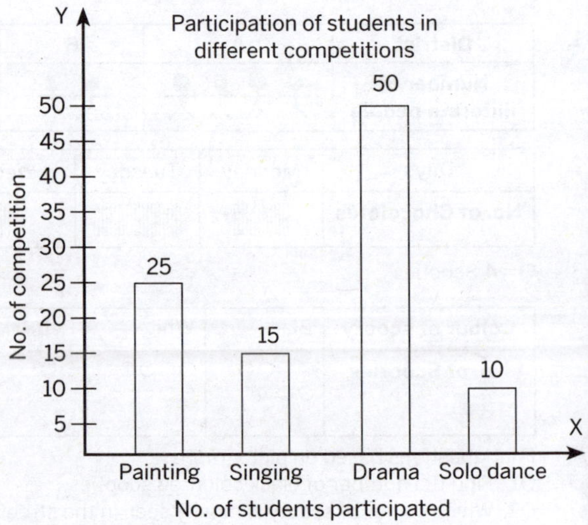

   a. 100   b. 40   c. 10
10. Mean = 21.5 °C, Median = 21.35 °C